D0946385

Career of Empire

By the same author, from The Johns Hopkins University Press

QUEST FOR EQUILIBRIUM: *America and the Balance of Power on Land and Sea*

BEYOND KISSINGER: *Ways of Conservative Statecraft*

STATES IN EVOLUTION: *Changing Societies and Traditional Systems in World Politics*

ALLIANCES AND THE THIRD WORLD

WAR AND ORDER: *Reflections on Vietnam and History*

IMPERIAL AMERICA: *The International Politics of Primacy*

NATIONS IN ALLIANCE: *The Limits of Interdependence*

EUROPE ASCENDANT: *The International Politics of Unification*

Career of Empire

AMERICA AND IMPERIAL

EXPANSION OVER LAND

AND SEA • *George Liska*

*The Washington Center of Foreign Policy Research,
School of Advanced International Studies, The Johns
Hopkins University*

THE JOHNS HOPKINS UNIVERSITY PRESS
Baltimore and London

Copyright © 1978 by The Johns Hopkins University Press
All rights reserved. No part of this book may be reproduced or transmitted in any
form or by any means, electronic or mechanical, including photocopying, recording,
xerography, or any information storage and retrieval system, without permission in
writing from the publisher. Manufactured in the United States of America

The Johns Hopkins University Press, Baltimore, Maryland 21218
The Johns Hopkins Press Ltd., London
Library of Congress Catalog Card Number 78–4576
ISBN 0–8018–2057–X

Library of Congress Cataloging in Publication data will be found on the last printed
page of this book.

For Anne

CONTENTS

PREFACE

The ensuing interpretation of the American imperial experience draws on propositions about expansion into empire, and the defense and decline of empires, as illustrated in the histories of the Roman and the British empires in Part One (and summarized, in regard to expansion, in the introductions to Parts One and Two). The two past empires admittedly differ from one another in several respects. But the very differences are actually of value for a statement of underlying uniformities, which are also of interest with regard to American expansion into a contemporary equivalent of empire. If the American world empire, as it emerged out of World War II and the cold war, combined differences with similarities relative to the older empires, its differences were yet greater when contrasted with the alternatives, equilibrium or balance-of-power model of political self-expression for powerful states and of political organization for primitive systems of states.

The American foreign-policy experience in the setting of equilibrium is the subject of another study,[1] likewise employing the analogico-historical method for interpreting basic policy orientations and structural transformations in international politics. It is the theme of that companion volume that the very existence of the United States distorted the working of the classic, Eurocentric, balance-of-power system in approximate parallel and unwitting complicity with Great Britain; but that, also, the most

THIS STUDY was completed under the auspices of The Washington Center of Foreign Policy Research, School of Advanced International Studies, The Johns Hopkins University, and is published as a special volume in the series Studies in International Affairs.
[1] George Liska, *Quest for Equilibrium: America and the Balance of Power on Land and Sea* (Baltimore: The Johns Hopkins University Press, 1977).

recent of the recurrent adoptions by the United States of the equilibrium approach in periods following upon a time of empire or imperialism could be viewed within the perspectives opened up by the record and tradition of the European balance of power. The present volume sets out to show, on the side of method, how closely the periods of empire in the American career can be fitted into a framework of analysis connecting the American with the earlier experiences of empire. On the side of substantive issues, this volume seeks to lay the groundwork for a considered answer to the question whether the latest American appointment with empire, on a world-wide basis, was to be accounted a success or a failure. It was a success if it prepared the ground for a global system of equilibrium within which the United States could perform a role partaking of the best (or idealized) elements of the British empire at its apogee; and it was a failure if an inadequate implementation of empire after a too facile expansion, and a premature withdrawal from it, were to leave the world in a condition apt to reproduce some of the worst (or caricatural) characteristics of the "dark ages" consequent on the disappearance of the Roman empire.

The uncertainty of the prospects was the reverse side of the ambiguities which mark the American performance in foreign affairs since the Republic's inception. And the ambiguities themselves reflected in large part the commonplace interlocking of the best with the worst in human intentions and social evolutions. But the uncertainty was also the surest sign of America's place as an organic element in the historical flow, rather than an aberrant, or exceptional, factor. As it continued to evolve, the contemporary internatonal setting was still recovering from the destruction of the "old world" of the Eurocentric system of states and empires at the point of collision, surfacing longer-term opposition, between the two outsized material forces of modern United States and unified Germany. Both were more potent in physical and technological power than in politico-strategic genius; and if the first accelerated propulsion into the future at a rate that exceeded the older system's capacity for adaptation, so the second, notably in its climax in the Third Reich, sought to impress or re-impress abidingly some features of the past upon a resistant present at the cost of deepening perversion.

The peculiar American responsibility for what came out of the collision is subtler than was that of either of the two latest German empires, and it continues to have a more profound impact on trends. How to judge the impact will depend in some measure at least on the assessment of the post–World War II American empire as a reordering force, growing out of the destruction of the anterior system and having the potential for channeling the emergence and shaping the crystallization of a new system. A projection of the American experience against the Roman and British backgrounds ought to lay a foundation for that judgment. It ought also to help guide as well as assess American performance during the post-empire period both in the central geostrategic balance of power, poised between preeminence and parity, and in the socioeconomic dimensions, pointing toward elastic stability or its opposite. It will matter which of the competing great, or world, powers in the emerging global system, and in the next phase particularly whether America or Russia, will best succeed in bending to the needs of the future—or transcending in new ways for better or worse—the qualities and the mechanisms exemplified in the major empires of the past.

Part One

ROME AND BRITAIN

INTRODUCTION. *Stages*
in Expansion

There can be no empire without prior expansion of more than mediocre scope; and the sources of the expansion of states are the vital, if latent, springs of all statecraft. They keep alive, as it were, the timeless mysteries which surround the pursuit and the exercise of power. Being elusive, the sources of expansion can be traced to man's psychology as a sentient being or to his predicament as a social one; to the innermost quality of states and other organized communities, doomed to either grow or decline in power, or to the vices of statesmen acquired through the exercise of power. They generate inhumane destruction in conflicts or inspire superhuman efforts for individual and collective self-realization. Whatever they be and wheresoever they may originate, the urges to expand are most grandly manifest in empires. Since empires are the products of an expansion which has exceeded the arbitrarily defined "natural" limits of a community, the determinants of expansion can best be traced in the imperial setting.

One needs to differentiate between the original drive and subsidiary incentives to expansion, and to explain why expansion does not always stop when the original drive has been either exhausted or appeased. And also, to perform the first two tasks with the aid of universally applicable categories reaching beyond specific manifestations and doctrinal militancies. Being a recurrent phenomenon of political nature, imperial expansion must perforce have uniform bases in need of a general explanation.

The original drive to expansion would seem to be on balance predatory, and to aim at a viable habitat conforming to the prevailing criteria of what is sufficient to insure survival. The drive itself is rooted in two basic needs. One is the psychopolitical need to assert self sufficiently to assure security within a competitive environment. It is brought home most forcefully by the fact or imminent threat of a hostile encroachment such as invasion or encirclement. The other need is the material one to acquire a measure of individual and collective sustenance that is sufficient to minister to the first, psychopolitical need in existing circumstances. And the somewhat derivative third need is to evolve and sustain a society or political community (or "system") with sufficiently diversified functions and stratified authority (and related status) to implement ever more effectively the basic conditions (security and sustenance) of survival. Expansion is, accordingly, a function of the inveterately erratic pursuit of the optimum framework for meeting the three interdependent needs of security and sustenance in society.

So far, the only difficulty lies in a useless effort to assess the relative weight or priority of security and sustenance as survival needs, without reference to the prevailing situation or systemic setting. The more meaningful, and soluble, difficulty is to explain why, in the absence of contrary frustration, expansion does not automatically cease when the original predation has secured more than should rationally be risked by its continuance; when the original drive slackened after it had stopped feeding upon itself. Such subsidence will occur for all but pathological motivations and for all but quite particular actors. The former will not outlast the lifetime of an individual conqueror and do not entirely either cause or explain most apparently limitless expansionisms, including those of Napoleon and Hitler most recently; the latter are limited to nomadic-pastoral hordes and trading apparatuses writ large without fixed territorial bases.

For an explanation of continuing expansion in most, or all "normal," conditions, it is necessary to reach beyond psychological and material urges to systemic factors. The latter will assert themselves in relations between effective forces or powers situated within reach of one another, whenever the predatory drive gives way to protective concerns implemented by preclusive strategies. When this occurs, the community expanded by the prior drive is virtually drawn into further expansion by interplays with likewise actuated external forces. Or, alternatively, a polity can be projected into continuing enlargement by interactions within the community's own political system. The common denominator is the recurrent near-impossibility for the ruling individual or elite to stop halfway, at the point of moderate expansion that would reflect and institutionalize a species of equipoise with the sum of still-autonomous external forces and with progressively emerging new political forces within. So long as they are at a clear disadvantage, the external forces will be reluctant to place themselves individually or collectively at the mercy of the largest single power, without a reliable guarantee other than its magnanimity. And the rising internal forces will be no less reluctant to accept permanent tutelage at the hands of the original ruling class, without compensations other than group pride in the original expansion.

In the first instance, an ineffectual external opposition or incipient counterexpansion will provoke an expansive response, carrying on the work of the predatory stimulus to expansion. The added thrust will be sufficient to engender a superior core-empire, and to insure for it a position of unassailable security in the relevant "state system" which has been profoundly modified as a result. The predatory bias of the original motive will have been transmuted in the process into a defensive-preclusive one. But a supplementary impetus, qualitatively different from the two original ones, comes into play only at a later stage, when the directing elite of the henceforth oversized power would halt expansion as a matter of deliberate policy. The resumption and increasingly reluctant continuance of expansion in scope, depth, or both, beyond core-empire to grand empire, is then due to subsidiary motives that are partially novel in either kind or, at least, mix. These motives or incentives reflect, first, the pressures for insuring or reinforcing the security of the imperial frontier, or periphery, against local threats. A related aim is to satisfy the expansive dispositions of friendly or dependent local, or peripheral, actors. The incentives reflect, second, the intra- or interclass conflicts and transactions of the mature imperial body politic. These conflicts and transactions will generate pressures for continuing diversionary or compensatory expansion as a means to internal political stability in the absence of radical external insecurity. And, third, terminal expansionary tendencies will reflect the interplay between strategic and economic factors, between security requirements and sustenance needs. They will be reunited, to the advantage of economic imperatives at a higher-than-initial level of complexity and intractability, in a late or even declining empire that has been again beset by challenges to mere survival from without or within.

The concatenation of the original and the subsidiary motives for expansion will easily obscure key distinctions in concrete historical conditions. One distinction is between predation and preclusion, protection (of either the frontier or the economy) and projection (of internal stresses due to surpluses of political energies and ambitions, or of material needs and outputs). A related distinction is between subsidiary and secondary motives or incentives. The first contrast with original (or initial) motives in both time and space, the second with those primary (or dominant) at any one time. And it is likewise necessary to differentiate between basic causes or determinants and mere preliminaries and precipitants of both expansion and the military conflicts which commonly attend expansion. Distinctions such as these are not always compellingly feasible. But they are indispensable for a disciplined approach to phenomena which, being both circular and multicausal, would otherwise have to be abandoned to either poetic intuition or ideologically colored imputation and invective.

I

EXPANSION INTO
EMPIRE. *International*
Determinants

The differences between the Roman and the British empires are various. They span the gulf between the primarily military and the primarily mercantile systems; one oriented chiefly to land-based power and one based mainly on sea power; one bestriding the central arena and one gravitating toward the colonial periphery; and one evolving toward institutional centralization and one tending toward diffusion of self-government. While Rome's universal empire comprised all the "civilized" world or "central" system, Britain's colonial empire did not, and the metropole enjoyed only a relatively brief spell of hegemonic primacy in Europe. The differences were most closely reflected in the external determinants of expansion, more or less closely related to power and its use.

I
The two empires' uneven rhythms of growth and unequal scope and direction of expansion can be traced back to a salient fact. Unlike Rome, the relevant English nucleus did not, at a sufficiently early formative stage, successfully overcome a severe threat to survival. While starting her career as a continuous actor on the European stage and before facing up to Spain, England had lost instead the nearest approximation to Rome's First Punic War, the so-called Hundred Years' War in France. The acute feeling of insecurity resulting from an early threat to physical survival

recurs historically as *the* traceable original impetus to expansion on a relatively large scale. Such a threat will vitally supplement the most primitive stimulus to the altogether initial enlargement, having to do with the most elementary ratio between the size of population and the amount of available sustenance. When the external threat occurs, it supplies a concrete, irrefutable, and (as it becomes legendary) lasting vindication of whatever diffuse anxiety may naturally permeate individual and collective psychology as a source of aggression; and, if successfully resisted and overcome, the threat impresses indelibly a corresponding ethos upon the body politic as a whole and, in particular, the ruling personnel which, having emerged from factional strife, have equipped the community for effective response. The ethos will be one favoring a forceful utilization of the enlarged resources in response to the dilemmas of existence posed, not least, by the conflict between the scarcity of finite resources and a dynamic conception of security encompassed in the protean notion of survival.

Like the wrestler that has been thrown off balance by the sudden yielding of a taxing counterforce, a body politic that has overcome a mortal threat will rush forward to regain its lost equilibrium—within an enlarged habitat. In addition to sheer momentum, expansion will be due also to the newly enhanced or discovered capacity to materially diminish the just-experienced vulnerability to subjection. Concerns with physical security and with economic sustenance will be thus typically combined in early expansion, focused on survival in a situation that is more or less exposed and defensible as to geographical location and more or less complex and exploitable as to geopolitical or "systemic" setting. If the challenge to survival in a given environment is to be bracing, it must be also manageable for an elite capable of effective leadership, make the populace display cohesion and high morale under stress, and vindicate whatever religio-mythical safeguards against premature extinction might supplement sheer luck or good fortune. Such underpinnings of initial survival add up to the requisite endowments of the expansionist as child or adolescent; they will be transmuted eventually into supports of an adult empire, and the relative importance of particular safeguards and stimuli will be rearranged in the process.

Being both strategically located and well-protected in terms of natural configuration, Rome was situated to both attract and successfully resist threats from greater aggressive peoples. Next to the Etruscans and the Gauls, these included also the Volscians and the Aequians, acting in alliance. Initially a reaction to such assaults and a consequence of withstanding them, Rome's gradual expansion merged with an ascent to supremacy extending to southern Italy. The process was sustained by material objects and was implemented by an institutional device. The earliest material object included supplemental arable and food-producing land for a growing population in a decreasingly pastoral economy; the device consisted of alliance, the Latin League, and Rome's increasingly successful contest for leadership in it. By the fourth century B.C. at the latest, Rome was allying with dependents and dividing adversaries for purposes of organization and control, and acquiring increasing numbers of slaves to work on a land agglomerated in part into large senatorial estates. Regardless of whether the slaves evolved into an independent incentive to war and expansion, enhancing their supply became a valued incidental reward for successfully concluding more or less hard-to-avoid periods of warfare. Without quite matching Seeley's famed dictum about Britain's expansion into empire, a modern historian of early Rome was able to attribute the crucial initial expansion to "bitter necessity" ruling out any "preconceived idea of planned conquest."[1]

Unlike early Rome, the post-Roman Anglo-Saxon England was not able to withstand repeated assaults from overseas. Nor, when the last Danish invader had failed to integrate the insular realm into a more than ephemeral politico-economic empire in the Baltic northern Mediterranean, was the conquering Norman dynasty, at a later stage, able to project lasting power southward toward the actual Mediterranean, in support of no more deeply rooted values than feudal fiefs and familial rights. It was, consequently, for ultimately victorious France to first display the effects of surmounting a threat to incipiently national existence, when pushing via Italy toward Europe's immemorial stake of colonial empire in Sicily. England herself had to wait for reconsolidating Tudor despotism and a withstood threat from Spain before bringing forth a full, defensive-offensive thrust outward.

The early events had done little more than outline the maritime-imperial and the continental-European options of later British policy, as opposed to insular self-confinement. With an underdeveloped sea power and an only feeble capacity for sustained and continuous warfare on land, the English had failed, in the typical first-stage effort of off-shore islanders, to expand onto the adjoining mainland. They entered thereafter upon an equally usual second stage of relative political isolation from the neighboring continent and trade-focused involvements overseas, before assuming a balancing role on the mainland by virtue of restored strength and revived interest. Instead of being absorbed through victory within an entity that was culturally and otherwise centered in France, England remained free to nurture her oceanic vocation and was compelled to energize her isolation by opposition to successive incursions from the Continent. The outcome of the Hundred Years' War also saved the emerging European state system from incurring prematurely the lot of the Hellenistic state system in the age of Rome. Early Europe was not

---

1. András Alföldi, *Early Rome and the Latins* (Ann Arbor: University of Michigan Press, 1965), p. 30; also pp. 402–05. Seeley spoke of a fit of absence of mind.

faced with an Anglo-French realm putting an end to autonomy in the Iberian and Low-Countries' subsystems and wresting Italy from a weakened Germanic empire. Nor did updated naval technology at a later stage find in the place of a mal-coordinated Habsburg conglomerate, based on Spain, an unassailable power complex poised to invade the world's oceans and Europe's peripheries.

If seafaring Britons would in time replicate, from a crystallizing balancer position in Europe, the Roman empire on a global scale, Rome herself had avoided being bogged down in a position of equal or, at best, balancer among coastal Mediterranean powers, with few if any prospects for compensations outside the land-sea area. Instead, Rome managed early to transcend the peninsular Italian base into the adjoining North African and Spanish land masses (via conflicts with Carthage) and into the Dalmatian coast (Illyria, via contests with local pirates and Macedon). While the very first of the three Punic wars with Carthage enlarged and provisionally secured Roman dominion on land, it also converted the so-far land-bound city-state into a first-class naval power, thus consummating the impression of its indefeasibility.

When the momentum of the Roman drive in and beyond southern Italy clashed with Carthage's preestablished security system and commerical sphere of interests in Sicily, the Romans were able to continue perceiving their expansion as defensive. The Gauls still represented a residual threat, as did opposition to Roman dominance by some Italians and Western Mediterranean Greeks aided by fellow Greeks from the East. Moreover, the earlier ramification of Carthage from North Africa to Corsica, Sardinia, and into Western Sicily (guaranteeing access to Spain) suggested that the trading sea power was not impervious to its kind's penchant for monopoly, aided by internecine contests among more land-bound and exposed powers. Any further extension of the Carthaginian sway in Sicily threatened to complete the strategic encirclement of southern Italy and to facilitate, in Roman eyes, tactical access across the Messinian "bridge" to Italy proper. The conflict was sparked when the dynamic Eastern Greek king, Pyrrhus, withdrawing from his earlier part in a triangular interplay, left the hitherto ambivalently related expansive powers face to face; it was implicit in Rome's growing reluctance to accept parity in overall standing with any other Italian or Italy-abutting state; and it acquired exceptional virulence from its character, denoting a schism of sorts between differently amphibious land-based military and maritime empires. Intensity grew in the Second Punic War, by which time the actors had virtually exchanged basic identities in consequence of the course and outcome of the first round. Rome had evolved into the dominant sea power from earlier dependence on naval allies; and Carthage was reduced to invading northern Italy overland from Spain, whose conquest had compensated the African power for the loss of Sicily, while enlarging both the area and the stake of the protracted contest.

At the peak of the Hannibalic threat, Rome ran the risk of shrinking to a marginal land and sea power, constantly threatened from the Italian rear—an equivalent of hostile Scotland ever-ready to ally with a weak England's French enemy. Survival in great-power status by a narrow margin sustained instead further expansion, despite provisional satiation[2]; it did so as fending off Macedonian and Syrian designs on enfeebled Egypt and divided Greeks drew Rome ever more deeply into the multipolar all-Mediterranean system of states. As a result, Rome's regional core-empire in the Western Mediterranean, comprising under partially direct rule Illyria, Sardinia, Sicily, and parts of Spain, was supplemented by an initially informal sway in the Eastern Mediterranean arena.

II

A Roman world empire comprising two discrete and problematically related, Western and Eastern, wings emerged from initial expansion in two distinguishable phases. A largely predatory drive of variable scope and intensity, originating in an expansive reaction to a direct and positive threat to physical substance, had accounted for the first phase; next came further expansion into which a power is drawn by preclusive involvement, designed to avert or anticipate upon more or less hypothetical threats to the congenial make-up of a larger system of security transcending mere physical integrity. Both motives to expansion combine elements of defense and offense; but whereas the first (predatory drive) does so sequentially, the second (preclusive involvement) commingles the two inextricably. The security of physical being in the first case has to do with self-preservation; in the latter case, it is the interests crystallizing around a progressively acquired role and image pointing toward self-propagation that are to be secured. Although the two phases and related types of security concerns, their objects and objectives, are analytically distinguishable, they are not sharply differentiated in the perception of policymakers and in their potency as determinants of policy.

The extension of Roman ascendancy into the three-power *plus* Hellenistic state-system (consisting of Macedon, Syria or "Asia," Egypt and the aggregate half-power of the Greek leagues and city-states) displayed some of the most basic tendencies of interstate relations. More important, be-

---

2. Thus Scipio Africanus, the victor over Hannibal, ordered his men to pray for the preservation of the Roman people's *imperium*, not for its expansion. Cf. Richard Koebner, *Empire* (Cambridge: At the University Press, 1961), p. 10. On the origins of the First Punic Wars, see B. H. Warmington, *Carthage* (London: Robert Hale, 1960), pp. 148–50; also Gilbert Picard, *Le monde de Carthage* (Paris: Buchet Chastel, 1956).

cause rare, is the fact that it consummated these tendencies in transforming an equilibrium system into empire. The conflicting internal
dispositions of the key actors compounded the uncertainties implicit in a
conflict among apparently but not really equal powers; and the tensions
that always attend the quest for parity in status among such states were
aggravated by the inherent instability of mere preeminence in favor of
one of them.

In its dispositions, the Roman senate seems to have vacillated between
the attractions of economy and the promptings of ethos. Economy entailed reluctance to expand further; ethos inspired disinclination to settle
for mere equality in the Eastern Mediterranean any more than before in
Latium, in Italy, and in the Central and Western Mediterranean. On the
adversary side, Macedonian policy displayed a blend of assertive ambition and defensive anxiety reflecting uncertainty whether and when to
fear more the power of Rome than of Syria. Syria's ruler, Antioch, appears to have likewise wavered, between the lure of an easier territorial
expansion eastward into Asia (partially at the cost of Egypt) and the
necessity to stand up to Rome at last, and then too late, in defense of
Syria's identity as a European as well as an Asian great power. At issue
for all the powers were immediately compelling strategic interests and
stakes, such as Illyria and Thrace respectively, open-ended future prospects, and historically generated rights (for Macedon and Syria) and
needs (for Rome, to establish an enriching rapport with the Hellenes).

Counteracting rival dispositions was the only abstract common interest
to define the terms of parity for equivalent regional empires, within
reciprocally acknowledged orbits, as a provisional plateau for coexistence.
Since all the parties were amphibious powers, parity entailed a comparable access to both sea power and (Greek) satellites in West or East,
within agreed-upon spheres of dominion or influence. An Illyrian (Dalmatian) coastal buffer zone could divide Rome from Macedon before and
after the First Macedonian War; and the narrow straits of the Hellespont
could separate Europe (Thrace) from Asia Minor, prior to Rome's climactic war with Syria. Largely suggested by nature, the lines of delimitation were either proposed or agreed upon in fairly good faith both before
and after conflicts; in due course, attempts to avert wars with the aid of
precise delimitations helped precipitate conflicts by removing ambiguity
from antagonistic claims. Macedon could not let herself be excluded from
the Adriatic and be bottled up, in fact or potentially, by a Roman-
Aetolian-Egyptian alliance in the Aegean; and for Antioch of Syria to
surrender his protectorate over all European Greeks would mean incurring a roll-back that would eventually encompass also the Greeks of Asia
Minor south of the straits. The Eastern powers could not accept the
consequences of defeat without succumbing in a prior test of strength;
and it was only deferring the evil hour for them to accept being confined

within a fixed frame of static power, while more dynamic Rome would continue to grow from within. On her side, Rome could hardly rest satisfied with a provisionally peaceful preeminence in the Western Mediterranean so long as there remained the risk of an adverse imbalance in the all-Mediterranean theater, henceforth incapable of lasting segregation into its two halves. Just as the intermediate Dalmatian coast had come to represent a physical nexus between contending East and West, so the policy link was forged by Macedon's two-faced orientation: friendly toward Rome's enemy in the West, Carthage, and hostile to Rome's potential allies for counterpoise, the Greek Aetolian League and Egypt, in the East.

Out of the confluence of such trends and dilemmas grew the pressure behind Rome's assertive prosecution of an essentially preemptive expansion. The expansion-stimulating possibility was that Rome might become permanently excluded from access to the Eastern Mediterranean by a firm alliance between Macedon and Syria, consolidated and enlarged by a predatory sharing of weakened Egypt between them. The reality, which facilitated the expansion, was in the lack of coordination between the two major Eastern powers, permitting Rome to conquer each in succession. Instead of jointly facing westward, Macedon and Syria indulged in separate eastward drives, meant perhaps to create diversions, score a gain in local competition, or compensate for Rome's aggrandizement elsewhere. In one's dimmed retrospect, rather than disclosing a fundamental unawareness of the balance-of-power principle, as might appear at first sight, these excursions seem to reflect confusion (primarily Macedon's) about the primacy of the regional eastern as against the all-Mediterranean balance, and miscalculation (chiefly Antioch's) regarding the relevant timetables for an effective containment of Rome.

The precipitant which converted the disparate underlying tendencies into a chain of events was the Macedonian alliance with Carthage at a critical point of the Second Punic War. The collusion followed upon what Macedon could not but regard as Rome's encroachments on the Illyrian coast. Thereafter, Macedon fought Rome repeatedly and in vain: for the balance of power on land and sea (under Philip V); for her own and Greek independence (under Perseus); and for sheer territorial integrity (to reverse punitive partition). While defeats were punctuating the way to disruption for Macedon, Rome evolved *pari passu* beyond equilibrium toward empire and then also within it. Syria was apparently a greater and more prudent power than Macedon. Feared more by Rome as a result, she fell in due course more readily when incited to action by the contentious small Greek powers, fearing alternately all of the greater states. The Aetolian League had first demonstrated to Rome the utility of a Greek alliance by applying pressure to Macedon's flank during Philip's anti-Roman thrust in the Hannibalic war. But, at a later stage, the League swung to Syria as counterpoise against a Rome that had become too strong relative to Macedon and too close for comfort. And Rome was incited to partisan action by the rival Achaean League and by Greeks (Rhodes and Pergamum) nearer to Antioch's power than to Rome's.

As before in the critical expansion across the Adriatic, Rome's self-defense merged with protection of lesser friends and allies. If protection of loyal Italians against Illyrian piracy had been pressing, protection in behalf of the ambivalent Greeks against Syrian primacy was only precautionary. It is fruitless to inquire whether Rome was propelled into the ostensibly least necessary or just war, with Antioch, primarily by growing momentum of expansion or by decreased control over policy, surrendered to seemingly necessary and deserving allies. Converging movements were, once again, prompted by preemptive or preclusive strategies on both sides. Macedon had kept crossing a line for fear of an irreversible constriction inland; Antioch refused to accept another delimitation lest he cease ruling a major power; and Rome preferred in the end to supplant all dividing lines (outside static Parthia) with a virtual circle around the inland sea. One objective was credibility with the strategically useful and culturally imposing Greeks: a compelling demonstration of power and will would prevent cumulative defection and impede countervailing alliances with a not yet wholly subdued original enemy, Carthage. The Macedonian stab in the back in the Second Punic War had been evaded with some difficulty; the threat's continuance was brought home by fugitive Hannibal's backstage intrigue with Antioch, as part of the Syrio-Roman "cold" war that preceded the real one.[3]

Rome had secured first the Messina strait and the Tyrrhenian sea bottlenecks between Italy, Sicily, and the Carthaginian promontory in Tunisia, previously dominated by the Euro-African power; she then wrested also the straits of the Hellespont (Dardanelles) from the Eurasian power. The larger result was Roman dominance over the Mediterranean lands and seas. Progressing rapidly from unstable parity to vulnerable preeminence, Rome's sway became empire when it had proved impractical to sustain a mere hegemony. The dominion became simultaneously one that could no longer be resisted, and one that might be only rebelled against. As local seekers for greater independence were driven to seek strength for revolt through small-scale imperialisms of their own, the unauthorized bids drew Rome, in turn, into ever-deeper involvement, replacing loose protectorates over half-willing clients with direct control over virtual subjects.

3. See E. Badian, "Rome and Antiochus the Great: A Study in Cold War," and "Notes on Roman Policy in Illyria," in *Studies in Greek and Roman History* (New York: Barnes and Noble, 1964). Also, by the same author, *Roman Imperialism in the Late Republic* (Ithaca, N.Y.: Cornell University Press, 1968).

III

Rome's progression to empire was ruthless and, even if not reluctant, unplanned. It was greatly eased by the inability of Macedon and Syria to combine effectively in time against the power rising at the other end of the sea. A similar inability of the European land powers smoothed insular Britain's progression to a world-wide colonial empire and a diplomatic hegemony on the Continent. But Britain lacked the power, and her expansion the momentum, to avoid the frustrating search for stable balance on land and for stabilizing parity with navally and colonially ambitious mainland powers. And she lost effective control over the continental equilibrium in due course, when a new Macedon rose in the guise of a Prussia-Germany straining toward the seas, and a new "Asia" was consolidated in the guise of a Russia encroaching, as had Antioch's Syria before, in the direction of both the Greeks, the straits, and the Indus. Before that had come to pass, however, England had first to start on the ascent that would eventually permit Lord Palmerston to equate the status of the British subject with that of the Roman citizen. Long before, at "greater" Britain's Elizabethan beginnings, aid to the Dutch estates struggling for independence (from Catholic Spain), in the name of common religious values, performed some of the functions of Rome's one-time pro-Greek proclivities. The Virgin Queen's assistance to rebels intensified the Anglo-Spanish antagonism that played a key role in projecting England into empire, not least by covering rapine overseas with the prestige of resistance to the Habsburgs' continental hegemony. England did temporary duty in the process for again-faltering France as the main counterpoise; in return for which a recovered French monarchy supplied ascendant England eventually with alternative stimuli to expansion by reengaging the insular power in the secular contention over Europe and, henceforth, also all the world's Indies.

Qualifying all parallels between British and Roman expansions is one great difference. Whereas the Roman empire was conquered from strength, England's expansion compensated for both intrinsic and relative weakness. A once rebuffed Carthage had expanded into Spain for her second encounter with Rome; having lost in the first round (in the Hundred Years' War), insular England had to move outward toward the Spanish Indies, and into what was to become British North America and India, before she could tackle the European continent again with effect. The compensatory character of England's initial expansion was due to two main factors. One was the paucity of her resources when compared with the first modern aspirant to hegemony, Spain, and when measured against the growing needs and numbers of her population in due course. The second reason grew in importance after initial colonial expansion had relieved the earlier basic needs. While the overseas and European theaters of competitive interaction grew ever more interrelated, each of the successive continental powers aspiring to preeminence in Europe and challenging England for parity globally exceeded its immediate predecessor in resource endowment and in the rigor of managing both men and matter.[4] The material needs of survival fuelled a predatory outward drive subject, as it responded to ever more complex motivation, to changing economic doctrines and political and administrative strategies; the systemic link between Europe and the overseas arena activated the preclusive mechanism that drew England, in two distinguishable phases and directions, into yet larger areas of final expansion. Situated as she was between the European continent and the colonial peripheries, England never achieved the comparative simplicity of purpose of either Rome, when facing for a time only one critical theater, or of the Portuguese trading empire, when facing away from the Continent. England was able to focus single-minded efforts on neither mercantile monopolies nor fair balances of military and naval power; nor, once her economic growth got under way, was England's dynamic of rising internal needs and the largely external means for satisfying those needs susceptible to relatively simple resolutions, such as agricultural and authoritarian Rome had found provisionally in a static economy and preindustrial trading Portugal in stabilized retrenchment.

In conformity with the norm, England's overseas expansion was substantially stimulated by the successful overcoming of a tangible threat to the survival of indigenous instititutions. The threat came from a Spain that had been herself propelled to expand by a threat from both land- and sea-based Ottoman power, in the aftermath of the final expulsion of the one-time Moorish invaders from the Iberian peninsula. The effort to outflank Islam for strategic reasons, circumnavigate it for economic reasons, and outstrip it for religious (i.e., ideological) reasons, led to Christianising new lands in the remote West as a substitute for linking up with legendary Christian powers in Islam's eastern rear. Strengthened by tribute more than by trade, the Hispanic overseas empire was soon to back the hegemonial pressure of counter-Reformation Spain in Europe. Since the resistance to it was headed by Protestant England at a critical juncture, a religious difference insured that the epochal turning point in the development of the Euro-global international system would have the ideological overtones commonly attending and confusing such beginnings. The effective factors were, however, less than purely doctrinal. One was the threat of Spanish military encirclement of England (by way of Scotland) and outright invasion (by means of the Armada); another, England's successful repulse of both. Inasmuch as the English escape was wrought by superior seamanship and strategy, it rehabilitated Carthage-

4. See Ludwig Dehio, *The Precarious Balance* (New York: Alfred A. Knopf, 1962).

like mobility of maneuver against Spain's land-like naval war-making that recalled in turn Rome's grappling and boarding tactics at one stage of the First Punic War, without replicating Rome's superior invasion capacity at another.

The reversal of fortunes for alternative tactics and strategies encompassed the reversion of empire to authentic naval power; and it both demonstrated and increased the capacity of the island country to escalate the defiance which English interlopers had already offered to the inefficiently restrictive economic monopoly of metropolitan Spain in her flourishing empire. A moral impetus was added eventually to the material incentive behind the Elizabethans' drive westward when commands of private conscience supplemented the attractions of profit from state-sponsored privateering in promoting colonies of settlement. Expansion eastward remained by contrast long responsive to chiefly material interests, inseparable as these were in the East as well as in the West from strategic concerns and military power equations in both the theory and the practice of mercantilistic political economy. Official fostering of the merchant marine continued to be a means to effective naval power as the Anglo-Spanish duel receded before an Anglo-Dutch contest over the carrying trade, and that contest was yet later overshadowed by the Anglo-French struggle over both trade and colonies.

Achieving preeminence over each rival in succession propelled England to global supremacy in all of the components of mercantilism's classic triad: command of the sea, as the warranty of commerce, based on colonies. The triad reached its eighteenth-century climax in the British triumph by way of two successive four-cornered interplays. The first pattern comprised two relatively small states and two great ones. Of the smaller ones Portugal pioneered overseas exploration, while the newly independent United Provinces began to perfect colonial explotation for trade. At different times the two smaller countries faced one another and their respective bigger neighbors, Spain and England, in competition. After losing initial advantages, both of the two lesser polities barely avoided a permanent union with the larger and less single-mindedly materialistic power. Being concerned mainly with the balance of an overseas trade, which it stimulated directly, the first quadrilateral interaction impinged less directly on the full-fledged balance-of-power system emerging in Europe. Spain had sought to prevent the birth of such a system, while Portugal worried only over the consequences which the system's breakdown into a Spanish universal monarchy would have for autonomy on the Iberian peninsula. And whereas, in defense of their independence, the Dutch vacillated between land-focused fear of France and sea-oriented distrust of the English, the latter were unsure whether to focus their enmity on the sprawling, but already declining, empire of Spain or an only reascending compact France as the best way to cease being themselves only insular and marginal and becoming imperial as well as, to a degree, European.

A later stage was marked when the interplay among four near-equal European powers, Britain, France, Austria, and Prussia, integrated fully the European and the colonial arenas, by the principal agency of the Anglo-French struggle over overseas empire and continental hegemony. The threat which France in search of both prestige and profit posed to Britain's Dutch protégés and competitors updated the ancient two-power rivalry; the consequent trilateral Anglo-French-Dutch permutations of alliances, mediations, and defections implemented the transition from the Anglo-French polarity to the vaster quadrilateral contest. In the process, the triangular diplomacy of the last Stuarts Europeanized British foreign policy, even if not yet England herself, to a degree easily consolidated by a king with wholly Dutch-continental priorities and fixedly anti-French propensities (William III). It remained for the quadrilateral contest to globalize for good the strategies for the European balance of power, even if not quite yet the balance of power as such, by interlocking the Anglo-French struggle over world empire with the Austro-Prussian contest over primacy within an older and, in name at least, holier empire of the German nation.

The transition from one to the other quadripolar pattern was matched by a less clear-cut transition from predation to preclusion as the principal original incentive behind Britain's overseas expansion. Prior to the early eighteenth century, the essentially predatory drive westward was manned by more or less lawful traders with willing Spanish colonies and by land-hungry colonizers in mostly unoccupied territories in North America; it entailed no major conflicts as a result. In the East, the English, just as the Dutch, profit-seekers had to deal with antecedent Portuguese bases as well as with greater local resistance. By yet more marked contrast, world-wide wars attended British expansion in the eighteenth and the early nineteenth centuries, while motivation became increasingly preclusive. The key systemic spring to British expansion in North America and the West Indies, to the detriment of the continental European powers, was embedded in the European balance of power. Critical stimuli were more locally centered in India, and French losses to Britain on the Indian coasts were correspondingly dwarfed by British acquisitions from indigenous powers in the subsequent preclusive expansion into the subcontinental heartland. Unlike the earlier and real Spanish threat to England, the much-advertised later menace of French hegemony for Europe was itself in large part a response to the equations of world power as they had been largely shaped by the Dutch and the British material advances outside Europe. The critical Anglo-French contentions tended to be provoked by colonial issues and overseas incidents and to be then decided in Europe.

The causal nexus was supplemented by a strategic link whenever British naval superiority produced enough of precautionary conquests of France's (or also Bourbon Spain's) colonies to permit their being bartered against anticipated French territorial gains on the Continent in a favorable or, at worst, tolerable peace settlement. As late as the Napoleonic wars, the West Indian sugar islands constituted a special case in the mercantilistic context. But the most conspicuous dividend from the British strategy had by then been Canada, the conquest of which was delayed because it was reluctant; and when it was finally undertaken for a mixture of sentimental, systemic, and security reasons, the ultimate effect was to release the American colonists from British rule for imitation, in North America, of a type of expansion the British practiced in the India-centered East against weak indigenous resistance and but token opposition by European powers.

Upholding the European balance of power defensively against France had helped complete Britain's North American empire by measures and acquisitions that could be attributed to preemptive concerns and strategies. The resulting upset in the balance of British and French forces on the North American continent caused the soon-to-follow retraction of that empire. If it had been difficult to effectively manipulate the two separate but interconnected balances of power in Europe and the Americas, it was even harder (following the Seven Years' War) to evolve a self-sustaining equilibrium between British imperial imperatives and American aspirations (themselves cast in the language of empire) in isolation from the intra-European balance generally and the French counterpoise to the local particularisms specifically. Difficulty became an impossibility when the requisite Anglo-American revisions got caught up in yet another and only emerging balancing act, within wartime England, between royal and popular favor as elevators to political office. The internal process further confounded the postwar British attempt to bring the preexisting external relationship between control over, and contribution to, shared Anglo-American concerns into greater conformity with the new balance of interests (between the motherland and the American colonies) and forces (between the colonists and their surviving, indigenous and European, antagonists).

As England's overseas expansion veered toward the second, India-centered, empire, a mere coincidence between European and local contests replaced (with minor exceptions) the closer interconnection of European and American balances and events that had first made and then unmade the Atlantic-centered empire. The greater distance; the initial absence of British settlers in the East (appearing only later and then chiefly in Australia and New Zealand); and the preference of both the English and the French East India companies for enacting on their own the politico-military features of their mercantile activities, conspired to transfer both the stimuli and the felt necessities behind expansion from a dynamic European equilibrium to a defunct local (Mogul) imperial order. Radical insecurity of even the minimal requisite facilities and immunities forced the companies into precautionary alliances with willing, and conquests of unwilling, local potentates, as part of mutually preemptive predatory quests for a henceforth seemingly unavoidable monopoly of profit-through-power for one of them. When they had bested the French in the coastal periphery, the British came up against indigenous (Bengali) counterimperialism inland; and after they had overcome what was itself a preclusive reaction by the local ruler to the anticipated northward spread of the interventionary Anglo-French competition, they were drawn into further expansion by deepening involvement in Indian politics and, later, security. Having replaced the Moguls, the British first reproduced in India the early Roman peace in Greece, moderating relations between dependent provinces and semi-independent princes on behalf of an ostensibly neutral suzerain. Only after the terminal conquest (in the Punjab), and still like Rome facing Greek inconsistencies and rebellious reactions, was the British arbiter forced into more direct administration. The mid-nineteenth-century Indian Mutiny had cultural sources rather than political objectives; this fact, and the revolt's failure, differentiated the Asian rebellion from the earlier American one and the western from the eastern core-empire for another century, without wholly annulling the fundamental unity and continuity of British overseas expansion.

Systemically rooted British expansion was resumed on a major scale after a pause, in the late nineteenth century. The resumption confirmed the secular drift, from predation to preclusion, in the self-conscious motivation of an increasingly defensive British statecraft striving to remain in overall control of private drives. By this time, the strictly European balance of power had become largely devoid of the means of compensation traditionally offered by its quasi-colonial southern and southeastern segments; and it was being tilted eastward in favor of the new German and the expanding Russian land empires. But the Eurocentric global balance continued to favor Britain with a provocative, but hard-to-redress, disparity between the dominant sea power with continent-related anxieties and the preeminent land power with maritime aspirations. The long-standing disparity was progressively aggravated by an apparently likewise irresoluble contradiction. Whereas the expanse of yet uncolonized non-European areas was limited and shrinking, a growing and potentially limitless gap was opening up between two classes of "civilized" powers. Continent-wide industrializing states, such as the rising United States and awakening Russia and, if it could be consolidated, Britain's intercontinental colonial ensemble, were seen as having an actual or potential, but in either case apparently unmatchable, advantage over mere great powers of classic dimensions, such as the new Germany and modernizing Japan—as well as a Britain that would prove unable to coordinate her imperial domain. A spell of free-trading had muted the divergence and the related issue; but the fading of economic liberalism not only resurfaced traditional dilemmas rooted in divergent land-sea power structures but also aggravated them by pessimistic appraisals of what exclusion from political control overseas was apt to mean for material well-being at home.

The old-new assortment of structures and attitudes needed only a precipitant to reactive quests for overall parity. To be equalized was the industrialized nations' status as world powers with extensive colonial domains and technologically advanced naval capabilities; the precipitating impetus was the newly awakened interest of late- and post-Bismarckian Germany in colonial compensations in Africa and beyond, in lieu of Bismarck's earlier use of colonial assets for advantage in European diplomacy only (to console Republican France and to either woo or embarrass England on the Continent). More significant still than any change in Germany's approach to colonies was her continuity with Bourbon France, however, as the belatedly consolidated nation-state moved to catch up with the Anglo-Saxon empire-builders before they succeeded in converting prior material conquests into touchstones of a new political morality, making the gains permanent.

Carrying on the eighteenth-century Anglo-French competition in one way, the later contention differed from it in another way. There was, at first, little direct causal and close strategic interconnection between grievances and rivalries in Europe and contests over spheres of interest or dominance overseas. Somewhat like the primarily predatory colonization in the seventeenth century, the largely preclusive colonialism in and past the late nineteenth century was not actually processed through the central balance of power after it had been precipitated by events in that balance. As a diversion, overseas expansion seemed even to be reducing pressures for a central-systemic conflict. Only in due course was the last-stage allocation of dependencies to have indirect or ultimate, actual or presumptive, diplomatic and material effects upon an increasingly stressful intra-European equilibrium, by preparing the spirits and augmenting the stakes for large-scale military conflict through the agency of controversial acquisitions (by France and Britain as well as Germany), antagonizing denials (mainly to Germany), and alliance-building renunciations and redistribution (among France, Russia, and Britain).

In the final scramble for colonial possessions, Britain even more than the other powers acted preclusively to earmark and subsequently to effectively occupy desired assets in advance of anticipated occupation by a rival. A largely reluctant expansion, following upon the likewise unwillingly permanent occupation of Egypt (in 1882), comprised territories chiefly in East Africa, a sphere of influence and strategic facility in China, and island positions in the Pacific Ocean. Reservation or effective occupation could be preemptive (in Africa, with respect to French and German designs) or countervailing (in China, with respect also to Russian ambitions); new colonies or spheres of influence came into being where previously there had been only strategic support points and zones of commercial interest. The transformation was reminiscent of the much earlier one in India. But, if the new assets were neither a match for the jewel of empire nor a significant distraction from empire's burdens, no one power or combination of powers succeeded finally in colonizing China as thoroughly as Britain had India.

IV

Completing as it did the second dependent empire, the last major wave of British expansion also interrupted a period of pronounced disinclination to expand further. The disinclination was no less real for being superficially belied by new acquisitions implicit in the old ones. The lull in imperial enthusiasm began with the end of the Napoleonic wars and deepened in the mid-Victorian period. Its Roman parallel, in the mid-Republican period in the second century B.C., saw the Roman senate reach the heights of opposition to further annexations east of Illyria. In both cases the lull expressed a resistance to the *force des choses* set in train by an earlier élan; a hesitancy before the final surrender to the many-faceted expansive dynamic of political and economic power at home and abroad.

Intervening between the creation of the core-empire and its completion in a grand empire, the lull evidenced the defensive inspiration of preclusive expansionism, while infractions of it denoted the activist manifestation of that peculiarly ambivalent posture. The Roman senate had merely rolled defeated Syria back to a new line in Asia, sparing her, as it had twice-defeated Carthage and Macedon; and it had resisted local invitations to annex other rich eastern realms. Similarly, the British returned to both the French and the Dutch most colonial conquests after the Napoleonic wars. The preference was for a preeminent role in a controlled balance of power, symbolized by Roman attendance at the Greek Isthmian Games and Britain's participation in the European Concert, and hopefully susceptible of being economically implemented with the aid of resources from the core-empires' treasure-houses, Sicily for Rome and India for Britain. An uninhibited recourse against the accumulation of antagonistic power by policing injunctions or interventions would be the essence of a nonimperialistic imperial order *par excellence*.

The desire for surcease from expansion was due to satisfaction, calculation, and frustration. The satisfaction reflected decline in systemic pressures and satiation of driving needs. Pressures decreased on Rome as she became clearly supreme on land and (barring pirates) on sea, on Britain, after she had acquired the naval predominance she was to retain until late in the nineteenth century. And both survival and security needs were more than assured by systemic preeminence. The material need was not central to Rome's midterm expansion, while British dependence on colonial control was lessened by the progressive dismantling (begun in the 1820s) of the mercantilistic system in trade and shipping.

Although factors militating against further annexations were mainly economic for Britain and mainly political for Rome, the equations were in the abstract similar for both. Costs and risks of continuing expansion weighed more and more heavily against its rewards; and the advantages of enlargement outweighed those of consolidating the already achieved dominion less and less. Since only few Roman and British dependencies were truly profitable at the critical stage, the costs of acquiring, managing, and defending additional possessions tended to exceed possible gains. For the British this was true most of all in the postmercantilist and preprotectionist era; for Rome, before she learned how to systematically exploit at least some of her dependents. A political liability in Rome was that expansion strained the oligarchical system of governance. Just as conquests raised the prestige of politicians successful as military commanders, so they debased the morality of both colonial administrators (proconsuls and other promagistrates) and of the people in Rome proper. Britain produced nothing quite comparable to, say, the Scipios in one respect and a Verres in the other, but her political system was not wholly impervious to the empire-related impacts of a Pitt and a Hastings, respectively. A steadily expanding empire will in all circumstances be hard to reconcile with a fixed structure of political power at home; extending sway massively will militate against containing the popular masses. The latent conflict had been sooner and more fully manifest in Rome than it was in Britain; but the resulting practical problems are bound to impress oligarchs anywhere with greater force than can any theoretical contradiction between autocratic administration abroad and liberty at home. Dominion came to entail demagogy in Republican Rome when an oligarchical empire gave way to a populist and an autocratic one; in Britain a comparable trend was at work only briefly (before World War I) and not sufficiently to entrench the empire. In both instances, however, intermittent regard for outside public opinion, Hellenic in Rome and European in Britain, completed the range of political factors discouraging indefinite expansion whenever past good fortune allowed the imperial power to indulge in calculated self-restraint.

Frustrations were always necessary to clinch the promptings of calculation supported by satiety. Britain's faith in expansion could not but suffer from the depletion of once-secure gains, mainly in the Americas. Military-political competition among the metropolitan powers resulted in similar losses for Spain and France. The first period of decolonization was substantially complete by the 1830s. It reinforced the argument for merely economic competition as against forceful political domination, dubbed "informal imperialism" in retrospect. Rome was spared worse than annoyance with the volatile Greeks in the East; but she, too, incurred frustrations connected with ugly little wars of pacification in the barbarian West (presaging Britain's in the hard-to-civilize East) and with the fine arts of stabilization everywhere (applied, by both empires, to entities with disparate degrees of residual independence and traditional pride). Macedon's repeated bids for recovery had epitomized the problem of stability for Rome, just as the Indian mutineers' commitment to restoring the Mogul empire combined the challenges of pacification and of stabilization for Britain.

v

The reasons for a halt were both powerful and intensely held, but in neither case did they finally prevail over new pressures for continued expansion, while intermittent reexpansion took place even during the lull. When subsidiary incentives to expansion take over from satiated predation or suspended preclusion in later empire, they involve, next to the self-perpetuating concern for imperial-frontier security, also the special needs of a matured ruling class and the increasingly difficult responses to ever more complex economic equations. The last two add up to something like "new politics," implying new subjective dispositions, and were responsible for Rome's second wave of expansion even more than for Britain's; the defense of a comparatively more, or more persistently, insecure imperial frontier was by contrast peculiarly critical for Britain, facing new major powers and new structural dilemmas.

With such differences in relative impact, some of the continuing expansion beyond core-empire was in both instances motivated or rationalized by the need for either natural or defensible frontiers. If Rome's abstinence from direct annexation in the middle-Republican period had been more effective than was mid-Victorian Britain's, this was because Rome's directly ruled provincial empire was more compact and less vulnerable. Exceptions, such as Macedon and Carthage, were carry-overs from the earlier stage. But internal strains in the late-Republican period, due to intervening transformations, intensified the second wave of major expansionism when it occurred in the first century B.C. on the strength of defensive reasoning due to become fully valid only in the third century. The later British empire was not immune to internal strains and resulting pressures for compensatory territorial extension or institutional tightening; but the dispersed character of the far-flung domain carried with it also in the middle period more or less real and imminent external dangers calling for remedial or precautionary action. As an empire expands, the growing risks and costs of continuing expansion will grow relative to rewards, inhibiting an aggressive expansionist drive. But so long as counterforces remain in existence they will tend to encourage an essentially defensive expansion, because of the risks inherent in avoiding action to insure future access at a time when present capabilities are known and equations of capability and challenge in the future are unknown. The strategic interests and the threats will often appear to be—or to have been—imaginary; but even pragmatic managers of empire will incline to do more rather than less when trying to preserve, if not to match, the achievements of the original empire-builders in less spectacular but often more difficult conditions.

The strategic frontier of an empire can lie on land or sea and will have both physical and ideal contours. It stretches along boundary lines or zones on land and traverses narrow passages and naval support points on the seas; and it will be defined by lines of communication vital for enhancing the coherence and defensibility of the empire, and by either concentration of antagonistic power or fragmentation of unstable power liable to endanger the empire's safety and compel its defense. Communications, power concentrations, and authority crises all can be located either within or outside the formal boundary, if there is such. And they will push the imperial frontier expansively outward in periods of growth and inward in periods of decay, as events and configurations create new conditions, needs, and capacities for access or control. Both the Roman and the British empires had their critical territorial and maritime strategic frontiers and expanded further as these were actually or hypothetically endangered by uneven threats from tribal, lesser-state, and major-power forces in particular. Disturbances which did not threaten the frontier failed to precipitate expansion, relinquishing it to the play of other specific forces and subsidiary motives.

The principal land frontier of imperial Rome was constituted by the belt of overland communications between Spain and Italy in transalpine Gaul, progressively extended to the Rhine-Danube line; by the frontier zone against Parthia (Persia) in Asia Minor, finally reaching the Euphrates-Tigris line; and by the Sahara Desert in the south. The corresponding British overland frontier covered accesses to the European continent and the Indian subcontinent. It comprised first Portugal and the Low Countries in the West, progressively reached the Rhine in the strategic thought and action of forward defense, and came to encompass the inner-Asia and Middle-East defense frontier of India in the East. On the seas, the Mediterranean and related communications, extending marginally to the Black Sea, were in the mid-period most important for the trading allies of Rome vulnerable to Illyrian and other pirates. In the eastern segment, they were initially protected by the allied island of Rhodes. The strategic importance of the sea lanes was less than that of the Roman roads; but the Republic still rose to power in naval engagements with Carthage and went down at the sea battle of Actium (between Octavius and Antony). The critical maritime frontier of the India-centered British empire extended from the home waters to the Indian Ocean and onward to and beyond the Malacca Strait, via either the South African Cape route or the Mediterranean-Suez route. Vital strong points were taken over from defeated, decayed, or defenseless possessors and developed anew. They extended gradually from Gibraltar through Malta to Cyprus, from the Cape of Good Hope and Mauritius to Singapore, and from Suez to Aden, as well as to the areas around them. The furthermost extensions of the two empires' frontiers coincided on the Rhine, facing eastward toward the Germans, and in the Persian Gulf, facing northward to Parthia (though only briefly) in Rome's case and to Russia in Britain's. The overland frontiers of both empires were marked by forts and fortified places, only late in Rome's case, but then extensively. And Britain's maritime frontiers in particular were dotted with key ports and strongholds. Frontier safeguards were supplemental to the central or strategic reserve. Its depletion coincided in both empires with increases in threats and decline in resources.

Various kinds of threats stimulated the protective expansion of the two empires along strategic frontiers. They comprised assaults by more or less primitive warlike tribes on the imperial power's prior presence; regional counterimperialism of lesser states, stimulated often by a greater past; and contrary advance or pressures by one or more major powers. Political or military warfare occurred on all of the three levels, and was more perfidious or brutal as the scale of the empire's adversary shrank and his status declined.

Rome was amply served with real or contrived tribal threats on her western land frontier. The early pacification of the Iberian and Ligurian tribes in Spain was carried over into transalpine Gaul in the late Republic; it overlept the channel into Britain under the Empire; and it came to rest on the Danube (by the conquest of Dacia) after efforts had failed to shorten the Rhine-Danube frontier by an eastward push toward the Elbe River against the Germans. In the east, Cilicia (off Cyprus) was annexed by the Republic to protect a coastal strip from hinterland mountaineers. The less extensive equivalents in the British empire are exemplified by the northwest frontier in India, the northern frontier of white South Africa, and the boundary of upper Egypt; threats came from warlike Sikhs, the Zulu warriors, and the Sudanese tribes under the Mahdi. And if the defense line in India was on land alone, the other two extended ultimately to the maritime frontier represented by the Cape-Simonstown and the Suez-Red Sea complexes.

Counterimperialism by lesser states was represented for Rome by resurgent Carthage (or, alternatively, by Carthage's Numidian neighbor in North Africa, in the period preceding the Third Punic War) and Macedon (twice, after being revived by Perseus and rebelliously reunified following a punitive partition). At a later point, locally expansive policies of Mithridates of Pontus, off the Hellespont strait, completed the cycle of wars leading to annexations. They marked a defeat for Rome's preference for nonannexation in favor of dependent "free" cities and client states. The British imperial frontier was threatened by the independent Afrikaner republics in South Africa. Their assertiveness increased when the prior British military action had relieved them of the warlike Zulus. But, in contrast to the comparable earlier British relief action against the French-Indian alliance in North America, a British victory over the Boer bid for independence contained the local counter-imperialists in the Union of South Africa at least temporarily. Yet another threat came from the drive of the Burmese empire into Assam and Bengal in the east of India, to be neutralized only by the annexation of Lower Burma. In all such cases, precautionary suspicions and outright provocations by the imperial power, its agents and dependents, helped impel the smaller-scale challenger toward an ultimately vain bid for autonomy via local supremacy. Both the Romans and the British reacted aggressively to the threat which a successful local self-assertion would represent for either overland or maritime access to a peripheral area or balance of power. And, more specifically, they acted to insure the security or submission of dependents (such as Rhodes-Pergamum and Cappadocia, the Cape Colony and Bengal) bordering on the local troublemaker.

The last kind of frontier threat was potentially most awesome but actually least acute most of the time. It came from great powers, meaning Parthia for Rome's and mainly Russia for Britain's eastern empire. The danger transpired more often in proconsular perceptions than in metropolitan designs on either side, not least before Parthia was regenerated under the Sassanid dynasty in the post-Republican period (after 220 A.D.) and Russia was fully activated as a world power in the post-British empire era.

After completing the containment of defeated Syria, Rome's client states in Asia Minor set the stage for treating unstable Parthia as both a quasi-client and a pseudo-threat, exposed to abortive schemes of conquest by individual Roman potentates in the late Republic. When Republic yielded to Principate and Empire, sporadic wars with Parthia led to a progressive absorption of the intermediate client states that had been previously semi-integrated through collection of tribute to Rome and division of labor with Rome in maintaining local order and security. Bythinia, Cappadocia following upon Pontus, and Judea were among these; and wholly new conquests had comprised Mesopotamia and Armenia before, in the final period marked by Sassanid renaissance in Parthia (or Persia), it was the latter's turn to invade some of the embattled provinces and to reactivate the see-sawing contest for the most critical, Armenian, buffer. Rome's Hellenized buffer states had their equivalents in the slowly "westernized" buffers on India's frontier under the British Raj. The buffers extended eventually from Persia in the west (against Russia) to Siam in the east (against France). If the British virtually absorbed Nepal and Upper Burma (in precaution against Russian pressures on south China and French advances in Indo-China), Afghanistan resembled in the Anglo-Russian setting most closely the earlier status of Armenia as the most evenly contested, and most nearly autonomous, buffer state. Rome had eventually to renounce converting resistance to the rising Persian power on the Euphrates-Tigris frontier into expansion, when increasing "barbarian" pressure on the Rhine-Danube frontier had made yet another buffer belt of recently Romanized Germanic kingdoms more urgent. Somewhat similarly, the subsidence of reciprocal British and Russian (and French) expansionisms was due largely to rising preoccupations with a Germany ascendant in Europe and ambitious in both China and Asia Minor.

While reacting to even imagined threats, neither empire rushed into remedial action against local disorder or anarchy that clearly lacked the potential for endangering frontier security. This was true even when internal troubles beset once major empires, as they tended to. Rome delayed taking charge of Syria and Egypt despite chaos in both and despite the fact that Egypt (like Pergamum before) was bequeathed to the Roman people by the last of the Ptolemies, until growing local disorders meshed with political struggles in Rome proper to produce action. Much the same was true for Pergamum and Egypt's offshoot, Cyrene (Cyrenaica). Similarly, late British imperialists preferred a mere protectorate in Malaya, while local disorders in East and West Africa, the Nile and Niger River area, failed to produce annexations before the final scramble got under way. Basic dispositions were similar in regard to the Ottoman and the Chinese empires, though the stakes were higher. Prior to the Ottoman Empire being finally liquidated in World War I, the British acquisitions at its expense had been related to the defense of the Straits (Cyprus) and of Suez (Egypt), while the contributing events inside Egypt were precipitated by an early instance of nationalistic disorders tied to economic development. In regard to China, too, Britain opposed partition, while seeking for herself only privileged access, mainly to the Yangtze River area adjoining Burma in competition with France. Preference for access everywhere over assured control of only a part also made Britain lease a military port farther in the north, as a countervailing measure to similar Russian and German acquisitions.

VI

Frontier threats or transfrontier disorders can precipitate expansive responses by the central imperial authority. Conversely, enlargements can be due primarily to local or subimperial initiatives. This happens when peripheral dependencies reproduce the motives and patterns of the core-power's expansion on a small scale; or when expansionist proconsuls project outward the mechanics of internal metropolitan politics.

Small powers dependent on Rome had little occasion for territorial subimperialism of their own. Always suspicious of uncontrolled foreign power, Rome tightened constraints when previously enlarged protagonists of the Roman order in the East, Pergamum and Rhodes, had failed to give wholeheartedly support in the last-but-one war against resurgent Macedon (under Perseus). The senate shifted thereafter definitively to fostering local stalemates (e.g., between Pergamum and Bythinia) by forcing local victors to restore gains to defeated rivals. Subimperialism flourished best, therefore, in function of institutional flaws: on a semi-private basis, by individual provincial clients of leading Romans preparatory to civil-wartime collusions; and in the economic arena, by Italian and Greek traders protected and promoted as a compensation for their political disfranchisement. Support for secure economic activities in exchange for political subordination played a comparable role in the British empire when the central government tolerated official expansive drives of white colonists and empire-oriented entrepreneurs. In Australia, New Zealand, and, later, East Africa, the peripheral imperialists pushed forward in quest of more indigeous land or labor; in South Africa, before the Boer War, British interests moved north from the Cape Colony into Afrikaner territory in pursuit of mineral wealth, and into Central Africa in quest of a counterpoise to Afrikaner attractive strength. And in West Africa, and perhaps elsewhere, the locally felt need to make previously acquired positions economically viable continued to foster pressures for enlarged control.

The other, proconsular type of subimperialism evolved still more differently in the two empires. Personal profit-seeking had tainted a Clive and a Hastings; but, when designing or implementing expansive security strategies, later British proconsuls sought not so much material profit as official promotion and politically marketable prestige. Noble Romans had shifted their priorities inversely, from earning the supreme civic and political reward (of a military triumph) inside Rome to collecting economic perquisites mainly in Asia. In Britain, a Curzon and a Milner were among the few whom proconsular service, in India and South Africa respectively, elevated significantly in domestic political standing; successful exploitation of promagistracies for a like end by a Caesar and a Pompey merely climaxed a rapidly evolving trend in the late-Republican polity.

Differences within each category of subimperialism and in degrees of importance between them had a larger long-term significance for the two empires. Starting with Canada, settler imperialism evolved soon into colonial nationalism and carried the British empire toward dissolution by way of the progressive disengagement of the white dependencies, in advance on the later and then more rapid decolonization of the remainder. On the other hand, the closer link between proconsular policies and metropolitan politics in Rome progressively undermined the Republican system itself. The British process turned an empire into a commonwealth; the Roman evolution altered a free commonwealth with an *imperium* into autocratic empire pure and simple.

II

EXTENSIONS
OF EMPIRE. *Domestic*
Dynamics

A preimperial community's concerns with irreducible security and sustenance are the original motives which initiate expansion. For the concerns to be effectively expressed, social cohesion and elite leadership, stabilizing equilibrium and galvanizing hierarchy, must have been combined internally in an ever so elementary manner. At a later stage, along with the need to secure the imperial periphery, the evolving political system will supply a subsidiary incentive to continuing expansion as it projects abroad internal stresses and reactions to domestic strains. The projective mechanism is always operative. But it will be most prominent as a source of expansion when the drives of predation and the dilemmas of preemption, relating the body politic as a whole to its international environment, are muted or temporarily dormant, and when the issues of survival in physical security and material sufficiency are matched by the problem of political stability within the metropole.

Security fears will tend to subside and problems of stability increase for a well-established core-empire. At that point of relative maturity, a threefold enlargement within the domestic system will be responsible for the further expansion of the empire, in its spatial extent or scope of organization, and will bring about its overall debasement in style and standards. The enlargements are related in one way or another to the empire-building ruling class or elite, tending toward oligarchy. And they will condition the likewise threefold changes, or three-phase evolution, in the posture and predicament of that class as it descends from the position of unchallenged trusteeship to collective trauma by the detour of transactions with upthrusting lower social groups. One of the enlargements affects the stakes which engage the attention and the energies of the ruling class as socioeconomic conditions change; it entails some deterioration in the quality of the ruling class and of its methods. Another enlargement is of the political system itself. That amplification results from divisions within the ruling class which activate the popular masses and tend to associate a new, aspiring political class of men in the management of the empire. The dilution of the constituent ruling class within an extended political system, along with the enlargement of the empire-related material payoffs, will be attended by yet another and final enlargement. The conception of the empire and its traditional values will be magnified to compensate for the symptoms of intervening corruption or the fears of impending decline.

I

The life paths of each ruling class and of each empire were all the more parallel in Rome and Britain because the two systems of power arose rather suddenly out of a previously isolated society, primitive even by the standards of its time. And inevitably involved in the eventual deterioration of the empire-founding ruling classes, attendant on one or several enlargements, was the ruling-class ethos governing functional responses to rival forces at home and abroad.

Both the Roman and the British imperial ruling class was a landed aristocracy. Its members were individually qualified for the exercise of political power by birth; they were selected on the basis of proven skills, which meant essentially the gift for command in Rome and for management in Britain; and they were rewarded for achievement by the honors and perquisites of office. Moreover, both groups succeeded an original, quasi-tribal ruling class that had been destroyed in early civil wars, between patricians and plebeians in Rome and among nobles alone (in the Wars of the Roses) in England. Consequently, they were both relatively new and dynamic at the critical junctures. And they soon established their right to rule by presiding over spectacular successes in foreign wars on land and sea, meaning the First Punic War in Rome and, in the England following upon the defeat of the Spanish Armada, the repulse of a French invasion attempt (in the sea battle at La Hogue), and victories in the French wars for empire.

The similarities in background prompted an increasingly self-conscious immersion of the British elite in the Roman exemplar. The similarities were offset, however, by differences in internal constitutions and in the constitutive principles or rationales of the empire itself. Whereas the Roman senate was a largely autonomous body, the British nobility-in-

Parliament had first to release its political power from strong dynastic constraints and, whereas the Roman empire was primarily militaristic in its nature and origins, the British empire was of an essentially mercantile character. The corresponding Roman concept of *virtus* emphasized fortitude under stress in regard to adversaries, *fides* to allies in adversity, and cohesion within political factions, patron-client sets, and military legions under the well-born commander-statesman. The British ethos emphasized instead pragmatic flexibility and, in due course, fair play, along with individuality. Class solidarity became a politically significant value only when the decline of divisive royal prerogatives was followed by the rise of socially inferior competitors with the aristocratic "cousins-in-Parliament." As long as adaptability exceeded assertiveness as the formula for routine political success, it relegated the more forceful personal mode to empire-building enterprises abroad by junior members of the aristocracy and aspiring members of the lower orders—a spectrum comprising over time a Raleigh, Clive, Raffles, and Rhodes. The exploits of British empire adventurers were matched occasionally by the flamboyance of individual British statesmen. But, throughout, expansive personal egotism was less an integral part of the British system of values and politics than it had become in Rome during the civil wars, perverting the ethos of firmness and denying that of cohesion.

A bias to deterioration will haunt every imperial ruling class, characteristically formed or crystallized in violent contentions, such as the Punic wars and the conflicts over the Protestant succession. The related crises will test the elite's commitment to a higher than individual or party interest, or at least demonstrate its capacity to identify a widely shared special interest with the state's welfare. Following the consolidation of the imperial state, heightened or newly defined partisan divisions will appear within the ruling class and foster its concurrent dilution. They both, divisions and dilution, will be related to the rise of socially subordinate elements, such as the middle-class financiers (the so-called equites) next to the plebs in Rome and the trading-industrial middle class and the mass electorate in Britain. At that critical midpoint, the aristocratic class will deflect the exercise of governing functions into efforts to retain power. It will adjust strategies for serving the state to the growing necessity to prove itself serviceable (to the ascendant middle classes) and to its declining capacity to elicit servility (from electorally activated lower orders), so as to avert or delay dispossession in favor of either despotic democracy (in Britain) or more or less popular despotism (in Rome).

The decline in the Roman aristocratic ethos appears to be sharper than that in the British, because the former ethos was pitched higher in its principles and had, therefore, deeper to sink in practice. The will-to-power took the wrong turn when the military empire veered toward the materialism of an exploitative one; when *virtus* came to be aimed at domestic adversaries as much as at external enemies. The overall tone of the British empire seemed to improve with time by contrast (though more so in India than in Ireland), and the actually applied standards seemed to rise; but they did so only as the domestic power of the ruling class declined along, perhaps, with the waning of its political talents.[1] In conditions of unmanageable social change, the British ethos of adaptation accelerated class debilitation. The sturdier Roman value of self-assertion suffered instead debasement in conditions of an accelerating social disruption. If the later British model was best betokened by the family duo Salisbury-Balfour, the Roman had been in the breakup of the Pompey-Caesar duumvirate. In the end, the skepticism of the last great Cecil was the British ruling class's only remaining antidote to the kind of internal scission which the first Caesar had brought to a head in Rome. Dispassionate pragmatism had to be summoned in one case to carry on with the managerial chores in a state of group dejection; in the other, domineering individual impulses were further exacerbated by the passion-play of empire in conditions of systemic decay. The common denominator was latter-day reexpansion, mainly defensive in the British case and still largely offensive in the Roman.

Relating ethos to functions, the deterioration of a political class and the coincident crisis of the political system will bear on the modes of acquiring, exercising, and retaining political power. Abuse in the exercise entails corruption, not least economic. Abuse in acquiring or retaining power entails violation of established rules of the game, by a resort to extraneous sources of power and arbiters of political success, including the military. Both abuses will be attended by new pressures for further expansion, giving rise to tendencies more fully revealed or consummated in the Roman case than in the British.

The early prerequisite of political power was, in both empires, relative and relatively ancient wealth based on land. In late-Republican Rome, however, political power also became increasingly a way of augmenting wealth, and very great, liquid wealth became ultimately necessary for the virtual purchase of power. The traditional polity of the aristocracy gave way to the new politics of demagogy; a species of intra-empire mercantilism (power, including military power, as a means to wealth) was combined with an early form of senatorial finance-capitalism (still

---

1. See Matthew Arnold's comment to this effect, in Wilhelm L. Guttsman, ed., *The English Ruling Class* (London: Weidenfeld and Nicolson, 1969), pp. 172–76. See also J. H. Grainger, *Character and Style in English Politics* (London: Cambridge University Press, 1969). On the Romans, see E. Badian, *Foreign Clientelae 264–70 B.C.* (Oxford: Clarendon Press, 1958); Frank R. Cowell, *Cicero and the Roman Republic*, 4th ed. (Baltimore: Penguin Books, 1967); Erich S. Gruen, *The Last Generation of the Roman Republic* (Berkeley: University of California Press, 1974); and H. Hill, *The Roman Middle Class in the Republican Period* (Oxford: Basil Blackwell, 1952).

greater wealth being derived from high-interest loans to clients and se-cured by military sanctions against default). The attendant corruption in the exercise of authority was in part a compensation for traditional in-hibitions on senatorial access to lucrative pursuits (e.g., the practice of trade under the Lex Claudia). It also revealed an inversion of traditional values whenever *virtus* migrated from effecting expansion by conquest to exploiting conquests by militarily enforced tribute and returns on pri-vate investment.

The British empire, in India and elsewhere, was familiar with like practices in its more predatory early stage. But the ruling class itself moved from personal corruption, in late dynastic politics, by way of residual political corruptness, in early electoral politics, to legitimate compensation for services rendered in managing empire. In the process the British elites were served, just as the Romans had been in effect subverted, by both law and social tradition and ethos. The English law prescribed that legal portions of paternal wealth go to younger sons. The assets became usable for trade or settlement in colonies, since the tradi-tional mercantile ethos permitted trade to produce respectable wealth and such wealth to be converted into possession of land and, with it, sociopolitical status. On their part, the great landed proprietors levied automatically a basic fee for managing the empire, both directly and indirectly, from the growing commercial and industrial prosperity. When, in due course, the aristocratic dictators of imperial policy subsided into decorative parts in company directorships, the debasement was one in political power rather than in the moral quality of its exercise. Mean-while, the Boer War was less directly caused and influenced by "capitalis-tic" interests (indictments by Hobson et al. notwithstanding) than had been Rome's Wars of Mithridates in the first century B.C. By the same token, official Roman harassment of Egypt in the same century can be more convincingly related to patrician investments than can Egypt's occupation in 1882 be attributed to governmental subservience to non-aristocratic English and foreign bondholders.

Likewise conducive to expansion, and a more basic flaw than occa-sional abuse of power, is the resort to traditionally untapped, extraneous sources of political power for the purposes of its acquisition or retention. In the case of Rome, the issue involved the recruitment, organization, and use of military legions; in Britain's case it was the organization of political allegiance. The early, preprofessional situation connected in both cases war and politics. In Rome, well-conducted war led to material booty and political preferment, including authorization to hold a tri-umph; in Britain, inept conduct of war could materially affect the dis-position of political office, inasmuch as it interfered with an uninhibited exercise of royal favoritism for one elite set by mobilizing popular favor for another. The fortunes of the greatest Scipio (Africanus) in Rome and the elder Pitt in England illustrate the mechanisms. They also stand for the first signs of the later transition to professionalism with popular overtones. In Rome, enlarged resources, drawn from "organizing" (i.e., fiscally exploiting) the province of Asia, fostered professional militarism; in Britain, movement toward political professionalism was due to increases in both the resources available to the government and the demands made on it within incipient industrial mass society. As the new resources were mobilized in both systems, the new political forces had to be appeased with the aid of either more expansion or more effective exploitation of empire, with consequences for traditional political arrangements.

Roman expansion was most clearly related to the new political resource, the professional legion. As a given condition, imperial expansion supplied the warrant for soliciting the authority to raise and command armies, increasingly necessary for the political success or survival of individual power-seekers. In regard to means, expansion produced new land and new wealth to distribute among loyal veterans. Expansion as a consequence was, moreover, the most patent demonstration of the driving genius of a politician as military commander anxious to gain and hold onto the personal loyalty of his troops. And, finally, expansion was also a key legitimating factor in so far as conquest or effective policing of peripheral disorders and boundaries covered up for other, less legitimate, uses of military power and personnel.[2]

The British context was more strictly political. But the elder Pitt's wartime pursuit of office by appeals from a reluctant king to the people, as the still extraconstitutional source of executive power, was a clear challenge to the preexisting political system; no less of an infraction was to be Joseph Chamberlain's resort to extraparliamentary bases of political strength, in a provincial political machine (or by Randolph Churchill to the Primrose League organization). In relation to imperial expansion, the new internal resource served less as the prime cause than as the more or less effective means. In Pitt's case, it helped conquer the king for an effective policy of imperial expansion; in Chamberlain's it was intended to sway the Tory party and through it the electorate for the empire's consolidation. The reverse connection, from imperial program to the domestic power struggle, lay in the program's actual or alleged benefit for either the mercantile interest, in the case of Pitt, or both the middle and the working classes, in that of Chamberlain. The new out-

2. The principal "illegitimate" uses were to employ military followers as the ultimate reserve in extralegal political acts, and as reservoir of votes in elections to magistracies or promagistracies. The last was vital, since uninterrupted official incumbency was the only reliable sanctuary against politically motivated legal prosecution by one's opponents. The practice, prefigured by Lucullus, initiated by Marius's settling of veterans on conquered lands, continued by Sulla and developed by Pompey, was consummated by Caesar in his integral expansionism, ending in well-nigh absolute power.

look promised to enhance the political standing of its proponent against more constitutionally orthodox and more firmly entrenched rivals.

Similarity in the functions of the Roman military and the British political machines meant that the British military was of secondary importance for political manipulation in the imperial context. One reason was that the Indian Army, a financially autonomous force, was largely immune to parliamentary control. It was left to actual military operations in the colonial peripheries to have an impact, not always unplanned, on the political fortunes of parties or politicians at home, not least with the rise of the mass electorate and no less than had major conflicts. A popular war would help a party in power, as the Boer War did the Tory party through the so-called Khaki election in 1900; and the party in opposition would profit from a mismanaged war, as the Whigs did from the Afghan and Zulu wars in the late 1870s. The only real, if unconsummated, parallel with Rome was thus the role which the professionalized army might have played in Britain's near-civil warlike situation prior to World War I, which fused imperial and social motifs in the focus on Ireland.

II

Deterioration in a ruling class will be commonly attended, if it is not caused, by internal divisions. Such divisions will create more direct pressures for expansion than does deterioration, and they will do so most directly by encouraging the formulation of conflicting strategies. The conflict of strategies will bear chiefly on military-political security in the early period of ruling-class ascendancy. It will focus mainly on socio-economic domestic issues at a later date, when new internal forces have risen and become targets for optional strategies. Whereas such rise terminates the power monopoly of the ruling class, it does not reforge the elite's pristine (and in part mythical) unity at any time before it faces imminent dispossession. Strategies formulated as contrasts or opposites will actually foment movement in both directions, as a result of compromises or alternation in power of the proponents. This will promote expansion whenever frustration does not produce temporary lulls instead of aggressive reactions, depending on circumstances.

In the middle period of the Roman Republic, conflicts over politico-military strategies revolved around both the degree and the direction of expansion. As to degree, the more restrictionist senate was pitted against more consistently ambitious politician-commanders; as to direction, the "barbarian" West rivaled for priority the politically more intricate, but richer, East. In the early controversy between Cato and Scipio, the East *vs.* West issue involved priority for either corrupting Greece or, presumably, still-menacing Carthage; at a later stage, Pompey's strategic concentration on the East contrasted with Caesar's on the West. In both instances the difference was tied to structures of values and also power at home; it was resolved through expansion at large in both directions; and the expansion reduced to the point of eliminating the much-disputed "counterpoise of fear," meaning the apprehension of outside enemies such as Carthage acting as a brake on the erosion of inherited virtues.

A different conflict over strategy arose in eighteenth-century England. At issue was the relative primacy of the European balance of power and of the overseas imperial theater. The purportedly converse strategies were at first identified with the Whig and the Tory factions, respectively. In due course, the "Europeanist" line led from a Newcastle and Carteret through Castlereagh to Gladstone, while the "globalist" line extended from Pitt through Canning (vs. Castlereagh) to Disraeli (vs. Gladstone) and on to Salisbury (vs. alliance with Germany). The representatives of the first lineage stressed the European balance of power or concert as the outside supports, at one time or another, of the Protestant succession, the conservative political order, or a conservative budget in the context of liberal free-trade policies; only the way of implementing the priority would change with the rise and the decline of Britain's capacity for military intervention. Protagonists in the second lineage were committed instead either verbally or by deeds to a more or less splendid detachment from European affairs, viewed as either distracting or negligible, and eventually as unmanageable; they would stress rule or influence overseas, in North America and India, Latin America and the Near East, and (as time passed on) in the Near East and Asia, as apt to produce profit, prestige, and (in due course) counterpoise to the rise of newly strong powers on the Continent. The issue of strategy was related in each major phase to a major internal issue with external implications, first that of Hanover (as a source of continental involvement) and later that of Ireland (as a portent of colonial insurgence). Meanwhile, the interacting conflicts made England move forcefully in both the European and the imperial directions in the early phase and intensified popular sentiment behind latter-day imperial initiatives. Sentimental support became valuable for an enterprise torn between waning free-trade doctrines and waxing overseas particularisms, including protectionism. It did not impede colonial adjustments with France and Russia as a preliminary to Britain's reinvolvement in Europe, which was to produce in due course final imperial conquests at the cost of the Ottoman and the German empires.

The connection between domestic and imperial affairs grows in intensity (and the connection between deterioration and division of the ruling class is most intimate) when constitutional issues acquire social contents and a divided ruling class enlarges the political system by contending over the allegiance of the popular mass. In Rome the critical cleavages had ranged from the conflict between the populist-aristocratic brothers

Gracchi and the traditionalist senate to the duel between still aristocratic if differently "popularist" Caesar and a reconstructed senate, still conservative if less uniformly aristocratic. In Britain, the most notorious encounter took place between Disraeli's Tory democracy and Gladstone's middle-class liberalism. However, more portentous in the long run was the conflict which opposed the radical social imperialism of Joseph Chamberlain to the free-trading conservatism of Salisbury and to the milder reformism of Liberal imperialists such as Rosebery and Grey. The key issue in both Rome and Britain was how to win over a politically mobilized people; the related question, how to make the populace visibly benefit from empire. The outcome, actual or desired, was to generate a new, mass-based drive behind the empire for its further expansion or more thorough organization.

Political mobilization of the people was always implicit in Rome's cleavage between the patricians and the plebs; it climaxed in the civil wars of the first century B.C. involving a reformed conservative senate. Britain's milder substitute for a civil war was the protracted competition over electoral reform in three nineteenth-century installments; it enlarged the electorate and produced a more responsive, if not yet democratized, House of Commons.

Key bids for popular support tended to coincide with famine in Rome and economic depressions in England, each sharpening popular receptivity to empire-connected remedies or bounties. The reform scheme of the younger Gracchus (in the 120s B.C.) had but slow and delayed effects. But the fiscal organization as a province of Pergamum, a hitherto spurned bequest to the Roman people, created a source of revenue for financing bread subsidies and thus a new, vital popular stake in empire. It was to fuel later annexations (e.g., of Cyrene) and new schemes for the economic exploitation of unannexed client kingdoms (by taxing them, as did Pompey). By dint of feeding and buying the people, the Rome of the Gracchi evolved into that of Caesar and, thereafter, of the caesars; as the bread subsidy spread, so did the conquered provincial land opened to colonial settlement. Social radicalism evolved somewhat similarly into socially based imperialism in Britain. Joseph Chamberlain's Free-Land plank had been aimed at landless laborers; it was extended subsequently to the search for new incentives to overseas settlement and new resources for internal reform in and through the empire, to be tied together by common imperial tariff and federal institutions. The objective—and a possible but not achieved outcome—was to simultaneously update Britain's social fabric and her position in world trade and power. The two-pronged strategy would supplant elaborate tactical gyrations, including the Palmerstonian variety of liberal imperialism making up for domestic conservatism; and it would put an end to the alternation of concern for internal social reform (thus from the 1820s to the 1870s and

again after 1906) with preoccupation with empire, as one set of accumulated frustrations fostered escape into another arena of meanwhile built-
up pressures and apparent opportunities for action. The failure of the
elder Chamberlain's efforts, to match the formal enlargement of the electorate with the enlargement of material payoffs from a reformed empire,
left only the decreasing facility of foreign-policy panache to compensate
for the penury of domestic programs.

The attempt to channel the unfocused demands of new voters, and to
transcend the waning system of rotten boroughs, recalled the Gracchian
effort to neutralize the waxing practices of aristocratic vote-buying by a
systematic approach to social relief. The Gracchian approach had degenerated in due course, while Chamberlain's proposed policy was first
deflected by the improved economic outlook in the 1890s into a final
burst of the so-called imperialism of free trade, and revived only in the
midst of the severest of economic depressions in the 1930s (by another
Chamberlain). And whereas the Englishman's policy was defeated by the
fear that imperial protection and reform would raise the domestic price
of bread, the Roman's had been undone by the suspicion that diffusion
of citizenship among Italians (faintly echoed in the idea of Imperial
Federation in England) would disperse the just-acquired bread subsidy
too widely and devalue it at the tribal center of empire. There was a
difference, however. The division in the Roman ruling class coincided
with the mere beginnings of its dilution by a rising new financial and
industrial middle class; dilution was more advanced at the critical point
in Britain. Accordingly, the aristocratic background of the Gracchi
brothers contrasted with the middle-class origins of both Disraeli and
Chamberlain, confining social change to the Gracchian alliance with
middle-class equites against the patrician senate and to the consequences
of that alliance for the interclass balance of power.

III

A middle class will sooner or later challenge a ruling elite for the
allegiance of a politically mobilized people. Before the contest gets fully
under way, however, the traditional class will attempt to overcome the
cleavage between itself and the new wealth through the less damaging
methods of compensation and co-optation, incurring further dilution and
new pressures for expansion in the process.

If ruling-class divisions had been foremost in producing expansionist
consequences in Rome, ruling-class dilution was prominent in having a
like dynamic effect in Britian. But the upper and middle classes were
similarly disparate in both empires. The older class leaned toward land
tenure and the newer toward seaborne commerce, while the former was
relatively declining and the latter relatively ascendant. Identical cleavages will occur between primarily continental and primarily maritime

territorial states; and the landed interest incarnated in either a state or a social class will display less mobile sources of wealth, be actuated by more pessimistic assessments of the advantages of change and the possibilities of expansion, and confine the expansionist drive within intrinsically more finite bounds than will the mercantile-maritime interest in both categories of actors. The cleavage in both interests and principles between a landed aristocracy and a commercial middle class would seem, moreover, to occasion as automatic a conflict as does the similar disparity between continental and maritime states. In practice, however, the domestic conflict can be postponed for sufficiently long to dampen its intensity or diminish its relevance, owing to the real or apparent possibilities of adjustment within any dynamic body politic and, notably, an expansive imperial one.

Moves toward accommodation will encourage expansion as the landed class promotes and protects the interest of the mercantile class in profit from trade, while reserving for itself, with the latter's initial concurrence, positions of authority within the empire, on account of its superior political power or, in the last resort, skill. The exchange intensifies as the middle class rises in political significance, if only because individual members or factions of the ruling class compete for its support and compensate it for provisional self-restraint, while the ruling elite as a group declines in actual power even while retaining positions of authority. Finally, the long-complementary preoccupations of the two classes will be propelled toward either antagonism or alliance, polarization or fusion, by the rising pressure from the third, popular, element in the overall field of political forces. As the upper and the middle classes decline and rise in different directions, see-saw at midterm, and finally decay and risk falling together, the populace will loom ever larger as a reservoir of potential auxiliary strength in electoral or other contests, as an alternative makeweight in internal alliances, or as a menace to both superior classes.

Interclass alliances can mute the conflicts between land-focused and sea-oriented domestic interests more effectively than foreign alignments habitually contain a comparable schism among states. But they are less apt to deal with the organic divergence between rising and declining classes. The politics of nonterritorial actors tend toward total victories or defeats in the absence of a merger or a jointly incurred transformation. Consequently, alliance between the declining class and the ascendant one will merely help to effect a more gradual, and thus more insidious, decline of the first, while conferring social acceptability, and thus initial legitimacy as present or future political players, upon the leading members of the second class. If the final interclass conflict occurs despite prior attempts at alliance, accommodation, and assimilation, the meanwhile enlarged political system will find the weakened traditional aristocracy attempting to reassert itself with the aid of one more, ideal, enlargement. The original ethos of service will reemerge, purified of vain compromises. More important, it will be reaffirmed conjointly with the exaltation of the empire, as the elite's finest achievement, to be secured in hoped-for alliance with the aristocracy's natural wards, the people, against a middle class that had been finally unmasked as determined to monopolize both material profit and political power.

The process through which the ruling class is transmuted, the domestic political system expanded, and the empire first augmented and then glorified, passes through three main phases. They entail for the empire-founding ruling class in succession the moral responsibility of trusteeship, implicit in unlimited control; the political exertions and strains of trans-actions, comprising co-optation and compensation or appeasement; and the psychopolitical ordeal of trauma, attending final conflict, collapse, or both. If trusteeship is the starting point for class deterioration, ruling-class divisions and dilution are typically related to intergroup transactions, while trauma attends the threat and, finally, the accomplished fact of dispossession.

IV

In the first phase of trusteeship, the ruling class has virtually sole responsibility for the common welfare, including economic. It is bur-dened with little if any accountability downward and rewarded with direct or indirect profit to itself. Following the conquest of land, the dominant elite conquers markets and other assets and insures the military-political protection of the mercantile class. The Roman aris-tocracy protected the interests of the disfranchised Italian traders to be joined, beginning with the second century B.C., by the emerging Roman entrepreneurs. It may have done so more consistently in the barbarian West than in the East, and Rome's Italian allies waited with growing resentment for Roman citizenship before finally fighting for it in the Social War. On the British side, military and naval power shielded the English merchant and planter in the West Indies more directly than his counterparts in India, where the East India Company long maintained its own army. And the British merchants, too, repeatedly expressed dis-satisfaction with public policy, thus when judging too generous and en-during the colonial concessions under the Peace of Utrecht with France in the early eighteenth century, while patrician politicians exploited commercial grievances as part of their exclusive and esoteric political games. However well-protected it may have been, neither mercantile group was a prime political actor at the early stage, despite isolated contrary appearances or even facts. Among the latter was the rise of the Italians to Roman citizenship which, coincidentally with massacres of their kin by an eastern potentate (Mithridates of Pontus), reinforced

long-term pressures for greater official involvement eastward; and the real
or exaggerated horrors of the Indian Mutiny and the Boxer Rebellion in
China were to have a similar effect in a later, post-mercantilist British
context.

Trusteeship evolved toward transactions simultaneously with the development of mostly informal links between individual profit and state
power. The new situation applied more pointedly in the British case
than in the Roman; and more to authentic Romans than to the just-
enfranchised Italians. As it grew in size and self-confidence, the middle
class became able to reward leading politicians for actions on behalf of its
economic interests both within and outside the limits of "formal" (i.e.,
directly administered) empire. The critical changes in the standing of the
new middle class were both formal and material. In Rome, the formal
change occurred in the 120s B.C., when the political alliance between the
Gracchi and the financial middle class (the equestrian order) put the
latter in charge of tax collection in the Eastern dependencies and, even
more significantly, of juries entitled to prosecute patricians for mal-
administration in the provinces of empire. The complementary, material
increase in middle-class power derived from the diffusion of Roman citizenship, which expanded the numbers, the capital, and the area of activities of the equestrian order inside and outside Italy. The first electoral
Reform Bill, of 1832, enlarged similarly the access of the British middle
class to political consideration, if not yet power, while the repeal of the
protectionist Corn Laws in 1846 expanded materially the volume of trade
and capital. To these enhancements were added the longer-range, and
largely unintended, effects of the later enfranchisements of urban and
rural voters. Mainly the material changes were progressively reflected in
both policy and political personnel, albeit more thoroughly within the
mercantile British system and ethos. In Republican Rome, the privileged
military functions and the legally constrained economic activities of the
ruling senatorial class had combined to impede a middle-class break-
through, while the Augustan order was such as to further inhibit transformations of the ruling class.

If to unequal degrees, the middle class rose politically in both empires
by gradual steps. Starting the process were selective handouts (of individual citizenship in Rome and limited vote in Britain) from contending
ruling-class factions, while more important concessions were fightingly
secured later with the aid of "new men" of middle-class origins previously
co-opted into the ruling class. The dynamic of midterm transactions will
commonly unfold in two main stages. In the first phase, the established
ruling class compensates the ascendant middle class for keeping it away as
a group from the direct exercise of political power. To that end, the
traditional sociopolitical elite tolerates the progressive social assimilation
of the rising middle stratum and co-opts its most effectively assimilated

outstanding members into the political personnel, with consequences for policy. In the second stage, a weakening ruling class will move beyond compensation to attempting to appease a meanwhile strengthened and potentially challenging middle class, with the aid of policies calculated to reward or revive its waning self-restraint and to retard a final bid for sole political power. As the social and political transactions become less productive, the dispossesion-prone political class will be progressively displaced nonetheless from the full range of government to foreign or imperial affairs and from elective to appointive office.

Co-optation of individual middle-class members was first spectacularly manifest in Rome in the rise of a *homo novus*, Marius; and it continued when his conservative opponent, Sulla, used middle-class equites to replenish a decimated senate. The weight of the ascendant class itself was employed with greatest effect to press the senatorial class for firmness in foreign and imperial policies. The scope of safeguarded economic activities grew as a result, as Marius pacified North Africa and Gaul, and young Pompey secured the Eastern Mediterranean from piracy. In the course of the crescending civil war, new areas of economic exploitation within and outside formally annexed territories were opened up by Caesar in the West and by Pompey, a man still closer to the equites, in the East. Such new outlets compensated a class which, like its early nineteenth-century British counterpart, was neither able nor anxious to actually replace the ruling class but could deny backing to its individual parties or factions. Less anxious to compensate and more anxious to appease were the aristocratic civilian governors and military commanders in outlying provinces who favored the economic interests of a class capable of punishing uncooperative patricians. Not only did equites control for a time the jury system reviewing administrative acts, they also increasingly influenced the assignment of military commands: e.g., when the Eastern command (against Mithridates) was taken from an unaccommodating Lucullus and given to Pompey.

In Britain, Lord Palmerston in his heyday supplied all the firmness abroad that could be reasonably desired. One of his objects was to impress the middle class, as well as the populace, with a vigorous foreign and imperial policy which, like the Roman analogue, was more novel in form and motive than in essence. By affirming British authority in the Eastern Mediterranean against both the French and the Russians, for instance, Palmerston set the stage for the occupation of Egypt by Gladstone. A policy for national prestige and for private profit aimed at fiscal order at home and a British peace abroad. Backed by a paramount Royal Navy, the policy was further supported by newly won facilities for trade, such as the acquisition of Singapore, the reduction of China in the Opium War, and the securing of a free-trade treaty first with France and then with others. As the nineteenth century moved on, it ceased being enough to either compensate or appease an aspiring middle class by acting forwardly abroad and co-opting internally spectacular "new men" such as Peel and Gladstone. It became ever harder for the Prime Minister, as contrasted with the Foreign Secretary, to sit in the upper chamber of Parliament; and the House of Commons, after changing its dominant concerns, also altered gradually its composition, as did the leaderships of the political parties. A thoroughly middle-class Asquith marked the transition in the Liberal (Whig) party, even as Lord Rosebery personified the displacement to imperial affairs of a ruling class approaching integral dispossession; the influx of businessmen into the Tory party had begun in the late 1880s, and raised middle-class Bonar Law to party leadership within little more than two decades.

The *embourgeoisement* took place after Disraeli, the most assimilated of the new men, had failed to reverse the trend by a Tory-populist alliance, while the evolution from Lord Salisbury to his nephew Balfour and within the latter's career was one of displacement from all-round class power to individual foreign-imperial expertise. Soon after the traumatic Tory defeat in 1906, the dispossession of the landed aristocracy as the ruling elite was formalized by the reduction of the powers of the House of Lords. Only by demonstrating superior political skill had the ruling class been previously able to retard its decline, while incidentally obscuring the backsliding of the imperial nation abroad. Part of the demonstration, and of the related appeasement, was the securing of the Suez and the Cape routes to India and of continued access to the China trade. Both involved major commercial interests. Less conspicuous, at least as critical, but less uniformly successful, was the diplomatic and consular compaign to insure "fair" trade by the rising foreign competitors in a decreasingly free-trading global environment.

Increasingly fruitless transactions, replacing effortless trusteeship with efforts at co-optation and compensations, will commonly preface upper-class trauma. A terminal conflict occurs when the traditional ruling class discards the protection of material middle-class interests for a last-ditch attempt at political self-preservation. The period is one of conservative reaction, following upon failures to tame the middle class and harness the popular mass; to sufficiently assimilate the middle class individually and socially so as to avoid being oneself superseded politically as a class, and to win over the mass while surrendering little of substance and less of status. The reaction will replace economic emphases with ethical ones, while electoral politics yields pride of place to the essential polity as represented by the traditional elites and backstopped by conservatively inclined elements in the middle and lower strata.

The last stage of an evolution will often stand for an attempt to revert to the first phase by repudiating the middle period. The empire, won by the ruling class at its onset and firmed up at its apogee, becomes then a key object of apotheosis in the face of decline. Since the empire consumed the best energies of the traditional elite's collective youth, it is now to lend *its* resources to regenerating the elite and, through the elite, the national society as a whole. Thus Cornelius Sulla, victorious in both Asia and Rome, combined a forceful conservative restoration in the city itself with a long-disused ritual, marking the territorial extension of the empire; his action was acclaimed by Cicero, the middle-class traditionalist *par excellence*. In Britain, following the rites of Indian Empire and Victorian Jubliee, the both economically and politically mutilated Tories looked to ex-proconsul Milner and the army for a new lease on life, by way of extraparliamentary procedures within a regenerated empire, fulfilling the ambitions of Disraeli. World War I helped avert the near-civil war situation. Modern Britain did not succumb to civil conflict and consequent despotism, unlike an earlier England and still more ancient Rome; nor did upper-class British go so far as to actually welcome the war as a diversion from or a solution to a traumatic crisis, unlike some of their counterparts on the Continent. But the coming of the war was accepted with relief as preferable to the choice between elite vegetation and domestic violence.

In Rome, the reconstruction of both metropole and empire fell to Caesar's kin, Octavius Augustus. Conjointly with the empire's final extension, ever-new and more alien ethnic elements were successively assimilated into ever-more central imperial positions and functions. In Britain, the decline of the middle class itself filled the hiatus between the failure of the elder (Joseph) Chamberlain to organize the empire under aristocratic auspices and the younger (Neville) Chamberlain's institution of imperial preferences. The political ascent of the middle class was paralleled by its economic decline, both absolute and relative to the products of more recent industrial revolutions; and its subsequent moral decay mirrored the gap between political ambition and political talent. Triumph over the traditional ruling class was soon offset by unease over a populace that was all the more unruly for being no longer truly ruled; that produced, and was henceforth mobilized by, its own demagogues in the persons of a David Lloyd George and a Ramsay MacDonald, ready to graduate from youthful social reformism to senescent imperialism in the setting of coalition politics with surviving traditionalists. The metamorphoses of such men blunted the spearhead of the radical antiimperial counterelite of Liberal-Labour vintage; thus they smoothed the way for the final extension of the empire, as part of the peace settlement after World War I.

Latter-day expansion of both empires, in space or in the depth of economic exploitation or institutional elaboration, externalized the internal turmoil of a political system; it was by the same token, if in unequal degrees, due in both empires to the dynamism of an ascending middle class. Such a class dislocates traditional hierarchies and balances of power with its economic drive and related political ambition, and generates new allies for competing ruling-class factions as well as a new set of incentives to preclusive expansion. Typically, the ruling class seeks to retain or recover political initiative by securing the material interests of the socially inferior classes with the aid of its own superior skill in the foreign arena; as a result, preclusion becomes the operative expression abroad of an underlying predation within; and the rise of the new predators occasioning preclusion will act as the subsidiary determinant of reexpansion most commonly at midperiod following a lull. Divisions within a ruling class may match or even overshadow its reactions to the upsurge from below in substituting for basic (or frontier) insecurity and lack of elementary sustenance as stimuli to expansion, so long as members of that class feel equally or more threatened by one another, and the absence of major "new (foreign) power" minimizes external restraints on escalating "new (factional) politics." Such was the case in late Republican Rome. Conversely, as in Britain, the rise of new internal forces to be compensated for may be critical and may coincide critically with the emergence of new outside rival powers. The domestic factors are then supplemental to the outside forces in motivating reexpansion, each being either primary or secondary in impact, depending on the momentary distribution of the two kinds of threats to the established system.

v

As the two empires matured, expansion ceased to be reducible to simple external stimuli and rudimentary collective needs. Of crucial importance then became the individuals who, being marginal to the traditional political class or system, aided and incarnated transformations as they broke up traditional molds and mediated between old and new interests.

Just as with new classes, so "new" or marginal men will push for inclusion in traditional frameworks that have been appropriately changed without being wholly undone. In consequence, they differ critically from outsiders who completely reject the empire. Whereas the ambition of a would-be coelite is essentially expansive, it is restrictive in the case of an authentic counterelite committed to reviving the supposed advantages or virtues of smallness. Thus the radical Liberal-Labour anti-imperialists in Britain opposed Little England to Greater Britain, while the anti-Italian Roman plebs and the aristocratic opponents of Caesar would resist the implications of Rome's expansion. And whereas potential coelites seek consciously no more than parity with the ruling class, the counterelite must aim at predominance in the political community. Parity for the would-be coelite can be achieved through its functional complementarity with the old class in a redivision of politico-economic labor. The resulting new balance between stabilizing traditional and vitalizing fresh political power can be firmed up by progressive social assimilation. Conversely, the counterelite must predominate if it is to transform societal values, even if not immediately replacing all of the governing personnel. The first process entails free or induced co-optation of ambitious new men into empire management; the second implies conversion to anti-imperialism of the most adaptable outgoing elites. Finally, in terms of absolutizing doctrines, the aspiring coelites will incline toward an ideological or romantic concept of empire, with organizational implications; and the aggressive counterelites will embrace the contrary extremes of tribal parochialism and either humanitarian or institutional universalism. Both orientations will deviate from the prudential pragmatism exhibited by the traditional ruling class at its peak, before it drifted into either the stoicism of *noblesse oblige* or an upper-class species of fascism seeking to merge the old nobility of birth into the new aristocracy of some kind of merit.

Much as they differ from the counterelites, the marginals are not a homogeneous group. Less significant are those who move outward themselves, in reaction to being unable or unwilling to weigh on the central political system. Here belong, in the British context against the background of a but intermittently "jingo" public, the very early merchant-adventurers, some of the nonconformist settlers, the younger sons of entailed aristocracy, and the ethnically marginal Scots and Anglo-Irish gentry. The Roman counterparts were, next to aspiring aristocrats seeking military and material fortune in the "barbarian" West, the profit-seeking equites and Italian allies-traders. Imperialism may thus at some point drain off marginals with domestically no longer acceptable and productive "primitive" upper-class behavior patterns. It can be then attributed to a form of atavism.[3] But more important than any atavism driving redundant individuals outward is the drive of salient outsiders for assimilating the home base itself. One category of such outsiders is the *social* marginals. They are typified by the "new man" of inferior social origins, who is co-opted into the traditional ruling class as a valuable reinforcement. The other category comprises the *political* marginals. These are the unconventional members of the ruling class, which shuns them as insufficiently responsible leaders or reliable team-players. Both types of outsider seek to narrow the distance between themselves and the political system, to assimilate what would otherwise remain dissimilar in kind and incompatible in action. But protagonists in each category distribute somewhat differently the elements in the change they seek in self

3. There has been ample comment over time on the role of ethnically marginal men, such as the Corsican Napoleon and the Austrian Hitler, as well as of marginal ethnic groups, such as the German *Grenzvoelker*, in imperialist practice and theory. On the role of "atavism" in imperialism, see Joseph A. Schumpeter, *Imperialism and Social Classes* (New York: A. M. Kelley, 1951).

and in the political society or culture, in style or institutional or material or moral substance. And the several differences in emphasis converge in a fundamentally different motivating concern.

The political marginals focus their energies on the imperial peripheries so as to mobilize there the resources necessary for overcoming the uncongenial conventions of their class at the center of empire. These conventions will appear to such men as constraints spawned by status quo mediocrity; as reflecting the virtues of collective middle-age, while contravening the ruling class' constitutive *virtus*. In this respect, the political marginals will share the atavisms which actuate the colonial expatriates of upper-class background, while sharing with the social marginals the commitment to changing the system.

In Rome, the outstanding political marginals were the brothers Gracchi, who initiated social conflict in an imperial context, and Pompey and Caesar, who brought it to near-climax. The first pair sought to tap the resources of the empire in order to overcome the corrupting, and the second pair the inhibiting, conventions of the senatorial-cum-consular class to which they belonged by right of birth. Caesar acted for larger ends than G. Gracchus, and with fewer tradition-bound scruples than Pompey, but was not essentially unlike either. He stands out as the prototype of the aristocrat who, half-renegade and half-reformer, would use the empire as the source of energy and the people as the battering ram against a decaying traditional system which he will have betrayed unless he reshapes it to fit the times and himself. In the virile phase of British imperialism, Pitt, Canning, and Palmerston were conspicuous as the proponents of limited system-change. They were unorthodox mavericks both politically and personally (and Pitt was, in addition, uncomfortably close to trade by family background). Obstructed by Crown, peers, or both in the pursuit and exercise of high office, they all employed flamboyant unilaterialism for imperial expansion or individual self-assertion in order to mobilize an impressionable public opinion against the conventional system; and they did this just forcefully enough to effect entry into the system and change its style, but style only, in their personal image. At a later stage, Lord Randolph Churchill and, in the period between the two world wars, Sir Oswald Mosley were to display the ambiguous reactions of political marginality to two different stages of decay, prematurely terminated in the first case and belatedly begun in the second.

Neither Pitt nor Canning nor Palmerston combined more or less tactical imperialism with strategies for basic internal change. They differed thus from Randolph Churchill's apparent intention and were more like Winston Churchill, the last major political marginal with imperial leanings. Unlike in Rome (e.g., the Gracchi), to combine expansion and change was reserved in Britain for social marginals, the middle-class men co-opted into positions of leadership at a time when the representative members of the traditional class were declining in either will or talent for changing domestic and imperial structures. The political marginals transfer political energies or attentions to the imperial peripheries in order to gain or retain key positions at the center. By contrast, the social marginals as individuals or group seek to transform and in the process amplify the political system as a means to positioning themselves automatically nearer its sociopolitical core. The political marginals will be prepared to employ illegitimate or unconventional means, as a matter of class-derived right; the social marginals in turn will typically employ formally correct means in order to legitimize their more or less revolutionary claim to responsible power.

For the social outsiders to enlarge the traditional system is to outclass the traditional elite and make it increasingly dependent on their co-operation and good will. In Britain, two new men leading the two principal parties, Sir Robert Peel and William Ewart Gladstone, mediated politically the enlargement of economic resource through industrialism and, as a policy consequence, free trade. Whereas Peel had presided over the institution of the new policy, Gladstone completed its expansion into the so-called imperialism of free trade. In Rome, *homo novus* Marius championed the economically expansive Roman equites and Italian traders. In both empires new men were foremost in employing the enlarged political resource, the mobilized people, in ways peculiar to the respective systems of politics. Marius used the people to obtain the military command preconditional to political power, in defiance of both tradition and the vested interest of the senate. Disraeli endowed the common man with the capacity to bestow political mandates, in order to entrench the Tory party with the masses, for the empire; from a higher office than Cicero, he too would marry an idealized people to a glorified empire with the aid of revitalized traditions, spectacular policies, and symbolic rituals. Gladstone brought the legally created electoral resource to life politically in order to prosecute the Turk, defeat the Tories, and transform a patrician Whig party into the Liberal party. And Joseph Chamberlain finally tried to tie the legally enfranchised and politically activated people to a reconstructed empire with the bond of material interest, and link the lower classes through the empire with both the middle and the upper classes in social peace.

An enlargement of the political and economic reservoir of power signifies for the new elite a more central position in the new politics, new economics, or both. It also spells a higher position in the new society. The social marginals will initially employ the mobilized people as an elevator toward the social summit and not only, as do the politically marginal members of the ruling class, as the battering ram against the inner sanctum of high office. The newly enlarged system is legitimated and group assimilation completed when the new men revive traditional values and institutions of the originally aristocratic body politic by reinterpreting them for use in the new framework. They thus effect a spiritual identification with a past in which the likes of them had no role and little place. The fact that the traditional ruling class in its great majority has deviated by then from the idealized version of the ancestral values will only complete the *translatio imperii* within the imperial system, pending transfer outside it.

When they promote the expansion of the metropolitan body politic, the empire, or both, the political and the social marginals must break up traditional molds if they are to act as brokers between old and new political orders. They can employ either demagoguery or statesmanship, and will commonly blend both, when bridging the chasm between the ruling class and the people and forging links between the upper and the middle classes. If political office rewards effective brokerage, mere breakage of obsolete molds can occur as a retaliation by marginals for being excluded too long by a frozen oligarchy or fearful oligarchs. But, the breaking up of congealed forms may be undertaken also as a constructive remedy. One possible distemper to guard against is the alienation of the lower strata from a society that has been undergoing rapid transformation in depth; such transformation was due to the Industrial Revolution in Britain and had been manifested in urban atomization in Rome. Another malaise may be the lost sense of purpose on the part of elites in a postheroic, but in any real sense prehumanitarian, phase of political and social evolution. Consequently, the broken bonds or limits can and will be both territorial, with the result of extending the area of rule or politico-economic access, and political, with the effect of revising the rules of the game and the structure of the amphitheater; and they will be also ideological or symbolic, with the intent of reshaping perceptions of past and future so as to produce a new rationale for the inherited imperial mission or rationalize its transformation. The common denominator is aggrandizement of the current design in order to avert decay, as the marginals strain toward the center of power, the unorthodox seeks to become the norm, and the so far normal offers vain resistance to becoming defunct after it has ceased being effectual.

III

EMPIRE AND IMPERIALISM. *Economic Dilemmas*

Marginal men mediate the interplay of social classes, easing and accelerating the resulting transformations. But it is up to the political dynamic in the aggregate to mediate the bearing of the economic factor on imperial expansion, in the sense of making that factor operational as a subsidiary incentive to reexpansion.

The mediation occurs mainly in the transactional period, when particular economic interests have been differentiated within, and from, a political system that has become more pluralistic while the economic system functions without much deliberate central management. That middling period follows upon the initial drive to insure a viable share of the material environment, external security, and internal peace, in behalf of a preimperial community under ruling-class trusteeship. Only in the final period, of more or less advanced elite trauma, will the upholding of collective power and of particular economic stakes tend to fully merge again, after the midterm separation. At that late stage, as different from the initial one as basic food supply is from high finance, conditions of advanced maturity or incipient decline will reunite concerns about strategic security with anxiety over economic coherence or viability by again raising the issue of survival as against that of superiority.

I

Whenever, and to the extent that, the economic factor affects imperial policy indirectly—i.e., by way of the internal political dynamic—the modes of promotion, to the enjoyment of political power or its fruits in different stages of power devolution, will matter more than do the modes of production. By the same token, the modes of compensating or appeasing the groups which have been denied direct access to political power will be more critical than are modes of economic competition or capital accumulation. Moreover, the essentially political modes, and resulting processes, reflect the recurrent patterns of evolution of the ruling classes or elites, rather than being tied to the evolution of any one particular economic system or social-class structure functionally deriving from that system. Only as a ruling class and the related imperial political system deteriorate will economic factors by and of themselves recover direct motivational force or significance. Economism will thus characterize late imperialism, and will do so more significantly than a narrowly defined imperialism reflects late-industrial capitalism—or any other economic system as such.

In the larger perspective, it is possible to reduce to a common denominator seemingly different economic stakes and rewards of expansion. Among these are booty as against profit; direct tribute as against surplus value; and free bread or games as against full employment or free welfare services. And, in the same perspective, it is important to distinguish not only between original and subsidiary motives of expansion but also between genuine motive and mere momentum. When, most commonly in maturing empires, a motivating drive merges with subsequent momentum as the mainspring of expansion, the preimperial community's relatively simple material and other deficiencies are likely to have ceased being the key or distinctive stimuli to expansion. They will have been supplanted and replaced by the multifaceted dilemmas bred first by surpluses of one kind or another and later by overall decline. Simultaneously, a clearly discerned and defined economic and related political "good" inviting largely predatory expansion will have given way to the defensive preclusion of economic and related political "evils" by a variety of methods, including reexpansion or empire consolidation. If such evils were incurred in part through prior expansion, they were so incurred commonly as an alternative to the more immediate perils of stagnation.

Both the Roman and the British empires experienced three differentiable relationships between economic factors and expansion, marking the transition from initial expansion through midterm empire to late empire. The corresponding three phases can be labeled formative war imperialism; informal free-trade imperialism (or just expansionism); and formally institutionalized, or formalized, protective imperialism.

In formative war imperialism, economic factors are indistinguishably intertwined with the strategic concern with state power or security, and may be only incidental to such concern, in the course of transforming a tribal or national polity into an imperial one. That period extended for

Rome up to about the middle of the second century B.C. (coinciding with the Third Punic War and the rise of the commerce-oriented equestrian order); for Britain, up to about the 1820s to 1840s (coinciding with the repeal of the basic mercantilist regulations and restrictions concerning navigation, colonial commerce, and home agriculture). The next informal free-trade (or free-enterprise) imperialism was dominant in the British empire up to about the 1880s and survived until 1932; its near-equivalent in Rome was dominant up to the latter part of the first century B.C. and survived until the second century A.D. In the informal empire, the economic factor is relatively separate from strategic security concerns. At the same time, particular economic interests become increasingly powerful and affect internal political stability (as part of the transition from trusteeship to transactions), while the imperial frontier generates subsidiary incentives to expansion more or less clearly differentiable from the economic stakes. The problem of frontier security continues in the last phase, that of formalized protective imperialism. But it tends to worsen again to the point of involving once more, if differently in kind, the fundamental security or survival of the imperial core-polity in terms of both military-political and economic competitiveness and viability. At this point of refusion, moreover, the issue of collective popular welfare will have been politicized and will compete for attention with the promotion of particular vested interests or interesting investments. A reactivated concern with economics to protect existing state power comes to be matched by preoccupation with economics as a matter of enhanced governmental function and responsibility. Protective imperialism was an issue for Britain's practical politics between the 1880s and the 1906 elections, and prevailed in 1932; in the Roman context, the ultimate form prevailed by the time of the second century A.D. under the Empire, following upon initial symptoms in the last decades or years of the Republic.

It is always difficult to weigh and compare strategic and economic considerations or compulsions behind imperial expansion; and the difficulty grows as the empire progresses toward its climax and decline. Not only do strategic gains and assets have incidental economic consequences, including possible benefits, and vice versa, but gains of one kind may be sought as prerequisites to goods in another category. Similarly, actual imperial conflicts (e.g., the Boer War) may be preceded by conspicuous preliminaries or surface precipitants of an economic nature without being principally caused by these. But, especially if they occur on as large a scale as between Britain and Germany prior to World War I, even waning economic and related rivalries can have predisposed both public and official moods in favor of warlike resolution of political or strategic differences as a matter of delayed causation. And, finally, social or political dislocations which can be attributed to economic transactions (e.g., in Egypt prior to 1882) may be the fundamental or critical factor behind the ostensibly determining strategic inducements to warlike action. Such circularities, replete with an inextricable concatenation of events, will make rough judgments about the relative importance of strategic and economic motivations depend on two contexts. More visible and conspicuous is the basic posture and relative position of the imperial core-community in the international environment; more esoteric is the background of doctrines and assumptions prevailing at different periods. Both contexts may be supplemented by broad inferences to be drawn from the internal hierarchies of groups and interests and the balances of power and aspiration within the imperial community.

II

Chronologically first is formative war imperialism. It was identified in Rome's case with the pristine militarism of a relatively united ruling class; in the British case (and likewise retrospectively simplified), with systematic mercantilism as policy. The basic initial posture of both core-communities relative to primary rivals was one of less than parity in power on both land and sea and in actual or readily mobilizeable wealth; it was, moreover, one of inadequacy relative to an actually or perceptually expanding overall environment. Internally, the public and private domains were considerably intertwined. The Crown both participated in chartered companies and supervised them in England, while the senatorial class was half proprietary and half submerged in both status and action in relation to the Roman state as it took shape conjointly with the conquest of land abroad and its controversial disposition internally.

The background doctrines defined or sanctioned the interdependence of military power with material wealth, and of both with the state and with war. In Rome, the nearest thing to a doctrine was the ethos of *virtus* as it related to offices, benefices, and, through war, to material gain. In the English context, the Protestant ethic of works reinforced the mercantilist tenets about war. If the ethic was a gateway to individual and collective well-being, the tenets guided state policy whenever the balance of trade was fostered to improve position in the balance of power, while favorable outcome was sought for a war as the surest way to a favorable balance of trade. War being profitable, to wage it successfully both required and insured one's being powerful. In expanding world conditions, to guarantee both profit and power required political and administrative control of the commerce with and of overseas colonies and, to insure it, adequate sea power, ideally culminating in the command of the sea. England's Navigation Acts were correspondingly designed to foster naval progress, toward and beyond parity, as the critical factor in implementing monopoly of trade with dependent colonies and frustrating the exclusiveness of prior monopolists. Supporting the distinctive Roman ethos, the Claudian Law had confined senators to ownership of the classic basis of military strength and virtues, land (in Italy); by debarring senators from practicing trade directly, the law insured that Rome would renounce commercial monopoly in favor of Italian and eastern allies, friends, and clients, to be protected and promoted in ways conducive to Roman power and to the material benefit of individual senators.

Colonies and clients were perceived as major wartime assets and resources, and early wars engendered major, if not always either intended or anticipated, economic consequences for both empires. Rome's Second Punic War had economic preliminaries in the guise of trade competition with Carthage, but hardly a basic economic cause. One reason was the failure in the first round of fighting to decide the issue of strategic security revolving around Spain. The war's economic consequence was, however, major. It brought to Rome important new wealth contributory to expanding the economy's base in estates and slaves. Britain's wars in the Caribbean were fought deliberately over the economic elements of power. But the mid-eighteenth century conquest of Bengal, inside the Indian subcontinent, was an originally unintended incident to the pursuit of wealth through trade from India's coast. It produced, nonetheless, a fiscal tribute which, along with concurrent rationalization of British agriculture, helped set off the Industrial Revolution.[1]

Illustrating the interlocking of strategic and economic concerns and consequences typical of militarist-mercantilist imperial systems, the pursuit of strategic objectives through war produced for Rome both tributes and slaves and both foodstuffs (Sicilian grain) and precious metals (Spanish silver), all helpful in developing further Roman power in general and her professional military forces in particular. Moreover, military successes enabled the Romans to do such things as secure access to a free port in Delos for their allies, restrictively regulate to allied advantage the culture of wine and olives in transalpine Gaul, and disrupt antagonistic monopolies and maritime blockades. By assuring a rough balance of material advantages from the empire for metropole and dependencies, such measures would prevent the disaffection or secession of useful junior partners in the imperial system; so would the comparable British manipulation of mercantilistic regulations and peace settlements. If the balancing effort had culminated in an oddly manifested success for Rome in relation to the Italian kin (waging the so-called Social War to secure Roman citizenship), it ended in failure for Britain in relation to her American kin (in the War of American Independence). But prior to that fiasco, the most important and most deliberately sought strategic benefit

1. It was that revolution which created a major difference between England's advanced, and Rome's agricultural-slave and only primitively industrial, economy, modifying the subsequent economic fortunes of the two empires and qualifying any functional parallels to be drawn between them.

incidental to economically profitable activities had been Britain's growing naval capability (next to resources for subsidizing land-bound foreign mercenaries). As a form of military power, the naval capability was inseparably dependent for both men and ships on the merchant marine, itself necessary for profitable trade in colonial groceries and dependent on militarily secured access to ship-building timber from the Baltic.

Security and sustenance tended toward fusion. Strategic prerequisites to economic gains and incidental strategic benefits from mercantile activities loomed larger in the policy-making counsels of formative war imperialism than did economic factors in isolation from strategic ones; but the distinction is hard to sustain for the period. Nor does the strategic-economic interlock make it any easier to assess the net economic costs or benefits of early empire. Compounding the difficulty was the triangular character of trade relationships, involving in one way or another Rome, her allies, and defeated enemies, and Britain, her colonies, and the European continent.

With these qualifications, the British colonial possessions would seem to have produced an overall profit over and above the costs of protection. The state could share directly or indirectly in this profit and find in it a reason for retaining such colonies, by force if necessary, even in the absence of a fiscal surplus from local taxation. (Such a surplus was realized only in India before 1770, at which time tribute yielded to trade only.) The costs of military protection for dependencies can be discounted if that protection is seen as constituting the forward defense of the British islands, and the islands themselves are viewed as beset by a security problem not wholly due to colonial imbroglios. By contrast with Britain, Rome's economic advantage was largely in fiscal revenues from tributes and provincial taxes, in the absence of a major direct share in trade. The net fiscal gains would have been larger had Rome continued to depend longer on citizen armies rather than on paid professionals. But Rome's initial independence of paid mercenaries, differentiating her from Carthage and the eastern empires, removes at least that particular source of a compelling need for foreign tributes as a self-sufficient economic cause of early Roman expansionism.

All considered, early empire paid, for both Rome and Britain and the gains were, on the whole, incidental to the pursuit of state power in conditions of initial insecurity and inferiority. Collectively gainful activities were not necessarily unrelated to individual and familial or dynastic material interests, however, insofar as it was possible to differentiate clearly the particular from the general in yet uncrystallized conditions (such as those facing, say, the Scipios in Rome) or in unsettled conditions (such as those confronting the later Stuarts in Britain). Economic motivation might be also deduced from Britain's peculiar mercantilist doctrine, holding that the balance of trade determined the balance of power.

But again, the concern with fostering either particular gain or general balance of trade did not unfailingly determine concrete policies so long as intraruling-class competition over individual role and status was highly politicized and the mercantile class rated low in both early empires. Being spuriously more simple and seemingly more determinate than their political counterparts, economic facts and data, concerns and calculations, will often appear to be determinant of actions and events, not least when political or prestige issues of security and status are more than usually ambiguous. The selfsame economic concerns may be for the same reasons discounted as the effectively primary incentives to expansion in a wide range of conditions, including those of formative war imperialism. They were nearly always supplemental to strategic stimuli, be it in a circular fashion (mainly in Britain) or in an incidental or secondary position (mainly in Rome); they clearly did not constitute a disincentive to expansion, but neither did they compel its indefinite extension.

III

Individual and collective economic gains of formative war imperialism create the material basis for midterm informal imperialism of relatively freer trade or enterprise. In facilitating further expansion, superior will and skill are then supplemented by superior military and economic resource, to a point susceptible of generating expansion as it were spontaneously. Informal imperialism avoids direct political control by way of annexation, as both unnecessary and uneconomical, but it does not spell independence from the network of strategic strong points and facilities for the pursuit of private gain by way of economic activities, including (free) trade. Imperialism is not coterminous with territorial expansion. But mere economic superiority and expansion, unrelated to strategic supports, is not imperialism in any but a peculiar doctrinal sense. It is not even one of free trade, and not even if that trade engenders a disguised tribute from inferior economies.

In the middle phase, as a result of the previously gained momentum, both empires enjoyed clear supremacy: primarily military, but also increasingly financial, for Rome; and primarily naval and economic for Britain. Both kinds of supremacy made it possible to collect a form of tribute even in formally unattached areas by conferring specially favored and protected access to economic opportunities. This tribute could be regarded as a tax levied in return for maintaining a pattern of relatively stable expectations, including predictable patterns of exploitation, which even the peoples subject to such an order could conceivably prefer to local forms of indigence, anarchy, or arbitrary rule, notably in the period following the initial erosion of indigenous traditions. Related to the passage from subparity to supremacy was, in this period, a change in the relationship between public and private interests, powers, and domains, from a tendency to fusion to relative separation. The imperial tax or tribute was in both empires levied by private entrepreneurs to a variable extent; the central authority and its incumbents derived mostly only indirect economic advantages, along with political or diplomatic liabilities, in return for managing and occasionally enlarging the supporting strategic framework, and for the more marginal role in distributing the rewards of empire among social groups.

The doctrinal background in Rome was the emerging thesis of the right of Roman citizens to freely enjoy the material payoffs of the Roman peace from sources enriched, mainly in the East, by the free flow of trade in the politically unified Mediterranean basin. While the people began to receive cheaper bread, military entrepreneurs commenced to supply the army at profit, publicans to engage in tax-farming in the provinces, and senators to loan money at high interest to oriental clients and purchase slaves at a discount from the debtors. The more explicit theory in Britain postulated freedom of the seas and of trade in the setting of a two-ocean naval supremacy, industrial quasi-monopoly, and a consequently profitable—if not, initially, unconditionally preferred—peace. The more optimistic tenets of the theory held that a natural division of labor between industrial Britain and primary producers would indefinitely perpetuate Britain's economic preeminence, if only she opened up her agricultural market to potential buyers of industrial products (and invested some of the trade surplus in the debtor countries). More pessimistic was the belief that only free trade in the largest, world context might or would avoid glut and depression for an overproducing, overpopulated, and underconsuming Britain. A like mixture of self-confidence and defensiveness underlay the bias against governmental regulation of economic activities. It corresponded to the hostile attitude of Roman financial entrepreneurs toward strict provincial governors. Freedom of contract, finally, meant usurious interest rates in Rome and, justified by equally great or greater risks, high profits and exploitation of labor in Britain.

Britain's mercantilist legislation, key monopolies and exclusions, were sufficiently dismantled by the late 1840s to give way to soliciting free-trade treaties with politically receptive countries, such as Piedmont in Italy and, during a spell of diplomatic détente, France under Napoleon III. Despite a concurrent trend to growing tariff protection of infant industries abroad, the British government was usually reluctant to identify with private commercial and financial interests in such areas of informal empire as Latin America and China; it would minimize the risks of diplomatic conflict with foreign powers in general and the United States in particular. Nor was the government anxious to underwrite ventures which private enterprise itself deemed too risky, mainly in

Africa. Rome's comparable hands-off official policy toward dependent but unannexed clients in economic matters complemented the curbing of supervisory gubernatorial zeal under the equestrian-dominated jury system. Most importantly, the Roman senate was apparently still unwilling at this stage (as the British government was to be at the comparable one) to allow the power of the state to be used for the recovery of endangered loans and coercion of defaulting debtors.

In part as a result, comparatively major wars were less imbued with, or suspect of, immediate economic ramifications in this period than were some lesser conflicts. Thus, despite encouragement by mercantile interests, Rome did not exploit the commercial site of finally destroyed Carthage right after the Third Punic War; and, after the survival wars with the first Napoleon had set the political stage for free trade, British commerce derived no immediate tangible profit from the neutralization of the Black Sea following Russia's defeat in the Crimean War. Nor were the smaller wars—Rome's for the security of the East Mediterranean perimeter in Macedon and Britain's for the safety of the Indian perimeter in Lower Burma or Afghanistan—designed to produce economic advantages additional to those implicit in the core-empire's existence. By contrast, private material interests were involved in some of the more "scandalous" small wars, such as Rome's against Jugurtha in Numidia (North Africa) or Britain's against China in the Opium War. But, even in these, official mismanagement had a yet greater impact than had official connivance.

The interplay of strategic and economic factors and considerations continued. And, even though the role of purely economic private and related public incentives to expansion increased, also continuing was the primacy of strategy in official thinking related henceforth to the defense of the imperial frontier and the status of economic advantages and opportunities as incidents to the implementation of that primacy. For instance, while leaving unused the prime commercial sites of not only Carthage but also Corinth, Rome levied tributes from other dependencies at least as much to undercut their capacity for revolt (and to maintain legions capable of crushing actual revolts) as to satisfy the economic requirements of the Roman political system in regard to the plebs in particular. The private economic drives of the most conspicuous entrepreneurs, too, were in many or most cases ancillary to political ambitions. At the same time, as an example of economic-strategic interplay, Marius's effort to expand the security of overland communications (between Italy and Spain) in Gaul engaged the legions in building an also economically productive canal (linking the Rhône estuary to the Mediterranean). A military drive, such as Caesar's later conquests in Gaul, would likewise incidentally open up the conquered areas to trade. And, finally, if trade followed the flag more often than vice versa, Pompey's clearing the Eastern Mediterranean of pirates in order to facilitate trade was beneficial strategically as well.

In Britain, the internal hierarchy of strategic and economic concerns complemented the international division of labor (between industrial and primary producers) characteristic of informal free-trade imperialism. While the landed ruling class continued its responsibility for the strategic framework, the industrial-commercial class was preoccupied with exploiting the framework's economic potential. Both specific and general economic advantages flowed from the official concern with the security of communications with India and her frontiers. Indian economic assets had become a vital part of a multilateral trading pattern; but the primary, self-conscious governmental concern was with a coherent strategic network befitting an evolving technology and distribution of power. At the same time, India as an economic asset spawned also a crucial strategic asset in the form of a materially self-sustaining Indian Army. Conversely, a port like Singapore, which had been established primarily to service and safeguard the commercial route to the China Sea off the Malacca strait, acquired progressively major strategic significance with the rise of Russia and Japan as Asian powers. So, too, Britain's positions would have become strategically crucial in the Caribbean and in South America, and her stake in the isthmian-canal project, had the course of Anglo-American relations taken a more antagonistic course. More generally, overall British naval supremacy in the world's two major oceans was the necessary precondition to securing an "open door" for the formally or informally protected British subjects in Latin America and China. The two were the principal areas of the informal empire of trade which, added to the trade with the United States, about matched the British economic stake in the directly administered formal empire of rule. The most significant economic side-benefit from naval supremacy came from the "invisible" exports. Along with returns on overseas investments, returns on shipping insurance and maritime transport replaced the earlier "unrequited" exports via Bengali tribute and reversed the navy's dependence on merchant shipping in the preceding mercantilist era. As the empire progressed, transmutations complicated the strategic-economic interplay further. Some dependencies which had had great economic importance in the mercantilistic period became most significant strategically. And previously marginal dependencies—notably the white-settler colonies of Australia and New Zealand—acquired major economic significance and eventually strategic importance as well.

The net economic costs and benefits of informal empire are even more difficult to calculate than are those of formative war imperialism. One reason is that a less direct and conspicuous interdependence of strategic and economic factors makes the costs of the strategic posture appear redundant. The direct fiscal gains continued to be crucial for Rome.

They provided the net asset for developing the military, political, and social systems of the empire on an administratively enlarged and longer-term basis. They were all the more important since increased gains from private financial transactions failed to find an economically productive outlet. And private benefits from mercantile activities in the intra-Mediterranean free-trade area began to be offset by liabilities from a growing autarky, accentuated by the Parthian barrier to the farther Asian economic universe. The British empire showed little or no net fiscal gain from the colonial empire of rule, the absence being compensated for by overall economic gains from some dependencies and from the informal segment of empire. Any resulting net gains were increasingly dependent on the strategically protected invisible exports, and receipts from India, as the always precarious British balance of trade in goods worsened with the relative decline of Britain's staple industries for export in an increasingly competitive world market. The naval establishment requisite for the command of the sea was the most costly single item. However profits-producing otherwise, it could not be meaningfully discounted for outlays necessitated by insular security proper, since intermittent naval activism on the Continent, such as the French build-up under Napoleon III, was itself inseparable from the challenge which Britain's naval power offered to the continentals.

British free-trade imperialism expressed more fully than the Roman the desire to expand trade rather than territory. The pre-Cobdenite assumption had been that a tribute by someone to somebody else was unavoidably implicit in irremediable economic inequality. Free trade was intended to support a British economic, and related naval-diplomatic, hegemony beyond and above mere parity with the nearest competitor. In the 1840s the fear was that unless other countries lowered or removed barriers to trade Britain would cease to be the "workshop of the world." Given the more optimistic climate of the prosperous 1850s and 1860s, however, strategic motivation remained dominant on the governmental level. Its primacy was fostered by the liberal era's relative separation of public and private concerns; and it was reinforced by the special political and economic status of India as a partially state-managed mercantilist survival in a multilateral trading system and free-enterprise era. As for the informal part of empire, strategic and diplomatic concerns were most strikingly shown to predominate whenever the British government avoided offending the United States (under the American interpretation of the Monroe Doctrine) by interfering on behalf of private economic interests in the Western Hemisphere.

By and large, the superiority of the two imperial centers, Roman and British, and the relative separation of private and public domains when compared with the previous period of formative war imperialism (and the subsequent protective imperialism), enabled governments to concentrate on the strategic aspects of empire and take the both self-sustaining and supporting economic system for granted. At the same time, governmental latitude to arbitrate among economic interests and between private and public interests was exposed to rising pressures in behalf of private economic needs and interests. Private interests rose in political significance even while they suffered increasing economic difficulties that could be attributed to official acts of commission or omission—in the Eastern Mediterranean vis-à-vis Pontus and Parthia in Rome's case and, in the British case, vis-à-vis increasing and increasingly "unfair" worldwide competition by the new commercial powers. Private wealth became more and more the means to acquiring power in Rome, while British statesmen had to become again most acutely sensitive to the critical role of strategic power in preserving national wealth in worsening conditions.

IV

Informal free-trade imperialism in Britain and the nearest approximation of it in Rome occupied a relatively short interlude between state-effected conquest of economic opportunities or goods and an officially sponsored defense of them. If conquest had been actuated by reasons of national power, the defense was also in behalf of politico-economic stability and sheer survival of the existing system. In the succeeding phase of formalized protective empire, the state will employ an expanding institutional mechanism to protect or regulate private economic activities. Internal and external measures and policies, mainly economic (in the British case) or military (in the Roman), aim then at remedying the economic (and, in the late Roman Republic, also political) incoherences within the empire and its actual or threatening inferiority relative to the outside.

The two empires declined in this period from the position of informal supremacy without (officially desired) annexations and direct or indirect taxation without (governmental) responsibility. The decline was both relative and, in a sense, absolute. It was relative when contrasted with the emerging rival powers; absolute when measured against conditions predating the rise of subimperial actors bidding for political power (in Rome) or for economic self-protection and military protection (in the British empire) and both able and disposed to look elsewhere (thus Pompey or Anthony to Egypt, Canada or Australia to the United States) for leverage within or salvation outside the traditional framework of the empire. By increasingly linking the survival of the empire or its existing forms to the satisfaction of individual, class, or provincial, desiderata, the public domain was reinvolved in the private. However, it was reinvolved henceforth in a relatively ancillary function and defensive posture. Britain's increasingly difficult commercial and naval competition with Imperial Germany embraced also France and the United States; and if conflicts between immediate commercial and longer-term diplomatic perspectives caused serious dilemmas, these were compounded by divergences between the dominions' movement toward protectionism and the still free-trading metropole. One Roman counterpart was the decreasingly only latent tension between the residual state power, symbolized by the senate in the aggregate, and assertive individual power-seekers in the Republic's interfactional alliances and rivalries; another, even before the resurgence of outside threats, was the deepening economic disparity between the Italian West and the East of the Empire. Topping all issues in both empires was the problem of satisfying, or appeasing, the economically threatened or politically demanding classes of the population.

The background doctrines were unequally explicit. In the Roman Republic, the unarticulated doctrine was one of statism. At the intersection of high finance and high politics, it entailed *de facto* official or quasi-official protection for those in a position to exploit the empire's clients and dependents directly. And the state assumed a similar role when distributing the economic assets from empire in response to the mass demand for politically motivated services, in the guise of "bread and games." When official monopoly of management and regulation under the Empire replaced the increasingly free-wheeling late-Republican oligopoly, the new order merely combined greater centralization with somewhat greater equity. In trade, autarky confined free movement of goods to the Mediterranean area, expressing in practice the overall structural-economic weaknesses of the empire and its geopolitical limitations eastward. Doctrines were more explicit in Britain, as proponents and opponents of imperialism were divided over the question whether Britain's economic and social problems had better be approached by instituting imperial tariffs (also to expand colonial settlement) or by redistributing income internally (so as to expand instead the domestic market). The assumption behind the doctrine of imperial development, protection, and colonization was that neither politically practical redistributive measures at home nor theoretically posited advantages of free trade at large could deal with Britain's problems of underconsumption, overproduction, and overpopulation sufficiently to relieve class conflict. Such pessimistic assumptions, involving the rate of profits and the size and security of alternative markets, had previously fueled the movement toward free trade. Now they were being increasingly redirected against economic liberalism, pending their being shaped into a theoretical weapon against imperialism.[2]

The doctrinal pessimism fed into the more practical preoccupation

2. On theoretical questions, see Bernard Semmel, *The Rise of Free Trade Imperialism* (Cambridge: At the University Press, 1970); also R. K. Webb, *Modern England* (New York: Dodd, Mead, 1968), and the literature cited therein on general economic conditions.

regarding the commercial and colonial powers that were more recently industrialized than Britain had been, and were less devoutly or reliably committed to free trade, if at all. The nightmare of doors being closed to British trade in conditions of an already declining share of world trade, chronic deficit in the balance of trade (minus services), and a protracted economic depression from the 1870s to the 1890s, imparted a concrete economic content to the precautionary bias always pervading international statecraft. The economic malaise served as a background for the reexpansion beginning in the 1880s. Free trade had been intended to counteract the externally protectionist North German *Zollverein* and avert popular revolution within Britain. Imperial protectionism was subsequently favored, in response to the colonial ambitions of an unreliably or "unfairly" free-trading Germany and a latent politico-economic instability in Britain. It was seen as a means to social reform and as a diversion of surplus population to colonies and of popular sentiments to "jingo" imperialism which was to peak around 1904 at the height of the German scare.

Each plank in the proposed solution had its Roman counterpart and involved immediate costs apt to inhibit both instant decisions and long-range planning. The British empire consequently drifted along, buoyed up by improved economic conditions after the mid-1890s and by the temporarily enhanced export position of new British manufactures after World War I. But others, including the white dominions, were more impressed by the apparently forthcoming system of protected economic ensembles. The new economic vision was backed by the widely shared belief (not least outside Britain) in the peerless material worth of the empire, and of India in particular, for Britain's power in the world. At the beginning of the nineteenth century, Britain had vainly tried to prevent free export and resulting diffusion of industrial machinery and skills; at the century's close, like futility befell the effort to inhibit the spread of protectionism by abstaining from policies in restraint of competitive imports.

In terms of actual policies, the minimum of protective imperialism meant official interventions to secure "fair" economic practices abroad; its maximum meant external and internal consolidation of empire with a view to managing foreign economic transactions. In the Roman case, proconsuls and other promagistrates used political and military resources to extract a "fair" return on private loans by Romans to local competitors for royal power in the client states. These shady politico-economic transactions tended to precipitate or even cause military conflict (e.g., with Pontus) and annexations or near-annexations (e.g., of Syria and Egypt). The more decorous British counterpart was to employ consuls and adopt either diplomatic or contractual measures to secure "fair" competition in world markets. Beyond that, the government insured future economic access in Africa by annexations. And weighty arguments were being marshaled behind the reluctant, and finally interrupted, movement toward giving up internationally safeguarded free trade in all China for politically secured fair trade or better in British-controlled parts, in the face of Russian, German, French, and Japanese initiatives. Finally, in the renewed economic depression of the 1930s, the principle of formalized protection was implemented through the Ottawa Agreements. Imperial tariff and quotas, within a system of periodic consultations, became then the nearest thing to the once-propounded Imperial Federation.

Comparable late developments in the Roman empire occurred in the second century A.D. At an earlier date, after his fellow-triumvir Crassus had vainly attempted to remove the Parthian barrier to Eastern trade, Caesar himself sought to shelter relatively declining Italian economy behind tariff barriers; he would also siphon off the politically explosive proletariat into colonization and control speculative finance. The continuing economic and financial crises induced a later caesar, the Emperor Trajan, to try for the last time a radical approach to the economic incoherences which were ruining the Eastern provinces and the empire's overall balance of payments. He followed the conquest of gold-rich Dacia (part of today's Rumania) by securing control of the overland routes to trade with India and China via the Persian Gulf, at the expense of the Parthian empire. The temporarily successful expansive military thrust into Mesopotamia promoted the trade-oriented Eastern provinces, but were to the detriment of the stagnant agricultural West. No single remedy could apparently cure economic imbalance within the empire, and of the empire with the outside. Similar dilemmas were to reappear in the discordant attitudes and, possibly, requirements of Britain and the self-governing dominions as regards free trade and imperial protection. Reproducing the position of "underdeveloped" Italy vis-à-vis the more industrial East in the Roman setting, the dominions sought to protect themselves against the metropole under both of the broad alternatives and helped undercut imperial protection without saving free trade for Britain in the longer run.

Before 1932, central responsibility for imperial defense in the British empire did not coincide with the will and, increasingly, the capacity to defend economic stakes by political and administrative means. In the later Roman empire, both before and after its administrative subdivision in the third century A.D., a growing bureaucracy drawn from the equestrian order struggled, finally in vain, to help rationalize military defense against rising threats and apply economic controls to chronic inflation internally and payments imbalance externally. Whereas the Roman empire's shortcomings were structural and probably incurable, the eventual British shift in a comparable direction may have failed because it was delayed too long.

In the wars of this period, economic factors would seem to have played an increasing role, even if not always or necessarily a primary one. The origins of the wars of the late Republic were clearly tinged with private economic interests in both West and East, relating to internal political ambitions. Rationalizations pertaining to frontier security could become highly questionable, witness Caesar's military activity in Gaul. The wars of the late Empire in Dacia and Mesopotamia had the just-mentioned economic rationales conjointly with the object of securing the imperial frontier in the Danube and Euphrates-Tigris areas. In the British period, the partition of Africa and China produced no wars among the European powers. Conspicuous economic preliminaries preceded, next to the occupation of Egypt, also the Boer War (affecting the Cape Colony relative to the Afrikaners) and World War I (affecting Britain herself relative to Germany). Yet the strictly economic issues were tied up with strategic ones, bearing on the Cape naval base and the Cape-to-Cairo railway in the South African conflict and with the Berlin-Baghdad railway in the global one. Moreover, the most spectacular of the economic discords had been attenuated when the two wars broke out for sufficient ostensible reasons, involving (in both instances) the political credibility of a British government and the security of imperial communications or (in the German war alone) also of England herself. As a result, the economic discords and growth-rate disparities do not qualify as the primary causes. But, since they did induce antagonistic reciprocal perceptions by the belligerents-to-be and, in the case of South Africa, also powerful if not decisive pressures on the official sector, they rank high among the secondary causes of the two wars.

Even as the impact of the economic factors increased, strategic requirements not only continued but grew in the face of gathering new threats, insuring a virtually inextricable interpenetration of the two determinants of action. The economic remedies which the Emperor Trajan presumably sought in the Balkans and in Mesopotamia had obvious incidental strategic side-benefits for the Roman empire (and vice versa). Similarly, controlling the Suez-Red Sea and Cape routes to Asia had both strategic and economic utility for Britain. So did having a military port counterpoising Russia's and Germany's within China: it would serve as a deterrent to both an unwelcome military-political partition of, and an intolerable commercial exclusion from, the decayed Celestial Empire. And, just as some of the new or enlarged positions with peacetime economic value could facilitate strategic deployments in military crises and conflicts (thus Australia), so the continued pursuit of security for the imperial frontier incidentally generated access to important new raw materials (e.g., oil in the Persian Gulf area).

With the passage of time, the economic and the strategic prerequisites and consequences merged in the larger fusion of "imperial defence" with economic strategies for survival. The survival of the empire was, in turn, presumed to be the precondition of the nation itself surviving in either political independence or internal social peace. If anything, the economic prerequisites to a tolerable strategic posture increased their claim on the attention of policy-makers. They did so as they increased in magnitude, even relative to the growing economic potential, with the rising cost of the naval arms race and the expanding scope of the relevant strategic theater, notably before considerations of economy impelled British statecraft to retrench by means of political agreements with the United States, Japan, France, and Russia at the turn of the nineteenth century.

When a mature politico-economic system has been caught up in internal decay or relative decline, it becomes futile in itself and irrelevant for policy to try assessing the costs and benefits of empire for the core-community. So much was true for Rome, as the spreading empire evolved into a polyglot, multi-ethnically governed politico-economic machine; Rome, the city, decayed into a mass-parasite of the enlarged empire; and Italy and the West declined relative to the East. But the resulting economic costs to the initial core-empire are meaningful only if, with the benefit of hindsight, they could be contrasted unfavorably with what would have been the position of Rome and Italy face to face with a triumphant commercialism of Carthage or as a result of some hypothetical alternative imperial strategies. Similarly, the steadily increasing costs of defense against barbarian invasions may be discounted for the attraction which the empire exerted on barbarians willing to be Romanized and anxious to share in the empire's defense.

Much the same is true for the British empire. The costs of both imperial and national defense were reduced in wartime by dominion contributions, although an adequate peacetime burden-sharing was sought in vain by British proponents of an institutionally unified empire. The net economic benefits of the empire prior to 1932 might conceivably be shown to have decreased, perhaps drastically. A negative factor was the competitive drive for actually or potentially protectionist colonialism which the empire's existence inspired in others; conversely, Britain's possession of colonial chips may have enabled her to bargain more effectively for the degree of free trade that was at any time in existence. Even a demonstration that empire is a liability would mean little in practice, however, when it has become impossible to return to the merely metropolitan framework and impractical to deflect affairs to a radically different politico-economic framework at acceptable risk. Nor would improvements in the metropole's post-empire standards of living prove anything for the different economic and strategic conditions prior to

World War II, let alone for conditions seemingly in the making in the nineteenth-century period of reexpansion.

Under apparently deteriorating and intermittently critical conditions, the all-important requirement to preserve the existing imperial and domestic structures will create necessities of its own, economic as well as political, related to military power and prestige. The period of informal empire coincides with the highest capacity to practice a sovereign economy of force, i.e., choose freely where and whether to act forcefully for either expansive ends or sporadic enforcement of the basic rules of an otherwise self-regulating and sustaining politico-economic system. Thereafter, the economy of force will be superseded by an enforced economy in utilizing resources for the protection of indispensable access and essential assets. In Britain, the need to economize had to contend with rising demands (for social services and economic development) in the metropole before World War I and thereafter also in the dependencies, even as it inspired efforts to minimize costs (through concessions of self-government or the practice of indirect rule) and maximize benefits (through imperial preferences in the last resort).

Just as vain as attempting to assess costs and benefits is to precisely discriminate between economic and strategic motives for either spatial expansion or organizational extension of empire in a period when the contemporaneous perception of a survival crisis fuses the two kinds of motives most radically. Foremost determinants of action in the politically contentious and economically primitive conditions of the late Roman Republic were surely the tactical requirements of success in domestic politics; determining during the late Empire were the strategic needs of effective imperial defense. On the other hand, individual political efficiency in the free-wheeling earlier setting depended greatly on the acquisition of conspicuous economic resource; and, as the subsequent decline of Roman power and prestige was being compensated for by increasing resort to sheer force in conditions of rising external pressures, the growing economic requirements and shortcomings could not but press for parity with politico-military criteria in determining strategic responses. In the British case, it is difficult to posit even nominal primacy with confidence. Thus to argue that just as Egypt had been occupied so the East African territories were formally annexed by Britain for strategic reasons, to protect the route to India, sidesteps the problematic question of the then perceived economic value of India—and the like value of the African territories at some later stage, marking the closure of protected economic ensembles. Whatever may be the estimate of India as an economic asset in itself and in the triangular world-trade pattern, it is unlikely that the subcontinent was valued chiefly for the contribution which the sepoys could make, on the French-African pattern, to the defense of the metropole or for its net contribution to naval-strategic capabilities after discounting deployments for the defense of India and her approaches. Nor does the ascription of paramount significance to strategic motivation at the late stage explain why West African territories, too, were annexed, while lacking strategic even more than an immediately apparent economic value.

Arguments such as these might be applied also to the period of informal empire or to any other phase or kind of imperialism. They can be so applied to the extent that politico-strategic-economic factors and considerations are always to some extent circular. There is, however, a significant practical difference. In a period of economic ascendancy or self-assurance, political action may and is likely to be governed by technically autonomous strategic considerations. Such a procedure becomes an unavailable luxury for any (including aristocratic) statecraft when economic distress or economically grounded apprehensions have come to reverberate in the domestic political process, and are not unequivocally counteracted by yet more astringent strategic imperatives of security and survival. In a compelling or at least obtrusive economic context, the political risk of not acting (i.e., not annexing or occupying a position, however reluctantly) becomes greater than that of acting (i.e., annexing apparently valueless possessions, representing possible liabilities in the longer run); and any implied embarrassment will be plausibly covered by appeals to unassailable, because by tradition legitimate, strategic canons.[3]

v

The incidence of economic considerations increases as the empire passes its zenith. The upshot is the economism of late imperialism; it followed in both empires upon two earlier phases. The first was a war-related imperialism of militaristic or mercantilistic vintage. Economic stimuli were secondary for Rome, if the supply of slaves for a gradually slave-based agricultural economy is plausibly identified as the reward of victory and empire rather than an initial stimulus to war and expansion.

3. The dilemma reappears in retrospect whenever the alleged strategic imperatives (e.g., those bearing on the access to India) continue being assigned primacy in an analysis which simultaneously decries them as imaginary or obsolete from a later vantage point. The debate can be traced, as regards the British empire, in D. K. Fieldhouse, *The Colonial Empires* (London. Weidenfeld and Nicolson, 1966); D. C. M. Platt, *Finance, Trade and Politics in British Foreign Policy 1815–1914* (Oxford: Clarendon Press, 1968); and R. Robinson and J. Gallagher, *Africa and the Victorians* (New York: St. Martin Press, 1961). On Rome, see E. Badian, *Roman Imperialism in the Late Republic* (Ithaca, N.Y.: Cornell University Press, 1968); and Tenney Frank, *Roman Imperialism* (New York: Macmillan, 1914), as against Cyril E. Robinson, *A History of the Roman Republic* (London: Methuen and Co., 1932), and H. J. Haskell, *The New Deal in Old Rome* (New York: Alfred A. Knopf, 1939). Also relevant articles in Tenney Frank, ed., *An Economic Survey of Ancient Rome* (Baltimore: The Johns Hopkins Press, 1937), vol. 4.

The British situation was more ambiguous, but conformed to type once the patently economic rationales of mercantilism are viewed as a facet of the strategic concerns of dynastic or "national" inspiration, and as being subordinate to these in cases of real or hypothetical conflict. The subsequent informal imperialism of free trade was characterized by a more or less conscious and successful attempt to disassociate empire and economics. A spontaneous equilibrium was then expected to take shape between supply and demand for goods and services of different kinds, and to permit strategic moderation and administrative retrenchment. But external projection of economic interests was increasingly mediated for purposes of policy by the dynamic of an increasingly plural domestic political system, since private economic interests and the official concern with the external politico-strategic environment were apt to work at cross purposes, in the absence of reconciling transactions. After a phase when the private and official, economic and strategic, agents had been too self-confident to be smoothly cooperative, finally, they became too severely subject to declining capabilities to be mutually supportive and helpful.

Somewhere along the way, as the empires matured, their economic overtones intensified as a result of varied and complementary factors. Most obvious is the progressive accrual of both private and, by association or extension, also public vested interests in the empire and in its profitable momentum. The accumulated economic stakes, facilities, and habits will survive efforts to discount the asset represented by empire in economically good conditions, while tending to enhance its value in bad ones. The evolving framework of economic and political expectations will be further strengthened when outside actors join in attributing a paramount economic significance to the possession of empire. Moreover, next to the accumulation of vested interests and the cumulative attribution of value, the ongoing requirements of adaptation to a changing economic environment will promote economic emphases. This will be true especially if the early challenge of a suddenly enlarged, but apparently fixed or static, economic setting, which is typical of mercantilism and war imperialism, is superseded by an economic setting which is dynamic or volatile in both volume and structure and secretes pressures for neo-mercantilistic management in time.

The bias to attribute value and the need to adapt to vicissitudes will make empire managers increasingly conscious of economic considerations. Precarious economic conditions will be intertwined with acute security issues, bound to resurface at some point in any evolving system of regional and global balances of power. The internal political system, too, will foster economism as the imperial ruling class seeks to provide for itself in an enlarged framework. It can do so by means of continuing political ascendancy and growing abuse of power and corruption, as it did notably in Rome; or, as mainly in Britain, by way of political transactions intended to appease the economically more dynamic successor-class, while also perhaps compensating the politically receding ruling class itself for the depressed value or lowered productivity of traditional landed assets. The economic stresses will be rounded off as ruling-class members compete among themselves or with the upcoming social stratum in offering material inducements to a numerically expanding and politically activated popular mass. In what is liable to be a deteriorating domestic political environment, political support can no longer be secured by awe-inspiring political accomplishments of the ruling class, as it was in the (comparatively speaking) heroic era of formative war imperialism. In the increasingly hedonistic eras of informal and protective imperialisms, support must be purchased in one way or another.

It is in some such manner that economism will become a corollary of late imperialism. As such, it will be a function of deterioration in the internal and external positions of both the imperial ruling class and the empire itself. The deterioration will parallel a growing differentiation of political forces and aggravation of economic dilemmas in the face of the elite's declining capacity to master one or the other, either at all or without substantially revising the original formula for the empire at home and abroad. Such revision will entail greater and more self-conscious emphasis on the economic factor at home and abroad. Not only will both diversification and decay in the political arena have brought to the fore a wider range of material self-interests, they will also have downgraded as irrelevant, or as irremediably compromised, the psychopolitical stimuli which made the early struggle for tribal survival climax in the conquest of the initial core-empire.

IV

DEVELOPMENT AND DEFENSE

OF EMPIRE. *Organizational*

Dead Ends

The career of empire starts with the learning process of expansion, is prolonged by the dreary task of management, and ends in the climactic agony of dissolution. The crucial midterm task is to insure cohesion at tolerable cost in resource available at the center and in capacity for endurance displayed on the periphery.

1

Expansion is often the most facile response, by means of a "flight forward," to dilemmas and dangers. It can be reversed into spatial retraction, which need not necessarily be ruinous for the retained domain. But management of a pluralistic empire involves the near-insoluble quandary of the proper degree of direct involvement. The issue is one of the ratio or balance between central control and local autonomy, between imperial tutelage and devolution of responsibility to dependencies. Economy of control in ever-changing contingencies is a yet harder science to practice than is economy of force. Over- or underinvolvement in depth is at least as fatal as is overextension in space; it is also harder to justify by uncontrollable pressures from the outside, in view of the seeming omnipotence of imperial authority within the orbit of prior expansion. Moreover, it will be a mismanaged assortment of authority and autonomy, superimposed control and spontaneous cohesion, *imperium* and *libertas*, that engenders the appearance of overextension. Just as overextension cannot be determined independently of the internal relationships, their mis-assortment will also foster the organic decay and relative decline which commonly set the stage for a final dissolution precipitated by hostile external forces.

The interrelation between the degree of authoritative control within the empire and the impact of anarchic power from outside is crucial for long-term survival. It is all the more so since the climactic outside challenges will tend to coincide with, or soon follow, a marked diminution of the capacity to modulate internal control both authoritatively and flexibly. Such a conjunction will undermine either moderation in action or mastery over events at the center and diminish either responsiveness or compliance at the peripheries. For this reason alone, which will be only reinforced by specific factors of decay, empires will secretly begin their decline near the end of the major wave of expansion, notwithstanding subsequent reorganizations and periods of resurgence. Even less than for homogeneous territorial states, there is no plateau of restful stability for pluralistic empires. Debilitating small wars will be prominent among the events that facilitate assaults by internal counterelites and external rivals or enemies upon the empire, encompassing its collapse and clearing the decks for its replacement by other powers or different principles of order and organization.

Even more than the expansion of the Roman and the British empires, their management was not a matter of deliberate planning. Instead, organization took shape in function of improvised reactions to local disaffection and central disappointments with existing arrangements. There were specific differences, however. The Roman empire had evolved toward more extensive and direct control from the imperial center. So, on the whole, did the America-centered first British empire and, initially, also the India-centered second empire. But the second empire came to be poised between a tendency, to decentralization in favor of its major dependent or constituent parts, and contrary aspirations toward reintegration into a unity that would emcompass far-reaching autonomy in function and parity in status for an ever-expanding range of dependencies. The Roman penchant for discretionary control at the center had made for stagnation in the empire's members; the experiments of the later British empire with devolution of responsibility fostered unruly local separatisms. Both the discretionary and the devolutionary approaches enfeebled resistance to the terminal shock waves originating from the outside.

II

While the Roman senate groped toward empire and before uniformity had set in, the clear preference was for diversity in types of control and a free hand over contractual or institutional limitations on Roman actions. Informal manipulation of local or regional balances of power, of the status of dependents, and of Roman commitments yielded only haltingly to institutional techniques of management, stopping short of or including direct administration.

Moving from West to East, the range of political space to organize by different means comprised initially very disparate segments. Spain was a colony of exploitation producing metals, corn, and recruits, and was subject to protracted unconventional warfare; Italy, south of the Alps, was managed through a confederacy of allies who fought eventually for Roman citizenship to consummate their informal equality and match the rising claims on their manpower outside Italy; and, finally, in Greece and Asia Minor the key differences centered less on types of confederates and more on how direct or indirect was to be Rome's management of the local balances of power and administrative involvements.

Early Rome's way of managing allies in the Latin confederacy had set the tone of Sicily, Illyria, and beyond. Mutuality of commitment and performance, governed by a treaty (*foedus*) with formal allies (*socii*), gave way to preference for "friends" (*amici*) without treaty. Applying only indirect control, by way of local oligarchies dependent on Rome, enabled the senate to interpret with increasing elasticity the obligations of clients and Rome's own commitments. In the process, contractual alliance was debased from genuine advance commitment to a device for justifying a war (under sacred law) as one undertaken in Rome's or an ally's defense. And just as the experience in Italy defined Rome's approach to commitments via formal or informal alliances, so Greece conditioned her approach to control via more or less autonomous regional balances of power. Whereas the disloyalty of some allies during the second (Punic) war against Carthage had colored the Italian experience, relations with Greece were shaped by the mere suspicion of disloyalty during the third war (of Perseus) against Macedon. Both experiences reflected the pitfalls of a flexible application of partial or intermediate forms of control to less-than-wholeheartedly acquiescent clients.

Rome's manipulation of the regional balances of power in Greece evolved from negative or indirect to positive and direct; the related control techniques tightened almost concurrently from remote via indirect to direct control. Rome had started out by merely denying to the Eastern Mediterranean great powers the right to interfere in local balances; later, the senate devolved to trusted middle-ranking allies a largely autonomous responsibility for maintaining a congenial order; and it finally merely delegated the execution of explicit senatorial mandates to reliably dependent, small or reduced, allies. Direct Roman management of a local balance of power worked against a discredited friend, such as Pergamum in the East, on a par with the defeated Carthaginian enemy in the West. Still falling short of direct administration, managing the balance directly involved imposing limitations on authorized arms (previously applied to the defeated Eastern great powers) along with control of both peacetime policies and war aims. The lesser states were denied resort to unauthorized self-defense as well as to offensive aggrandizement, while Rome empowered herself alone to define intolerable threats—and exercised that power in favor of the party momentarily least suspect of threatening Roman interests. Inhibitory control of offensive capabilities or intentions was supplemented with structural measures, moreover, such as the fragmentation of resurgent Macedon. Throughout the early period, so long as Roman policy-makers alternated between the urge to disengage and actual drift into ever-deeper involvement, the lesser states remained uncertain about both the intent and the extent of controlling authority. The resulting ambiguity of conditions and attitudes fostered arbitrariness in policies, pending the emergence of authoritative institutions for the empire in its entirety. An early controversy about the Greek problem had adumbrated a theoretical contrast between an essentially disinterested or internationalist approach, favoring assistance in response to local needs, and an essentially self-interested imperialistic approach, looking to a clear choice between unilateral control and integral abstention from involvement. Mixes of the opposites permeated in the event the gradual shift from philhellenic hesitancies to hegemony over all the Hellenes.

Local security was initially allocated by means of *ad hoc* (senatorial) investigations of disorders. But the Roman senate could never attain a degree of consistency which would cumulatively evolve readily recognizable and locally assimilable standards in the application of sanctions and rewards. Consequently, a protectorate based solely on remote control via locally internalized consistent signals from the center had to be largely replaced by indirect control via dependent oligarchical regimes. The more far-reaching system of maintaining order meant that substantial limitations would be imposed on lateral communications and trade between local powers; and it entailed drastic sanctions, such as territorial division (of Macedon), physical displacement (of Carthage), and deterrent terror (the razing of Corinth). The final mode was direct control by civilian-military resident promagistrates and tax collectors. It was resorted to under the pressure of fear—not least of German tribes beyond the Alps (as, before, of Carthage in Sicily); of material needs, thus to finance social services; and of sheer failure of the alternative approaches. Only territory close to Rome, such as Gaul south of the Alps, was annexed and administered as a matter of preference. When Greece came to be administered as a province, as late as 27 B.C., the progression was complete from intermittent Roman interventions to continuous influence through indigenous pro-Roman oligarchies and on to the institution of permanent Roman residents.

When the Empire eventually followed upon the Republic, direct regulatory administration was applied in a widening compass, while assimilating some of the supplanted Eastern models. Management combined then three cardinal elements: a deified emperorship, for unity; a professional army intertwined with imperial bureaucracy, for protection; and, for support, cosmopolitan elites standing above the heterogeneous and inert masses. As upholders of the *pax Romana*, the emperor and the military-civilian bureaucracy represented central authority within the *orbis Romanus*, while the provincial elites, endowed with the ethnically and culturally ever more neutral status of the *civis Romanus*, were the ones to mediate between the central order and local diversity. Formal autonomy for provincial cities was fairly highly developed, so long as local candidates were available for local administration. So was actual tolerance for local mores and material interests by a government which inclined at first to merely react rather than originate and, later, regulated but ineffectually. The right to present collective petitions promoted cultural regionalism with political side effects, notably when senators drawn to Rome from the provinces came to "represent" the area of their origin at least as much as they continued to transcend parochial antecedents.

Such trends notwithstanding, local or provincial autonomy had but a limited impact on both imperial power and popular support in the phase preceding a late administrative subdivision of the empire. Following the earliest indirection in management, and reflecting senatorial reluctance to administer directly, decentralization had meant in the middle Republic no more than delegation of executory functions to trusted dependents. More effective decentralization emerged temporarily in the late Republic, when provincial clients gained influence as part of the fight of powerful Romans for control of central power. Under the Empire, assimilation of provincials to Graeco-Roman culture, along with their access to Roman citizenship and highest imperial offices including the emperorship, did for the psychopolitical condition of local elites what decentralization and autonomy had done earlier. Assimilation and co-optation extended progressively from southern Spain and Gaul via the Greek East and Africa to the Danubian area; they probably assured elite allegiance to the empire more efficaciously than could any practical extent of local self-government and regional representation.

The problems of the British empire were similar. But the empire's long-term record was different once attempts to centralize, or rationalize, the structure and administration had produced the American fiasco, and the fiasco itself conditioned the second empire. The main working compromise of the first empire was to temper metropolitan regulation by colonial evasions. That informal *modus vivendi* was replaced by differentiating formally between matters of imperial and of colonial concern; and the shift occurred when interest in economic tribute from dependencies within a mercantilistic empire had been overshadowed by the pursuit of economies, to result from diffusion of local self-government, within a system of free trade. As part of the process, a species of indirect rule by way of chartered trading companies and proprietary settlement colonies in the first empire was supplanted in the second by indirect rule through indigenous elites (previously practiced by some of the trading companies themselves). By and large, whereas the Roman empire had evolved toward uniformity in assimilative subjection, the second British empire veered toward differentiation in degrees of responsible colonial government. Moreover, and again contrary to Rome's centralizing arbitrariness, de-concentration of governing responsibilities was matched by a heightened formality and mutuality of commitments, especially in relations with the self-governing white-settler colonies (to become dominions). In a way, the beginning of the Roman empire in a confederacy with autonomous Italian allies (and in semi-autonomous client status for the Eastern realms) was the penultimate stage of the British empire as it evolved via a commonwealth toward the uniformity of indiscriminate emancipation.

So long as the fundamental trend away from direct control did not manifest itself uniformly, it accounted for status differences. Thus the change in India was from supervised (East India) company rule to an enlightened civil-service despotism applicable also to Egypt and the crown colonies. But, outside these domains, the impact of the Indian Mutiny on imperial sentimentality fostered disengagement. Indirect rule through indigenous potentates was perfected in due course in Africa; but it constituted only nominal delegation of authority when compared with the effective devolution implicit in self-government and dominion status. The grant of colonial self-government was initially possible because Britain's supremacy at sea alleviated the problem of military protection; it was available to dependencies with sufficient European population to run and material endowment to finance self-government; and it tended to be pressed upon eligible colonies beset by protracted, costly conflicts with indigenous peoples such as the Maoris in New Zealand and the Bantus in the Cape Colony. When the desire to avoid the costs of localized military skirmishes evolved in due course into the urge to share with the more important among the white-settler colonies the inevitable expenditures on larger defense against resurgent old and ascendant new European powers, Canada had led on the road to autonomy (in the 1840s, following the trail-blazing Durham Report); she was eventually joined by the Australian colonies, New Zealand, and, finally, South Africa in dominion status. And when, soon after the late 1860s and 1870s, as part of the trend from informal free trade to formalized protective empire, the British Conservatives sought to reverse the trend initiated by the Liberals (anxious to withdraw permanent British garrisons from the self-governing colonies on grounds of economy), they attempted to use the new basis of autonomy and, hopefully, burden-sharing for remilitarizing imperial ties.

The object was to offset the loosening of other bonds, including economic, and to implement the shift of concern from small colonial wars to potential bigger conflicts directly involving the metropole.

Any design to complement devolution with reintegration had to come to terms with the example set by the final institutionalization of the Roman empire. The Empire had promoted provincial elites to highest functions in the imperial government, while the (British) dominions were attracted to a status more like that of the autonomous Greek and Italian allies during the early Republic. The vision of restructured unity was, moreover, at variance with the unwillingness of the metropole as well as of the dependencies to incur and endure the implicit transformations. A broad positive agreement about general direction was overwhelmed by quarrels and quandaries as to when and how. When would the white-settler colonies be materially and psychologically ready for reintegration on the basis of parity with the mother country? And how should the transition to common political institutions be implemented: by means of military defense measures only or also of common protectionist economic policies and representative political organs? If common institutions were to command universal support, they would have had to transcend a merely consultative conference format and be compatible with British as well as dominion autonomy.

Other differences bore on attitudes toward the several balances of power. British recourse to mercenaries or military allies on the Continent as "swords" in European wars, in return for economic subsidies or protection of friendly trade, resembled somewhat Rome's early practices in Italy. More important were the differences between Roman and British approaches to commitments and to regional balances of power. The British approach to equilibrium on the Continent was notoriously elastic (or opportunist), even in the period when that balance was circumscribed by British hegemony in the last resort. If, therefore, the only commitment that had a firmness matching Rome's *fides* at its best was to protect the closest or most dependent allies (Portugal and the Low Countries) and Britain's own colonies, it was, ironically, the reciprocal commitment by the self-governing dominions that became eventually susceptible to the kind of arbitrary interpretation and optional implementation that Rome had often practiced vis-à-vis dependents. And whereas the British did not delegate intervention to indigenous actors (other than the Indian Army) in regional balances of power outside Europe, they acted, if to a controversial extent, more like Rome when employing the techniques of divide-and-conquer for manipulating precarious balances of local power in Malaya, the Persian Gulf area, or on the Indian subcontinent between Hindu and Moslem.

As the empire matured and moved to dissolution, the critical balancing by the imperial power shifted to relations between white settlers and indigenous majorities, notably in Africa, in an effort to reverse divide-and-conquer for empire into unite-and-retain for essentials. Prior to that, too, the techniques of management had been primarily political and institutional. But military force and occasional acts of punitive and deterrent terror could not be wholly absent at all time from Britain's imperial register any more than they had been from Rome's. If a comparable scarcity of available human and material resources required sophisticated resourcefulness, systematic ingenuity had also to be accented by occasional intimidation.

III

Different as they were in specifics, both empires sought to find stability midway between all-out centralization and radical deconcentration; and they did so in the face of a structural dichotomy that persisted and deepened within their orbits. They engaged in comparable efforts to bridge disparate structures when organizing the empire for effective defense; and they suffered from comparable vulnerability to political strains and military conflicts which were contributing directly or indirectly to their eventual decline.

In the phase of expansion and ascendancy, the critical cleavage for both empires was one between "barbarian" and "civilized" wings. For Rome the first meant the West, the second the East. The barbarian West, including Spain and Sardinia, was conquered in near-permanent and inhumane warfare, while a vicious circle of annexations, revolts, and repressions strained Roman political institutions and morals alike. The East was initially characterized by higher standards of civility in both the Hellenistic concert of powers and the subsequent indirect Roman sway. The corresponding difference for Britain in the seventeenth and eighteenth centuries and beyond was between overseas territories and the European balance of power and occasional concert. The worldwide periphery (lying beyond the "line" drawn west of the British isles) was successively excepted by common consent from the benefits of European peace treaties, of the canons of chivalry (as inapplicable on the high seas), and of the basic norms of international law (as linked to an unspecified level of civilized conditions). But Britain experienced also, in due course and in her own way, the internally corrosive effect which the disparity had had in Rome, without reliably enjoying abroad (at the hands of sporadically attentive Europeans) the advantage Rome had derived from Greek indifference to the lot of the barbarians. Furthermore, intramural conflicts had been rife in Britain over strategic priorities, as between the continental and the colonial theaters, from an early time on; they were followed by divisive intraempire debates over colonial contributions to overall imperial capability, as part of the continuing interaction between power struggles on the Continent and contests over colonies among the leading European states.

Both empires resolved in the end at least partially or superficially the conflict of attitudes and techniques implicit in simultaneously managing a colonial empire of exploitation and a hegemonial orbit of influence. Whereas Rome assimilated the Greeks to the barbarians for political purposes, Britain allowed the gap to narrow between the colonies of settlement and continental allies for strategic purposes. The line of cleavage had by then begun to shift, however, to bedevil the climax and decline of the two empires. Rome, the city, and Italy were eventually to become the core of the Western or Latin empire as distinct from the Eastern or Greek empire; the corresponding British intraempire division was between the western wing, represented by Canada, and the eastern Australasia.

In the earlier phase, the critical differentiating factors had been types of warfare, forms of imperial control, and kinds of economic exploitation. The critical new difference became, next to the magnitude of economic resource and the identity of the principal security threat, the disparity between land and sea power. It was a disparity that had been previously secondary for the Roman empire, while pervading in the British case both colonial and continental relationships. Maritime-mercantile Eastern Rome faced the combination of Persian and barbarian military pressures, while no conventional major power beset the agricultural West alongside the Germanic invaders; but the East had both greater material resources and a shorter line of defense. Once the West had been separated from the East in both organization and vital sea communications, it lost the ability to adequately provision and pay its land armies; the Eastern empire lived on to fight the Islamic successors to the Persian menace, and did so with superior sea power and an ultimate weapon (the so-called Greek fire). The analogous cleavage in the British empire was between Canada's exposure to the long-feared United States on land and the exposure of economically weaker Australia and New Zealand to naval threats from Russia (largely imaginary even before the Anglo-Russian entente) and Japan. The disparity hampered efforts to organize common defense before World War I. Near-disaster ensued in World War II, when it took America's globalized sea power, backed eventually by a nuclear version of the "Greek fire," to prevent Japan from permanently severing Britain's imperial sea communications.

Dealing with two-wing structures while pitting diminished material resources against rising external threats required a twofold effort at unifying the defense system. One effort was narrowly strategic, another more broadly organizational. Matching the tension between authority and autonomy in the politico-administrative sphere, the key issue regarding concentration and dispersion in the military context was between stressing central strategic reserve and relying mainly on peripherally stationed forces. Within that fundamental choice, the burden in the Roman empire rested with territorial troops (and a relatively small fleet, principally against pirates), while the naval branch was critical for the British empire (next to small land-army effectives in peacetime).

In the Roman empire, the secular trend in strategic concept and practice was, on the whole, from concentration to dispersion; from initiative to response and from delegation (of responsibility for peripheral order to Rome's clients) to dependence (for defense of central core on romanized cohorts); and from mobility for offensive purposes to mobility as but a marginal corrective to static defense. The attendant increases in the size of armed forces and in material cost went with an eventual decrease in morale and efficiency. The overall trend overcame intermittent efforts, such as Emperor Hadrian's in the middle of the third century A.D., in the face of intensified assaults from Germanic tribes and Sassanid Persia, to mitigate the loss of initiative and enhance mobility; to supplement static-line defense with defense in depth; and to add new strategic roads to frontier fortifications along the Rhine-Danube defense perimeter for use by an improved and professionalized army command backed by increased financial resources from reorganized taxation. The Roman legions, for long the relatively small core of the military system capable of successively underwriting the Roman peace and withstanding intrusions by much bigger barbarian forces, reflected the trend toward localism. As they grew less mobile, the legions were increasingly recruited where they were stationed. They were supplemented in manning fixed frontiers by indigenous, and originally noncitizen, auxiliaries fighting under local chieftains and only gradually used also outside their areas of origin. In the Latin West's climactic crisis of the fifth century, finally, the Roman forces gave way wholly to "civilized" barbarian allies authorized henceforth to settle after as well as during campaigns inside the limits of the empire.

The assimilative effect of military organization helped transcend localism, just as efforts at improving unified defense delayed the full manifestation of the structural disparity between West and East. But not indefinitely. In the East, a strong professional "Roman" core-army survived to be only supplemented by occasionally employed foreign (including barbarian) legions and allies, and remained under adequate civilian control from Constantinople long enough to sustain the defensive subtleties of late Byzantine diplomacy. In the West, by contrast, progressive deterioration marked the transition from offensive-defensive salients, such as Dacia (conquered in the first century A.D.), to the protective belts manned by the Germanic "allies" in the fifth century. Across a longer time-span, a like worsening informed the change from protected *socii* with *foedus* (treaty) to protecting *federati*, the former mercilessly controlled and the latter mercifully conquering in the end.

The most far-reaching effort to transcend the structural dichotomy by reorganization acknowledging its existence was Emperor Diocletian's reform at the end of the third century, including a quasi-federative hierarchy of senior and junior emperors and caesars in West and East. Decentralization was to channel authoritative guiding energy to the different wings and sectors; the senior Augustus or emperor was to insure the irreducible degree of unity. In actuality, however, the top-heavy collegial emperor system may have promoted disruption instead of fostering coordination of common defense; it helped transfer the point of gravity eastward, while deflecting military pressures westward. The post-Diocletian breakup of both fiscal and strategic unity was completed by a moral cleavage wrought by intrigues between the different imperial "palaces" and by doctrinal controversies consequent on the adoption of Christianity. In the long run, the two wings came to be related mainly by competition over primacy in status; by reciprocal conquests, perversely expressing the ideal of unity; and by the abandonment of each party by the other in its final crisis, consummating the fact of decentralization.

Serious problems of defense had arisen for the Roman empire in the third century A.D. and culminated for the West in the fifth century. They began for the British empire with the military setbacks in the late 1870s, including those in Afghanistan and associated with the Russian threat; and they culminated in the erosion of British naval supremacy, associated mainly with the German challenge in the 1900s. Just as the Russian menace sparked concern with centralizing "imperial defence," so the German threat stimulated naval deconcentration within the empire, as well as outside it via agreements with newly allied or friendly foreign powers. The largely impractical ideal was to have an effective empire defense without impeding economic progress in the colonies and imposing heavy fiscal burden in Britain; to allocate controls, commitments, and commands in ways that would reflect the material contributions and political aspirations of the self-governing colonies, while safeguarding the British government's monopoly in formulating foreign policy and military strategy. The underlying question was whether military coordination could be effective without politico-economic integration in depth or whether it would lead soon enough to such integration; whether imperial defense was possible without imperial preference or even federation.

The favored strategic concept behind "imperial defence" was to continue concentrating the main naval forces in Britain's home waters. They would act as a deterrent against major-power attack, as a strategic reserve for outlying theaters, and as an offensive striking force against enemy concentrations in war. If outlying dependencies or dominions were invaded or overrun, they would be relieved after the Royal Navy had won decisive naval engagements in the principal theater, while continuing to protect the "imperial roads" (i.e., the sea lanes) for the transport of troops and essential trade. The concept was analogous to the Roman one of mobile legions backing local efforts by clients. It was inimical in theory but not in practice to naval proliferation, which the Admiralty espoused even less ardently for the colonials than for the continentals, long preferring to complement an exclusive British naval responsibility with primary colonial responsibility for local defenses on land. Only just before World War I was the division of labor modified to assign naval missions to the colonials, against locally confined smaller-scale threats to ports, facilities, or coasts temporarily eluding the Royal Navy. Simultaneously, the commitment of dominion naval and land forces to imperial (meaning effectively British) supreme command in wartime became technically a voluntary one. The instantaneous dominion involvement in the war caused such infractions of a centralized "imperial defence" to be no more than symbolic; but they proved to be substantive enough in the longer run preceding World War II.

Actual capabilities for a cooperative naval defense of the empire developed only gradually. The practice evolved in comparable stages, from the colonies making financial contributions to the Royal Navy for specific ships or general purposes, to their actually operating auxiliary ships in peacetime, and on to establishing national navies within the framework of the Royal Navy after acceding to dominion status. But, whereas land-oriented Canada was foremost in resisting any contribution to British sea power, the most exposed (and consequently most loyal) maritime colonies of New Zealand and the Cape clung longest to the lowest stage (of financial contributions). It was Australia's evolution toward a Royal Australian Navy by 1907 which typified the basic trend for all, once the intermediate stage (of individual "auxiliary" ships) had run aground on admiralty obstructions. In the last resort, the intraempire "one-fleet" principle broke down only along with the collapse of the "two-power" standard globally, as the proliferation of foreign navies (German, American, and Japanese next to the French and Russian) made nonsense of opposition to autonomous dominion navies. Advantages could then become mutual. The rudiments of dominion navies, just as colonial gifts of ships to Britain, were not necessarily counted for "arms-control" purposes in the Anglo-German controversy over naval constructions, while expanding the actually available sea power. And even small steps toward a *de facto* division of the spheres of naval responsibilities with the dominions (matching that with Britain's allies and entente partners) amounted to extra insurance for an Australia or a New Zealand, exposed to hypothetical future dangers from an expansionist Japan in the Pacific as much as from a restrictive British strategy when focusing on the North Sea.

Land forces caused fewer frictions for good and sufficient reasons. The central defense of the empire was virtually consigned to the sea, following the retraction of British garrisons from the self-governing colonies to the British islands. If the increased vulnerability of the denuded colonies could be expected to encourage them to accept British leadership in empire defense, assuring the impregnability of the insular metropole was once again to become the ultimate safeguard of the whole empire. Moreover, unlike sea power, the remaining land forces were not susceptible to either instant destruction or an unavoidable intermingling in action, requiring close advance coordination. Whereas the Australian colonies typified the naval issues on the way to becoming the Commonwealth of Australia, Canada set the pattern for matters connected with the territorial army. The Canadians had first opposed the withdrawal of the British garrisons; they then replaced the garrisons with volunteer militia, and finally opposed the reintroduction of British forces. This did not preclude British technical assistance, inspection, and role in effective local command. The mother country's willingness to deconcentrate and proliferate on land, in marked contrast with the naval arena, made it possible for its military style and traditions, and for standardized equipment, to permeate and virtually imperialize (if not wholly integrate) the dominion militias even before the emergence of an Imperial General Staff in the early 1900s. The unwittingly creative British detachment reflected the absence of meaningful threats, as the American threat to Canada became academic (and, should it revert to real, unmanageable); local threats (e.g., from the Fenian raiders in Canada and the Maoris in New Zealand) disappeared; and the diplomatic crises in Europe were not yet such as to awaken concern with empire-wide preparation for expeditionary forces.

The strategic concepts evolved in peace managed to contrive an imperial-colonial mix of both substantive and symbolic components that proved sufficient to sustain combat operations and avert the military destruction of the empire in World War I. Conversely, the failure to advance the political organization of empire insured that the principle of naval proliferation, adopted in 1907, would evolve over the next three decades into the Statute of Westminster, provisionally codifying effective institutional deconcentration bordering on dissolution. A widely acknowledged axiom had held that dominion representation was at the heart of imperial defense. If Britain's stake was in perpetuating command and control, also as a condition of efficacy, the dominions were bent on securing voice and visibility: voice in the making of foreign and imperial policy; visibility for contributions to common defense, also as a condition of domestic support for such contributions. In due course, there was no shortage of institutions with the prefix "imperial" and with *ad hoc* or nominal participation of dominion representatves; but there was no peacetime increase in effective colonial participation in the shaping of British policies. Empire loyalists, such as the New Zealanders and the Canadian Conservatives just before the "great war," seemed anxious to abstain from naval independence in exchange for policy coordination. Admission to imperial councils was to be had, however, and even then only temporarily, less through abstention in peacetime than through actual assertion of dominion capabilities in wartime. By and large, the measure of effective consultation was a function of tactical considerations, as the British sought to extract binding advance commitments and the colonials to eschew them.

The impediments were more or less real. One difficulty lay in the tendency to overstate the requirements and the consequences of meaningful imperial institutions. Whereas the British raised the specter of a colonial bloc in the House of Commons and colonial Trojan horses in the Cabinet, the colonial autonomists agitated the bogey of restored British control posturing as empire-wide consensus. The pragmatism of the British governments, addicted to piecemeal steps in multiple directions, conspired in avoiding an earnest search for the middle ground with the dogmatism of an emerging colonial nationalism, prone to relegate "imperial federation" to a future so remote as to become nonexistent. British statecraft had learned previously when and how to loosen colonial ties in order to avoid losing key parts of the empire altogether; it failed now to tighten the bonds of empire in depth on a new basis, for fear of stripping the metropole of its essentially national prerogatives in conducting foreign policy and foreign trade as well as in managing the empire. Timely sharing with members, any more than with rivals, was not seen as a practical method for consolidating the residuum. The obstacles seemed forbidding at any one point in time, not least because the relevant time dimensions were different for the parties. The British were primarily concerned with short-term financial relief; the less-developed dominions could not grant it at once in a magnitude sufficient to justify giving them a major voice in policy-making. The longer-term functional concern of the dominions was in economic development; growth would be retarded in the short run by major outlays for defense. The curve of dominion economic potential was rising relative to the stagnating level of British economic capacity-in-being; the two did not intersect in time to create a material basis for expressing in institutions the imperatives of unified naval strategy and massive military capability.

Only an imperial customs union slanted in favor of industrial development for the dominions might have concretized the possibilities implicit in a common racial and cultural background. It might have given the dominions a unique stake in the Royal Navy, as the protector of intraempire trade routes, and softened the rift between Britain's globalism and dominion parochialism. Lacking a material base, mere defense coordination in and for war was not enough. Lord Salisbury's imperial *kriegsverein* failed to spill over into either economic or political integration in conditions that would enable Britain and the empire to consolidate a viable position within the emerging new global balance of power.[1]

1. The preceding account is based on Richard A. Preston's *Canada and "Imperial Defense"* (Durham, N.C.: Duke University Press, 1967), though my conclusions are contrary to the author's. See also D. K. Fieldhouse, *The Colonial Empires* (London: Weidenfeld and Nicolson, 1966), on imperial management. The discussion of the Roman Empire in this and the following chapters draws on Fergus Millar et al., *The Roman Empire and Its Neighbours* (London: Weidenfeld and Nicolson, 1967), articles in the *Propyläen Weltgeschichte*, edited by Golo Mann, (Berlin: Im Propyläenverlag, 1963), vol. 4, and, next to the literature cited in previous chapters, on A. H. M. Jones, *The Decline of the Ancient World* (London: Longmans, Green, 1966), and Joseph Vogt, *The Decline of Rome* (London: Weidenfeld and Nicolson, 1967).

V

DECLINE AND DISSOLUTION OF EMPIRE. *Terminal Distempers*

The difficulty in striking a satisfactory and enduring balance between central authority and peripheral autonomy is such as to verge on an impossibility. It will prepare the terrain for the terminal agony of empires. The waning of great realms is habitually attended by disproportionately petty circumstances; the greatest of empires will be mortally wounded by the smallest of wars, and will fall prey in the end to challenges and challengers vastly inferior to threats and trials they had withstood before with real fortitude and apparent success.

I

Inadequate as it was to be in the long run, a mere—and a merely military—cooperation between Britain and the dominions proved itself in World War I well beyond the degree of concord and concert realized in the earlier and smaller wars of the British empire. Such small, peripheral, and mostly inglorious, wars did not threaten the existence of either the British or the Roman empires. But they contributed to internal malaise, which had weakened both empires when they came to face larger threats. Among the lesser conflicts of the Roman Republic were the so-called Viriatic and Numantine wars, fought in the barbarian Spanish wing (in the late second century B.C.), and the Numidian war in North Africa against Jugurtha. The Eastern emperor Justinian was to fight a comparably strenuous war of reconquest and pacification as late

as the sixth century A.D. after the fall of the Latin West and North
Africa. The British empire labored under relatively small-scale wars of
pacification first in North America and later in South Africa (against the
Zulus and then the Boers); the Crimean and Afghan wars, while not
technically major, differed by involving contest with another great power.

Common to such disparate conflicts are their character and purpose,
their internal repercussions, and their effects on key aspects of empire. All
were limited wars and most of them were also protracted wars, not least
because the imperial powers abstained from mobilizing their full resources at all or promptly enough. They would avoid involving politically hostile greater powers, such as Persia in Justinian's war and Russia
or Germany in Britain's small wars. Except in the Crimean War, the
battlefield situation did not as a result accurately reflect the actual power
relationships, all the more so because a more often than not inefficient or
insufficiently supported military command had typically to cope in difficult terrain with an uncommonly tenacious adversary. The result was
repeatedly frustration at home and inhumane combat in the field, distributing extraordinary strains and stresses about evenly among the
metropolitan body politic, the imperial troops, and the indigenous
populations.

It did not help much that to conspicuous flaws could be opposed
essentially valid objectives. Even if they were not parrying immediate
and mortal threats to either the empire or the core polity, the small wars
provided against the cumulative effects of inaction as regards both pacification, of actually or supposedly rebellious forces, and prestige, in relations with actually or potentially rival powers. Hence the Roman
empire's concern to counteract Persia in the East and Britain's to
check Russia in the Eastern Mediterranean, and the need for the latter to
impress Germany in South Africa. Stakes and purposes of this kind were
intangible and made the conquest of territory into a secondary objective
at best. But failure to win a clear-cut victory was tantamount to defeat.
And if peace negotiations were typically less than either candid or conclusive, their flaws only reflected the nature of both the underlying issues
and the military procedures.

The varied repercussions of the small wars within the imperial polities
tended to exceed their magnitude and dwarf even their immediate external significance. The most visible crises were political, entailing discredit
for the executive power and, by extension, the entire regime. Initial
popular support for a war tended to wane with the war's prolongation.
In Rome, both the Spanish wars and the North African war activated in
due course demagogic plebeian tribunes against the senate, to the successive advantage of the elder Gracchus and of Marius and his equestrian
allies. Until later in the Empire, however, when an idle populace in
circus assembled would pressure emperors during games to terminate

unpopular wars, the fundamental necessity for the wars of pacification had been largely recognized. By contrast, the critique of corresponding British wars tended to comprise not only their conduct but also their presumed cause, imputed to governmental inadvertence or special-interest intrigues. Moreover, the popular British press outdid Rome's popular tribunes in undermining confidence in the ruling class. The wide repercussions of the Crimean War were due to its being the first war covered by newspaper correspondents in the field; near-instant publicity for shortcomings quickly produced demands for official inquiry hostile to the governing system itself. The demagogy surrounding the Spanish wars in Rome on the side of both the popular leaders and the aristocrats (typified by a late Scipio, Aemilianus) had set the stage for Rome's civil wars; the political crisis set off in Britain by the Boer War eventuated in a deepening malaise before World War I.

In all circumstances, protracted wars drained material resources beyond the measure warranted by readily identifiable stakes and competed with rising internal needs or demands. But specific social and economic effects differed, depending on the general economic situations. Waged in conditions of material scarcity, Rome's Spanish wars provoked rapid urbanization along with substantial economic recession. The result was unemployment and money shortage, conditions that aggravated the general insecurity fostered by simultaneous slave rebellions in the agricultural sector. Rome's North African war, just as the South African war of Britain, took place in more prosperous conditions. But prosperity exceeded poverty in exposing the ruling class to charges of corruption or subservience to obscure and irresponsible economic interests. Later on, Justinian's war of reconquest was initially subsidized by the reconquered provinces, but it progressively burdened also the Eastern empire heavily and ended by importing a real (as distinct from the more frequent figurative) plague from the war arena into the civilian rear.

Other major domestic problems included, on the military side, the tendency to overreact to military setbacks in the field, not least by demands for fundamental changes in the supporting military organization. The overall drift was toward professionalism, as a remedy for either the incongruity or the incompetence which a war had revealed. The incongruity in Rome was between a citizen militia, originally intended for relatively short survival wars waged close to home, on one side, and both protracted and peripheral conflicts of empire management on the other. To evade the draft required selling the family farm carrying with it the obligation to military service; the flight from the land fostered excessive urbanization with its attendant political and economic evils. The growing difficulty of recruiting by other methods shifted emphasis to "volunteer" or professional forces, severing the vital link between citizenship and military service by the time of the Spanish wars. Conversely, professionalizing the officer corps as late as the third century A.D. completed the elimination of another pillar of early Rome, the senatorial politician-commander. Britain was always professional with regard to ranks, but it took the failures in the Crimea and the setbacks in Afghanistan to change the selection of officers from social to professional criteria in the 1870s, while still higher-level reforms were set off by the incompetencies revealed during the Boer War.

The effect of wars on the armed forces could thus be, on balance, positive. No such possibility existed for their impact on the imperial ruling classes and the empires themselves. Rome's self-perpetuating wars in Spain debased internal standards generally; only the refusal to make material concessions under unfavorable battlefield conditions contained the scope of elite intrigues related to the war. And the metropole's reputation suffered from the tendency to play off clients against one another, as during the Jugurthan war, and to conduct or conclude peace negotiations with less than thorough integrity, as, for instance, in the Spanish wars. Britain's imperial structure was strained by efforts to either mobilize or retain the support of self-governing colonies for individual imperial wars. The causes of some of the military activities were regarded as not sufficiently just, as in the Sudan; and the grievances behind others were not judged to be sufficiently serious or the challenges sufficiently threatening, as in the case of the South African war. Official Australians may have agreed to view participation in the Sudanese war as a case of "offensive defense" of their own country; but important sections of public opinion in Australia regarded the Sudanese no less as fighters for liberty. Such differing appreciations were even more common inside Britain. Setbacks in both the Crimean and the South African wars encouraged internally divisive attacks on the imperial establishment; and events such as the Indian Mutiny caused the elites themselves to become discouraged with imperial tasks, in favor of some unspecified alternative arrangement among the great powers. But it was the Boer War that provided the sharpest focus for the previously developing critique of empire. In the view of the emerging radical counterelites, the empire hampered social reform and political democracy at home; and it also impeded an effective maintenance of either the balance of power or the British moral leadership at large. Overt attacks were directed more systematically at public expenditures for the army and the navy than at the empire itself; yet it was a markedly anti-imperial bias that inspired both the economic interpretation of the Boer War in particular and the advocacy of "peace, retrenchments, and reform" as opposed to "war, waste, and reaction" in general. High-level criticism was unable to undercut immediately the then climaxing mass support for the empire;

but the discredit cast on the political system did bear fruit soon enough at its center, even more than in the colonial field.[1]

II

Three problems: the two-wing structural cleavage within the empires; the wavering distribution of emphasis on the center and the peripheries in organization and strategy; and the centrally taxing peripheral conflicts, were the most conspicious sources of near-insuperable challenges. In the Roman empire, the overall trend toward centralized authority in the imperial administration atrophied spontaneous plural forces without preventing the polarization of divergently evolving western and eastern wings, under war-induced stresses. In the British empire, the accelerating tendency to decentralization inhibited an effectual central coordination, especially in peacetime. Beneath the basic difference lay significant similarities. Neither empire evolved the kind of working internal balance between coordination and autonomy that would keep augmenting material capabilities steadily enough to match external forces. Ascendancy had removed the counterweight of fear represented by Carthage for Rome and by France for England; and the subtly dissolving effect of safety surfaced when the period of decline produced no equivalent counterpoise to depression. A diminution of elite self-confidence communicated itself to the populace as lessened trust in the elite and, consequently, lessened responsiveness to government. It also created an opening for a terminal assault on the empire as fact and idea by internal counterelites and extraneous enemies alike. An empire nears its end when the elites have perceived it as unmanageable, unnecessary, or both, while the counterelites simultaneously have discovered that destruction is practically feasible.

The moral crisis of empire will open when the political class has reacted to apparently unmanageable peacetime and wartime problems by withdrawing into private, self-indulgent irresponsibility. A declining empire can be simultaneously beset by material deficiencies overall and by concentrations of private wealth. A resulting, ostensibly decadent or hedonistic, elite attitude will then reflect the waning of worthwhile purpose when possibilities have disappeared to exercise power efficaciously. As a subjective response to the vicissitudes of existence, rejection of petty striving for mediocre ends will then not only succeed to previously abundant readiness for selfless or (in the military context) reckless service, it

---

1. See, in particular, A. E. Astin, *Scipio Aemilianus* (Oxford: Clarendon Press, 1967), on the Spanish wars. On the Crimean War, Olive Anderson, *A Liberal State at War* (London: Macmillan, 1967). Radical critique of empire in Britain is covered by Bernard Porter, *Critics of Empire* (New York: St. Martin's Press, 1968) and by A. P. Thornton, *The Imperial Idea and Its Enemies* (New York: Wiley, 1965).

will be also qualitatively on a par with the more inspiring attitude. But the abandonment will play nonetheless potently into the hands of two sets of counterelites. One, internal, set is oriented negatively toward the state as such or the empire, as a matter of fundamental psychological and philosophical bias. Its members will seize upon material crises to relax or do away with the secular disciplines implicit in the exercise of power, to which they can meaningfully relate only as objects or opponents. The creed of the domestic enemies of empire is essentially abstract; it will for that reason assist no less powerfully the very concrete objectives of the second set of counterelites from outside the empire's political system, who seek its downfall in order to supplant it with power or empire of their own.

The intramural confrontation is between flagging, self-consciously aristocratic, and ascending, inherently proletarian mentalities. The confrontation will commonly entail mostly unwitting collusion between differently motivated internal and external enemies of empire. And confrontation and either collusion or mere coincidence will join to bring to a head, in conditions of distress, the intermingling of material and moral components in the decay or deterioration of imperial polities.

Internal decay is not coterminous with either decline from supremacy or final dissolution; empires fluctuate typically between high and low points before passing away, and elements of decay exist within viable imperial structures. Moreover, corruption can overcome material limitations more efficaciously than will moral dejection or political ineptitude; and private opulence, often identified with decline, can be employed as readily to subserve political ambition as to cushion political prostration. Roman elites were more corrupt in the late Republic and early Empire than in the late Empire, and the surviving Eastern empire was in many respects as decayed as the Western. Nor was either Pompey or Caesar inferior in riches to the functionless senatorial landowners of a later era. Similarly, the British domestic and imperial systems were more corrupt in the eighteenth century than in the subsequent era, and were apparently more decayed before both world wars than during either of them or immediately after the second. Also, the landed aristocrats were both relatively richer and substantially more devoted to public business in the eighteenth or nineteenth centuries than in the twentieth.

It is equally true, however, that elements of decay can be more than the momentary symptoms of social ferment or malaise. Over the longer term, they can be sufficiently critical as preliminaries to be among the prime causes of overall decline or final dissolution of empire, having helped to erode the material bases of the original strength and early expansion; undermine attempts at compensatory replacements or corrective adaptations; and enhance the efficacy of emergent adverse factors.

But even then, as contrasted with preliminaries and primary causes, the final precipitant on the plane of events will often, and even typically, be a more or less dramatic invasion of the empire by forces extraneous to its territorial or systemic boundaries. Consequently, eventful and prestigious as it well may be, the history of empires will merely fill a hiatus between two cardinal events: the core-community's successful resistance to invasion, which initiated expansion, and the empire's incapacity to resist invasion or encroachments at its peripheries, which sets off or climaxes the contrary chain reaction.

In the critical fourth and fifth centuries A.D., symptoms of decay were more pronounced in the Western than in the Eastern wing of the Roman empire. The symptoms included demise of civic spirit at large, inadequately compensated for by an expanding bureaucracy; decline in the sense of responsibility and in the readiness to take risks on the part of elites; and the juxtaposition of concentrated private wealth with the exiguity of a fiscally ever more exacting state in conditions of overall material insufficiency. Beginning under the Republic and culminating in late Empire, revulsion from military service grew with spells of prosperity and with the growth of casualties in civil and frontier wars. Forcefully conscripted armed forces became less disciplined and mobile, and it was more difficult to divert a sufficient quota of manpower from internal policing to frontline service against barbarian assaults. A formally military "civil" service saw its internal standards of performance decline as it grew in size and scope of functions. A parallel growth in personal danger and expense attaching to imperial public service and local self-government accelerated the elites' withdrawal to the countryside. Military leaders of non-Roman origins came to fill the vacuum of leadership at the center by becoming effective or shadow emperors, and imperial administrators did the same in the provincial cities.

Just as the civilian elites avoided the personal dangers of public service, moreover, so they eschewed also the risks of industry and trade. The traditional neglect of economics by Romans continued and spread even as it had ceased to be incidental to pursuing a prominent role in politics. Nor was this all. A nonproductive economy and a decrease in the supply of gold meant increasing the taxation of a diminishing population in order to pay for the armed defense of an again endangered empire. The conflict between a rationalized system of budgeting and tax collecting on one side and a materially deteriorating base on the other was at first relieved by an extensive nonapplication and evasion of the multiplying regulations. But, aided by chronic inflation and consequent reversion to a barter economy, the growing activism of the late imperial administration contributed nonetheless to the progressive constriction of the key unit susceptible of economic self-sufficiency, from the Mediterranean to a manorial one. The parasitic city of Rome yielded in the process to the rural commune the position of the empire's dominant unit of social organization; its moral decay was partially redeemed by its incurring also material and political decline.

Actual decline got under way when the decay had helped derange the constitutive elements of imperial greatness. The political system deteriorated at different levels. It was fractured at the top when the classic unity of civilian-political prominence and military command under the Republic was replaced by competition between increasingly powerful and heterogeneous military elites and the increasingly functionless senatorial elites. While the equestrian order was moving over into the bureaucracy, the senate sank gradually to the level of the praetorian guards, as merely one of the several political pressure groups and mediums for socioethnic assimilation. Flexibility in policy degenerated into discontinuity with the increasingly rapid turnover in the emperorship, and the office itself was militarized in a setting defined by ostensibly intractable security problems. As a deliberating influence, the simultaneous growth of social and class conflict was second only to the spread of civic apathy in the wake of an indiscriminate diffusion of Roman citizenship that had reduced its value as the very foundation of the imperial order. No less compromised were the professional legions, the order's centerpiece between the emperor at the summit and citizenship at the base. They were inflated in size and bereft of both cohesion and strategic initiative. The socially damaging cost of either static or in-depth elastic defense was not requited by guaranteeing an ultimately effective protection. One-time strategic advantages were passsing or were being inverted into their opposites. One such asset had been the unity of the Mediterranean basin; another, a makeshift balance of power among the Roman, the Parthian (Persian), and the Kushan (Indian) empires, entailing only intermittent frictions while resting on either political détente or physical distance; and still another, the contrast between the empire's superior military or diplomatic efficacy and divisions among the less adept assailants, which shielded the imperial frontier from intrusions by the Germans (from behind the Rhine-Danube line), the Arabs (from across the southern desert frontier), and the Scots (from beyond the Hadrian wall in the north).

Just as decay helped erode the sustaining bases, so did it finally abort successive adaptations to decline via reorganizations of the empire and its key military and fiscal operations. Adjustments prolonged the life of the empire beyond the major crisis in the third century, but they also caused civilian-military contentions and social conflicts, as well as the ultimately fatal organizational division of the empire. In the end, however, it was the emergence of new ideal and material factors that accelerated decline and precipitated the "fall" of the Western empire. In the absence of disruptive major nationalisms, apathy of the masses and alienation of the elites fostered sentimental or symbolic identification with the barbarians, to be followed by outright defection to them, in a way complementing the earlier increase of anti-empire attitudes on the part of counterelites. The originally non-Roman military men and allies manifested resentment of the empire's surviving classic forms as they conquered the residual empire from outside its traditional political system rather than being co-opted into it. Likewise corrosive, if with less immediate potency, were the long-submerged and henceforth reemerging local subcultures and the intermittently persecuted religions. Without being a sole or even principal cause, Christianity in particular could not but contribute to the empire's decline and dissolution. Its values were contrary to the Roman ideal of *virtus* and to the ethos of devotion to the secular state; instituting it as the dominant church, in charge of spiritual welfare services, increased the material burdens on an already overstrained public domain. Moreover, the Church's mere existence as a parallel and potentially substitute framework of social organization may have weakened the deterrent effect which would have inhered otherwise in the mere prospect of the empire's disappearance. On the material and military side, finally, more even than Sassanid Persia, the Huns came to exert a massive pressure from behind the Germanic tribes, whose final push into the Western empire was aided by their also undoing Rome's long-lasting technological weapons superiority.

The British core-polity incurred its share of decay before outlasting the empire, unlike classic Rome. And the decline of the empire itself was likewise due to derangements in its bases, structure, and setting, before culminating in dissolution. The rather late-coming and short-lived enthusiasm of the British masses for the empire faded when incipient redistribution of power, income, and welfare at home had begun to evolve an alternative to developing the vaster but hard-to-mobilize imperial resources. Among the elites, mass apathy was matched by aversion to taking risks—economic on the part of the mercantile middle class, political on the part of the traditional ruling class. The latter was drained emotionally by the political crises preceding World War I, decimated physically during the war, and finally discouraged or diverted to the pursuit of utopias in the conflict's aftermath. With the drift into terroristic politics, begun in Ireland, elite attitudes toward the pseudo-aristocratic facist regimes of Italy and Germany (and Japan) became sufficiently ambivalent to compound the desire to avoid risks with the incapacity to decide between counterpoising the "dynamic" powers by traditional methods in Europe and Asia and appeasing them within a redefined Euro-global power field. Indecision as to the basic diplomatic strategy entailed hesitancies (in the 1930s) about economic policies: whether to stimulate the flagging economy through military rearmament or continue the pursuit of longer-term changes in economic structures within a both politically and economically defused global setting. As previously in Rome, the connotations of decadence seemed to fit growing numbers of both upper- and middle-class social elites as they withdrew into private pursuits within either suburban or country surroundings, and as they offset a growing fiscal burden with a declining birth-rate amidst an interwar depression pursuant upon a general agricultural decline in the late nineteenth century. Only the self-contained colonial bureaucracy seemed to enhance its sense of mission beyond maintaining order to promoting socioeconomic development in the colonies from a thin resource base.

From the mid-nineteenth century climax on, a for long nearly invisible erosion affected all of the three props of the British empire: not legions, but sea power; not senatorial, but industrial paramountcy; and not the freely distributed privilege of citizenship, but goods and services freely traded in privileged conditions. With the rise of potentially hostile and uncertainly neutral or associated navies of other nations, the two-power-plus standard had to be jettisoned. And as British naval capability descended from universal supremacy to only localized superiority, naval proliferation made it more than ever difficult to tie together the scattered parts and shield the exposed frontiers of empire, at a time when safe and secure access to overseas trade and to colonial raw materials in peace and in war was sought by more industrialized powers more ardently than ever before. The sharing of naval responsibilities before, and the updating of export industries after, World War I improved somewhat Britain's adverse balances between resources and needs and between the empire and its great-power rivals. But even the partial success was only temporary once the Great Depression set about dislocating trade and exasperating competitors who continued to view empire as still the best available token of virile strength and world power.

The 1930s saw some of the home-grown social consciousness and economic engineering being extended to the empire, but not in time to offset rather than exacerbate the either new or newly accelerating adverse developments. Political nationalisms began to occupy in the dependencies the place held in the Roman empire by religio-ideological creeds and schisms, with indigenous elites being intermittently persecuted and indigenous masses remaining passively tolerant of an empire apparently indefeasible at any time before it faltered in World War II. Imperfect assimilation and social acceptance of native by imperial elites had meanwhile fostered resentments that made conquest from within or without the empire's political system appear once again preferable to co-optation. And the verdict went almost simultaneously against the empire inside Britain as well, in the debate over its quintessential quality, as either a bloated extremity weighting down the national body politic or its driving heart; a diversion from domestic social reform or a reprieve from the "sordid controversies and the sometimes depressing gloom of insular existence."[2] Beset from without and within, the empire could hardly belie forever the assertion that "empires, and especially great empires, when they crumble at all, are apt to crumble exceedingly small."[3]

The tendency, sustained by changing ideas, was aided on the material side by the rising political and economic costs of maintaining a colonial empire that had ceased to be fiscally self-sustaining and either qualified or clamored for technical and economic assistance. Moreover, successive technological revolutions generated a new type of not only mass-producing industrial competitors but also mass-mobilizing politico-military rivals. The British empire would have had to meet especially the latter's challenge in a radically changed environment, even as new weapons and modes of projecting power downgraded sea power in favor of air power and elevated the capacity to organize resources and concentrate assault above the capacity to improvise response. Amidst so many adverse circumstances, final abdication followed naturally an ultimate affirmation in World War II, also because of the simultaneous appearance of an alternative, ostensibly anti-imperialist and internationalist order. In dividing up and revising an empire's commingled ideal and physical constituents, the concept of the United Nations and the power of the United States were expected to replace an outgoing British empire worldwide yet more immediately and efficaciously than the Church of Rome and its secular supports had filled the void left behind by the defunct Roman empire in the West.

III

An intermittent and cumulative decay went hand in hand with a declining capacity to manage or reconstruct the empire and to either copy or convert its enemies. Both empires were critically weakened by partially deflected pressures converging upon a too-long imperial frontier. They finally succumbed to forces which, weaker than those previously withstood, received a decisive impetus from a setting that was intrinsically antagonistic to their continuance. Decay and decline fostered together dissolution by either producing or reflecting a redistribution of power amounting to the reemergence or restructuring of a multistate system.

Rome "fell" finally to by then wholly barbarian mercenaries. The collective superiority of the migrating peoples was due to better coordination, arms, and motivation rather than to greater numbers. They subdued in the second half of the fifth century a Western wing of empire

2. The characterizations and quotations are from Lords Curzon and Rosebery, respectively, as cited in George Bennett, *The Concept of Empire* (London: A. and C. Black Ltd., 1962), p. 356.

3. Ibid., p. 284.

that had been weakened by exposure to successive onslaughts from the third century on, including the exhausting resistance to revitalized (Sassanid) Persia in the East, and gave way before forces deflected westward from the more resistant Eastern wing blessed, among other things, with a shorter and more defensible frontier. Circumvention completed the work of deflection in the end, when the Vandals isolated the city of Rome from a vital grain supply by seizing what had once been the possessions of Carthage. Britain's hold on empire had been comparably weakened by two world wars fought stubbornly with waning strength against increasingly powerful adversaries, only to be finally broken by infinitely weaker anti-imperialists of both colonial and domestic vintage. With the white dominions virtually sovereign, the accelerating process of dissolving the dependent empire began with independence for India and continued with the peeling off of India's protective colonial layers in ever-widening circles. The real beginning of the end was not so much in 1947 as in 1942, however, when India had been nearly lost to the invading Japanese, deflected southward from China by American prewar diplomatic strategies among other things. When, in complementarity with German military advances, the Japanese came close to circumventing the British moat by cutting the imperial life lines in the Middle East, the near-disaster in the East compounded the strain that Britain had imposed on herself and her empire in the West by adding to the already long imperial a national defense line on the Rhine, in exchange for allied relief on the maritime frontier.

Decline in relative power was not relieved for either empire by lastingly favorable dynamics in the environing field of forces. Neither the Germans and the Persians in the third century nor, later on, the Germanic peoples among themselves, competed sufficiently to reduce the residual pressure left for use against the Roman empire; the particular cleavages that did exist (between the Visigoths and the Vandals) actually encouraged the massive thrust of Attila's Huns behind the final waves breaking over the Western regions. The managers of the faltering empire sought to make up for insufficient conflict among the barbarians by playing off Romanized mercenaries or allies against non-Romanized tribes and the latter among themselves; the strategy and the similarly motivated alliances with the successor "states" of the Visigoths, Burgundians, Franks, Alamanni, and the like, against the Hunnish "world tyrant," merely eased the temporary substitution of the *pax Gothica* for the *pax Romana*.

The British sought somewhat similarly to blunt the convergence of the newly empire-conscious old and new great powers against a *pax Britannica*, which had been sustained previously by foreign acquiescence as much as by British strength. The more or less costly naval accommodations with the United States and Japan, and ententes with France and

Russia, implemented before World War I the intention of perpetuating British naval superiority vis-à-vis Germany (by making the continental-European parties equally immune to connection with and coercion by Germany); they enabled Britain at first to participate in allied victory also on land. But, in World War II, Britain came finally to depend for survival on allies of whom the continental one promptly substituted Soviet Russian for the Nazi German challenge and the maritime one an American order for the British peace. Classics-bred British statesmen were at all times fascinated by the land-oriented Roman empire, only to become increasingly sensitive to the omens implicit in the decline of the maritime-mercantile empire of Venice. Fittingly, after concentrating on continent-based threats from France, Russia, and Germany, the British hold on empire was broken in and after World War II by qualitatively different but effectively converging pressures from essentially insular sea powers. If the United States was the self-consciously preordained successor on the grounds of fundamental affinities and the higher logic of history, Japan was unwittingly conforming to a law of geopolitical configuration affecting the life cycles of offshore islands. And if Japan's forceful pursuit of imperial extension onto the adjoining Asian land mass was of a kind that an earlier England had vainly pursued in France and the lagoon-based Venetians wrought with greater provisional success on the Italian *terra ferma* (as a prelude for both to a more modest mainland role as would-be balancer on the strength of economic expansion overseas), the very act of thwarting the Axis powers in an increasingly unequal alliance with the British set off quasi-insular America on a like career in Eurasia.

The transformation of allies from subcontractors or surrogates into candidates for succession was accompanied in the case of both empires by their own transformation into state systems. The Western wing of the Roman empire, already dislocated into semiautonomous domains of senatorial potentates, was superseded by competitive congeries of Germanic kingdoms, initially managed (from Ravenna, by an Ostrogoth king) with the aid of dynastic marriages. The structure and the strategy presaged the eventual European dynastic balance-of-power system, after overcoming reemphasis on the competing idea of a universal polity by Frankish and German patrons of the Roman Church. The collapse of empire-type monopoly had cleared the way for the shift of power from the Mediterranean world northward. It also revived, in due course, for both the secular and the ecclesiastical successors to the Latin empire, the issue of parity and the tension between parity and preeminence, previously disposed of in the Hellenistic system by the conquering power of Rome.[4]

The dissolution of the British empire, too, cleared the decks for the

4. See chap. 1, pp. 10–22. Also George Liska, *Quest for Equilibrium* (Baltimore: The Johns Hopkins University Press, 1977), chap. II.

slow and turbulent growth of a multiple-state pattern within the empire's one-time colonial orbit. But a no less important long-range effect lay elsewhere. So long as the empire was ascendant, it was a provocation agitating the European balance-of-power system, while helping Britain to act intermittently as a barrier against attempts to overthrow either the system itself or the British conception of it. The empire's decline removed an obstacle to the globalization of the balance of power by interaction between the American and Soviet world powers although, in contrast with the dichotomy of post-Roman secular vs. spiritual powers, the perennial issues of parity and preeminence continued, in the post-British context, to bear upon the relationship of principally sea- to principally land-based power.

The Roman empire in decline had been the delayed victim of Rome's prior success in superseding the inchoate equilibrium system in the Mediterranean, to be only belatedly and inadequately replaced by the interplay of the two halves of empire with one another and with reemerging strong outside forces. British expansion and empire were long the beneficiaries of the crystallizing European balance of power, and the resources of accomplished empire helped Britain neutralize for a time the most prominent members of a fully developed balance-of-power system. In being differently poised between equilibrium and empire, both the Roman and the British core-powers passed from masterfully manipulating unevenly firm allies and variously formal alliances for maximum effect with minimum effort, to being first dominated and eventually supplanted by their allies: Rome by the "federates" and Britain by a domineering confederate, completing the process begun by increasingly ally-like dominions. Previously, the Romans had rejected parity on land with respect to Carthage, Macedon, and Syria, just as the British were to spurn it on sea with regard to France and Germany. The result left Rome without either significant allies or stimulating adversaries, and Britain with only a weakened and dispirited major ally (France) in Europe.

Whereas the fall of the Roman empire had spawned the rudiments of what was to become the European state system, the British empire and the Europe-centered international system collapsed simultaneously in their jointly attained maturities. The synchronized collapse was either encompassed or at least accelerated by the British organizing their national policies around the one-power pole and their colonial-imperial doctrines around the multistate norm, while rejecting equality or parity among the few. Thus, Britain herself became the preeminent power in the Europe-centered politico-military balance and leader in the liberal-economic order; her statecraft was strenuously focused on identifying and then resisting the continental European aspirant to like monopoly at any one time; and she first forwarded thereby and later also favored succession by the United States alone. A concurrent British imperial doctrine looked to multistate pluralism to replace empire in due course, by way of a gradual progression to colonial self-government under British auspices. While the long-range doctrinal goal was but a species of moral standard for the shorter term, it was overtaken by movements for all-out independence when the British managers of empire, having omitted to meaningfully co-opt notably the non-white educated elites into the empire in the period of ascendancy, lost both the will and the capacity to constrain the rate of emancipation in the later period of weakness.

In paving the way for chaotic pluralism of many new states, without significantly regulating the rise of the first one, the British precluded in the last analysis a concert of several older great powers in a reciprocal balance that would include a dependent empire for each and prolong independent national existence and overseas sway for them all. As a consequence, a joint extinction of an imperial order and a state system concluded the cycle of events, with its center in Romanized Europe, that had begun with the First Punic War and ended with the Second German War. The end of one cycle only set the stage for the next, however, involving the contest for succession to either the Roman-type imperium or the British-type role in equilibrium between unevenly Europeanized wing powers, converging from the outer margins of the depleted world center.

Part Two

AMERICA AND EMPIRE

INTRODUCTION. *The Political*
Economy of Expansion

On the basis of the history of the Roman and British empires, an attempt has been made to distinguish particular processes, kinds of stimuli, and phases, ignoring peculiarities of specific economic systems or political cultures. Such singular characteristics will affect the institutional and other manifestations of imperial expansion, but they do not shape underlying motives and visible patterns unless they create a radically novel environment of moral dispositions, psychological expectations, and, consequently, political responses to situational predicaments. The following discussion of the American experience with expansion and empire may be usefully prefaced with a brief summary of earlier findings, employing the economic factor as an entering wedge without treating it as the dominant weight throughout.

The conquest of a materially and psychopolitically viable habitat occurs typically for coequal and indistinguishable, or fused, objectives of elementary security and sustenance. Thereafter, the economic factor becomes gradually incidental to the concern with strategic security at the center of the relevant system or space. Even aggressively pursued economic goods become a means to political power at home or abroad, and the product or consequence of superior military power and skill. In both the Roman and the British instances of the correspondingly denoted first stage, of formative war imperialism, an authoritative ruling class acted as a trustee for the body politic and exercised a largely unfettered command and control over community resources.

In the second phase, identifiable as one of informal free-trade or free-enterprise imperialism, the strategic and economic factors are largely separate even while being variably interdependent. The strategic factors are more than ever autonomous in the considerations of governmental policy-makers responsible for the security and coherence of the established order in a technologically or otherwise changing environment. Economic concerns affect state policies and imperial expansion principally by way of evolving interclass transactions within an internal political system that has become more pluralistic and competitive. A thus mediated economic motive remains largely incidental, but now to the pursuit of internal political stability of the imperial body politic. The shift from external security to domestic stability as the key concern occurs while the imperial frontier continues to be locally endangered even though the imperial polity is at its most secure in the central balance of power. Continuing expansion is therefore only intermittently and marginally impelled for strategic reasons and is alternately undesired by and imposed on policy-makers for reasons of political economy in the broadest sense of the term.

The final phase of expansion is associated with formalized protective imperialism. The economic factor emerges—or, looking back to the conquest of the initial viable habitat, reemerges—as a direct and coequal or even primary stimulus to expansion. As such, it is subsidiary when viewed in relation to the original stimuli which actuated early large-scale expansion for security and sustenance; but it has ceased being secondary to the previously ascending strategic and political determinants with which it is integrally re-fused. As a matter of fact, it is the concern with strategic factors that tends to become ancillary to the continued enjoyment of critical economic goods, endangered by growing incoherence within the empire and its subsequent decline relative to outside forces. Increasingly precarious internal transactions by a weakening and deteriorating ruling class shift from voluntary efforts to compensate rising social groups for their self-restraint in the political domain to enforced attempts to appease ever more assertive challengers. The more or less original empire-founding ruling class undergoes final trauma in economic corruption or social dilution and political division or dispossession, as part of a drift toward civil strife, demagogy, or autocracy. Strategic insecurity will simultaneously tend to exceed local threats to the imperial frontier. While internal and external "barbarians" besiege, or prepare to besiege, the empire as it was originally constituted, along with major "civilized" powers, the political elites multiply attempts to relate survival of the empire to material payoffs that are meaningful for the popular mass. They may, but do not necessarily, reinfuse the empire with one more period of dynamism before it subsides into a terminal phase within protective economic or military barriers and either effectively centralizing or only nominally unifying institutions.

The overall process of expansion is informed by a range of pervasive tendencies. One of them is progressive differentiation and deterioration in the sociopolitical class structure internally. Another is the secular shift among the stimuli to expansion from primitive predatory drive for a viable habitat or survivable core-empire toward preclusive or preemptive, essentially defensive or protective, concerns. Changes in emphasis in central (or authoritative) policy-making do not rule out the conditioning of official policies by private predation throughout. But the altered emphasis tends to predominate as the problem of preserving and consolidating the enlarged possession dwarfs any rational or responsible desire for further extension in circumstances when no alternative politico-economic frameworks of organization appear capable of superseding the empire without fatal cost to the imperial core-community. By contrast with the secular trend toward protection, its objects are subject to cyclical changes. Protective concerns gravitate from central to peripheral security and back to central, and from physical security to the safety and survival of the supporting political and economic systems and back again to physical security of the empire's territorial core.

The cycles are related to yet another trend concerning the projective mechanism. Somewhere at the climactic midpoint of an empire's evolution, the external environment will be relatively pressure-free and permissive. A species of institutional projection will then exteriorize internally self-protective political transactions of the ruling class in the form of outside expansion. A different psychological form of projection will typically climax at a later stage, in a relatively constraining and threatening external environment. At that point, a trauma-prone ruling class will impute to outside actors the earlier tendencies of the henceforth declining empire. It will attribute to ascendant outsiders expansive designs on the imperial assets and treat their ambition as illegitimate in presumably changed overall conditions. The Roman senate had done some projecting onto defeated Carthage, Macedon, and other suspected lesser-power challengers at an early stage of expansion; the mechanism played a more critical and ambiguous role later, however, when the autocratic Roman empire was being assaulted, saved, and taken over by barbarian claimants to succession. Imputations of both expansionism and illegitimacy were still more marked in the British case, Imperial Germany following upon France overseas as the most conspicuous target. Where such a projection exceeds the norm, it exceeds also the early predatory drive for expansion and the later preclusion of counterexpansion in adding to the conflict over empire as a mundane fact the passions aroused by empire as an idea suspended between supreme good and absolute evil.

VI

AMERICAN EXPANSION.

International Determinants

Predatory drive and preclusive defense succeed one another as original stimuli to expansion, and physical security and material sustenance are variously conjoined at different stages as stakes encompassed in the goal of community survival. Of critical early significance is, for most or all preimperial communities, the incidence and the intensity of a shaping threat to existence, to be overcome defensively and transcended expansively. Yet if, in the American case, the initial threats to the survival of the colonists were less than a supreme test, the withstanding and overcoming of these threats would not have been either sufficient or necessary to supply the critical extraneous impetus for the subsequent expansionist drive. Actual impetus differs from imputation just as an authentic reason for expansion does from its rationalization. Was not, in fact, any defensively unleashed driving energy only supplementary at best to the pull of a virtually empty space on the acquisitive instinct? And was that instinct not fortified by the sense of an absolute right to fill the void—a right that, being conferred providentially, did not have to be established preclusively? From returning inconclusive answers to such questions, moreover, it would be only one step (if possibly the wrong one) to making an assumption: if preclusion of external threats, opposition, or counterexpansion had been fallaciously affirmed as the principal cause and sufficient warrant for expansion at its beginning, preclusion was by the same token even less genuinely operative in revitalizing a flagging (or saturated) predatory drive at a later stage and in conditions of greater power.

Actual conditions varied for different stages of American expansion, from continental sway to regional core-empire and beyond to world empire; but both fact and fiction about them go back somehow to the critical formative experience.

I

The American record is replete with challenges from man and, even more, from nature; for the expanding American body politic and, even more, its individual members and sectional components. But was there at the beginning, or indeed ever, a single and concentrated extraneous threat to physical or political survival in the form of invasion or encirclement which, repulsed, would implement the wrestler metaphor and carry the community forward as it was recovering its equilibrium?

The initial threat for the American colonies, starting with New England, was one of overland encirclement by the French, in an arc stretching eventually from Louisbourg to Louisiana. It first coincided with and, after subsiding, was succeeded by intensified British efforts to either wholly dam the territorial expansion of the colonists or at least divert it from the Mississippi River, and to contain the settlers within bounds consistent with streamlined imperial, mercantilist and defense, systems. British containment efforts culminated in outright invasions on land and in actual or attempted naval encirclements, first during the War of American Independence and later during its attenuated replay in the War of 1812. For a time after independence, moreover, Spain's territorial encroachments from the south and Britain's from the north kept the young Republic in a pincer-like squeeze encompassing nearly half of its territory. Throughout, the European powers drew on the native tribes for crucial reinforcements. During the critical war for independence, more over, parallel to protracted guerrilla action by the Indians was a similar type of warfare waged by pro-British American loyalists. It was they who may have constituted for the insurgents the most serious or most intensely felt of the threats to survival.

The succession of threats was real enough to serve as a formal warrant for expansive claim or action. But, on the face of it, the individual threats were not serious enough to add the decisive stimulus to the pre-existing imperial mystique of the colonists. Nor were the threats capable of fusing into transparochial solidarity the factional politics within and among the colonies. The French threat was backed by too few people locally and enjoyed too little support from the metropole. The all-important Indian allies were divided and poorly organized and motivated; they had been too dependent on the French before the Seven Years' War and were thereafter helpless to constitute a mortal threat or even a strategically menacing force. Moreover, once the Americans had come into more direct and sustained collision with the French beyond the Appalachian Mountains (as part of the warfare in the 1740s), the henceforth more directly involved British offset the French pressure in the North. Conversely, the decisive French financial and military engagement on the side of the colonists in the War of Independence diluted fatally that particular threat to survival, while the British effort itself was being undermined by both European and domestic complications. Establishing a pattern for decolonizing "new nations," French more than American military exertions, and Britain's diplomatic calculations more than her coercion by either, crowned with political triumph the military deficiencies and near-disintegration of the fighters for independence. The postwar Anglo-Spanish-Indian encirclement was removed by (Jay and Pinckney) treaties negotiated from a position that offset economic weakness by tactical politico-diplomatic strength. The overseas powers assigned a clear priority to intra-European conflicts (in the wars of Napoleon) when entering into peaceable adjustments as much as when waging wars with the Americans (the British, in 1812). That priority mattered more than could any effective primacy the Americans might be able to assert in and over their rising coastal empire and beyond as a matter of national will forged in a sacred union against overwhelming odds.

As matters turned out, a mortal threat and corresponding testing of viability was delayed until the onset of the Civil War, and then was not external. The two world wars, and the greater ordeals of the subsequent peripheral imperial wars (in Korea and in Indochina) came too late to a mass society shielded by great collective power from a complex environment to wholly make up for the earlier absence of trials that make nations out of populations and prepare nations for empire. The American expansion westward does not, therefore, elicit the image of the wrestler propelled forward into the void created by the felling of the adversary. It suggests, instead, the metaphor of an advancing current receiving sufficient momentum from its tributaries to effortlessly flatten minor natural obstacles. In the American expansion, the incoming waves of immigrant populations were the tributaries; and the presumed (European) defenders against the expansionist current were most of the time busy removing the artificial barriers from before the momentum as part of pursuing their competitive and individually disabling immediate self-interests.

Objectively weak, the early threats engendered nonetheless a strong subjective impression in the first Americans when projected against scarce available resources. The paucity of resources tended to enhance the felt impact of threats to a point where the threats would suffice to represent plausible grounds for an expansion offering, in addition, and initial reinsurance against the consequences of internal disunities. Economic and financial weakness, notably relative to Great Britain, made the original geographic space and the location of the newly independent Republic into its basic resource. The space had been from the outset divided among reciprocally isolated, self-contained and competitive, settlements; and as the resulting coastal nuclei, or hubs, fanned out inland, they did so under the impetus of paper claims to additional territory that exceeded even the substantial effective energies fueled by vulnerability, chiefly from the sea, and sustained by the remedy against that vulnerability available in a succession of ever-receding natural barriers. The first-line barrier was constituted by mountain ranges and rivers (except initially in the South); it promised to relieve or wholly prevent a squeeze by hostile forces from land. However, as insecurity was greater from the sea, and overland expansion with an anti-British bias enhanced further the seaborne threats, an increasingly important duality was fostered between the continental (farming) and the maritime (mercantile) factors and interests. The cleavage inhibited a concerted defensive effort had it been necessary; but it promoted uncoordinated offensive responses to the pull of the open continent, the push of the coastal urban-mercantile civilization, and the pressure of outside efforts at mercantilistic control or competition.

Threats were not sufficient to unite in a hierarchically stratified sociopolitical equilbrium for concerted resistance and coordinated expansion, least of all if others disposed of the threats as it were vicariously. But the dangers were sufficient to crystallize diffuse anxieties into a psychic basis for aggression and to consolidate a communal ethos favorable to dealing forcibly with the moral dilemmas and practical problems engendered by an expansive approach to scarcity. The greater-than-usual anxieties were rooted in either personal experiences or in the group memory of ordeals suffered before, during, and after arrival in the new habitat; they could not but be perpetuated, directly for the successive pioneer waves and more subtly for sedentary political elites, by the unknown character of the beckoning continent. The early experiences may indeed have been the true American equivalents of the formative ordeals of imperial Rome and England; and the continental vastness may in itself have represented a challenge that made up for the absence of powerful, but clearly identifiable and predictable, political adversaries. Vast emptiness enhanced anxiety by creating mystery. It also deranged the normal givens of existence by creating a more than passing opportunity. And the opportunity blended easily into the temptation to equate survival with near-automatic and unresisted material growth. From that equation it was only a step to viewing any and all man-made constraints, representing scarcity, as a malignant obstruction inviting and warranting forceful or forcible removal.

Anxiety interacted with avidity to enhance ambiguity regarding the relative weights of (physical) security and (material) sustenance in conditioning survival and motivating early expansion. Initial American expansion resulted from a predatory drive and the pull of a vacuum of power, and it was a response to the challenge of an ever-receding natural and political frontier rather than to the threat from an advancing foe. Sustenance was consequently the primary or original aim that could not but exceed security on balance, however much the two would be intertwined and the operational priorities change in specific conditions. Thrusting beyond the Appalachian Mountains into the Ohio country in the mid-eighteenth century (with British assistance) meant abandoning a secure physical barrier for an enlarged sustenance, if at first mainly for land speculators. Similarly, the safety sought in the control of the Mississippi River was mainly one from economic strangulation by Spain or France and from internal dislocation due to a consequent defection by the West. And the pursuit of individual and group security from increasingly martial Indian tribes ever farther west was only incidental to the basically acquisitive motive behind the thrust forward.

Underlying the extensions were dualities significant for the standing of the security concern. A two-level, hierarchical relationship between British empire defense and the subimperialism of the colonials was critical before independence; a more egalitarian two-track relationship operated between both pre- and postindependence American authorities and private interests. The hierarchical relationship involved conflicts over both priorities and objectives; the more egalitarian relationship was characterized by complicity. The conflicts complicated responses to the French-created security problem while it was still real, and might have rendered the problem unmanageable had it been serious. The complicity was sufficient to exaggerate the total or composite threat, without reliably producing the capacity to deal either promptly or efficiently with isolated and minor insecurities.

In the strategic perspective dominant before the late 1750s at the imperial center, both mercantilistic and military criteria favored checks and balances intraregionally within North America and interregionally between North America and Europe. The balancing outlook entailed only moderate imperial expansion in North America. As a result, even as the implementation of the outlook drew heavily on colonial manpower and resource, the security deemed adequate for Britain's imperial possession and frontier in North America spelled chronic insecurity for the colonials. Simultaneously, the conditions of stability for Britain's mercantilist system vis-à-vis the West Indies implied confinement for the Americans. The subsequent reversal of British strategic emphasis away from Europe to overseas, effected by the elder Pitt in the course of the Seven Years' War, meant assuring the security of the American colonies from non-British forces, and doing so moreover by primarily British efforts. In exchange, however, the issue of economic sustenance for the colonists was henceforth to be even more firmly subordinated to the requirements of imperial defense. The new policy made for bounded economic opportunity, and started off that particular limitation on its career as a partial or even integral substitute for physical insecurity in "causing" American expansion, while outright economic crises became expansion's habitual preliminaries or immediate precipitants.

After independence, private pioneers or profiteers and public powers became roughly equal parties in a collusion that replaced the earlier disparities—in fighting involvements and strategic aims of the imperial center and the colonies—in regulating expansion. It became henceforth more than ever the part of the public powers to invoke hypothetical insecurity in order to better convert paper reservations in colonial charters, projecting the coastal nuclei westward toward the Pacific, into paper occupations by international treaties concluding a war or a purchase, pending the constitutional consecration of territorial expansion by statehoods resulting from intersectional deals. Actual insecurities were implicit in the progress toward effective occupation. They were in large part surrendered to the private parties, acting as spearheads of aggression and triggers for officially organized defense, most conspicuously though not only in the Indian wars. A similar division of labor helped implement the motive implicit in the drive for economic sustenance. It was then either the profiteers who staked out claims or the pioneers who actually broke the soil in preparing the ground for officially effected or sanctioned expansion, in the area between the Mississippi and the Rocky Mountains before the 1840s and thereafter mainly, though not only, westward as far as Hawaii.

Differences in the security equations before and after independence were illustrated in a special way by Canada, claimed by Americans from early on as a matter of both national security and imperial vision. A still French Canada was partially but futilely breached by the temporary conquest of Louisbourg (Cape Breton Island) by colonial troops in the warfare of the 1740s, as part of their tactical contribution to imperial strategy. Her eventual conquest by primarily British forces disclosed before long the ultimately self-defeating nature of the Pittite imperial strategy in North America. When Canada had become Britain's residual bridgehead in North America, she came to represent the only genuine insecurity for the newly independent United States. But neither private nor public American efforts were able to encompass her annexation as a matter of either predation or preclusion. Instead, the United States was to·establish security from, and in due course for, British Canada across a safe (and eventually undefended) frontier as part and parcel of global strategic equations involving ambitions by and responses to third powers. Similarly, Canada's safety *for* the French had been previously a token of the larger equation, while the subsequent failure of the Americans to take Canada *from* the British was an early intimation of how limited would be the potency of their preclusive response to genuine threats or opposition in the absence of readily usable overwhelming material superiority or diplomatic leverage.

Protection by the British on the North American continent had been reliable in the last resort; following independence, the only possible real threat from the British in Canada was self-confined. So long as either condition obtained, only an exorbitant view of what constituted security could engender a sense, or justify the pretense, of insecurity that would be sufficient to leaven materially inspired predation with the yeast of morally legitimizing preclusion. Actual insecurity was at all times reduced by the operation of a European balance of power lopsided enough to impede a timely checking response to American expansion by the competing European powers acting individually or in concert. Rome and Britain had been similarly favored, but only at a somewhat later stage of imperial expansion. No concerted, coalition-type response carried into the postindependence period an equivalent of the (Franco-Spanish) Bourbon counterpoise to Britain in North America. Instead, variations in the position and alignment of declining Spain between first revolutionary and then Napoleonic France and Britain engendered major initial gains for the United States (in the Mississippi-Florida sector). And the conflict between France and Britain permitted only intermittent and inconclusive efforts to implement either jointly or simultaneously their shared opposition to unbounded American expansion. When Britain sought to confine the colonists in the imperial framework, the French helped break it up; and when the French tried to confine the expansionism of their ally-protégé in its bid for independence, the British counteracted the attempt by offering the Americans territorial inducements to a virtually separate peace. Nor did the later containing efforts by the two European powers converge sufficiently in the American South, the Caribbean, and the Western Hemisphere at large. Being ill-coordinated, the southern confinement strategy was no more successful than had been the western strategies, when unilaterally and competively pursued by the two European powers.

American diplomacy did not have to divide in order for the executive organs to conquer. And it did not take a real danger of rival conquest for an expansionist response to follow mere psychic discomfort from territorial contiguity with alien powers or forces, potentially contentious rather than actually contending, dangerously weak rather than perilously strong.

From the beginning and for a long time, the makers of American policy would strive to preclude the mere possibility of disputes with neighbors. Overt hostility might be clearly absent as, say, in relations with Napoleon after he had taken Louisiana from Spain; early Americans took refuge in the presumption of an automatic adversary dynamic, which made contact unavoidably result in conflict and justified the equation of self-preservation with self-aggrandizement. When it was patently absurd to impute aggressive or hostile intent to a grossly weakened power, the guardians of American interests postulated the unavoidable replacement of the weak by a stronger power to justify interposing the United States in the chain of succession. So extreme a conception of the nature of security implied the pursuit of the perfect natural frontier; it was superficially vindicated when Louisiana had been transferred to Napoleonic France and worked substantially against the Hispanic powers, Spain and Mexico in particular, first on the mainland and eventually also (in regard to Spain) in the insular realm. The attitude reflected the presumptions governing all international statecraft. It was peculiarly American, however, in the degrees of the intensity with which it was held, the intolerance with which it was applied, and the self-delusion with which it was deemed to be moral rather than merely natural—i.e., not only deriving from the nature of the system of states, but justified by the unique character of the American polity and the human experiment for which it stood.

The ideologically exaggerated sense of right to expand corresponded to the equation of security with total immunity and of sustenance with unlimited growth. It was matched by a likewise exceptional absence of immediate necessity to expand at any particular time, corresponding to the absence of dangerous counterexpansionists compelling instant preemptive action.

One result was the capacity to provisionally suspend or apparently abandon an expansionist move in momentarily unfavorable domestic conditions, or while awaiting a favorable configuration of extraneous conflicts, only to resume expansion and complete the acquisition at a later date. Conspicuously postponed was the outreach for Oregon in the Northwest, Texas in the Southwest, and Hawaii and Cuba overseas—as well as, in due course, for global power itself. The exceptionally big margin for delays and replays before finally rolling back the contrary force or influence translated into the dimension of time the continent's underpopulated vastness in the dimension of space. It also mirrored an international system that was sufficiently permissive locally to tolerate a deviation from the principle holding that favorable opportunities for positive action recur less frequently and reliably among than within nations. So favored, Americans were able to overextend claims (and paper "reservations") rather than capabilities (and material resources), and avoid both rushing and being rushed into prematurely upholding claims or disclaiming ambitions forever. Disclaimers did not have to be forthcoming even in exchange for matching self-denials, e.g., when

Britain's Canning renounced annexations in Latin America prior to the one-sided American enunciation of the Monroe Doctrine, or when both Britain and France imposed upon themselves a self-denying ordinance with respect to Cuba in the 1850s.

The practical capacity for delay and replay made it possible to mix, and thus partially obscure, predation with prudence. The ideological counterpart was to view foreign tenure of possessions or resources earmarked for eventual claim and appropriation as being provisionally in trust for the United States. Since the custodianship was inalienable, it implied the radical incapacity of the momentary possessor to transfer the asset to an alternative claimant; and inalienable custodianship meant further that the United States would actually appropriate a good at the conjunction of effective capacity (to seize and hold) with a hypothetical contingency (of a suspected possibility of, or a simulated belief in, an impending transfer to a non-American successor). The principle was implicit quite early in Jefferson's attitude toward Spain's possessions in America; and it covered conduct that would be wholly unprincipled when judged by other criteria, as with respect to the war with Mexico in the 1840s. Moreover, the theory placed the United States implicitly in an exalted position relative to less privileged parties and provided a warrant for treating them with corresponding condescension, not least when offering to purchase Spanish and Mexican possessions as an alternative or supplement to using force.

Just as the exceptional American capacity to defer or repeat bids for territory or rights made it unnecessary to reciprocate self-denials by others, so the custodianship principle overrode all duty to reciprocity in positive performance. Thus the independent United States would no more reward *de facto* naval protection by Great Britain with a "federative" alliance at an early stage than it would tolerate later on British power and possessions in either the Pacific Northwest or the Western Hemisphere at large in exchange for such protection. Britain's naval supremacy (and, as time went on, the entirety of her ordering imperial involvement) was presumptively America's in function and effect before passing to the United States in fact and exercise. It was as if the preordained end, America's imperial succession to Great Britain, was immanent in the beginnings of America's secession from the British empire; and as if the end shaped accordingly the intervening process of American expansion, while sanctioning its irregularities. These irregularities were again in keeping with, but exceeded the customary degree of, the non-reciprocity which will reflect the relative inferiority and express the situational advantage and moralistic or ideological pretense of weaker and newer states relative to stronger and, for expedient reasons, tolerant older and established powers. The American pretension was only unusually sweeping because it was shaped by the view of the United States as being in turn a trustee for rising forces in the transformation of the world, rather than being merely the beneficiary of one more transfer of imperial primacy from one orthodox power to another.

While the crowning pretension was being put to the test of cruder realities, the ascendancy of predation over authentic preclusion had to run its course and gradually fade in the process. The fading occurred as the American "imperial frontier" receded westward from the original eastern nuclei (or hubs) of expansion, correspondingly decreasing America's advantage over the more assertive of the European powers and Japan and causing even an inordinately strengthened United States to evolve toward preclusion. Predation had exploited either the unevenness in a bilateral relationship of forces with another state or the instability in the net margin of power that could be used against the United States because it survived the reciprocal neutralization or nullification of national capabilities by the balance-of-power mechanism among the Europeans. Preclusion was responding to the possibility that the mechanism might be supplanted by a rival claimant to imperial succession either in specific areas of interest to the United States or in the world at large. Thus, even before the two world wars, and especially the second one, had produced an apparently abrupt qualitative change, there was a gradual shift to preclusion as a plausibly genuine and ultimately compelling determinant of American expansion. The shift unfolded while provisional custodians were being replaced in the position of critical reference points by prospective competitors in a geopolitically enlarged and diversified universe.

II

If the concept of the Manifest Destiny stood primarily for the weakly resisted drive across the continent, the Monroe Doctrine stood for a more even interplay between preclusion and predation. The exclusion of extraneous threats and encroachments was both the reverse side of, and the prerequisite to, the pursuit of positive American interests and influence in the Western Hemisphere generally and in the Caribbean in particular. Materially founded drives were for land and furs and for plantations and plantation slaves on the continent, and for commerce with agricultural and manufacturing products beyond it. And the mere assertions of insecurity pointed to preclusion as coequal with predation as a determinant of expansion, without indicating clearly which of the two original stimuli was dominant in the absence of an authentic threat or clear and present danger among the more or less real and serious specific challenges to security.

The most common danger throughout was to be preempted by others. Preemption would rule out either immediate access or eventual succession to a critical territory; and it would imperil either American physical security, by extending European militarism (or navalism) to the Western Hemisphere, or jeopardize American economic well-being at the hands of an exclusive European mercantilism. Threats of that kind seemed to be implicit in the half-hearted effort of the dying *ancien régime*, and the effort's apparent if brief revival by Napoleon, to replace the New France lost in the North with one based on New Orleans in the South; they could be also read into the suspected British naval designs on or in Florida during the War of 1812. It mattered little that American apprehensions along these lines, and the remedial counteractions, were no more well-founded in actualities than had been earlier fears of suspected Spanish expansionary moves from Florida toward the Carolinas, which had inspired expansion into the Georgian buffer. The suspected European schemes represented individually or collectively less of a real danger for the several colonies, and, after independence, states, than competition among the colonial assemblies over Indian lands in Virginia and the Ohio River area had constituted before independence.

While continental expansion continued in the 1840s, the feared threat to which to react was competitive expansionism by independent Texas toward California (comprising the future New Mexico) and reported British (and French) designs on the San Francisco Bay area—and on Texas itself. Beyond California, the American absorption of Hawaii was ostensibly vindicated by early French pressures (in the 1850s), British proximate acquisitions (Fiji, in 1874), Japanese naval visits (1897), and overland thrusts by the Canadian Pacific Railway. Farther west, the French and the Japanese menace to the Philippines was overshadowed by supposed German ambitions, encompassing also Samoa; and either collusion or competition among the foreign powers in China was sufficiently suspect to prompt the Open Door notes and other paper reservations and diplomatic interventions in behalf of the right of Americans to freely trade and build railways in the Celestial Empire. Finally, extending American possessions or power into the Caribbean and Central America was anticipated from the early nineteenth century on, in opposition to European designs on the continent's "natural appendages" and the "American seas," illustrated by the French in regard to Cuba, the British in Central America, and, in due course, Imperial Germany in Haiti and the Danish West Indies. Germany eventually replaced the British as the principal suspected threat when the Venezuelan crisis in 1894 had written finis to the *pax Britannica* in the area, in favor first of Anglo-American naval and commercial parity and subsequently of sole American police power and dollar diplomacy based on naval and commercial preeminence.

Throughout, putative threats to American interests consisted in either too little order, while indigeneously maintained, or too much of it, if or when it was imposed by a rival of the United States. Disorder, or anarchy, was peculiar to southern or colonial areas such as Florida, Cuba, Mexico, Central America and the Caribbean at large, and, eventually, China; it could be replaced without being removed as a provocation by imitative nationalisms with anti-American bias, such as Mexico's opposing voluntary sale of national territory prior to the war of 1846. The threat of too much non-American order was peculiar to northern actors, be it Canada before and after federation and unification in the mid-nineteenth century or the European powers or Japan. The basic idea, to keep rival claimants out by removing or forestalling disorder as a pretext for their intervention and occupation, was merely made more explicit in the positive reformulation of the Monroe Doctrine. The Roosevelt corollary expressed an increase in American capabilities, mainly naval, since the doctrine's original enunciation; but it also reacted to enhanced outside threats to American control, susceptible of like implementation.

In the preceding period, the threats to the United States were largely self-created, grossly exaggerated to the point of being simulated, or both. The threats were self-created mainly when American claims or aspirations were either premature or already obsolete. Premature claims addressed and risked provoking a preestablished and still stronger rival in the area. One such rival was Britain in the 1830s and 1840s in relation to Oregon, earmarked by anti-slavery northern interests as a counter to southern pressures for annexing Texas. And increasingly obsolete aspirations in relation to Canada, after her mid-century reorganization had been stimulated by local fears of wholesale or piecemeal absorption by the United States, served only to enhance her status as an impediment and competitor on the North American road to India and to the Far Eastern trade generally. A rival, rather than a threat, was self-created when New England merchants blocked the annexation of Texas, only to fear the designs of independent Texas on California. And, most generally, threats and dangers were self-generated as fear (e.g., of British actions) rose as well as fell with greed (in relation to Canada before 1812, and in the 1840s in relation to Texas, California, and Oregon).

Unwitting generation of threats tended to merge with their deliberate fabrication, and genuine security fears became hard to distinguish from simulated alarms. Thus the War of 1812 was ostensibly fought to defend neutral maritime rights against British encroachments, while being opposed by the most directly concerned, northeastern maritime states and favored by the agrarian interests in the West and South (interested in Canada and Florida). And the pretended British arms supplies to Indians east of the Mississippi, which contributed to the War of 1812 and were to be the object of its key achievement on land, were only slightly more authentic than were to be the rumored British designs on the San Francisco Bay in the 1840s, prior to an abortive American attempt at annexation. The justifications for American actions in the two cases had been only relatively less contrived than was President Polk's later assertion of Mexican aggression north of the Rio Grande, serving as the formal grounds for a war which finally gained California. By contrast, no preclusive expansion deeper into Mexico met the more real threat from Napoleon III's venture in the 1860s. Sufficient inhibitions were imposed by the simultaneous American Civil War over the meaning of the U.S. Constitution; they were to be matched by Woodrow Wilson's quandary over the bearing of constitutionalism on civil wars generally, when a later opportunity for self-protective expansion was passed up at the time of the Mexican Revolution in 1911. Both instances coincided, moreover, with subsidence of the predatory expansionist drive.

Other threats were more genuine and at least semi-real. One was that from the western, trans-Appalachian Indian tribes. They replaced territorial squabbles among the colonies as the critical indigenous threat. Another was British interest in Texas before its annexation, in the Southern Confederacy during the Civil War, and—more single-mindedly in the 1840s than at any later stage—in Central America and in the projected isthmian canal. Buffers under British protection would inhibit American expansion; the denial of Texas to the United States and a lasting secession of the Confederacy would have entailed also an economic threat (by curtailing the American cotton monopoly); and Palmerston's policy for Central America was a challenge to American aspirations to naval and commercial parity (or better) in the area. Finally, semi-real to real threats had been implicit in Japan's designs on Hawaii and the Philippines in the 1890s, before the diversion of the frustrated Japanese toward the Asian mainland sowed the seeds of a later and bigger threat from that quarter.

Had the United States abstained from annexing the Philippines and exerting control in the Caribbean, finally, the German interest in both might well have become a source of danger. But, all considered, the sense of threat was most genuinely rooted in the inhibiting *pax Britannica*, notably in the Western Hemisphere. That threat was brought home most directly by the naval experiences in the Civil War with respect to the West Indies stations, while a different kind of threat was intensified by the decline of British overseas supremacy, at first especially in regard to China and to Asia as a whole. On land, be it on the North American continent or in the Western Hemisphere generally, the United States was never really threatened by a stronger adversary; nor was it beset, as it grew strong, by dilemmas of the kind which hard-to-stabilize parity or mere preeminence short of hegemony generate for less advantageously situated expansive land powers. But the issue of parity vs. preeminence in naval capabilities did involve the United States as a maritime power in at least potentially (and thus plausibly) threatening relations and contingencies. The first partner in contention, Britain, was followed by other rising sea powers, even before the regionally delimited issues merged with continental-European complications in the two world wars.

As a determinant of American expansion, preclusion rose thus in importance relative to predation at once unevenly and imperceptibly. It came into play as the United States ceased to be solely favored by the operation of the European, or Eurocentric global, balance of power and as it became more directly involved in the peripheral ramifications of the balance as a maritime and commercial actor.

The involvement in the larger system imparted a degree of authenticity to preclusive concerns that had not been present in the sporadic and either self-created or at the most semi-real threats on the North American continent. The predatory drive itself was ebbing concurrently. Not only had real needs for more land become less pressing, and additional space on the continent less readily available; but the mythical character of overseas means (such as the China trade) for meeting temporarily exaggerated or merely hypothetical future needs in the economic domain had also been gradually revealed. Once both needs and means became more like the felt threats, i.e., dubiously real or genuine, a more realistic equation could interrelate all of them as bearing on expansion. The growth in geographic distance between the original nuclei of expansion on the east coast and the receding imperial frontier might not have sufficed to dampen the impetus behind expansion. But physical distance was supplemented by an increasingly felt and likewise growing moral distance between the constituent community ideals of the American Republic and the actual consequences of a continuing momentum of expansion, threatening to encompass racial and ethnic groups ineligible for full citizenship within an ever-expanding empire. The result was a weakening of the commitment to a centrally underwritten, if often locally and individually promoted, expansion aiming at annexations. The correspondingly rising preference was for extending merely informal influence, if any. The background event, which catalyzed the convergent developments into a new basic orientation, and which consequently dated as well as determined the onset of a major lull in expansiveness, had inevitably to do with the key factor shaping the experience of the American body politic and provoking its reactions. Since that factor was the British empire, the background event itself was the final supersession of British dominance in the Western Hemisphere by the ascendant American core-empire.

The regional American empire in the Western Hemisphere took shape in the last stage of annexationist expansion preceding the lull. It was shaped by a preclusive response to the threat or fear, first of British encirclement and later of the consequences of Britain's enfeeblement. Encirclement threatened outside the continent if the British-controlled West Indian island chain were to be complemented by Britain acquiring comparable naval facilities off the Pacific coast. In the late nineteenth century that possibility engendered in the Americans acute psychic insecurity which was transmuted into hostility by virtue of a pervasive inferiority complex, even while the hypothetical security hazard found intermittent expression in positive scares. Britain's gradual enfeeblement failed to appease the fears. It raised instead the issue of succession to British naval supremacy, at first locally, and opened up the prospect of more cogent threats to physical security at the hands of suspected successor powers drawn into a post-British vacuum. In the actual course of events, the British complied with being locally superseded by the United States itself when they yielded on both the Venezuelan and the isthmian-canal issues to the American desire for status primacy and strategic security in the Western Hemisphere. The reallocation was also on the British side a preventive response to the rise of new threats, outside as well as within the Western Hemisphere; but if the growing signs of Britain's anticipated decline made America's would-be imperialists keenly aware of the remote threats, local concessions satisfied their more immediate regional goals.

The dominant American attitude fitted the essential quality of preclusion in that it merged defense and offense in an expansive method of dealing with more or less hypothetical future threats. The synthesis of offense and defense differs from the initial sequence, when offensive predation follows upon a successful prior defense against a clear and present threat to existence. But it corresponds all the more to the nature of the threat, which is hypothetical; and it conforms to the object, which is no longer an irreducible communal habitat assuring viability, but a sustainable make-up of a larger system of power.

That larger system was delimited for the United States by both principle and practice. The elastic concept of Manifest Destiny and the reactivated and revised Monroe Doctrine were supplemented by the Open Door principle in inspiring and rationalizing action in behalf of maritime defense and mercantile designs and, in part, delusions. The outward scope or orbit of the interplay was in part accidental, being defined by sporadic reactions to disparate forces and events as much as crystallizing systemically compelled, preclusive responses to unequivocal threats; the internal structure of the larger system of power expressed no less erratically the respective advantages and liabilities of mere control and of actual possession. Whereas *de facto* control would suffice for protection and was preferable to annexation if it could be made reliable and effective, formalized possession appeared to be the natural consequence of geographic propinquity, unless contravened by the absence of cultural or ethnic affinities. The scope of the core-empire which actually evolved was sufficient to assure American dominance in the relevant international system or environment, encompassing the Western Hemisphere and the adjacent islands, while its emergence transformed part patently and part latently the Atlantic-European and Pacific-Far Eastern balance-of-power systems that were marginally abutting on, and were impinged upon by, the core-empire. The regional empire acquired, consequently, the characteristic structure consisting of an inner core, bounded by the imperial frontier, and an outer zone of less reliably influenced or less directly controlled parties.

III

The critical environment of a core-empire is defined by the conjunction of political topography and military technology. The former refers to the configuration of territorially based concentrations of power, the latter intimates the strategies that are technologically suited to dealing with consequent threats to security. Policy-making also will be conditioned by dominant assumptions about the character and the requirements of the material, meaning chiefly economic, bases of political power and its military application. The economic factor will do more than condition and will actually shape policy when politico-military strategic threats or responses are not compelling as to intensity or determinate as to specific identity.

The pertinent technology for America's regional empire concerned mainly sea power and bore directly on both threat and defensive strategy; the economic environment was defined by the rise of the industrial system and of new industrial powers, and had both direct and indirect implications for the threat-defense equation. Evolutions in both technology and economy made the relevant political topography expand rather abruptly beyond continental North America, the northern regions of South America (covered by a species of balance of power among notably Argentina, Brazil, and Chile as the indigenous powers and the regionally involved European powers), and what John Quincy Adams had called the "natural appendages" to the northern continent. The newly critical, broadened arena comprised as outer zones the concurrently recrystallizing West European-Atlantic and East Asian-Pacific regional theaters of the still Eurocentric global balance-of-power system. Even more so than Latin America, the Asian theater combined indigenous powers (Japan, Asiatic Russia, and China) and regionally present European parties (Britain, France, and Germany). For the United States to expand into a core-empire with offshore maritime defenses against overseas powers was the near-unavoidable consequence of a prior failure to allow a balance of power to develop among indigenous entities on the North American continent; but the precise configuration of the inner core of the regional domain, and its relation to the outer zones or peripheral balance-of-power theaters, was less predetermined and consequently more problematic and controversial.

Technologically determining was the near-total reliance on steamships and the resulting need for sources of coal supply fairly close to one another. The inner security zone was, conversely, defined by the imperative to control, so as to withhold from potential enemies, the "keys to the ocean approaches," meaning the islands situated at standard cruising distance from the mainland coasts and equipped with coaling depots and other base facilities. Since the waters along much of the mainland coasts were shallow, moreover, deep-sea harbors offshore were desirable; and, in view of the prospective tendency of an isthmian canal to draw European naval powers into the Caribbean (*en route* to the Pacific), yet another need was for directly controlling and fortifying the outposts of a simultaneously enlarged and modernized naval force. The strategic rationale adequately covered insular positions relatively close to the mainland in both the Caribbean-Mexican Gulf and the Eastern Pacific; and it continued to predominate when justifying on military grounds the interest in remoter bases situated close to the main trade routes. (Such bases alone allegedly provided needed facilities for raiding hostile commerce in wartime, the traditional forward-defense strategy of a relatively weaker naval power. The rationale was not foolproof inasmuch as an inferior navy, inadequate to insure defense near the coasts, would be also unable to bar hostile retaliation for the commerce-raiding strategy.) Any weakness in the strategic rationale enhanced either the force of or the dependence on economic motivations, postulating the utility of remote coaling stations for peacetime naval protection of seaborne trade and, insofar as commerce follows the flag, its promotion.

Remote coaling stations met the prevailing technological requirements of steam navigation. But, so long as facilities could be securely held, neither technology nor the consequent doctrine implied the need for permanent and direct political control over territories surrounding the facilities and propelling the imperial power beyond core-empire toward world empire. However, the case of the Philippines more than any other showed the difficulty of confining acquisitions to strategic *points d'appui* in practice.

Technologically conditioned security requirements, and the related consideration of status, defined the inner core validly and persuasively. The balance of considerations for and against extending the radius of involvement was different when delimiting the fluid outer zones of the core-empire. The controlling perception was then one of supposed economic necessities in conditions of an actual or threatening neo-mercantilism. If the consequent danger to internal stability was less solidly based than was that to external security, it was experienced no less intensely at the critical juncture. The materially rooted anxieties were greater in regard to the vaster Pacific theater, whereas security considerations tended to preponderate in regard to the smaller theater of the Atlantic. Consequently, it was in the Pacific, combining the lure of the China trade with the vision of Japan as a threat, that the first if inconclusive step beyond regional to world empire took place (in the form of the Philippine conquest). Conversely, enclosing the islands situated near the mainland in the core-empire put into effect expectations that had been long in maturing, while entailing the rejection by the McKinley adminis-tration of the just-preceding Cleveland administration's last-ditch resis-tance to abandoning continentalism for the sake of "distant acquisitions." The thereafter more or less directly and permanently controlled islands (Cuba and Puerto Rico, pending the acquisition of the Virgin islands, on the Atlantic side and, on the Pacific side, Hawaii and Guam, next to the American stake in Samoa) were unevenly suited for satisfactory harbors and strategic bases and facilities for defending the mainland coasts and the approaches to an isthmian canal. But to the extent that their acquisi-tion derived from the war with Spain, it also revealed the continuation of a long-standing, self-sufficient concern to extrude decaying empires from America's proximity, for the sake of excluding potentially encroaching rising ones.

The timing was propitious. By the end of the nineteenth century, the original target (Britain) had no longer any real intention of impeding the completion of the American core-empire and the British admiralty had correspondingly ceased to rival the American search for bases in the Caribbean and, with qualifications, off the Pacific coast. Moreover, nei-ther Germany nor Japan yet had the means and (therefore) a serious intention to threaten American coasts any more than to deny America access to the insular "outworks of continental defenses" (in Senator Henry Cabot Lodge's phrase). But the overall concept may have been less impeccable. Since Germany was the more feared of the two ascendant powers, the growing U.S. naval forces were concentrated on the Atlantic (or Caribbean) side of the prospective canal site. The massing plugged the surviving lacunae, represented by Santo Domingo-Haiti in particular; but it also made the American core-imperial security system markedly lopsided before a two-ocean navy "second to none" arose as a result of World War I. The imbalance compounded the unsatisfactory nature of base and harbor facilities in and east of Hawaii, overstraining the Ameri-can capability to defend the newly acquired Pacific possessions. More-over, whereas competition among European great powers militated against a naval invasion across the Atlantic, the dynamic of Russo-Japanese relations substituted entente for the war of 1904 with the result of eroding the previously self-sustaining bases of American security and access in the Pacific theater.

For practical purposes, security threats can become no less acutely felt if they have been promoted by unbalanced perceptions and premature precautions. American perception of the German threat as superior to Japan's had begun to emerge in the 1880s and was crystallized by the turn of the century, in both economic and military dimensions. The growing German economic penetration in the southern portion of the Western Hemisphere was seen as having direct political implications for the penetrated parts. It had also indirect domestic political consequences for the United States itself, insofar as German exports reduced the capacity of American trade to compensate abroad for economic depressions at home, while concurrently increasing the costs of an augmented military (i.e., naval) preparedness. Moreover, German activities would have been responsible for a major threat to American interests if the European powers were to rush into partitioning also Latin America, next to Asia and Africa, in response to the Bismarck-wrought intra-European stalemate. And, finally, a direct military-strategic threat for the West Indies immediately, and the continental United States ultimately, would result from a German seizure of a Caribbean island (such as Cuba or Santo Domingo), preceding a naval blockade of the mainland and an eventual military invasion.

The ascendancy of mutually antipathetic expansive leadership personalities, Theodore Roosevelt and William II, added the psychopolitical dimension to hypothetical military reasoning and planning in the two countries. The conjunction strengthened the appearance of verisimilitude attaching to the idea of a German-initiated war on the United States, however belied that plausibility may have been by the professional German planners holding such an initiative to be "unthinkable" in the then existing conditions of German naval and military capabilities and commitments.[1] In that intramural judgment, a chronically volatile European situation made it impossible for Germany to assign the bulk of her naval forces and a large army to the Western Hemisphere. But, if the conditions in Europe warranted discounting the immediate American security fears, they also supplied reasons for American concern over the longer-term direction of Anglo-German relations as potentially too friendly before they became acutely hostile. The concern underlay the mechanism which converted the American political elites' growing emotional hostility for Germany and an only economic rivalry into a military conflict propelling the United States beyond core-empire in two installments.

Before that happened, real or imagined German provocations had taken place in Chile and China, Haiti and Samoa, Venezuela and the Philippines. They served not only to couple the Atlantic and Pacific outer zones into a whole for initially only diplomatic-strategic purposes but also to provide the Pacific arena with a specific focus. Such a focus had been lacking previously in the complex politics of inter-great-power

1. See Johns A. S. Grenville and George Berkeley Young, *Politics, Strategy, and American Diplomacy* (New Haven: Yale University Press, 1966), pp. 306–07.

transactions and was only insufficiently supplied by the economics of the China trade.

The imbalance between the Atlantic and Pacific theaters with respect to American deployments, perception of dangers, and expansive designs was accompanied by a discrepancy intrinsic to the Pacific arena itself. Whereas the Pacific was perceived as more important than the Atlantic for the balance of world trade and empire in the long run, it was the subject of yet greater uncertainties of analysis and of no greater readiness for sustained action in the short term. Incipient moves by the great powers to partition China in the latter 1890s aroused both economic and strategic concerns; but there was no settled assessment of the configuration of the threat and of a proper response to it. It was not settled whether the main menace was economic and immediate, and came from Russia in Manchuria, or was also eventually strategic, if Japan extended her aims to Hawaii and Central and South America. And the critical threat could evolve in one way if power came to be concentrated in one regionally dominant state, as an alternative to a stable regional balance of power and an analogue to a hegemonic Germany in the Euro-Atlantic theater; or it could, in different ways and more immediately, result either from competitive seizures of ports and spheres by powers engaged in a dynamic balancing of assets and facilities for access or from the non-American powers accommodating their respective acquisitive goals in more or less formal concert.

The different configurations of threat were illustrated alternately in Russo-Japanese relations and in related policies of the European powers in the first decade of the twentieth century. Similarly, both competition and concert of foreign powers threatened to exclude American interests from China, even if not to precipitate immediately hostile intrusions in the American home waters as might one-power ascendancy. And, finally, compounding the uncertainty as to the identity of the power embodying the greatest threat and such a threat's precise complexion was uncertainty about the kind of reactive strategy to be applied. It was possible in principle to promote the Japanese counterpoise to Russia in Manchuria and Korea; to cooperate strategically with Britain in the Yangtze valley; or to compose differences with Russia and deepen thus the anti-German bias which had crystallized in frictions over Samoa and had been intensified by the German seizure of Kiao-chow in China. And the United States itself could either participate in preemptive seizures of bases and positions in China, and literally contravene in Asia the kind of principles enshrined in the Monroe Doctrine; or American statecraft could extend the application of the doctrine and adjust it to Asian conditions by insisting on an Open Door in China and on China's territorial integrity.

The Pacific uncertainties were accurately reflected in the ambiguities surrounding the annexation of the Philippines. Since the archipelago was situated beyond the mid-Pacific line, it was not eligible for inclusion in the core-empire on the strategic-technological grounds conferring legitimacy in the case of Hawaii. Being time-bound in the sense of imitative of prevalent imperialist modes, the annexation was as a result also only chronologically part of the expansion that completed the core-empire. Analytically, in terms of its specific motives, the annexation represented a deviation from the structurally conditioned lull in expansionist élan that attended the completion of the geopolitically defined core-empire in all other respects and areas. In any larger view and longer perspective, the annexation was anachronistic to the extent that it anticipated a much-later extension of the American core-empire into world empire; it was aberrant inasmuch as the preponderantly economic bias of the underlying motivation differed from the primarily strategic determinant responsible for the insular core-empire; and it was accidental since, in lieu of being strategically motivated, it was the byproduct of strategic naval planning before the outbreak of the war with Spain, envisaging a naval diversion in Philippine waters as a means of facilitating success in the critical Cuban theater.

In terms of economics, the possession of the Philippines related to the China trade as the perceived analogue to Britain's prime stake in India; insofar as it could be at all plausibly rationalized in terms of strategic considerations, it was reminiscent (and possibly imitative) of Britain's actions with respect to Egypt and Suez, inasmuch as the Philippines were likewise seen as a point of access or a stepping stone to a paramount economic prize (China and India, respectively). The inorganic connection of the Philippines with the core-empire was strikingly manifest when the intention to occupy only Manila Bay, and then only the principal island (Luzon), had been reluctantly surrendered in favor of annexation of the entire archipelago. The expansive dynamic of preemption was revealed further, and the initial hesitancy was vindicated anew, when progressive disenchantment set in with the strategic worth of the insular complex. Its vulnerability to Japan was not compensated for by marked economic value, moreover, either intrinsic or relative to China; and the Filipino rebellion, by dramatizing the political liability represented by the archipelago, had only strengthened the perception that was to inspire in due course the strategy of disengagement.

Since the annexation was disjoined from the original determinant of mainstream expansionism in the postpredatory preclusive stage, it had to draw on subsidiary motives of a kind that had actuated extensions beyond a completed core-empire in comparable earlier situations. One such motive was the defense of the core-empire's "frontier" in the outer zone, to be distinguished from the metropolitan boundary. But, given the still largely self-neutralizing Far-Eastern balance of power, this rationalization from defense needs was likewise insufficient to cover the Philippines, and created the need for additional or subsidiary incentives. One is to be found in the domestic political arena, since the push outward expressed the reluctance of the dominant Anglo-Saxon class, receptive to the tenets of Social Darwinism, to be confined and submerged by the swelling numbers of immigrating alien ethnics; another was lodged in the economic arena, since the push implemented the need for outlets, seemingly augmented by the just-experienced depression in the United States and by the overseas implications of the mercantilist policies favored by the non-Anglo-Saxon imperial powers. Such particular subsidiary motives were only secondary to the original, principally strategic and preclusive, determinant of the regionally bounded expansion; their salience beyond it denotes the qualitative difference of the Philippines from the core-empire, just as their soon-to-occur weakening or virtual inversion confirmed America's unreadiness to reach beyond the core-empire and sustain an Anglo-American cooperation in the Far East that would build on the brief if superficial honeymoon of 1898.

The subsidiary determinants of expansion were weakened or inverted into opposition to expansion as the ruling class (typified by Theodore Roosevelt) veered from hopes for mass-supported imperial progression to progressive political reforms at home; the primacy of the home market and of economic ties with Europe dwarfed the actually feasible China trade and American big business became strong enough in Latin America to dispense with direct governmental support; and a progressing naval build-up in the Atlantic combined with Rooseveltian "large policy" in the Pacific theater to remove any immediate threat to the security of the continental-maritime regional empire. If diplomacy sufficed to help push back Russia without immediately Asianizing the Far East by helping Japan to immoderate aggrandizement, less direct or effective American assistance helped China escape all-out Africanization in the guise of definitive partition. Intermittently promoted by the government, American railway diplomacy in China was a weak example of informal imperialism and an inferior counterpart of the dollar diplomacy practiced in the Caribbean. Only that diplomacy was sustained by military force, ostensibly placed in the service of an international policing mission under changing ideological auspices, when implementing in the period from Theodore Roosevelt to Woodrow Wilson the strategic and economic requirements of the core-empire in both the unstable insular realm and in revolutionary Mexico. Checking local disorders that might precipitate rival intrusions was necessary for avoiding the need for further annexations while plugging strategic lacunae (e.g., in Santo Domingo and Haiti) by less drastic means. That end being secured, employing only limited means and informal methods of control reflected the limited immediate objective of consolidation, pending eventual devolution of responsibility for internal order to indigenous agents. A so adjusted American posture was consistent with the existence of a structural lull in the overall expansionist dynamic, also because self-restraint in the south had its parallel in the final acceptance of the new Canadian constitutional order as a bar to forcible annexation in the north.

IV

For it to be "structural," a pause in officially promoted expansion has to follow a discernible conclusion of a prior expansionist cycle in a provisionally consolidated, secure compass. Taking off from a more-than-regional achieved scope for a range of reasons, Roman reexpansion into grand empire followed upon the lull in the second century B.C. and the similar British reexpansion upon the mid-Victorian lull. In partial contrast, American reexpansion was from an essentially only regional into a world empire following World War II, and was at first primarily due to the emergence of a new and apparently compelling threat to national security in the central balance of power. In all cases, however, the structural lull between two major periods of expansion differed from the surface subsidence of expansionist energies that commonly follows upon the termination of taxing wars. Such subsidence will reflect nothing more than the depletion of energies, or their diversion to internal tasks of political or economic reconstruction intended to remedy disruptions and implement possibilities that were either generated or revealed by the turmoil of war.

There were several, not all necessarily structural, lulls in the American case. The first and limited one coincided with the institutional consolidation of the newly independent Atlantic coastal "empire," in the period between 1783 and the Spanish transfer of Louisiana to Napoleonic France (in 1801). The second followed upon the war with Mexico and was extended into the reconstruction period consequent upon the Civil War. And the third followed the Spanish war and the related Filipino rebellion, while the fourth marked the post–World War I relapse into isolationism. Of these, only the first and, more significantly, the third lull were structural. Both followed the acquisition of two different but likewise viable territorial habitats of a regional scope. Each could be stabilized by a corresponding, intracontinental or intercontinental and oceanic, balance of power. By contrast, neither the second nor the fourth postwar lull were of the structural kind. The second lull marked the completion of the purely continental scope of expansion, which was strategically incomplete and untenable in the long run, while preceding the subsequent expansion into the two-regional Atlantic-Pacific overseas empire. The pause was conditioned by domestic intersectional turmoil, and it was facilitated by a coincident introversion of European power politics culminating in Italian and German unifications. The fourth lull represented effective regression from an initiated movement toward a global, back to the two-regional Atlantic-Pacific (or western-hemispheric), empire.

If the second, superficial lull was made temporarily possible by the turning of dynamic European balance of power back upon itself for a final adjustment preceding its deterioration, the fourth pause (and related retraction) was likewise impermanent because it depended on artificially contrived, arms-controlled European and Pacific-Asian balances. The second lull ran its course for the post-Civil War United States when continental European introversion had turned into a deadlock, to be relieved by overseas politics abutting on peripheral American interests and hypothetical security margins. And the fourth lull ended when the several "dynamic" powers finally pressed home their revisionist assault on the decaying powers in Europe and Asia. They engendered as many incentives to massive American reexpansion in the form of less than hypothetical threats of global scope or, at least, global significance. Different in other ways, all of the lulls except for the first tended to coincide with periods of either marked economic growth or unusual economic effervescence. Heightened productivity and deep-seated crisis were alike in imparting a material aspect to the subsequent periods of expansion; both permeated self-consciously preponderant defensive-preclusive motives with variable doses of predatory acquisitiveness.

Temporary subsidence of expansionism following foreign or civil wars is consistent with actual expansion, so long as the latter is due to sub-imperialism by nongovernmental actors. It is also compatible with official designs which remain unimplemented on paper. Schemes of the Hawaiian sugar planters and of Secretary of State Seward illustrate the deviations in the period following the Civil War. Nor is a genuinely structural lull, arising out of the completion of a viable orbit and the consequent erosion of original expansive stimuli, incompatible with actual expansion. In the American case, expansive deviations were related to wars and did not arise out of independent proconsular or subimperial departures from official initiatives, as had been the case in Rome and Britain. One such deviation was the annexation of the Philippines, if it is seen as the result of an uncontrollable dynamic of war rather than of any previous design for expansion in that particular direction. Another was American participation in World War I and its expansive concomitants, if the second (and principal) authentically structural lull is viewed as extending from the conclusion of the Spanish-American War to the onset of the American-Soviet "cold war" growing out of World War II. When they occur, the deviations from and interruptions to the lull are actually testing mechanisms. They test the continued efficacy of the objective conditions and the subjective predispositions that were originally responsible for the pause as an expression of more or less realistic satisfaction, rational calculations, and irrational frustrations relating to previous expansion and its attendant or resulting features.

Satisfaction with the regional core-empire and consequent pause in expansion were warranted on grounds of both security and status. Growing American naval power was supplemented by a partially American-promoted stalemate among other powers in Asia (including the Russo-Japanese peace) and elsewhere (including the Franco-German competition in Morocco). The two together ensured national security, while the fact of being acknowledged as mediator between big powers and policeman within an orbit of small powers reflected America's status as one of the imperial powers of the age. Nor did the limited scope of the American colonial empire entail real, as contrasted with apprehended, limitations on the metropole's economic well-being. Whatever hypothetical advantages there were to additional colonial acquisitions, as either protected markets or chips in bargaining over world-wide economic liberalization, had to be measured against real costs. Whereas drifting into colonial protectionism on a wide front would further compromise American advocacy of the open door abroad, internal costs would attend adjusting the advantages and the liabilities accruing to different special agricultural and industrial interests from alternative tariff policies and regimes vis-à-vis multiplying dependencies.

In such conditions even a rough cost-benefit calculation militated against immediate further expansion that was, in addition, apt to enhance domestic instability by encompassing ever harder to assimilate ethnic elements. Prudence dictated instead a pause that would permit the elites to assimilate the already admitted foreign ethnic groups into the national framework, and to evolve the capability for indirect approaches to the limited goals of law and order and security outside the national boundaries but within the core-imperial framework. The task was difficult at a time, including the Wilsonian period of Caribbean diplomacy, when deliberate national policy ruled out supplementing policing military interventions with governmentally funded and implemented economic inducements on the pattern of the later assistance programs. Calculated self-limitation was also to lead eventually to attempts at naval arms-control in the Pacific in the 1920s and to a species of devolution (including suspension of military interventions) in the Caribbean by the 1930s. Whereas the former was designed to forestall reactivation of a massive threat in the East, the latter was in part responding to its re-emergence in the West.

More compelling than either satisfaction or calculation were, however, the frustrations implicit in the imperial experience. They arose, dramatically, out of the Filipino uprising consequent on annexation, were reinforced by the elusiveness of a profitable and voluminous China trade, and were perpetuated by the policeman's "unhappy lot" in the Caribbean. Neither drawback was adequately compensated for by a striking economic advantage from existing colonial possessions. And the sense of frustration was only amplified by two interrelated factors. One consisted of the excessive expectations which Americans were wont to attach to far-out ventures; another, of the either limited or unstable measure of realistically assessed necessity to meet immediate security and other needs, which necessity would first compel the resort to wide-ranging ventures and subsequently constrain the anticipation of beneficial effects. Propensity to frustration cut short the first imperial élan; and it ensured that intervention in World War I would not reactivate the élan on a sustained and enlarged scale in the absence of a postwar security threat more compelling than was the indirect and hypothetical one of social revolution in Central and Eastern Europe.

American intervention in World War I had key points in common with the annexation of the Philippines. Both deviations from the structural lull were ultimately, if not consistently or single-mindedly, rationalized as constituting forward defense of the core-empire security system. They were both stimulated by congruent factors in domestic politics: ethnic factors, having to do with dispositions of the Anglo-Saxon ruling class; and economic ones, having to do with peaceful trade with China in the earlier case and wartime credits to the Allies in the later contingency. And the two initiatives were linked together by the perception of a growing German threat to a full range of critical values. Moreover, once the gradually enlarged objectives of the American intervention in the "great war" went beyond the defense of the mid-Atlantic security frontier of the core-empire, the intervention became as premature and incomplete a move toward world empire Roman-style as the annexation of the Philippines had been toward an overseas colonial empire British-style when reaching beyond the offshore imperial frontier in the Pacific in the Spanish-American war. Finally, the United States recoiled from the implications of involvements in both Asia and Europe in a fit of disillusionment aggravated by prior emotional mass-commitment.

To argue thus is not to assert that the initial recoil by an Anglophile statecraft from U.S. dominance in postwar Europe was without parallel in the initial reluctance of phil-Hellenic Romans to dominate "liberated" Greece; nor is it to assert that the retreat from Europe and the world generally was complete, or that a perfect parallel obtains between the earlier Asian departure from the structured lull and the later European deviation. The post–World War I withdrawal was qualified by the continuing residual impact of factors and forces that had been responsible for American wartime involvement, such as Anglo-American ruling-class politics, high-finance economics, and concern for naval primacy within overall limitations. And, as a result of America's decisive intervention against the Central Powers in the European war, the position of the American core-empire in the interstate system remained potentially much closer to that of Rome and Britain following their wars with comparable (Macedonian-Syrian and French-Napoleonic) threats to the Mediterranean and the continental-European balances of power, than it had been after America's earlier war with Spain. The American core-empire had grown meanwhile in both potency and the influence it exercised abroad, even while becoming again a passive referent rather than a sustainedly active element outside the hemispheric compass.

The lull period between core-empire and grand empire has a characteristic that reflects the tapering off of the original predatory and preclusive stimulus behind expansion and the still embryonic state of the supplementing, subsidiary pressures and determinants. The characteristic trait is for the core-empire's policy-makers to seek, if they seek anything outside their orbit, no more and no less than a privileged access to cost- and risk-free influence. In seeking such access to the key balance-of-power arena or arenas, the policy-makers will draw on either the resources or the prestige of the core-empire in order to impede the crystallization of comparable and rival power concentrations by means that do not include a further extension of direct control over foreign territory or policy. Such were the essentially traditional unilateral diplomatic methods employed by Theodore Roosevelt, after 1900, as an alternative to both the Cleveland-style Western Hemisphere continentalism and the annexationist world imperialism of the McKinley era, while Henry Cabot Lodge propounded in due course a similar posture as an alternative to the Wilsonian multilateral internationalism. Secretary of State John Hay's notion of a concert of the powers in China was yet another variant on the approach, and one similar to Woodrow Wilson's notion of concerted force behind the League of Nations all over the world. The first, more traditional, view of concert would apply the principle of Open Door to economic competition, its updated version (and the later Briand-Kellogg Pact) would close the door on forcible infringement of territorial integrity. Throughout, the preferred means tended to be no more forceful than the refusal to recognize territorial gains resulting from military aggression, in the several Hay-Bryan-Stimson formulations. The largely declaratory diplomacy amounted to declamatory dress rehearsals for an effective world role. As such, it carried on the American tradition of paper reservations commenced by the claims of the colonial charters to territorial conquest, continued by the Monroe Doctrine's pretension to political control, and carried over into the strategic dimension by the first, Clayton-Bulwer, canal treaty. The common purpose and partial effect of these and similar instruments was to neutralize, or at least delegitimize, competing claims or acquisitions pending the growth of American material and moral ability to actualize the positive thrust immanent in the anticipatory symbolic acts.

The platonic approach proved ultimately insufficient. One reason was that involvements in the Philippines and with the warring Europeans left behind hostages to more aggressive or active local powers. In Asia, contractual and other limitations on local American naval engagement and defense measures rendered the Philippines virtually indefensible and helped inspire the long-ambiguous (and ultimately provocative) American reactions to Japan's expansive moves in mainland China (and eventually to the south of China). In Europe, the self-imposed limits on effective politico-diplomatic engagement in the central balance of power after World War I engendered fundamental policy conflicts between Britain and France, which correspondingly aggravated the issue between the satisfied and the dissatisfied powers. The intra-European balance of power became unmanageable by indigenous means as a result, a fact which eventually inspired the British appeasement response to German resurgence and an initially ambiguous American reaction. And if the European and the Asian issues interplayed increasingly by way of Anglo-American interactions, parallel Germano-Japanese actions were to span both of the two key theaters sufficiently to consummate America's military involvement in World War II.

Participating in the first full-fledged Eurasian war marked a further, but still not final, U.S. step beyond the preliminary and preparatory core-empire stage and pattern. The desire to equal Britain as a global colonial empire had led the United States to acquire in the Philippines a source of conflict with Japan, geopolitically the "Britain" of Asia and eventually the most direct precipitant of American reinvolvement in a climactic Eurasian conflict through the Pacific back door. If the British had not precisely foreseen that back door, they had provided for it by tolerantly condoning America's access to Asia via the isthmian canal and her acquisitions there in the aftermath of the war with Spain. Britain's crowning acts of appeasement of America in Asia by the late 1890s were the necessary preconditions for effective American reinvolvement, beginning in the late 1930s. And it was that reinvolvement alone that enabled Britain to cease appeasing Nazi Germany in Europe (because she was no longer alone in facing Japan in Asia) and thus to bring indirectly to a close the odd half-century long lull in American expansion.

v

Exposed as it was to a chain of events, the lull in expansion beyond the core-empire could continue only so long as existing structures perpetuated, conjointly with the capacity of the British empire to act as a provisional surrogate for the United States, the potential of the balance of power for surviving in two interrelated manifestations. Principally non-American parties had to retain the ability to contain the intraregional balances of power in the Atlantic and Pacific theaters in such a way as not to release in Western Europe or East Asia a margin of sea-borne capabilities usable with effect against the American security system; and the two interacting (Atlantic and Pacific) regional balance-of-power theaters had to continue being, to an irreducible minimum degree, separate from one another in operation and both distinct and distinguishable from the Eurocentric global balance-of-power system in scope, participants, and alignments.

So long as the interdependent conditions prevailed, there was no imminent prospect and present threat of either a concentrated or a coordinated action against the United States by any single power or plausible combination of powers. However, the several arenas would remain separate and distinct only so long as the regional (Atlantic and Pacific) theaters continued to be the ramifications of the Eurocentric global system without being its integral reflections. That general fact was in turn due to a number of specific factors. As a coastal state with offshore insular possessions, the United States was a direct if remote and restrained participant in both the Atlantic and the Pacific systems; but it was only a reserve or background factor, albeit potentially decisive, in the European center of the global system. By contrast, Russia had a more weighty impact on the central balance of power than on its Pacific extension, especially after the 1904 war with Japan, and had a more direct impact on the European than on the Atlantic theater, which she affected mainly by way of competitive French and German reactions to Russia-in-Europe. While increasingly central to the Pacific theater, Japan had a still more indirect bearing than Russia on the Atlantic theater, at first only as an alternative to Germany among British options in 1901–02 and subsequently, in the 1930s, as a stimulant to American involvement in the Pacific readily extensible to the Atlantic theater. Between the two dates, Japan was also largely peripheral to the Eurocentric global balance of power. Germany was the cardinal factor in Europe, but was much less steadily and evenly involved in the two oceanic systems over time. And, most comprehensively, the European powers had different priorities and espoused intermittently different policies and alignments in relation to extra-European (including Asian-Pacific and African-Atlantic) colonial matters than they did with respect to continental issues of national security inside Europe. The discrepancy had been most marked in the period between the 1880s and the Anglo-French-Russian entente before World War I, and it resurfaced with the collapse of that entente during and immediately after the war.

A decisive change occurred when the so far partially autonomous Atlantic and Pacific regional balance-of-power theaters ceased to be separate in operation by virtue of collapsing under German and Japanese military pressures. Their fusion was complete when a power encompassing Europe and Asia, the Soviet Union, consummated the prior inorganic merger of the two theaters by the German-Japanese Axis and was at least temporarily joined in close union by Communist China. The result was a restructured and, initially at least, simplified global balance-of-power system on one level only, no longer decomposable into regional and global planes and orbits any more than Eurocentric in the old sense. The new system was focused on Eurasia as the key embattled object, and on the American-Soviet interaction as the principal process. The fact that Russia and America were brought together, first in rivalry over preeminence, was the predictable consequence of Anglo-German hostility, just as an Anglo-German accommodation before World War I would almost certainly have promoted concordant U.S.-Russian action for shared parity with other powers within a less radically revised, traditional international system. A related and concurrent development was the wartime weakening of the British empire. It raised the issue of imperial order-maintenance, distinct from but interrelated with the state of the balance of power in conditioning American self-confinement. At the latest by 1947 the older empire was manifestly veering toward the dissolution of what had previously appeared to be the principal counterpoise to any new Eurasian power bloc and its most likely principal target.

Taken together, the decline of the custodian of the Anglo-Saxon role in world leadership and the rise of a potent new claimant to imperial succession challenging America's natural right to near-total security, removed the bases from under self-isolation within a regional core-empire. As a posture, isolationism always depended on its actually sustaining conditions in—and the self-sustaining potential of—the very global system that America's isolationist policy came increasingly to subvert. It ceased henceforth to be either safe or responsible to assume that no single power, or predictable combination of powers, could preclude the United States from taking decisive action at acceptable cost in circumstances critical for the global system, or could bar the United States in normal circumstances from access to political and economic associations within the several regional theaters. A combination of actual military and potential economic power inherent in the Eurasian Russian state alone, or in a Soviet-controlled complex comprising Germany in Europe and China or Japan in Asia, might or might not be immediately or spontaneously expansionist. In either case, one or the other aggregation of power added the fact of central location to the possibility of future access to major sea lanes and naval allies or capabilities in constituting a long-term threat of some kind of exclusion for the United

States. The threat could, moreover, be plausibly seen as superior to the menace previously offered by the existing or likely future capacity of the German-Japanese Axis to coordinate encirclement of the Western Hemisphere in war or, following a victory, aggregate insuperable land- and sea-based power in nominal peace.

The so-called cold war got under way in the aftermath of one more American attempt to subside into the habitual postwar posture or, differently put, to resume the interrupted lull posture. A rapid demobilization responded to internal domestic constraints. But it also mirrored a provisional uncertainty about the kinds of external threat that would flow from Soviet-controlled power along the lines of a new dominant conflict, shaped by reactions to war-created vacuums of power. The Soviet pressure might have receded somewhat in Europe and a global conflict might have crystallized around an ascendant Soviet Union's challenge to a gradually retreating British empire. In such a case, the United States could have withdrawn once more into the accustomed role of a third party, free to either retreat from world role or advance only gradually and selectively toward defining such a role in peacetime. But as initial uncertainties waned and the long-range implications of the nuclear revolution became clearer, pressures rose for a prompt active response to conventional-military insecurity in the central system. If the preclusive determinant of reexpansion was initially self-sufficient, however, it was also gradually reinforced and its globally expansive manifestations were perpetuated by the subsidiary stimuli implicit in the defense of imperial frontier, domestic dynamics, and economic dilemmas.[2]

The initial, preclusive American response was to the demonstrated power of the Soviets and their ostensibly expansive behavior or suspected expansionist intentions in the Eurasian heartland. That original impetus entrenched the United States in positions seized in hot pursuit of the retreating Axis powers, expressing the will and implementing the compulsion to withhold major reservoirs of power in Western Europe and Japan from rival control with the aid of newly acquired strategic positions in the Atlantic and the Pacific. A subsidiary motive, identifiable with the subsequent defense of the imperial frontier, expressed in continuing expansion the intent to shield the essential elements of the emergent world empire and global power distribution from erosion by more or less well-organized forces related in one way or another to the centrally threatening major power or (following Communist victory in China) powers. The establishment of American protection over the key areas was thus followed by American penetration into peripheral areas, substituting American presence and control for the remaining authority on the periphery of the Western European powers protected at the

2. See chaps. 6 and 7 for domestic dynamics and economic dilemmas respectively.

center. Staging effective defense against rival subversion required plausibly, and came to imply nearly automatically, the supersession of less efficacious dependent allies.

An apparently effective Russo-Chinese complex in Eurasia was an analogue to the for long apprehended Russo-German coalescence in Europe. It came into being almost coincidentally with Soviet Russia's accession to nuclear capability and postwar material rehabilitation (1949); and it was almost immediately followed by an acute threat to the security of Japan (Korea, 1950). Although Japan's integration into the American empire was, unlike that of Western Europe, the consequence of her defeat, the difference was only superficially significant. Japan's defeat merely restored the high degree of American-Japanese compatibility in politico-economic relations whenever there was a settled world order, and affinity against an assertive Russia in regard to China when the world situation was unsettled. Furthermore, the American occupation policy under General MacArthur merely reactivated an earlier policy of restraining Japan by cooperation with civilian political elites, concurrently restored to domestic predominance. Prewar Japanese military expansionism had been to a great extent a reaction to the mismanagement on both sides of the basic American-Japanese compatibility in conditions of a progressively disintegrating world economic order. To that same extent could it be disavowed in Japan as part of readjustments which included an American guarantee of Japanese security and access to both raw materials and markets.

The United States both replaced and outdid Britain as the Western great-power sponsor and protector of Japan, after it had helped disrupt the Anglo-Japanese connection and set in motion Japan's drive for an Asiatic empire. A Japanese continental-maritime complex would ultimately have threatened both Britain in India and America's Pacific and possibly also hemispheric positions. Its frustration was followed by the distortion of an intended consequence. The desired reconsolidation of a Chinese empire on the mainland did take place, but under a hostile regime suspect of expansionist ambitions in the Asian rimlands and off-shore insular realms. The triumph of the Communist regime appeared to postpone indefinitely the American ideal, of a China matching efficacy at home with restraint at her outskirts and constituting a useful buffer between the United States and the Soviets in the Far East. Instead, the Maoist takeover apparently undid the remaining constraints on Chinese xenophobic nationalism and culturally supercilious regional imperialism. It appeared thus to complement the Soviet-controlled mass in Eurasia, and to compensate for the relative weaknesses of the Soviet Union in the Far East in ways that would compound any threat from Communist China proper.

Upholding a new balance of power with the enlarged and activated powers in Asia seemed henceforth to require American actions of a kind needed also for insuring the security of the enlarged American empire at its remote frontiers. In this connection, direct responsibility for the security and welfare of Japan was combined with ultimate American responsibility for averting forcible subversion of both the diminishing number of European colonial possessions and the growing number of independent Asian countries nominally headed by recently decolonized India. Just as the European and related peripheral theaters, headed by the Middle East, merged with the Asian sectors into an interdependent strategic entity coterminous with the outline of a crystallizing American world empire, so the original preclusive determinant of American wartime and postwar expansion merged through the defense of the imperial frontier with one of the several subsidiary motives of continuing expansion. Rather than only interrupting, the key lull between periods of American expansion preceded sustained expansion on a global scale; as a result, frontier defense was even less patently segregated from the anterior security impetus by time or quality of action that it had been in either the Roman or the British empires. Moreover, it was possible for a time to identify the transfrontier threats to the American empire and its dependents with the major Communist powers, pending the rise of relatively autonomous smaller-scale imperialisms and strictly indigenous forms of disorder.

America's imperial frontier was no different in kind from those of her imperial predecessors. It was essentially an ideal notion defined by vital strategic bases and lines of communications by land, sea, and henceforth also air, for the purpose of ensuring access to both specific material assets and to immaterial influence determining the terms of such access. The United States originally denied to the Communist powers the right to recolonize areas within or adjacent to the frontier and progressively also assumed the corollary positive obligation to maintain order. Imperial American statecraft globalized in the process the two levels or stages within the Monroe Doctrine in relation to a growing range of more or less dependent lesser powers and more or less defensible "isthmian canals." The expansive thrust of the frontier-defense strategy conformed to the classic, concentric pattern of an imperial security system. It did so as the security of Western Europe became an extension of the Hemispheric-Atlantic matrix of American national security, and was upheld in ever widening circles. These encompassed progressively Greece and Turkey in the traditional Near East, as well as the wider Middle East, extending westward to North Africa and eastward by way of East Africa and the Persian Gulf to the Indian Ocean areas. The latter constituted, in turn, also the outermost fringes of America's own defenses, centered in Asia on the Japanese linchpin of the U.S. security system in the Pacific region and extending concentrically from Japan via East Asia (Korea),

Southeast Asia (Indochina), and South Asia (Pakistan-India) to Western Asia (Iran) as part of the greater Middle East. In such a scheme, Western Europe was for the United States what the Low Countries (and Portugal) had been for British security, while the Euro-Japanese industrial aggregate took the place that India had occupied as the centerpiece of Britain's empire. The forward zones of a military-political defense for Western Europe and Japan intersected in the Middle East. But since the United States was unwilling to effectively defend the traditional Near East in Eastern Europe, as had done the most energetic of anti-Russian British statecraft in the past, it had to be all the more strenuously defense-minded everywhere else.

Enlarging the scope of the Monroe Doctrine in a concentric pattern was expressed symbolically and implemented materially. The symbolism was conveyed through a globe-circling series of foreign-policy doctrines, starting off with the Truman doctrine for Greece and Turkey; extended by the Eisenhower doctrine to the Arab Middle East; continuing in the implicit Kennedy doctrine for Southeast Asia; and reverting to the Western Hemisphere in the guise of Johnson's restatement of the Roosevelt corollary for the Caribbean. Routine implementation was through American alliances and alignments; it was occasionally raised to the level of military intervention, mostly in civil strifes with international ramifications, such as those in Greece, Korea, Lebanon, the countries of former Indochina, and the Dominican Republic (following disguised actions in Guatemala and Cuba).

The interventions were but the visible tips of the iceberg, as the more than half-concealed American world empire grew in the chilling climate of a cold war. The empire gradually acquired a world-wide scope in the 1950s and 1960s, while threats to imperial-frontier security originated in the three categories of events familiar from the earlier empires. Most serious and soonest to arise were direct threats from the Communist great powers themselves, ranging in time and space from the early Soviet demands on Turkey and Iran and for the Italian colonies in North Africa to China's claims in regard to Taiwan and the offshore islands. Only somewhat less serious, if subsequently more frequent, were threats that arose from the actual or presumed association or identification of the Communist great powers with the regional imperialisms of lesser states. Such were the ambitions of Tito's Yugoslavia with respect to Greece in Southeast Europe, of North Korea in East Asia and North Vietnam in Southeast Asia, and, at one remove from Communism, of Nasser's Egypt in Lebanon and the Middle East generally, Nkrumah's Ghana in sub-Saharan Africa, Sukarno's Indonesia with respect to West New Guinea, Malaysia and the "Indonesian ocean" generally, and Castro's Cuba in the Caribbean and Latin America at large. The third category of threats, and one least apt to provoke an expansive American counteraction, comprised the breakdowns of post-colonial local authority and other forms of disorder that were largely insulated from or reliably impervious to take-over bids by foreign would-be imperial successors. Here belonged the often trivial interstate conflicts and the more violent civil-war upheavals (e.g., in the Congo and Nigeria) in Africa as well as in other parts of the turbulently modernizing Third World.

Expansive American reactions to actual or suspected threats to the imperial frontier had a general purpose and more specific objectives. The general purpose was to prevent unfriendly (or uncongenial) substitutions for receding European empires from taking root and exploiting the extra-European and anti-Western revolutionary activities that had been succes-sively fomented by the receding Japanese and the advancing Communist imperial powers. The strategically more specific objectives were several. One was to prevent the envelment and economic strangulation of Western Europe by an indirect, southern, Communist strategy by-passing the high risks of a direct military approach to Western Europe, somewhat as Napoleon had tried to circumvent Britain's insular fastness via Egypt and India. Another was to bar any development that might isolate Japan definitively from her natural strategic-economic environment in Asia. In terms of interests, free access to Western Europe and Japan was essential for American security and material well-being. If free access to Japan was the preferred alternative to unfriendly control, free access to Western Europe was required also for psychological well-being. In terms of action, safeguarding outlying Western European assets and Japan's far-flung access routes meant that American capabilities (and control) would gradually and nearly completely substitute for those of principal allies. It also meant, as a result, America's tactical emancipation from those allies. The rationale for defending vital allied interests was the two-faced one of American national security in the strict sense of territorial immunity and as ultimately tied up with the integrity and cohesion of a U.S.-centered imperial or world order. Hence, as the rationale took shape, it effaced step by step the distinction between the hemispheric core, the essential industrial segments, and the preindustrial peripheral areas, as assets and responsibilities immediately at stake.

In the actual process of American expansion, fending off suspected indirect Soviet approaches to Western Europe via Greece and Turkey and to Japan via Korea in the immediate postwar, Stalinist, period stim-ulated an American strategy of encircling the Sino-Soviet heartland by way of the Eurasian rimlands and offshore islands. In the post-Stalin period, the dynamics and the strategy of frontier defense were kept alive by Soviet efforts at counterencirclement on a global scale. The primary focus of Soviet world policy, in once-British India and her Middle East-ern and Southeast Asian defense zones, reactivated the traditional concerns of Tsarist Russia; the updated anti-Western initiatives came to be directed at least as much at Communist China, increasingly only a nominal Soviet ally and *de facto* rival, after eliciting appropriate American responses in places such as Lebanon and Laos. Insofar as Stalin had countenanced or actually inspired the North Korean military initiative against South Korea as a move to offset the rise of Mao in East Asia, that early incentive to the American defense of the imperial frontier was also the initial source of the Sino-Soviet divergence. And as the unfolding split radicalized Chinese declaratory policies, it also helped propel America's anxieties over the imperial frontier to their climax, as part of containing China proper.

A combatant U.S. involvement in the protracted Indochina conflict marked in due course the farthermost displacement toward Asia in the center of activity—even if not necessarily of gravity—of America's world empire. It also recorded the empire's inner evolution through a change in rationales. If American action in Korea had been rationalized in terms of collective security through the United Nations, the decisive reason for it had been the defense of Japan against a threat carried out from the Asian mainland under presumed Soviet auspices and with effective later Chinese participation. Intimate American decision-making, as well as public Japanese responses, were different by the time of the intervention in Indochina. Not least because North Vietnamese expansionism was only ambiguously and competitively backed by China and the Soviet Union, the protection of Japan as a motive for the increasingly controversial American response was submerged by a less clearly focused all-imperial concern to demonstrate firm opposition to ideologically neutral small-nation imperialism using the label of "wars of national liberation."

VI

As a historical fact, American expansion from a regional to a world-wide empire was due to Axis aggressions, Soviet-Communist ascendancy, and European-colonial decline. The Axis compelled the United States to fuse the hitherto disjointed strategic, economic, and institutional elements of an American-inspired world order into an at least theoretical unity in the form of sweeping wartime planning. Subsequent controversies with Soviet Russia forced wartime blueprints to be progressively concretized and adapted to evolving contingencies. And the politico-economic weakening of the European powers supplied the most critical contingency, compelling the application of essentially imperial methods on a world-wide basis.

The stage had been set for the new departure by the bankruptcy of a policy only occasionally breaching the façade of regional isolationism between the two wars; involvement being tantamount to renewed and sustained expansion had been made first possible and then unavoidable by the resumption of leadership in the second war; and the momentum was kept up by a sequence of incentives to fitfully escalating postwar interventions. Of the three steps or stages the first two were related to the regional core-empire in the Western Hemisphere more directly than the third was to be initially. Linking the first two phases was the Japanese military attack on the Hawaiian outpost of the core-empire that imparted, through the potent security incentive, a new thrust and scope to the interwar American groping for a chiefly economic liberal world order. Post–World War I dollar diplomacy had ranged from extending loans to defeated Germany in liberal doses to liberalizing the diplomacy's application to its original Caribbean testing ground (notably in the Hughes-Hoover era as part of a shift to be dramatized by Franklin Roosevelt as the "good-neighbor" policy). It took the mounting Japanese military-economic initiative in the Far East, its German counterpart in Europe, and the spread of economic depression world-wide to help demonstrate the insufficiency of geographically and functionally limited, and arbitrarily selective, responses. No less futile proved to be the interwar American effort to either promote a world security system or construct a national security system by noncommittal methods such as concerted limitation of (chiefly naval) armaments and the outlawing of aggression in tenuous association with the League of Nations on the one hand and neutrality legislation supplementing the open-door principle and supplemented by an incipient naval build-up on the other hand.

Breaking with the immediate antecedents, the approach was radically different during and after World War II. An early trend was toward renewed acquisition of bases and reservation of strategic resources, both in the old Atlantic and Pacific haunts and in the newer hunting grounds of the Middle East. What had begun before actual American belligerency, continued during it and as the spoils thereof; the wartime acquisitions were both preparatory to a shooting war with a winning Axis and resulted from the hot pursuit of the receding Fascist powers. They could still be seen as a logical completion of the core-empire so long as isolated acquisitions, or acts subversive of European colonial dominions in Asia and the Middle East, could be regarded as objectively necessary for the conduct of the war or subjectively arbitrary with an American president carried away by his war powers and projects for peace. The situation changed when attention continued to shift from the Western Hemisphere to Western Europe, Japan, and Afro-Asia in the decisive phase of expansion after the war's end. The interplay of regional and global concerns was thereafter sharply limited as well as lopsided in favor of the larger arena to the detriment of the older and narrower empire. Since the implications of the new American world posture for strategic security were least critical in the Western Hemisphere, the political and economic instruments supporting that posture favored only stintingly the area that had seen the original development of the techniques. The interplay was consequently reduced during the early postwar period mainly to the secondary, if conspicuous, institutional level of the new structure of world order whenever America's hemispheric clients supplied the initially critical votes for the automatic American majorities in the United Nations.

The actual scope of expansion was enlarged by the initial American uncertainties concerning the identity of the primary threat, Communism as an *idée-force* or Soviet Russia (and later China) as a power; of the primary theater, European or Asian; and, relatedly, the principal instruments of response, economic or military. There may have been an inconclusive drift over time toward stressing the second-named factors in each pair (Communist territorial powers, Asia, and military instruments), but the fundamental resolution of quandaries was still the expansive one of combining every menace and method in different assortments in different situations. The finally predominating principle of indivisible containment, in regard to both scope and kind of response, became a precept for action because it reflected a fact (the rise of Communist China) and a need (for a bipartisan domestic consensus on foreign policy).

Pressures for expansion were inherent in both the objects of concern and the remedial strategies, in both the conceptual dilemmas and the internal political dynamics surrounding unresolved priorities. The stimuli were only partially offset by the absence of an all-encompassing and driving, positive goal, an absence that was in turn not unrelated to the controversies over priorities, and did not materially suffer from the weakness of "subimperial" expansionists.

The actual objective was neither universal dominance for American power and principles nor total security for the nation. Just as American policy was less deliberately aimed at superseding the decaying empires of allied dependents than it was firm in resisting rival attempts at imperial succession, so the makers of policy sought less to perpetuate and more to approximate as much as practically possible the "total" security that quasi-insular America had carried over from the continental to the regional arena in the past. Least of all did the United States, as the leading representative of a particular institutional ordering of society, consistently aim at eliminating abroad all non- or antidemocratic forms of either authority or disorder as a self-sufficient purpose. American aloofness from many or most local disorders did not materially differ from either British or Roman self-limitation in that respect. But the absence of clear and sustained imperial purpose differed from both and from Roman self-affirmation in particular.

The lack of a settled purpose may have set a limit to expansion, but it also implied a handicap for the substantial expansion that occurred nonetheless. Much the same was true for the absence of successfully expansion-oriented American proconsuls abroad, with the conspicuous exception of General MacArthur, and the weak influence on major policies of bureaucratic sponsors of foreign clients at home. There was, furthermore, little scope for regionally expansionist dependents, with the qualified exception of regionally subimperial Israel and the not even partially successful militarily activated regimes in South Korea and South Vietnam. The gaps in nongovernmental subimperialism were partially filled by the preponderantly American organisms operating as multinational enterprises. They influenced economic and political conditions, not least in the peripheral areas, in ways that could supplement even unrelated politico-military incentives to official American involvement. But they were less visibly or vociferously related to American global expansion as its stimuli than had been the land speculators in Texas and Maine to continental acquisitions and the sugar planters of Hawaii to regional expansion. And the multinationals were even more dependent on the infrastructures of officially created order and security than had been their Roman and British subimperial counterparts.

At least initially more stimulating than any excess of either enterprising subimperialists or multinational enterprises was a fundamental fact of existence, similar to the emptiness of an unfamiliar continent that early Americans had turned into a stimulus to advance. Its postwar equivalent was the global vacuum of friendly power, conjoined with an intrinsically unknown major adversary with an alien ideology, an ultimate weapon with unpredictable technological and political potential, and gradually emergent minor postcolonial powers with unfamiliar cultures. If the chief adversary in particular was largely unknown, it was also unknowable in the absence of sustained interactions as part of an expansive engagement.

Ignorance, mystery, and related anxieties reduced the efficacy of limitations, including unsettled priorities and unfocused diplomacy, upon America's purpose and expansion. For instance, even if there was no *a priori* grand design to dispossess either the British or the other European empires, their replacement by American power did occur whenever economy and efficiency in defending the imperial frontier seemed to require the United States to deny the European powers the capacity to weaken the American (and presumably common) effort by holding onto assets that the Europeans could use only less effectively or at a local cost unacceptable from the global viewpoint. Culminating in the 1956 Suez crisis, the process of substitution worked most conspicuously against the British and most exasperatingly against the French empire. It was accelerated by the shrinkage in the time span between the decline of the European custodians of imperial assets and the rise of actors other than the United States capable of staging a bid for succession. The substitution was further stimulated by the related fact that, even if the United

States did not aim at an integrally democratic or any other institutionally specific order, initial local reactions to the decline of European colonial empires assumed self-consciously antithetical radical expressions that made them legitimately suspect of association with Communist (Soviet or Chinese) initiatives and intentions. The resulting frictions and expansive implications for American imperial policy were aggravated by the failure of the new nations to accept the idea of responsible reciprocity in performance and restraint vis-à-vis the United States. It did not much matter that the failure merely reproduced that of the new American nation vis-à-vis the European powers in an earlier phase.

Similarly, and most critically, if the United States neither did nor could seek total security under existing conditions, the novel technology of the nuclear setting placed a premium on locating widely dispersed land-based facilities as far from the vulnerable homeland as possible. This particular stimulus to expansion was to be gradually somewhat reduced by developments favoring mobility and fostering seaborne deterrents. But these deterrents kept also alive and reemphasized, in conjunction with lower-level military contingencies in the third-world peripheries, a recurrent phenomenon. Northern insular or quasi-insular maritime powers will tend to gravitate toward outlying continental rimlands and islands as part of a typically southern strategy to offset the advantages which are presumed to attach naturally to continental heartlands in terms of space for both creating and dispersing power and of inner lines for coordinating its projection. The United States was bound to be even less impervious to this tendency in the face of plausible dangers in the global phase than it had been immune to it earlier, when perceiving less real indigenous or extraneous threats to continental or regional security.

When it came to delimiting the scope of American expansion, more important practically than any continuities in motives were the actual interactions of global and regional concerns. The interplay, initially lopsided to the detriment of the old relative to the new empire, began to be equalized as soon as the defense of the world empire's frontiers gravitated back to America's regional orbit. It was the Cuban crisis that assimilated the Western to the Eastern Hemisphere in terms of the quality of threat (strategic Soviet, as contrasted with the ideological Communist one previously agitated in Guatemala), of stake (parity with the Soviet Union in nuclear capability and imperial status), of context (third-world revolutionary), and of American response (massive aid program to potential targets). The Cuban crisis at the antipodes to Indochina expanded the scope of world-imperial politics to its extreme range, drawing attention to the possibility that America was overextending herself to the detriment of concerns nearer home. The crisis started in the depths the process of restriction even before the involvement in Indochina, the be-

ginnings of which predated the Cuban imbroglios, brought the retrenchment syndrome into the open. America's being countercontained by
Soviet-backed revolutionary forces in the Western Hemisphere threatened to complete the diplomatic countercontainment under way in
Western Europe with the aid of traditionalist, or Gaullist, tendencies.
The immediate American response was to renew emphasis on the
Western Hemisphere, most conspicuously through the so-called Alliance
for Progress. The partial redressal of priorities between globe and region
did not immediately extend to their reversal, however. Any such further
step would follow only a prior regression from essentially liberal imperial
to more constraining imperialistic policies in a narrowed regional scope.
Intensified constraints, marking the retreat from world-wide to regional
empire, would aim at containing either revolutionary infection (from the
third Afro-Asian as well as the second Communist worlds) or also conventional attractions (from industrial Europe and Japan) in the region.
Either form of penetration would have been prepared by the preceding
degree of dissolution of the American core-empire in the larger imperial
setting; and it would be positively responded to in the southern part of
the hemisphere as either counterpoising American dominion or compensating for American abandonment.

VII

The American regional core-empire retained a measure of separate
identity within the world empire. It was also the subject of a special
concern that reemerged as a check on further expansion when preoccupation with regional security had exhausted its earlier stimulative effect.
The continuing distinctness of the inner zone points to a major difference between the American and the Roman empires as regards their
universality, but the relation between core-empire and world empire
points up more generally both similarities and differences among the
Roman, British, and American empires with respect to their structure
and scope, and their kind.

The American empire has expanded concentrically, from the continent
by way of the two-regional empire in the Western Hemisphere into a
global scope focused on the metropole. So did, basically, the Roman
empire, from Rome-Latium by way of Italy and, when Carthage had
been subdued, from the resulting Western Mediterranean core in all
directions. By contrast, the British insular metropole formed the core of
only a microcosmic imperial security system, extending to the north- and
southwestern coastal reaches of the European continent. Notably the
second British overseas empire was excentric in relation to the metropole,
while spreading out concentrically around its Indian core. This meant
that the central, i.e., European, balance of power was interposed between
the insular metropole and the imperial core (India) both spatially—as a

matter of geography—and systemically—as a matter of politico-military interactions. Nothing comparable intervened between Rome's Western Mediterranean core-empire and the critical balance-of-power system in the Eastern Mediterranean, while the Europe-centered global balance of power intervened only systemically and not spatially between the American core-empire and the adjoining regional balances of power in the Atlantic and the Pacific. The last-mentioned interposition applied, moreover, only so long as the central balance of power, not yet comprising the United States, conditioned the operation of the regional systems more directly than did the United States as marginal participant or wholly passive background factor in the regional interplays.

The British-type interposition of a balance-of-power system between metropole and the dependencies tended to deflect expansion into creating a colonial-peripheral rather than a central-systemic empire. Next to its direction and result, the configuration affected also the scope of expansion, if more ambiguously. On the one hand, interactions with the central balance-of-power system were apt to stimulate expansion overseas by supplying motive, mechanism, and momentum. In the British case, the pervasive basic motive was to make up for the intrinsic weakness and comparative vulnerability of the home base. The mechanism was illustrated by the eighteenth-century war- and peace-making, requiring the British to compensate by conquests overseas for French gains in Europe; modified in and after the wars with Napoleon, it remained favorable to Britain in end-result. And a continuing momentum resulted from changes in primary continental rivals, from France to Russia and Germany, each successive rivalry fostering concurrent overseas competition. On the other hand, the dualistic configuration of metropole and empire and the consequent problems of priority tended also to limit the scope of imperial expansion. Concern for the efficacy of strategies for home security, linked to the adjoining European balance-of-power system, placed a limit upon securing India expansively. Available resources had to be carefully allocated and acceptable risks weighed. It was just as risky to spoliate and alienate a potentially valuable European ally in the colonial realm as it was to overburden tolerance for disparities between a policy of balance in Europe and a tendency to colonial-cum-maritime monopoly overseas. British colonial restitutions after the Napoleonic wars, for instance, were a partial offset to indebted continental allies for adopting British ideas on the law and the actual command of the seas.

The combination of stimulation and limitation wrought by the interposed balance-of-power system was the result of Britain's inability to supersede the central system either before or after being drawn into its conflictual interactions as a balancer of sorts. The relatively more powerful Roman and American core-empires extended their control to the central balance-of-power system as they were drawn in by conflicts within that system. Rome acted more decisively than America, and may have had the easier task in relation to the inchoate and lopsided all-Mediterranean and Eastern Mediterranean balances of power. Moreover, the relative distance (even as conditioned by different technologies) between the metropole and the central balance was greater in America's than in Rome's case, while both the (only systemically interposed) central European system and the (geographically adjacent) regional Atlantic and Pacific systems enjoyed a relatively greater initial degree of autonomy and self-sufficiency than had their Mediterranean counterparts in antiquity. These differences help explain why, in contrast with Rome, the principal lull preceded American expansion into the central system and extended even beyond the tentative false start of that expansion in World War I.[3] In addition, the western and the eastern offshore semicircles in the regional American core-empire were more uniform, in both kind of powers or forces and controlling strategic concepts, than had been the far-western barbarian and the civilized eastern segments in the Roman empire. The Roman imperial expansion in the two sectors was in consequence less synchronized as to sequence and more unevenly coercive in style than had been the American. But the difference was less significant for the final scope of expansion in the aggregate, and less significant overall, than was the similarity between Roman and American empires when compared with the British empire in regard to the alternative, concentric and excentric, basic configurations of an imperial metropole and the dependent empire.

The scope of British imperial expansion was an almost self-adjusting compromise result of constant latent, and occasionally manifest, tension between stimulation and limitation, compensations and complications, deriving from the intervening balance-of-power system. In the British-type configuration, moreover, the empire became less of a threat and more of a temptation and a target for other expansionist states when the maximum scope of the empire's expansion consistent with the overall balance of power had prompted a shift from a preclusively expansive to a more passively defensive stance. By comparison, the scope of the American and Roman empires was more a function of a one-time shift or transition from one extreme to another. The geographically coherent and continuous structures of the two core-empires entailed a considerable safety margin and warning time against massive threats consequent on breakdowns of the balance of power in the outer zone. That condition made it possible in principle to prolong self-confinement indefinitely,

---

3. In Rome the lull occurred after the annexationist consolidation of the core-empire, including Carthage and the Illyrian coast, *and* the extension of indirect influence into the Eastern Mediterranean, following the defeats of Macedon and the roll-back of Syria; in Britain it occurred following the defeat of Napoleon, when the insular security system was already paralleled by a far-flung, if uncompleted, colonial empire on a global scale.

while its very strength represented both a threat and a target for powerful and ambitious actors tempted to seek stability through symmetry by replacing constraints from a balance of power with a core-empire of their own. Since the existing Roman and American core-empires constituted a basis for dealing effectively with such actors and attempts, they were actually subject to an intrinsically unlimited expansive dynamic, tending toward the supersession of critical balance-of-power systems.

When realizing that tendency to an uneven degree, both Rome and the United States profited from disunities among the major (Hellenistic and European) actors in the central balance-of-power system. They were drawn eastward by the actions of, and responses to, a power looking in two directions: Macedon, facing the Illyrian coast and the adjacent sea and the continental Greek state system; and Germany, with eyes on both the world oceans and *Mitteleuropa*. In this fashion, both Macedon and Germany were liable to act as links between arenas that might otherwise have remained separate. Whereas Macedon linked the Eastern and the Western Mediterranean, Germany mediated between the European center of the global system and the regional Atlantic system (via alliance or conflict with Britain before World War I) and between the Atlantic and the Pacific regional theaters (mainly diplomatically before World War I and in World War II also militarily, by way of the alliance with Japan that was as opportunistic and casually implemented as had been Macedon's with Carthage in the Second Punic War). Macedon and Germany were consequently the critical symbols, even if they were not the only effective causes, of the ultimate impossibility of keeping indefinitely separate the several segments of the respective balance-of-power systems in the period before being themselves partitioned.

The inseparability enhanced, and was further enhanced by, the feeling in both Rome and the United States that preeminence or hegemony in the core-empire area—the Western Mediterranean and the Western Hemisphere—was insufficient so long as it was exposed to the possibility of an adverse distribution of power in the larger, all-Mediterranean or Atlantic-Pacific global, theaters. An imbalance could be due in both cases to a power aggregation, combining by conquest or collusion the major Eastern land powers: Macedon and Syria, and Germany and Russia or, after World War II, also Russia and China. Such aggregations risked overwhelming the weakened or declining, predominantly maritime, powers: Rhodes and Egypt in the Eastern Mediterranean and Britain in the Atlantic and either immediately or ultimately (next to Japan) also in the Pacific. Macedon and Germany remained comparable when, after their first defeats, they became the foci of an only artificially restabilized distribution of power. As such, they became also the sources of possible upheavals, with critical bearing on the central challenge or dilemma facing the two imperial powers so long as they remained poised between incipient and accomplished empire. How was either of them to consolidate a preeminence short of hegemony in the overall system with respect to inferior powers located within the radius of war-won control and to independent major powers outside it? And, failing that, how was the imperial power to confine the geographic scope of an ultimately unavoidable hegemony to limits that would be consistent with its material capabilities and political dispositions?

If the structures of power facing Rome and the United States were similar, their fundamental dispositions—or spirit—were not. The disparity accounted for the differences in results, including the maximum scope of expansion, while one of its possible sources was in expansion's sequence. Roman involvements in the Western and Eastern Mediterranean succeeded one another in time (despite the casual Macedon-Carthage alliance in the Second Punic War); and hegemony in the West was secure before Rome tackled, or was drawn into, the Hellenistic balance of power in the Eastern Mediterranean (from which the yet unconquered far-western "barbarians" were—and were to remain—separate in terms of a system-like interconnection). The American involvement, too, was successive if it is traced from the supersession of Britain in the Western Hemisphere, via America's militant involvement in the Atlantic balance of power in World War I, to engagement in the Pacific theater in World War II. But unlike Carthage's in the Western Mediterranean, Britain's opposition in the Western Hemisphere was too weak, and America's first involvement among the modern European equivalents of the Hellenistic great powers too inconclusive, to shape lasting dispositions. If World War II is, therefore, taken as decisive for the transition of the United States from core-empire to world empire, simultaneity rather than sequence will characterize American involvements in the Atlantic and the Pacific balances of power. A militarist (Shinto) Japan expanding into China in the Pacific theater becomes the analogue to Spain-centered (Hannibalic) Carthage, transformed in the more testing Second Punic War to the point of becoming almost as different from the conservative-mercantile Carthaginian empire of the First Punic War as the Britain of the 1890s was from the Japan of the 1930s and early 1940s.

The Carthage-Japan analogy takes fully into account the Pacific bias of America's Western Hemispheric core-empire. The Western Hemisphere proper becomes Rome's Italy-cum-Sicily won in the First Punic war; and, if the Western Mediterranean is equated with the Pacific theater, the Atlantic assumes—or retains—the position of the Eastern Mediterranean in the earlier context. But, in the absence of sequential involvement, the United States did not enter the decisive struggle with Nazi Germany and Soviet Russia over succession to European world empires steeled by a prior life-and-death struggle with Japan and matured by the consequent organization of a West-Pacific empire on Japan's ruins, any more than it had been tempered previously by the much milder contest with Britain over the Western Hemisphere when entering the "Hellenic" European world militantly for the first time.

The resulting difference in spirit between Rome and the United States reduced the significance of the substantial similarities in structures and the superficial similarity in time sequences. In the aftermath of their respective wars with Philip V of Macedon and Imperial Germany, both powers attempted first to withdraw from direct political control and peacetime involvement in the culturally imposing Graeco-European world to the East. They attempted to preside instead over world order at little or no cost, in contrast to their greater readiness to entrench themselves in the Mediterranean-Pacific West. There is a difference, though. Rome had withdrawn from locally irritating direct control conditionally, as a matter of a calculation anticipating the conflict with Syria further east and sustained by a contrived balance of power among the Greeks. The post-Wilsonian United States withdrew as a matter of mood or doctrine and its isolation was sustained by nothing better than widespread disenchantment in America and a precariously contained disequilibrium of mobilized and potential power in Europe. Whereas Rome gambled on the possibility of absentee preeminence, the United States gambled on the safety of absence—on the mere chance that preclusive reinvolvement might not again become necessary or could be resisted on the strength of the new awareness wrung from the earlier loss of innocence.

The difference in spirit became manifest—and conditioned the scope of ultimate American expansion—when the United States failed to extend political influence to Eastern Europe over Soviet opposition in and after World War II. The United States did not reproduce the refusal of ascendant Rome to tolerate equal or near-equal great-power adversaries outside as well as inside her immediate regional orbit and, consequently, to accept as permanent any line of separation between the Roman orbit and the spheres of other great powers in the Eastern Mediterranean, any more than before in the Western. If anything, the American-Russian relationship inverted the earlier disparity between the forceful style of the Romans and the hesitancies of their Hellenistic opponents. If the United States was not another Rome as regards invariably resolute self-assertion, Stalin's Russia replicated Antioch's Syria in relative geopolitical location but not in indecisiveness of purpose. The differences showed as the two modern powers contested—like the ancient ones, with the aid of inflated propaganda—each other's influence over the contemporary equivalents of Eastern and Western, Asiatic and European, Greeks. In the classic setting, the lesser parties had stimulated the climactic Roman-Syrian conflict only to fall within Rome's virtually universal empire in the Mediterranean world. Remote and irreducible Parthia-Persia stood for China rather than Russia in the modern setting. As part of the latter, the lesser powers in both Western and Eastern Europe were caught up within not one but two hegemonial spheres and, in addition, in a protracted contest over the question of whether parity between the two superpowers, or else either one's preeminence or hegemony, was to define the overall global theater in due course. It was that conflict which stimulated American world-wide expansion but also limited its scope short of a universal one.

If the parallels with the Roman empire are in the last analysis superficial, the parallels with the British empire are largely nominal. Both the British global and the American regional empires were somehow related to interactions among four great powers. The earlier ones, beginning with the mid-eighteenth century, had involved Britain, France (or the Franco-Spanish alliance), Austria, and Prussia (replacing the United Provinces). Beginning with the 1890s, the key great powers were Britain, Germany, Russia (or the Russo-French alliance), and Japan. Unlike England, the United States was not directly included in either of the two quadripartite processes. It had emerged to independence from the early Franco-British interactions as the benefitting third party, and became the only latent, if codetermining, background factor in the later Anglo-German and the Anglo-Japanese relationships. The resulting American-British-German triangle especially was a close modern parallel to the tripartite Anglo-Dutch-French pattern in the seventeenth century. In both periods, the relatively declining maritime power (the United Provinces in the first instance, the United Kingdom in the second) played an ambiguous role at first between the navally ambitious major land power (first France, then Germany) and the ascendant sea power (Great Britain in the first case and the United States in the second), only to opt finally for accommodation with the more congenial sea power.

The choices had major consequences for the ensuing phases in world politics. Repeating what it had done previously for England, the three-power interplay Europeanized American foreign policy, even if not at once also the United States itself. The growing sense of affinities on the part of the American political elites for the British counterparts and their viewpoints did in that respect what dynastic associations (via the Dutch king and the Hanoverian dynasty) had done for assimilating the continental viewpoint into British foreign policy. Moreover, as it reproduced the pattern of the earlier interplay, the later interplay revitalized the result of the former by globalizing anew the regulation of the European (or Eurocentric) balance of power—even if globalizing the balance itself in full was left over for World War II and its sequelae.

Most of the time Britain had been actively involved as a direct participant and link in the simultaneously operative balance-of-power system and related conflicts and alignments. Conversely, for a long time the United States was largely remote and absent from comparable transactions, much as those transactions had conditioned American expansionism before an expanded United States itself became a key catalyst in defining the diplomatic options open to other powers and eventually also the source of a potentially crucial military capability in major conflicts. A related difference bore on strength. When involved, the relative strength of the United States was greater than Britain's had been when sprawling Russia and compact Germany replaced a sprawling Spain-centered conglomerate and compact France as primary rivals. A matching escalation had the United States face Imperial Germany with Austria-Hungary, followed by National-Socialist Germany with Japan, and the latter two by Soviet Russia (with Communist China), within concurrently expanding areas of disputed control. America's material advantages enabled her to match the growth in antagonistic power with more expansion for the United States, resulting in a concentric empire unlike the excentric British one. But, being both stronger and geographically more remote from rivals than Britain, the United States was also better qualified for the alternative British-type option of "splendid isolation."

Aloofness from the central balance of power expressed repeatedly the national reluctance to pursue actively a mere equilibrium. American statecraft would not follow the British into becoming bogged down in a both frustrating and, given America's ultimate immunity or self-dependence, seemingly unnecessary role of balancer over an indefinite period of time. Isolation as a theoretical option and recoil from participation as instinctive disposition combined with inherent material strength to contain the American will-to-power and confine its manifestation to intermittent expansion. Abstention prevailed whenever no imminent and major adversary threat dictated otherwise; propensity to expand was blunted by attributes and circumstances different from Rome's, mainly in the realm of spirit, but also of structure when the growing size or potency of America's successive adversaries is contrasted with the declining strength of Rome's in the period between Barcid Carthage and much-later Sassanid Persia.

The fundamental starting difference between Britain and the United States was that the English had not established, during or at any time after the Hundred Years' War with the French, a sufficient continental base for directly dominating the central system. The actual bearing of the difference was reduced by the American failure to consolidate a dominion in continental Eurasia to the detriment of Soviet Russian (and Chinese) counterforce. One result was the survival of a balance of power in Europe, albeit subordinate to the American and Russian wing powers, after the European balance had worked one-sidedly in favor of British colonial expansion and American continental expansion. The American confinement in Western Europe came to resemble the limitation of Britain's overlordship there to the northwestern Low Countries in the period before Britain herself lapsed into the condition reminiscent of once-imperial Holland's. The United States was as a result likewise diverted to the peripheral realms outside Europe as a way of dealing with, if not compensating for, the limitation. The diversion occurred in ways and for reasons sufficiently different from Britain's to modify only marginally the preponderantly Rome-like, central-systemic character of the American empire. But the remaining measure of similarity with the peripherally situated colonial empire had implications for style of action and solidity of achievement as well as for its scope. It helped account for the failure of the expansionist tendencies implicit in a concentric structure to work themselves out in the American case as fully as they had in the Roman.

Rome and the United States were alike in opposing the concentration of any Eastern power to the detriment of either the Greek or the European balance of power in physically comparable, Mediterranean and Atlantic, geopolitical settings. Rome's opposition was rationalized by defining as a just war any defense of lesser-power friends and allies against stronger powers. As the United States grew into a military imperial power on a world scale, it adopted a comparable principle less unequivocally and applied it less decisively. In the Anglo-American context, the principle of just equilibrium helped translate only nominally similar structures into comparable concrete reactions to powers aiming to combine naval ambitions with an indefinitely expansible continental base —Germany in Europe and Japan in Asia. Such a power would be automatically superior to narrow-based Britain, and even a merely psychic threat of unwonted parity in both land- and sea-based power could evolve into a real threat for the United States in conjunction with intensified industrial-commercial competition and technological transformation. In the final analysis, the American expansion was structurally a replica of the Roman up to a point, beyond which it tended to subside into British-type molds and limits. The expansion was stimulated by the reception into American statecraft of Britain's cardinal preventive principle, after it ceased being a reaction to Britain's expansive practices in the Western Hemisphere; and the expansion's scope was determined by the only partial revival of Roman principles in regard to major adversaries and lesser clients.

Defined from two sides and conditioned by both structure and spirit, the process of American expansion from core-empire to world empire produced a provisional result intermediate between the two antecedent extremes. One is outright domination and ordering of the central international system, consummating in full-scale hegemony the tendencies implicit in the precariousness of mere preeminence. Another is the mere balancing of forces in the central system from an off-shore insular position reinforced marginally in the central system and more substantially at its periphery. If the first pattern transposed onto the global stage the tendencies which the United States manifested previously on the North American continent and in the southern reaches of the Western Hemisphere, the latter reflected the kind of recoil before effective opposition which had previously saved British Canada from inclusion in the North American continental empire.[4]

4. The most useful sources on the international determinants of American expansion include: Albert K. Weinberg, *Manifest Destiny* (Baltimore: The Johns Hopkins University Press, 1935); Richard W. Van Allstyne, *The Rising American Empire* (New York: Oxford University Press, 1960); Walter LaFeber, *The New Empire* (Ithaca: Cornell University Press, 1963); John M. Blum et al., *The National Experience* (New York: Harcourt, Brace and World, 1963); Julius W. Pratt, *Expansionists of 1898* (New York: P. Smith, 1951); Howard K. Beale, *Theodore Roosevelt and the Rise of America to World Power* (Baltimore: Johns Hopkins Press, 1956); John A. Garraty, *Henry Cabot Lodge* (New York: Alfred A. Knopf, 1965); Akira Iriye, *Across the Pacific* (New York: Harcourt, Brace and World, 1967); R. G. Neale, *Great Britain and United States Expansion 1898–1900* (East Lansing: Michigan State University Press, 1966); Kenneth Bourne, *Britain and the Balance of Power in America* (London: Longmans, Green, 1967); Johns A. S. Grenville and George Berkeley Young, *Politics, Strategy, and American Diplomacy* (New Haven: Yale University Press, 1966); George Monger, *The End of Isolation* (London: Thomas Nelson and Sons, 1963); William A. Williams, *The Tragedy of American Diplomacy* (New York: Dell, 1962); and Walter LaFeber, *America, Russia and the Cold War 1945–1971* (New York: Wiley, 1972).

VII

AMERICAN EXPANSION.
Domestic Dynamics

A genuine threat to security was a late international determinant of American expansion to world empire, having been preceded by predation and by preclusion of more or less spurious threats. By contrast, internal political conditions impinged on expansion from its continental beginnings, although in varying degrees and fashions. Independence from the British empire was acquired and the initial movement westward followed within the general framework of a hierarchically graduated social equilibrium. The populace acknowledged the elite's capacity to lead for survival and security in the already colonized areas, while a degree of friction between elite and populace made expansion beyond those areas into a condition of social peace and stability. Later expansion was sustained less unequivocally and continuously by domestic factors, in the form of an outward projection of identifiable pressures, conflicts, and deadlocks involving a well-defined ruling class, an ascendant middle class, and a progressively activated popular mass. But domestic interclass, or intergroup, dynamic as a process, and domestic political stability as a purpose, were nonetheless present as subsidiary incentives to expansion. They supplemented predation and preemption of real or imaginary security threats in a secondary role routinely, and sporadically superseded or mediated either of the two original determinants. They did so notably outside the continent, when the ruling-class factor asserted itself in ways which, though modified or even diluted, were reminiscent of earlier Roman and British patterns.

I

The very notion of a ruling class can be used in relation to the American experience only very loosely. There are impressive conceptual and philosophic obstacles to the application of both the class (as against the elite) concept and the ruling (as against governing or political) function. In most of the American experience, the notion of a class cannot evoke any firm idea of unity as distinct from mere uniformity among members. Unity is commonly based on shared economic, educational, familial or any other background, but shared functional experience and acquired social style will suffice to engender relative uniformity in individual mores and group consciousness. And the attribute "ruling," denoting the role or activity of a class, must be in that same experience reduced from anything approaching dictation to mere coordination of particular purposes and management of group conflicts within institutional constraints. Sufficiently scaled down, however, the notion of a ruling class is no less useful than is any substitute term, such as "governing elite"; nor does it connote merely administrative or bureaucratic specialization. Any revaluation of the ruling class as concept, and any weakness of it as phenomenon, will be communicated to its correlate, the middle class. The two depend more frequently than not on competitive interaction for external identity and internal cohesion. Conversely, to deflate the ruling-class notion and correspondingly inflate the middle-class concept will depreciate the concept of the popular masses. No more helpful than ideologically inspired definitions of the middle class (e.g., as capitalistic bourgeoisie) will be denegations of the existence of such popular masses in the United States in favor of an all-encompassing middle class. A middle class may be simply identified by its position, as the group situated at any one time between a higher or upper layer and a lower stratum socially and economically and, most of the time, also politically and functionally.

Retaining the term "ruling class" is not the same as asserting that the role of the corresponding group in American experience and expansion has been either identical in kind or equal in weight with the role of its counterparts in the Roman and British imperial settings. The American colonial elite displayed the rudiments of the classic cleavage between a land-owning ruling class and a mercantile middle class, in the form of the Southern feudal slavocracy on one side and of the Northeastern merchant oligarchy on the other. And the Roman-British pattern of domestic dynamics might have been *grosso modo* reenacted if the Southern landed aristocracy had firmly asserted itself as the national ruling class, to be only progressively challenged by an ascendant northern mercantile class, and if the contest had been devoid of the distracting slavery issue. Instead, the early American polity was more realistically differentiated between two basic social types: authentic or self-perceived aristocrats or oligarchs, facing urban and rural artisans and operators. That differentiation did not sufficiently coincide with the dominial-mercantile cleavage, however, nor was it sufficiently controlling politically, to compensate for the insufficient crystallization and continuity of a landed—or any other —ruling class steadily interacting with comparably well-defined lower orders.

The ruling-class deficiency was due to historical events as much as to political institutions and to socioeconomic ideals and realities. Historically, so-called proprietary rule had aborted as the principal formula of prerevolutionary colonization and, consequently, the fountainhead for an authentic Americanized landed aristocracy. Thereafter, the Americans loyal to the British empire failed to preserve themselves in the War of Independence and, more importantly, the secessionist colonial elite failed to form itself into a unified political class capable of withstanding either its own economically conditioned heterogeneity (evolving into the Federalist-Republican cleavage) or a soon-following first status revolution (implicit in the Jacksonian onslaught). The War of Independence was itself an insufficiently testing collective ordeal to crystallize a traditional political elite endowed with a distinctive unifying ethos by its own formative experience and with an unquestioned trusteeship position by a grateful and yet unformed populace. That particular sterility of the constituent event of the American Republic aggravated the actually occurring degree of economic differentiation and diffusion. And the vaguely felt consequent vacuum was hospitable at a later date to a substitutive mythology, glorifying next to the Founding Fathers the Constitution itself.

The initial cleavage within the ruling class helped the existing social mobility to a political expression, while helping to convert the original composite ruling class gradually into a disempowered social caste. Social mobility in the United States was a function of physical mobility westward, it was rationalized by an egalitarian ethos, and it was kept alive institutionally by the developing mass-based electoral system and the professionally managed political party system. Whereas a strong elective Executive was a hindrance to the creation or recreation of an independent collective ruling class, socially mobile egalitarianism depressed the level of preeminence or privilege that could be either institutionalized or openly avowed. But the ostensibly complementary individualistic ethos simultaneously gave free rein to differentiating both actual power and acquired status in fact. Such differentiation was matched by growing specialization of function as industrial society kept developing in conditions of economic change and instability. The variety and salience of the consequently expanding specialized elites and functional hierarchies militated steadily against both the rise and the recognition of an identifiable political ruling class, standing above both social and functional hierarchies as a tribute to the paramount social utility of its particular specialization.

The actual tendency was to discount or deny the existence of anything approaching a ruling class with inherited or acquired upper-class social status. Within a correspondingly expanded definition, the middle class became an ever more inclusive occupational category and a generic social-class term for virtually all Americans. But the ideologically posited civic uniformity was at least partially contradicted by social and political realities. Although it became commonplace to affirm the existence of social pluralism and consequent diffusion of political influence, not least within local communities, action in the national and international arenas entailed clearly the application of power, graduated hierarchically and productive of a degree of cohesion and complicity at the higher levels. If the cohesion was not one of a hereditary socioeconomic class, it was that of a functional political class or at least coterie. America experienced a succession of thus loosely defined ruling classes (or ruling-class generations), both before and after the Civil War. The several "generations" differed from one another in dominant social and economic characteristics, and even the variably important economic components of a political ruling class varied in predominant type as mercantile, industrial, financial, and managerial elites succeeded one another. But, again, any such discontinuities were mitigated, and the rags-to-riches frontier myth was contradicted, by the successive elites displaying a considerable degree of uniformity and continuity in their (relatively high) inherited socioeconomic standing and their (Anglo-Saxon) ethnic background.

The most important paradox is to be found elsewhere, however. The bulk of the traditional, or old-stock, social upper class—more or less plausibly deriving from the original political ruling class—may have lapsed into a rigid and politically irrelevant social caste. But the individual "aristocrat" as political leader and popular demagogue has been all the more crucially in evidence at critical junctures of American politics and expansion. He was present, furthermore, on the strength of a recognition from below that his special, status-related presumptive aptitudes were relevant to particular situations; the recognition itself reflected the fluctuation in social needs and, consequently, valued critical skills in even the most fluid or mobile and ostensibly classless society. The conclusion is inescapable. If the American social structure has been sufficiently ambiguous as to allow individuals and groups of variably ancient stock to attribute to themselves aristocratic status without imposing much strain on an officially classless society; and if mass attitudes to political leadership have been sufficiently ambiguous as to allow a doctrinal repudiation of the idea of a ruling class to coexist with an occasionally keen popular receptivity to authentic or self-perceived individual aristocrats as having a special fitness to lead and, in effect, rule the body politic, then the ruling-class factor cannot be discarded as wholly irrelevant to American experience and, as part of it, to expansion.

Historical conditions and the social structure rendered the role of the ruling-class factor less than central and continuous. But the role was intermittently all the more critical for that very reason. The career of American expansion has not been either parallel or coterminous with a constituent, empire-building ruling class as it had been to a considerable degree in the Roman and British cases. But, if the two did not coincide, they intersected at critical—quite possibly mid-career—junctures in ways that helped extend expansion beyond the scope that can be sufficiently accounted for by the working of either acquisitive (or predatory) drive or defensive (or preclusive) instinct.[1]

II

The complexion and the corresponding dominant ethos of the American and the Roman and British ruling classes were sufficiently different to shape differently the critical three-fold enlargements of the material payoffs, the political system, and the ideal concept of empire. Moreover, in the American case, substantial enlargements preceded rather than followed expansion into oceanic core-empire, owing to the scope offered by a vast continent and a steady flow of immigration from the outside. Consequently, the effects of the enlargements on both the ruling class and expansion also tended to be different and, if anything, more ambiguous.

Material payoffs, as stakes of concern to the ruling class of the moment, increased in the American as in the other cases with territorial expansion and economic development. But their effect as an added incentive to further expansion, corrupting elite performance and ethos, was muted by the essentially materialist character of the American ethos itself. Apart from the early quasi-feudal undertones derived from European antecedents, the rapidly ascendant ethos was one of individual enterprise and of material success as both the consequence and the evidence of personal worth and virtue. Whether described as Whig ethic or Protestant-capitalist ethic, the value system differed fundamentally from the patently corruptible idealistic-military ethos of the empire-formative Roman ruling class; it differed also, if more subtly, from the British

1. On the problem of the "ruling class" in general and in America in particular, see T. R. Bottomore, *Elites and Society* (London: Penguin, 1967); Robert Wilkinson, ed., *Governing Elites* (New York: Oxford, 1969); Arnold M. Rose, *The Power Structure* (New York: Oxford, 1967); C. Wright Mills, *The Power Elite* (New York: Oxford, 1956); Suzanne Keller, *Beyond the Ruling Class* (New York: Random House, 1963); G. William Domhoff, *The Higher Circles* (New York: Random House, 1970); and Edward D. Baltzell, *The Protestant Establishment* (New York: Random House, 1964), and *Philadelphia Gentlemen* (Glencoe: Free Press, 1958).

mercantile ethos, so long as material acquisitiveness was constrained in Britain by the feudal-aristocratic values or pretensions of a well-rooted landed aristocracy. Acts and attitudes transpired in the American experience that might pass for individual corruption. They included the land speculations of the Founding Fathers (e.g., Benjamin Franklin's in the Ohio Valley), comparable activities of later senators (e.g., speculations in Texas land and scrips by the pro-annexationists in the 1840s), and still later associations between political and economic interests with respect to areas eligible for annexation (e.g., Hawaii and Cuba up to the 1890s). Such abuses inspired latter-day aristocratic critics (such as Brooks Adams) to equate the business-connected senatorial class in the United States with its corrupt analogue in late-Republican Rome. But, within a materialistic social context, financial and similar operations did not in themselves denote a marked deterioration of the ruling class and debasement of the early imperial system.

Enlarging the material stakes and potential payoffs promoted expansion directly. The connection became more ambiguous whenever it was not individual advantage that was concerned, but the well-being of the increasingly complex economic system in fact or in action-controlling suppositions. Such was to be increasingly the case at the later stages of regional and global expansion.

A similar situation prevailed in connection with the enlargement of the political system. Expanding effective participation was in the American political system (unlike the Roman and British) congruent with the spirit of its laws, while being impeded by initial oligarchical practice and comparable later inhibitions. The early inhibitions actually favored expansion by stimulating the westward movement in search of more democratic self-government and individual autonomy locally, and of solid property basis for effective exercise of civic rights nationally. Whenever this happened, a horizontally unfolding sociopolitical diffusion across the continent supplemented the relatively weak hierarchical crystallization of ruling class, middle class, and popular mass. Intense divisions and interactions along the vertical social-class axis had been a key factor in expanding the political systems of the older empires and, concurrently, their external domains. But even a smaller measure of class differentiation and both intra- and interclass competition sufficed to help enlarge somewhat the American political system. The process had begun with the seminal rivalry after 1800 between the still-aristocratic Jeffersonian Republicans and the no-longer purely elitist "young" Federalists, revolving around party organization and electoral agitation; and it was taken one step further in the 1820s by the Jacksonian Democrats in the first bid for leadership by an emerging middle class. When competition was more than usually intense it tended to reflect greater than usual social and political malaise or even crisis. The crisis was sectional in the mid-1840s, civic in the later 1890s, economic in the early 1930s, and racial in the 1960s. And the consequently expanded or intensified effective participation in the political process tended also to coincide with war and external expansion, in an uncertain relationship between cause and effect and between an expansionist party platform and its actual significance for electoral victory or defeat.

When only economic and social-class divisions or distinctions had been involved, the premium of full political participation had been secondary to the prize of an easy access to land or to other material goods. Having a part in the political process became more conspicuously at stake as a value in itself when ethnic and racial disparities and divisions came to the fore. These also raised to the fullest extent the threat of dilution for the ruling class, previously contained within the ethnic compass of Americans of English or Anglo-Saxon descent. The mere danger of an enlarged political system mobilizing the so-called hyphenate Americans tended to enlarge the concept of a ruling class to encompass, in the nativist view, all Americans of Anglo-Saxon origins, regardless of social status and political function. The tendency was to be of importance for the international posture of the United States, notably in regard to Europe's wars in the twentieth century.

The rise of ethnically or racially alien Americans promoted American expansion by one kind of Anglo-Saxon reaction (overseas imperialism) and impeded expansion by another reaction (continentalism or isolationism). The common denominator lay in the entity that could be the object of the third and final enlargement in the peculiar American context. Since no traditional ruling class was continuously identified with world-wide expansion, it was not an accomplished empire that could be exalted into an ideal defender of the ruling class against dilution and dispossession. Instead, it was the Anglo-Saxon element itself that was idealized and amplified into an inclusive ruling class.

On that basis, the strategy of class defense could choose between two empire-related formulas. It could take the form of identifying with one early American conception of empire, connoting independence from Britain and uniqueness as an example for the world at large. This strategy pointed to opposition to annexations outside the North American continent and isolation from Europe or, at least, the European continent. Or the defense strategy could take the form of positive identification with the British empire or of its competitive imitation. It was then part of a still more ancient tradition antedating independence and pointing to imperial expansion overseas. The natural isolation and the primitive nature of the early Roman and English polities had facilitated the association of their imperial growth with a ruling class concurrently evolving from a trusteeship position. By contrast, America's reactive isolationism as well as her imitative imperialism overseas were related to more or less intense traumas of both authentic and imaginary Anglo-Saxon elites resisting submersion in the more primitive, at once recent and ethnically alien, segment of the enlarged American political system.

Ethnic nativism opened a gap and engendered tension or outright conflict between the constituent national ethos and subsequent practice. It did so more acutely than could any form or expression of economic materialism and may have had an at least equal, if more indirect or reactive, effect on expansionism while it was in force. But the more fatal and lasting gap was between the ethos peculiar to a particular ruling class and the reality reflecting or affecting its performance. One such gap opened ultimately between the Washington-Hamiltonian feudal-aristocratic ethos, mercantilist in the stress on managed organic growth and unqualifiedly elitist in denying responsibility downward for such management, and the open geoeconomic frontier and related political democracy in the West; another, between the Jefferson-Jacksonian ethos of rural democracy and the expanding commercial-industrial order; and yet another between the succeeding free-enterprise capitalist ethos and the (temporary) closing of the economic frontier in the series of economic depressions culminating in the 1930s. All these gaps and disjunctions mirrored the failures of successive elites to adapt to changing conditions, or diversify their composition or commitments, and helped dispossess them in more or less crisis-centered conditions and integral measure. In return, discontinuities in the ruling class reduced or shortened the gradual collective deterioration to which any one group was liable *qua* incumbent ruling class. This was the case within the Federalist-Republican-Jacksonian Democratic-Whig sequence before the Civil War and remained true when the war had precipitated a more basic mutation.

Changes in the ruling class were moderated by the co-optation and assimilation of ambitious individual members of the previous ruling-class generations. Even thus qualified discontinuities sufficed to rule out the protracted class deterioration peculiar to continuous ruling classes, renovated only marginally and finding it ever harder to exercise and retain power. But discontinuity in America's ruling class may also have intensified different moral-political dilemmas as a factor in and for expansion. The drive to reacquire a share of power individually may raise as difficult issues as do collective efforts by a class to retain power. Moreover, and conjointly, some of the deterioration that the successive ruling classes escaped while they were incumbent was shifted onto the longer-lived American political system itself. The costs included the relative abruptness of class-substitutions, the relatively brief periods of tenure in commanding positions of both the successive ruling classes (typically rising to dominance while still too young in political experience) and the individual ruling-class members (typically too old in physical age when attaining supreme leadership responsibilities), and the resulting short-comings of the political parties as either vehicles or instruments for the momentarily ascendant class.

The deterioration of the political system was most conspicuously manifest in the increasingly hard to manage geographic sectionalism along South-North lines; and it was also apparent in the intermittently radicalized Western populism, as well as in the transitional phenomenon of Anglo-Saxon nativism. All were in various ways at variance with the universalist American ethos while also reflecting the potentialities of spatial vastness and the actualities of growing economic and ethnic heterogeneity. Sectionalism and populism expressed the material discrepancies within the regional triangle of South, North, and West; nativism would augment the critical distance between early and late immigration, between Anglo-Saxonism and Americanism. In doing one or the other, North-South sectionalism dramatized the failing aptitude of the political system to adjust peacefully the competing economic interests of the Southern slave-owners and the Northern employers of free labor; Western populism reflected the specialized interests of the commercial farmer in conditions of lessened prosperity, and distorted the political system by projecting a separate political leadership that was parochial in orientation but national in impact and unpredictably peculiar in its positions on foreign policy; and nativism defined the American political system as one that isolated a particular group, the so-called hyphenates, as essentially extraneous to the political system. A special appeal or resort to that group in interelite competition became as little or as questionably legitimate within the context of nativist politics as activating the lower orders is more commonly in oligarchical politics.

Suspended between enlargement and deterioration, the American political system influenced expansion when it supplemented concern about common security and sustenance with mainly intersectional transactions before the Civil War; and when it later added transactions involving sociopolitical and ethnic groups, most pointedly in the periods preceding and immediately following the war with Spain and American participation in World War II. In the earlier period, crucially operative were two partisan concerns and one all-encompassing constraint. One concern was to build up and maintain a core-coalition of geoeconomically defined and relatively stable sectional and special interests; another was to maximize prospects of electoral success by means of party platforms appealing to momentary popular sentiments on expansion among other things. So long as it lasted, the constraint was lodged in the imperative to avoid straining, beyond the breaking point, the constitutionally enshrined intersectional, chiefly North-South, equilibrium.

III

The flawed way of applying the universalist ethos intensified the normal divisions within a ruling class and between that class and the masses. It also conditioned such common phenomena as the fact or threat of ruling-class dilution (ethnic as well as social) and the conflicts between proponents of different strategies for expansion and consolidation (continental vs. overseas; focused on Atlantic or Pacific, Europe or Asia). There were differences between the earlier empires and the United States in such things as degrees of ruling-class continuity and the identity of salient, ethnic or social class, distinctions. But the American modalities of ruling-class division, dilution, and dispossession affected expansion no less in conjunction with the passage from ruling-class trusteeship to transactions and on to trauma.

The place of trusteeship in the American experience was in keeping with the peculiar character and circumscribed role of the ruling class itself. In principle, trusteeship stands for a posture of limited accountability downward by a united political class that was consolidated and legitimized by its prior performance in safeguarding the body politic in the face of critical security ordeals. In America, trusteeship was subject to the formal constraints of a representative political system and to the persistent group factionalism institutionalized by that system. This meant that political transactions for managing and adjusting divisions among groups would begin at an earlier stage than they had in the Roman and British imperial polities. It also meant, conversely, that the American political system would be relatively less exposed to the obverse of trusteeship, the group trauma of an empire-building ruling class clinging to a reduced hold on power and specialized political competence. But it did not mean that trusteeship as phenomenon and philosophy, eschewing total discredit because at no time absolute, could or would not periodically emerge as a corrective to uninhibitedly transactional intergroup politics.

The founding-father model originated the American version of the aristocratic trust mystique and set the pattern for the type of trustees, the propitious situation, and the appropriate response. Preeminently eligible for the leadership function were individuals whose generalized political skills and commitments were sufficiently intense to contain and subordinate factional differences (originally in economic interests and backgrounds between Northeastern merchants and Southern planters). The fitting situation was one of political and economic external threats (initially from the mercantilist empires of France, Spain, and Britain), potentially explosive internal social pressures, or the combination of both. And the corresponding response and apparent solution was expansion, as a safeguard against external pressures and a safety valve for internal tensions, complementing the measure of social change feasible internally and diffusing more widely the growing supply of material goods without jeopardizing the essentials of the existing order.

So long as the public remained somewhat detached from salient issues of national security and well-being, the trust posture was compatible with tactical divisions within the ruling class (e.g., over the issue of neutrality between France and Britain or the purchase of Louisiana from France) and was also capable of outlasting the temporarily galvanizing effects of intraelite divisions and other distempers on the populace. The first period of trusteeship began nonetheless to reach the end of its life span conjointly with the passing of its originating conditions. The growth of an effective central government made the polity less dependent on an effective and cohesive ruling class for a modicum of order and justice; and the Louisiana purchase, the commercial accommodations with France, and the understandings with Spain over Florida in the aftermath of the War of 1812 assured the Republic's long-term viability against the mercantilist empires. The reassurance within and without occurred, moreover, on terms that, while immediately consistent with the diverse economic interests represented within the ruling class and among its sectional allies, contained also the seeds of future intergroup conflicts over sensitive issues such as the external tariff.

The early trusteeship experiment did not endure because the external threat was insufficiently serious and long-lasting; because the two principal (landed and mercantile) wings in the ruling class were coequal in status and power; and because the ostensibly synthesizing, agricultural-commercial, West acted more to divide than to depolarize the older sections. The trusteeship phenomenon was to reappear, however, in the aftermath of the Civil War to the benefit of the emergent laissez-faire capitalist business elite, and twice in favor of more traditional or aristocratic forces represented by Theodore and Franklin Roosevelt. The business elite had masterminded successful postwar economic reconstruction and economic expansion; but since its qualifying domestic performance lacked a foreign-policy complement, the business elite did not acquire the all-round legitimacy that would shield it against popular reactions to its crowning lapse in the Great Depression. By contrast, the two Roosevelts managed confluences of foreign and domestic crises along proven aristo-demagogic lines by combining an essentially conservative reform internally with a revolutionary (i.e., innovative and expansive) foreign policy.

The first, Republican Roosevelt blended domestic progressivism with a "large" foreign policy, while he positioned himself as the trustee of both a traditional and a (socially) "new" nationalism and promoted the United States itself as the trustee of a nascent world order. His variety of the trusteeship mystique and mentality reached back to and updated the traditions of the Hamiltonian-Federalist aristocratic Republic that had been dormant ever since John Quincy Adams was supplanted by more democratic chief executives and political party managers. Being originally a reaction to the political consequences of both the early industrial revolution associated with Jacksonian Democracy and of its post–Civil War capitalist flowering, the Rooseveltian trusteeship was brought to full fruition when the second and Democratic Roosevelt revived Jeffersonian aristo-demagogy in substantially more critical conditions. It was his presidency that institutionalized the reemergence of the trusted aristocratic leader, implementing with only limited accountability a broad popular mandate, and initiating the process that was to culminate in the "imperial presidency" under the stress of the cold war and the impetus of John F. Kennedy.

A strong central government had helped inhibit the early development of an independent and continuous ruling class with a settled socioeconomic profile and status. At the later stage, the merger of strong institutions with reascendant trusteeship mystique in a resumed process of empire building spawned the nearest equivalent of such a class. The substitute was a political class and bureaucratic elite deriving its power from the president-trustee. As long as the class remained effective, broad mass support and only ineffectual challenges from a middle-class counter-elite would endow it with virtual irresponsibility vis-à-vis the principal representative organs, notably in matters of foreign-imperial policy.

IV

Elements of trusteeship, while not absent from the American experience, became qualified in the aftermath of the initial Federalist dominance, sustained by the prestige of the first president and the prior Federalist achievement in averting wartime defeat and postwar chaos. More characteristic than trusteeship were the multiple transactions involving the likewise manifold divisions within the body politic, including the ruling class itself. But since the horizontal North-South sectional division along geographic lines penetrated the original ruling class itself, sectionalism interfered with a coherent political manifestation of vertical social differentiation or stratification.

The early (Hamiltonian vs. Jeffersonian or Federalist vs. Republican) split along sectional lines was between the primarily Northeast-based mercantile oligarchy (or "plutocracy") and the South-based plantation aristocracy (or "slavocracy"). The former was avowedly elitist, because more immediately threatened locally by rising socioeconomic forces; the latter was more ostensibly democratic, because immediately more immune to the forces of change. The split within the self-consciously aristocratic stratum had a greater practical impact on the political order than had the absence of authentic feudal antecedents, since (conjointly with the absence of a sustained foreign threat) it weakened constraints on always-present routine intraclass divisions and precluded a common class-preserving response to the rise of the so-called common man in the 1820s and 1830s. In conformity with the Roman and British precedents, the response would have taken the form of an expansionist strategy, which the ruling class would manage as a means to compensate a rising (commercial) middle class for its political self-restraint or to appease the material grievances and desiderata of the popular masses. Instead, Jefferson's Republican pseudo-revolution of 1800 overthrew Hamiltonian Federalism, only to be displaced itself in 1828 by a Jacksonian Democracy which reflected the initial impact of the industrial revolution in the United States and was more truly revolutionary in sociopolitical terms than its predecessor had been.

Sectionalism impeded common ruling-class action. It also provided in the rapidly emerging and growing West a stake for intraruling-class competition that either supplemented or wholly substituted for socially lower groups along vertical lines of stratification. The land-hungry Western commercial farmer became the key object of competition not only between the older, Southern and Northern, sections, but also for the new political party organizations that had replaced the founding-father leadership generation with a new breed of professional politicians and party managers.

Within the political party framework, the cross-cutting geosectional and sociohierarchical divisions surfaced in the guise of a standing danger of conflict between the principle of equilibrium and the accomplished fact of or tendency to expansion. Equilibrium between or among sections, with respect to senatorial representation of slave and nonslave states, was a condition of national cohesion or even integrity; it was also interdependent with equilibrium within political parties, between mainly Northern and Southern influences and voting support, as a condition of the parties acquiring or retaining a national character. Potentially unbalancing expansionism was, conversely, implicit in the periodic compulsion of party managers to forge winning presidential coalitions, as a condition of access to federal power and patronage. A conspicuous instance of the resulting tension occurred in the 1840s, crucial for completing continental expansion under the aegis of Manifest Destiny. During that period, the more aristocratic Whig party was more keenly conscious of the limits that intersectional and intraparty equilibrium placed on expansion; the more demagogic neo-Jacksonian Democratic party was by contrast readier to risk disrupting the party along the North-South cleavage in an effort to wrest electoral victory from an intraparty transaction along South-West lines, accommodating the West's integral expansionism. Actual commitment to further expansion resulted from the West being projected to decisive third-party influence by a near-stalemate between the South, subordinating expansion to its anticipated impact on the relative position of slavery, and the even more ambivalent Northeast, compounding growing opposition to slavery with developing internal divisions between mercantile and industrial economic interests.

The issue of slavery progressively overshadowed other sectional differences in the period following the Louisiana purchase. That acquisition removed a closely constricting envelopment by foreign powers, while showing that ruling-class trusteeship was at all times shot through with transactional features. Ever since the 1790s, it had been necessary to appease the potentially secessionist Southwest, and to compensate it for tolerating or supporting the political leadership of one or the other segment of the Eastern-seaboard aristocracy by insuring uninhibited traffic and outlet via the Mississippi River. The purchase promoted that objective, while the ensuing expansion also raised a contentious issue in the contractually pledged incorporation of racially alien Louisiana creoles as United States citizens. But the ethnic issue was a portent of conflicts over expansionism to arise in the late 1890s, rather than a beginning of the contention over slavery, culminating in the 1860s. Only in connection with the Missouri Compromise of 1821 was the Louisiana territory to be caught up in the interplay between equilibrium and expansion in the context of slavery. At issue was, however, only the extension of statehoods and not of national territory, when the transaction admitting the slave state Missouri to the Union jointly with nonslave Maine formalized an expansion already accomplished materially. A comparable compensatory scheme focused on British Canada as a Northern offset to slavery's expansion in the Hispanic South. It was no more sufficient to energize expansion into Canada than had been the simple predatory drive for land and furs, rationalized by the Anglo-Indian threat to security, and were to be ethnic motivations implicit in the fast-growing anti-British Irish vote in the United States. Consequently, the seemingly most effective and effectively system-preserving intersectional transaction took place in connection with Texas. Its annexation as a slave state was paired off with the Oregon question, and California was more ambiguously paired off with New Mexico, as part of a coupling foreshadowed in the Democratic party's electoral platform (of 1844) and implemented by the twice-victorious Polk administration.

Intersectional compensations were easier to bring about when the expansive thrust of chiefly economic group interests coincided with the apparent practical requirements of a dynamic constitutional equilibrium between states' rights and national power, subordinating the issue of individual rights to social mobility and sectional harmony. Transactions were correspondingly impeded when differences in changing social beliefs and economic interests were raised to the status of constitutional dogmas, making it impossible to resolve intersectional discords expansively. The interest of the mercantile Northeast in Pacific harbors and in trade with the Orient lent itself in principle to a transaction with the South. But the partially economically motivated Northern opposition to extending slavery by way of sectionally balanced expansionism inhibited the full thrust of the mercantile motive until after emancipation had removed slavery as an obstacle. At an earlier date, Northern unwillingness to preserve internal peace along the lines of Madison's maxim had thwarted the extension of Polk's annexationism to still wider areas of Mexico (although the South was more interested in Cuba as more suitable for a slave economy); and a like reluctance frustrated the designs of the Pierce administration in the Caribbean (in the 1850s) while inspiring President-elect Lincoln to prefer the South's secession over slavocracy's expansion.

Only in the aftermath of the Civil War was the aboriginal conflict between diverse expansionist strategies reenacted via updated trans-actional dynamics and, as is common, resolved expansively. The Southern slavocracy's early vision of a feudally managed tropical empire had fo-cused on the Hispanic Caribbean, away from the pathways of expansion followed by the Northwestern trappers, traders, and trail-following farmers. The 1890s revived the question whether to be aimed at was an empire of the seas or merely an overland empire and, as a corollary, an annexationist empire with feudal-type paternalistic responsibilities or a merely informal, mercantile and exploitative, empire. The expansionists of the 1890s failed to resolve the divergence conclusively, causing delays that dimmed the resulting empire's prospects for long-term stability; but they began nonetheless to combine southward directions of expansion into the Caribbean with the more northward-directed push across both the Pacific and the Atlantic. Nor was it entirely accidental that the conflict over direction was being expansively resolved under the impetus of an element within the ruling class harking back to the era before the Civil War and combining resuscitated Southern-type "feudal" disposi-tions with Northern-mercantile background. A newly structured, ethni-cally defined inferior class was about that time also beginning to condition the unfolding of an additional or substitute conflict of strate-gies, between Atlantic-European and Pacific-Asian foreign-policy priori-ties. The conflict divided the East from the West coast and was politicized by the identification of one strategy with the more popular-hyphenate Democratic party and of the other with the more upper-class Anglo-Saxon Republican party.

It was not until the 1950s that the second-generation conflict over directions could achieve an expansive resolution on the basis of the interdependence of Europe and Asia within a balanced global strategy. The dénouement displayed once again the pervasively two-sided, both limiting or delaying and stimulating, effect of sectional conflicts on ex-pansion. Moreover, a parallel segmentation influenced throughout the ways of resolving conflicts over strategies. The supplementary cleavages, with effects on spatial expansion, were the vertical social ones between the ruling class and the lower classes.

V

In the overall expansive thrust of early America, the popular masses appear to have been more expansionist in the continental phase and the upper or ruling class in the overseas phase, while the fluid middle class is indeterminate. Within the ruling class itself, the Federalist-Whiggish component was more conservative or limitationist in the face of land-grabbing expansionism westward than was the Jefferson-Jacksonian component. The Federalist-Whiggish group had its core in New England and tended to be "nationalist," in the sense of favoring internal economic consolidation and development through a functionally expansive government; it was not territorially expansionist for the sake of expansion. Its concern for cheap (if free) labor, next to high external tariff, was at variance with the mass desire for vast tracts of cheap (and as nearly as possible free) land. The Jefferson-Jacksonian ruling-class component was largely focused in the South and was states-rightist, antimercantilist, and more responsive to mass demands. It was thus more prone to countenance the kind of territorial expansionism that either enlarged the domain of slavery or kept it in balance with free soil.

The divergent basic predispositions were in due course subject not only to the deepening constraints of the slavery issue but also to the stresses of intraruling-class competition over the allegiance of the Western farmers as the mass element. In that connection, the opposition between elitist "nationalism" and both grass-roots and aristo-demagogic expansionism was confounded by differences in attitudes toward expansion on the one hand and toward expansionist wars on the other.

In 1803, the declining Federalists were disposed to woo the West away from Jeffersonian Republicanism by calling for war with Spain (over the closing of the Mississippi-New Orleans outlets), but they opposed and obstructed the expansionist incorporation of Louisiana (including New Orleans) on half-specious constitutional grounds. By the 1840s, the emphasis was altered when the Whiggish perpetuators of Federalist "nationalism" showed at least as great a repugnance for the war of aggression on Mexico as for subsequent territorial acquisitions. When the elite and the populace inverted their respective attitudes toward expansion as it reached out overseas, the reversal was manifested over the entire nationalism-war-expansionism spectrum. In the 1840s, the land-hungry West had wanted expansion, but war only if not otherwise feasible; by the 1890s, an economically depressed populist West was hot for war (on Spain over Cuba) but cold on expansion (to the Philippines). Conversely, the business elite within the composite ruling class of the 1890s was initially against war and subsequently for expansion, while the aristocratic element was ready and even anxious for both war and expansion. The simultaneous reorientation of the ruling class from economic nationalism to a species of economic imperialism was in the process overshadowed in determining importance by a species of (economically conditioned?) popular chauvinism. But popular moods were to prove as unstable on the issue of war as they were incapable of sustained support for overseas imperial expansion.

The ruling class became expansionist when the search for markets and raw materials superseded the quest for land and furs. At least as importantly, the flight of the populace inland away from coastal oligarchies was replaced by self-perceived aristocrats escaping overseas from continental mobocracy; as stimulus to expansion, social decompression westward gave way to an increasingly world-wide functional displacement of elite roles from domestic to foreign and imperial politics. One set of reasons for overseas expansion was economic and manifested the gradual prevalence of the original artisan social type in the shape of the post–Civil War capitalist or big-business elite; another set was political and marked the reemergence of the aristocratic social type as a part of the new, composite, ruling class. The big-business element synthesized the early Federalist-Hamiltonian stress on economic development with the Republican-Jeffersonian (and Jacksonian) emphasis on laissez faire by the federal government; the neo-aristocratic posture combined the Federalist political ethos, viewing rule as a right implicit in rank and entitling to trust, with the Jefferson-Republican (and, to an extent, Jacksonian and post-1800 young-Federalist) stress on the aristocracy's obligation (as well as capacity and need) to secure mass support for rule by political transactions. Such political transactions might well come to encompass in due course the penchant of the early Federalists for an economically interventionist, "big" government. Accordingly, in the setting of the 1890s, the residuum of the high-Federalist elitist ethos made the politically reactivated upper-class elements seek escape from the swelling masses in areas of geography and policy suited for uninhibited rule based on trust. But the Jeffersonian and young-Federalist ethos was simultaneously put to work at building bridges to the populace whenever it was translated into a policy that was "large" not only abroad but also at home, socially as well as imperially.

As mass-favored expansionism evolved into mass support for isolationism, and a massive escape from oligarchy to opportunity westward set the stage for ruling-class escape from democracy into the world at large, the forces to be harnessed were ever less those of raw nature and ever more those of politically rudimentary populace. Competition for the allegiance of that populace declined gradually within the new Republican elite into the limited controversy over whether to couple imperial expansion with elements of socioeconomic reform; the ascendant strategy, of compensating for policies overseas by domestic programs, differed only partially from the one-time Jacksonian approach combining intracontinental expansion with a semblance of reform via enlarged access to cheap land. Concurrently, as the conflict over basic external policies became one with the Democracy of Bryan, it could subside within the composite Republican ruling class into issues of style and method. If the ex-artisan capitalists preferred informal mercantile expansion, direct colonial administration held a greater attraction for the neo-aristocratic conservatives (subdividing into Rooseveltian aristo-demagogues and more orthodox Hamiltonian elitists such as Henry Cabot Lodge). The very heterogeneity within the (Republican) ruling class enabled both its modern and its more traditional elements to adapt creatively to changed conditions the older ruling-class tradition of trust alongside or even over against transactions. At the same time, however, a basic cleavage was continued by the fact that only some of the members of the upper class, defined socially, adjusted to modernity. But whereas the irreconcilable opposition of high-Federalists after 1800 to the expanding and usurping West had culminated in New England secessionism, continuing little-Americanism led dyed-in-the-wool upper-class conservatives on the later occasion into no more than unwitting and largely tacit alliance with both the old-stock Populist rural, and hyphenated-immigrant urban, masses.

As early mass immigration augmented the demographic pressure on land, it fostered the westward continental expansion directly. Later immigration had a more indirect or dialectical relationship to expansion, insofar as it augmented the pressure on the Anglo-Saxon ruling class to seek functional displacement outward. Somewhat similarly, the much earlier movement north-westward of Scotch-Irish immigrants had directed the sights of the Southern slavocracy to a colonial-tropical "empire of the seas," as a means of restoring the demographic and electoral balance. Situated between the hierarchical extremes of the upper and the lower classes was the shadowy middle class, as intermediate on the class ladder as it tended to be indeterminate or vacillating on policies. In the era of the nationalist mercantile aristocracy (or plutocracy), the artisan middle class inclined to the side of the mercantile system and its bias in favor of economic consolidation rather than territorial expansion. An exception consisted of the middle-class elements engaged in commercial farming and land speculations. When the artisans had evolved into the later big-business elite, their place as middle class *par excellence* was taken by members of the liberal professions and by liberal intellectuals spearheading Anglo-Saxon Progressivism in the 1890s and ex-hyphenate

Radicalism of the 1960s. The new middle class inclined toward anti-imperialism on the side of the politically ascending, and more often isolationist than expansionist, masses. The expansionist exceptions, more analogous than comparable to the land speculators of the earlier era, were the militantly anti-Communist and the imperial-bureaucratic members of a middle class that evolved out of World War II and along with its sequelae.

VI

The dynamic of mainly intersectional transactions stimulated expansion as a subsidiary determinant or motive quite prominently in the last continental push beyond the Rockies in the 1840s. Before that time, the mountain range had been long viewed as a potentially terminal natural boundary and divide. But the internal political dynamic did little more than mediate, or make effectively operative, the predatory drives that were strongly at work in the body politic. Both the drive and the dynamic were at the same time rationalized by the need for a preclusive response to threats to security. The domestic dynamic became more fully and independently prominent relative to material interests and security concerns when expansion beyond the continent set off in the late 1890s a short-lived imperialist phase and a longer-lived expansive foreign policy.[2] The end of the nineteenth century witnessed the full flood tide of two interconnecting sociopolitical processes. One was the rise of a new, economic or business elite and its juxtaposition and progressing synthesis with elements harking back to the older political class. Another was the influx of a new type of immigrant and his confrontation, pending a much later and more partial synthesis, with the antecedent Anglo-Saxon community as a self-perceived ruling class writ large. The issues linking the two processes consisted of threatened dilution and dispossession; actual marginality; and varied co-optation. They were all related to expansion by way of a range of transactions, as an alternative to individual or group withdrawal into trauma and its diverse private or public policy manifestations.

Following the failure of the North and the South to keep reconciling expansion and equilibrium, the ultimately successful Northern drive for profit and preponderant power reduced the South from the seat of empire to the status of an exploited colony. A half-century after the critical 1840s, in a comparable context of war and expansion, a new composite and nation-wide ruling class combined the shrunken residues of the Southern aristocratic ethos (and imperial thrust) with magnified traits of Northern artisan enterprise (and economic drive). The socioeconomic effects of the Industrial Revolution that had begun in the 1820s and

2. On the relationship of domestic-political to other determinants of core-imperial overseas expansion applicable to the Philippines, see chap. 6, pp. 127–29.

1830s were accelerated in the aftermath of the Civil War, only to see the resulting conditions and beliefs challenged, in the 1890s, by opposing values and interests rooted in the antecedents as much as in the consequences of laissez-faire capitalism. The challenge occurred, moreover, in conditions compounding an apparently irretrievable shrinking of economic opportunities at home and openings abroad with an apparently unassimilable inflation of ascending social and alien ethnic forces internally. The resulting question was whether expansion abroad was not the only workable approach to reestablishing a political equilibrium between groups, as it had been previously between sections, rather than merely retarding and subsequently aggravating social and interethnic strife.

The business elite which emerged out of the Civil War was the first major American ruling-class type with a truly national base. It engineered America's economic independence as an industrial power and eventually also a creditor nation, complementing in peacetime the nation's war-won political independence. The accomplishment legitimized the newly dominant national force and model; but the economic elite could not be a self-sufficient ruling class so long as it relied on professional politicians. Neither was it internally uniform so long as purely economic differentiation amplified and refined the pre–Civil War cleavage between merchants and manufacturers. Since the subcategories were largely only functional, they divided less than had the earlier geosectional ones; but, in the late 1890s, that fact did not prevent international financiers and domestically oriented bankers, the money men and the producing industrialists, from significantly differing on issues of war and expansion. More enduringly at odds were economic elites with specific or specialized interests (e.g., in sugar and tobacco) and representatives of more generalized or diversified interests. The former had quite precise ideas on particular directions of territorial expansion, but were not necessarily able to determine government policy; the latter were keyed only to the overall expansion of the economic system itself, while differing among themselves as to the social and political implications of intermittent economic deflations and depressions. That which was to matter most in the long run, however, was a divergence, in basic ethos, between the early risk-taking entrepreneurs, who founded the several corporate "empires" after the Civil War, and the risk-shy institutional managers of corporate mergers and cold-war crises in the succeeding century.

Given its distance from the routines of daily political process and its internal divisions, the new business elite could evolve into a genuine ruling class only by co-opting individual members of the traditional political class *par excellence*. Co-opting such individuals differed critically from employing and ultimately controlling professional politicians;

it presupposed some form of mutually acceptable transaction entailing a division of labor.

Since the principal elite types were present on the American scene by the 1890s, for the subsequent internal dynamics to unfold required only scissions within both the self-perceived political (or aristocratic) elite and the economic (or ex-artisan) elite and, parallel to successive splits, co-optation-related secessions from the two elite groups. Successively co-opted into active political roles were upper- or ruling-class individuals who preferred to share power as part of a political compromise to sharing impotence within a social caste; who chose defection from their kind over nostalgic regression to forms and rules associated with their group's formative or trusteeship period, be it a politically free hand for the first-generation pre-democratic aristocracy or unshackled economic free enterprise for the business elite in its predepression heyday. The dynamic of scission, secession, and coalescence was repeatedly related to external expansion. Offshoots of a previously dispossessed or discredited ruling class were displaced in such cases to new kinds of performance, corresponding to changed conditions but marking essential continuity in worthwhile roles rather than petrified rules, functions rather than forms, and compensating for the material or status costs necessarily implied in domestic transactions with the newly ascendant group and with the still merely upwardly mobile forces.

The first post–Civil War scission occurred unavoidably within the older, aristocratic class. It erupted over the issue of active cooperation with "money power" in corrupt party politics and led to the co-optation of the more adaptable aristocratic elements epitomized by Theodore Roosevelt into the new business-centered ruling class. Subsequent and likewise hard-to-avoid scissions developed within the business elite itself, first over Progressivism and later and more critically over the New Deal as responses to prior deficiencies in the elite's performance. The New Deal marked the fuller reversal, insofar as it was by then a reascendant political aristocracy, epitomized by Franklin D. Roosevelt, that did the co-opting. The more adaptable offshoots of the business elite, such as Averell Harriman, followed then the precedent which a George W. Perkins had set in the Progressive era by supporting the first Roosevelt. The cycle was provisionally completed when the economic elite was politicized wholesale in the Eisenhower administration as part of its accepting and administering the imperial-welfare state across the board.

While the co-optation-prone individuals alternated as junior and senior partners in ruling coalitions, the unco-optable members of each group fell off successively into privatism (or humanitarian philanthropy) internally and anti-imperial isolationism (or nationalist unilateralism) externally. The two kinds of reaction to social change made up the essential political history of the United States; in immediate importance if not otherwise, ruling-class mergers as political transactions mattered more than did the ethnic melting pot as process.

Throughout much of the nineteenth century, so long as they remained marginal to national politics, the surviving members of the one-time traditional ruling class (or "gentry") had a fairly uniform fundamental outlook on issues concerning socially and ethnically lower orders. A split within the local or provincial upper class occurred only when philosophic uniformity had been exposed to tactical differences over the ways of conserving status while restoring role in the midst of both the capitalist and the socialist manifestations of an accelerating industrial mass-production and a rapidly-augmenting mass-immigration. Standing still were the older-generation aristocrats called Mugwumps, opposed to further expansion and immigration alike. Their anti-capitalism and little-Americanism were co-optation-resistant formulae rehearsing the nostrums of an earlier age of less acute social crisis and of unreal security threats from the British empire. Overwhelmingly opposed was the more dynamic younger "Tory" generation. It mixed domestic reformism and foreign-policy expansionism in variable doses, but was uniformly willing to co-operate with both the dominant business elite and the regular political party organizations in coping with the real internal threats of social and ethnic class-engulfment in a period of reintensified imperialism world-wide. If the older ruling class was typified by succeeding generations of the Adamses (from John Quincy by ways of Charles Francis to Brooks Adams), Henry Cabot Lodge represented the conservative and Theodore Roosevelt the progressive tendency in the co-optation-prone aristocratic component. Analogous nuances differentiated the politically aware business elite, or "industrial gentry," into conservatives *à la* Hanna and progressives *à la* Perkins, while the group's potential for politicization over time was typified by succeeding generations of the Rockefellers and the Harrimans, among others.

Reaching out to both the plutocracy and the aristocracy was the naval aristocracy symbolized by its most conspicuous public spokesman, Alfred T. Mahan. Standing in the forefront of the ascendant Anglo-Saxon nativism-cum-imperialism, American naval officers did more than identify professionally with the Royal Navy. They also shared the ethos of the British land-owning ruling class in their half-subservient and half-condescending *noblesse-oblige* attitude toward commerce as both the ward of sea power and no more than a rationale for morally (and strategically) self-justifying maritime power. At the opposite end of the spectrum, facing plutocracy and aristocracy more or less antagonistically, was rural Populism, spearheaded by the Democracy of Bryan, and the predominantly Catholic urban proletariat, organized by the boss system. The two mass elements constituted an identifiable, both immediate and long-term, domestic challenge ramifying abroad by way of its source (immigration) and implications (the Populist silver vs. gold issues), a possible response and remedy (expansion) and potential involvements (in Anglo-continental complications in Europe).

The British empire had to be superseded as America's rival over continental empire in North America and a regional one in the Caribbean before it could emerge as a positive focus of domestic American dynamics related to global empire. The Anglo-American ruling or upper class retained a measure of ambivalence toward the rediscovered mother country so long as the non-English-speaking immigrant masses from southeastern Europe, following upon the Scotch-Irish and German waves, did not critically magnify the ethnic threat, and the anti-British Populist advocates of silver did not constitute a social (or "revolutionary") menace. A threatened American ruling class came thereafter increasingly to identify with Great Britain on the ethnic score and with the British upper class on the social issue. The kindred country and class were both potential moral allies in a successful resistance to domestic pressures, while the kindred upper class was also a social and cultural bridge for escape from the consequences of defeat. Such a defeat, threatening engulfment, would follow from the inability to secure for the ruling class a successful displacement of leadership function from domestic to foreign affairs and for the body politic an effective diversion of lower-class pressures and collective solutions in the same direction. To avoid the jeopardy, an irreducible dose of ruling-class demagogy had to be previously marshaled in an attempt to vanquish agrarianism and socialism at home with conquest and colonization abroad; to exorcise domestic troubles, no longer freely exportable westward, by internally popular action overseas; and to essay imperial expansion as the elites' alternative to either expatriation or internal exile.

VII

The Social Darwinian vision of Anglo-Saxon superiority and solidarity, as embraced by the American upper stratum, was the ideology of a near-traumatized ruling class searching on a trans-Atlantic basis for a counterpoise to the ethnically heterogeneous populace. The ideology manifested itself more conspicuously in conjunction with successive foreign wars than in association with domestic militarism. But the outlook aimed nonetheless basically at consolidating a congenial or, at worst, tolerable internal order as part and parcel of a world order under Anglo-American auspices. Moreover, if critics saw America's end-of-century imperialism as amounting morally to a conquest of the United States by Spain, the acute social polarity reemerging along ethnic or racial lines on a nation-wide scale in the decades following the Civil War represented a posthumous moral triumph of the ante-bellum South over the North. The North's moral "conquest" by the South was, however, one which helped heal the

North-South cleavage. It presented old-stock Americans from both sections with a common problem, to be again approached by way of expansion. Only, this time, the needed new equilibrium involved instead of geographic sections political functions to be performed by and in behalf of different social groups.

Sectional and factional differences had militated against ruling-class cohesion during the struggle with the British empire, when the American population was predominantly English in origin. A North-South ruling-class mentality fused at the later date as a reaction to non-English mass immigration and as a matter of largely reunited opposition to the populist-isolationist West. The simultaneously sharpened sense of affinity and interdependence for class survival with the British social and political elites was anything but an automatic renewal or updated version of a perennial, if intermittently tacit, alliance. On the one hand, the rapprochement had to overcome the mix of attraction and revulsion within the larger Anglo-American family, although the continuing nuances within the American ruling class itself were but pale reflections of the earlier splits between Federalists and Republicans, between outright Anglophilia (e.g., that of the New England merchants) and virulent Anglophobia (e.g., that of the self-perceived victims of British mercantilism). On the other hand, if the feeling of interdependence was new, it was also reminiscent of the earlier Hamiltonian attitude toward the British empire, perceiving in a positive relationship (pending prevalence of the American factor) a safeguard for the postcolonial ruling class against Jeffersonian mobocracy, typified by early Irish immigration. The fact that even neo-Hamiltonian Henry Cabot Lodge had to twist the (British) lion's tail in order to propitiate the (Irish) voters in Massachusetts staked out the intervening departure from pristine Federalist elitism and Anglophilia alike. But it also expressed the continuing elite resentment of British condescension toward the United States as a navally encircled and negligible nation. Only as the 1890s moved on was the attitude and the policy of the British ruling class set on the course of change from apparently calculated contumely to conciliation and from conciliation to courtship. The earlier American ambivalence, streaked with animosity for things British, evolved concurrently into a form of amity translatable eventually into alliance.

The metamorphoses coincided with America superseding Britain's regional supremacy in the Western Hemisphere, clearing the way for solidarity with the British empire globally. The attitudes of an Olney, Henry Adams, Roosevelt, and Lodge moved thereafter closer to unreconstructed Anglophilia of a Hay or a Mahan (extending thereafter through a Woodrow Wilson to a Dean Acheson). A final psychological decolonization of the American ruling class required the prospect of Britain's imperial decline. The intersection between Britain's decline and America's ascent was the event necessary to reduce to a common denominator imperial succession by the United States and survival of the composite Anglo-Saxon ruling class in national leadership within the United States. Only as that conjunction approached, could the American elite find in transient equality of status with Britain overall (including U.S. supremacy in the Caribbean) the cure for an inferiority complex, and embrace Olney's "patriotism of race" (joining America to Britain) as an answer to the danger of perversion by forces alien to that particular race's common heritage in America. In Britain meanwhile, the negative attitude of the ruling class toward the United States had been epitomized by Palmerston and survived in political significance down to a Neville Chamberlain. But, beginning with the Venezuelan crisis, the dominant attitude moved along an Aberdeen-Joseph Chamberlain-Winston Churchill trajectory ever closer to the traditionally positive pro-American attitude of British commercial interests and the popular masses. If the result was convergence on the higher Anglo-American levels, however, the same process deepened the divergence between the American ruling class and anti-British, Irish or German, ethnic elements, creating a new disjunction between the dictates of personal sentiment and the imperatives of electoral strategy for a Lodge and his likes.

The Hobbesian drives of the American ruling class for aggrandizement abroad and self-preservation within came together and mellowed elite attitude toward the British empire most conspicuously in wars. Wars actuated the trend by raising the issue of American intervention for, just as overseas expansion involved the issue of imitation of, Britain, as opposed to either neutrality or passivity and thus possible preemption by third powers. Conservatively inclined American aristocrats had been as much opposed to war with Britain over neutral rights (and Canada) in 1812 as they were to be to conflict over Oregon in the 1840s. They also sided by means of a biased neutrality or worse with preeminent British sea power against its continental challengers, France in the late 1790s as much as Germany a century later. The war of 1898 was the occasion for a sentimental public reconciliation with Britain, based on misrepresenting both British and German naval acts and dispositions in Manila Bay; it was also the prelude to diplomatic intimacy on the Open Door and related questions, based on overrating the Russian threat in China. Since Francophile Jefferson himself had seemed willing on one occasion to "marry" the American cause to the British fleet and nation against France, it was correspondingly easy for later Jeffersonians to follow Hamiltonian biases on issues pitting Britain against Germany. But even when underpinned by a spate of actual Anglo-American upper-class marriages, the Anglo-American alliance failed over two world wars to save either the British empire or the Anglo-Saxon ruling class in the United States from infiltration and eventual subversion by inner barbarians. As the failure became apparent, representatives of American unilateralism, from Lodge by way of Franklin Roosevelt to Douglas MacArthur and John Foster Dulles, proceeded to disengage imperial American policy from both overt and multilaterally disguised privileged connection with Britain. The disengagement enjoyed the support of the earlier ethnic objects of trans-Atlantic Anglo-Saxonism in America, who had meanwhile graduated to integral Americanism in the form of anti-European isolationism by way of service in the first war and in the guise of expansive anti-Communism following participation in the second.

VIII

Even though the British empire and ruling class were the key external factors, domestic political equations remained decisive for the American aristocratic elite's survival-through-rehabilitation. The upper-class American expansionists at the end of the century were the offshoots of a self-perceived hereditary, but in no way feudal-military, aristocracy. Any primordial atavism could not, therefore, but be largely spurious and only marginally supplemental to more mundane determinants domestically, even as the expansion-fostering attitudes themselves were imitative of external imperial models. This fact enhanced the importance of political transactions in the critical 1890s. The transactions themselves were somewhat different and less clear-cut than in the Roman and British instances, however. America's equivalent of a constituent ruling class was not fighting off deposition from a dominant position by a rising mercantile middle class, but was itself reascending from a narrow base to partnership with a politically dominant capitalist class. The aristocratic element was consequently neither self-confident enough as to its position nor sufficiently despondent as to its situation to embrace the populace fully as a natural ally against either the dominant business elite or the progressive-reformist anti-business middle class.

The more limited was the possible scope for effective alliances and transactions between the expansionist aristocrats and both the popular mass and the middle-class liberal professions, the more critical became the transactions within the composite plutocratic-aristocratic ruling class itself. By the same token, the merger of traditional and contemporary upper-class elements by transactional or more organic means became the most critical domestic determinant of expansion. The interplay on an essentially horizontal social level virtually replaced the deficiently operative vertical interclass dynamic, which offered only very limited possibility to mobilize a stable lower-class support for overseas expansion as a good in itself or a corollary to domestic reform.

Strictly confining the scope of possible vertical transactions was the only tentative reformism of the old-stock aristocrats and the ultimate conservatism of American labor. If the former feared that improving the conditions of labor beyond a certain point would politically strengthen labor's collectivist organization, the latter feared the economic implications of opening up access to low-paid nonnative labor by unbounded overseas expansion. And if the reformist zeal of a Theodore Roosevelt was ardent only when compared with Senator Lodge's, the popular élan behind expansion did not outlast the jingoistic alliance with combative aristocrats for war with Spain against initially hesitant economic elites and political party managers. The working masses recurrently came to oppose overseas expansion in order to foreclose the diffusing of material opportunities beyond the absorptive capacity of even a dynamic economy. On its part, the Progressive native middle class, chiefly urban but also rural after Populism declined with economic recovery, wanted to avoid diluting American citizenship beyond the assimilative capacity of even an elastic political ethos. Both were correspondingly indifferent to the interest of the aristocrats in reallocating governmental roles, or even power, within a framework of foreign or imperial policy sufficiently expansive to offset the mass-democratic implications of an expanding domestic political system.

The aristocrats' limited access to the masses was increased only by failures of the economic system, such as the recession in the early 1890s. The theoretically firmer basis for transactions between the aristocrats and the Anglo-Saxon or native, professional and Progressive, middle class was laid by shared enmity for supposedly illegitimate power concentrations. Such could be monopolistic big business, standing for corrupting materialism; local power-monopolizing urban bosses, standing for corrupted machine politics; and, incipiently, the labor unions. All such agglomerations denatured old American values of self-reliant individualism, while the city and labor bosses also impeded direct access to recent immigrants as clusters of latent force. In the domestic theater, the community of middle- and upper-class views was the possible foundation of an alliance for trust- and boss-busting in the interest of fair, if not necessarily perfect, political and economic competition under the aegis of materially disinterested and politically enlightened traditional, or at least tradition-perpetuating, elites. However, it took World War I and interventionism in England's favor to rally the Progressive middle class behind an active foreign policy. Prior to that, there was no solid middle-class support of overseas expansionism to exchange for a commitment by the aristocratic elite to sweeping political (and related socioeconomic) reform.

Like Lord Curzon in Britain, a Theodore Roosevelt would ventilate the American "domestic slum" by opening the door onto a "large" foreign policy, hopefully habit-forming if initially more grandiloquent than grandiose. The typical middle-class Progressive reformer would instead extirpate the slum by hopefully cumulative and ramifying measures of institutional reform, however minor or superficial individually. A potential division of labor inhered in the very divergence of the two strategic priorities. The potential was tapped for occasional overt alliances and implied transactions during Roosevelt's presidency and, more conspicuously, while he attempted to recapture the White House in the 1912 elections. But the scope of actual cooperation was limited by two disharmonies. The parties differed over the practical capacity of Progressivist strategy to secure the avowed democratic, and the implicit elitist, goals and to do so either at all or at an acceptable cost in hostile rivalry with regular political party organizations and their entrepreneurial sponsors. They also assessed differently the bearing that overseas expansion would have on both the assimilative process (in regard to alien ethnes) and the democratic representative purpose (exposed to the impact of an empire-bred aristocracy).

In view of the sundry obstacles, the flirtations of aristocratic expansionists could not go very far with either the masses, in the setting of pro-war chauvinism, or with the middle class, in the context of anti-boss reformism. The liaisons were more tentative and tactical than seriously transactional, and their main ultimate significance was in strengthening the hand of the aristocrats vis-à-vis the business elite, whose position as the sole trustee had been weakened by the near-catastrophic economic misperformance in the early 1890s.

As a result, it oversimplifies but also illuminates matters to single out as fundamental the end-of-century transaction between the residual (but revitalized) political aristocracy and the shaken (but reprieved) business oligarchy, and to reduce that transaction to one basic exchange. The American aristocracy would extend support for the survival of the American plutocracy via expansion of foreign markets and containment of the domestic popular mass; in exchange, the economic elite would support the political revival of the social elite via effective empire-building and reform-boosting action or rhetoric. The reciprocal compensation would bridge the gap between a static and a dynamic conservatism and would be implemented through a successful competition with radicalism. As the key intermediary between the moneyed oligarchy and the populace, the aristo-demagogue (Theodore Roosevelt) would do battle with the period's facsimile of a system-threatening popular tribune (William Jennings Bryan). In performing the appointed task, with some help from moderate middle-class allies, the aristo-demagogue would launch intermittent moral crusades against the extreme embodiment of economic growth and vehicle for economic order, the trusts, even while propagating in a more sustained fashion an expansive foreign policy as the morally superior alternative to stagnation and remedy against the dangers of sociopolitical anarchy.

One basic premise behind the *de facto* ruling-class coalition was that an internally and externally expanding economic system could be expected to go on insuring upward mobility and contain irrepressible social discontent as a result; another and related one, that sustained cooperation between the aristocracy and the plutocracy was the best way to institutionalize the dynamic American way of confining grassroots mobilization for radical change within tolerable limits. The transaction was mediated in principle by the more progressive elements in the business elite. Its concrete terms centered on delimiting the domains reserved for each party, and entailed moderation for both in tolerating overlapping jurisdictions. A limited reform carried out under aristo-demagogic auspices would respect the reserved domain of the business elite in regard to the essentials of the capitalistic system, such as protective tariff and financial monetary policies based on gold. And, following Theodore Roosevelt's ascension to the presidency, the business elite and its senatorial spokesmen would concede to the aristocratic chief executive a free hand in appointing key colonial administrators and perpetuating expansionism in appropriately adjusted forms.

The moderation of Roosevelt's onslaught on economic bigness was the obverse of his latitude in foreign policy. The business elite's condoning grandiose diplomacy was in turn part and parcel of tolerating a moderately reformist regulatory interference with integral laissez faire as the least damaging way to appease or anticipate severe popular discontents. At the root of the transaction was a substantial complementarity of interests. Just as a directly administered patrimonial colonial domain might terminate, British-style, the long-lasting underemployment of dispossessed aristocratic types in public functions, so enlarging assured access to either a protectionist American empire or a reciprocally opened up freer trade with other overseas domains might prove necessary to keep afloat an overproducing American private enterprise at some future date. In such a perspective, the annexation and administration of the Philippines was justified as a step on the road away and toward something: away from the (all-too-real) trauma of a functionless political class within the United States; toward the (mythical) increment of trade with the unclad masses of China. And gains in domestic stability accruing to the economic elite from aristocratic charisma warranted tolerating aristocratic indulgence in both gratuitous diplomatic forms and more onerous naval symbols of great-power status. Each of these luxuries had, moreover, an either marginal or potential usefulness for the business elite's more direct or intimate concerns.

Despite frictions and shifts in gravity, the aristocratic-plutocratic bargain within the Republican party endured (and with it America's first phase of world policy) long enough to establish a pattern and set a precedent. The policy itself subsided into the less conspicuous dollar and railroad diplomacy under Roosevelt's more orthodox conservative successor in the White House, William Howard Taft. In that form it continued, except for the Wilsonian interlude, until the domestic collapse of the capitalist elite reversed the relationship of forces within imperial America's composite ruling class.

IX

The Great Depression of the early 1930s terminated the post–Civil War phase of the economic development masterminded by the business elite. It dwarfed the economic depression of the early 1890s, just as the remedial combination of the New Deal with world policy under Franklin Roosevelt was to reduce Theodore's variations on expansionism and reform via the "square deal" or "new nationalism" to the standing of a mere dress rehearsal. The business elite which presided over post–World War I normalcy, and was typified by Herbert Hoover, had been largely purged of the end-of-century aristocratic component and ethos. When it met the depression with a paralyzing reluctance to substantially compromise the laissez-faire doctrine that had sustained its trusteeship posture along with its economic performance, it consummated the previous failure to expand its trusteeship base functionally into the area of foreign policy in a way capable of dwarfing unavoidable internal shortcomings.

The unwillingness to move away from free enterprise reflected the desire of a still inherently nativist and again integrally conservative ruling elite to avoid mobilizing the popular masses by interventionist governmental policies. But the foreign-policy default was due at least in part to an inability. A business-centered ruling class was unable to even try to transcend the considerable congruence between domestic interethnic and European internation divisions within a more realistic configuration of power for world order than underlay the rejected League of Nations system. The compound of unwillingness and inability to strike out in new directions at home and abroad generated a posture conservative in doctrine and middle-class in mood. Whereas small government prevailed in domestic affairs with respect to the essential supply-demand equations of economics, little-Americanism was maintained in foreign policies with respect to military-strategic and diplomatic equations even while these were being again increasingly separated from the balances of foreign trade and high finance. After reaching its nadir, middle-class–conservative quietism could be relieved and redeemed only by infusing into an ostensibly ultraliberal doctrine the essentially aristocratic blend of conserving reformism and foreign-policy activism.

It took two stages to reinstitute the reformist-expansionist political formula by the second generation of aristo-demagogic Rooseveltian leadership. And the formula was replicated in the Kennedy presidency as part of the search for a Roosevelt-surrogate in connection with a continuing global crisis and conflict. In the domestic part of the two-pronged approach, the aristocratic leader would inject his personal charisma into the bargaining among capital, labor, agriculture, and other specialized interests, and legitimize the outcomes routinely mediated by congressional and party politicians. In the hands of the younger Roosevelt, the formula entailed the expansion of both the socioethnic basis and the functional scope of government, as a prerequisite to social reform and economic revival before it became their consequence. Enlarging the basis meant bringing fully into the political process the previously marginal second- and third-generation hyphenates within the lower (or only recent) middle class, as allies and supporters against conservatives identified with deflation of the economy and restrictions on immigration; expanding governmental functions meant combining a responsive big government with an intensified foreign-policy response to crises in Europe and Asia. Both kinds of enlargement, while activist and interventionist, were also quieting and restorative. The expansion of domestic base and governmental function in the New Deal phase was mainly instrumental in provisionally appeasing the disaffected popular base. The expanded view of foreign policy was more significant in attenuating divisions within the ruling class. It smoothed the co-optation of business and high-level professional elites (such as Nelson Rockefeller and Dean Acheson) who had been either alienated or insufficiently attracted by the domestic economic policies.

When viewed from the perspective of the just-preceding presidential election, the deliberate and successful mobilization of the hyphenates in 1932 was a species of political revolution. Conversely, the subsequent co-optation of the previously ruling business-elite element into an initially junior position entailed merely a revision of the balance of power within the reconstituted composite ruling class. The reversal between its aristocratic and its plutocratic components was epitomized by the relative positions of the elder and the younger Harriman in relation to the two Roosevelts. The New Deal's fading in wartime soon softened the lapse of the business elite from co-optator to co-optee, however, and selectively liberal businessmen were able to reassume nominal leadership in the first genuinely postwar administration, as the more conservative of the two main parties reached once again for the military hero as a substitute for the popular aristocrat and savior from continuing dispossession.

The Eisenhower restoration, following upon the Rooseveltian *reprise*, consummated the revival of ruling-class trusteeship in both the internal and the external functional arenas. But if the restoration symbolized the acceptance of interventionism as the basic principle for both arenas by the business elite, it also substantially did no more than adapt to a mobilized domestic and militarized international setting the elite's basic post–World War I formula of liberalism in foreign, and conservatism in domestic, policy. An essentially liberal foreign policy was updated in economic matters and extended to the politico-strategic arena in conditions of nominal peace, while a conservative domestic posture was again becoming viable electorally in conditions of inflationary prosperity. Concurrently, the reconstructed business elite itself was being politicized in collective outlook, individual career roles, and standards of personal success. As the elite disassociated itself from the ideologically rigid architects and casualties of the great-depression trauma, it adjoined unto itself the high-level military and civilian functional elites of indifferent social and ethnic backgrounds that were growing in numbers and importance along with the expanded role of government at home and abroad.

Restored ruling-class trusteeship was nourished before, during, and after World War II from several sources. One was the ascription of the special title to govern in a crisis to the aristo-demagogue, especially by the metropolitan-urban population, and to the military leader, by the rural and small-town folk in particular. Another was achievement, uncompleted in the domestic economic crisis but initially consummate in the foreign field. And yet another was assimilation, encompassing newly habilitated lower-class elements or second-class citizens. No trusteeship could be either complete or stable, however, in a representative democratic setting intensified by an ongoing two-faced crisis and recovering from a just-preceding major ruling-class debacle. It was contingent upon unfailing elite performance and supporting transactions between the transformed ruling class and the middle- and lower-class forces committed to continuing transformation at home and, increasingly if less firmly, in the world at large. While the conditionally renewed ruling-class trusteeship rested precariously on a confluence of ascription with achievement and assimilation, the trust-qualifying parallel interclass transactions assumed gradually the specific if equivocal forms of compensation or appeasement within a changing social setting.

In the phase covering the rise of the United States to world empire, the restoration of both the unity and the authority of the postdepression composite ruling class was inseparable from a dynamic and effective foreign policy. Only the latent social radicalism of the Great Depression era stood to profit from a continuing separation of domestic politics from a foreign policy that would foster employment through economic recovery by nonradical means; and only much later would resurgent radicalism be able again to stage a drive to relieve domestic reform needs of the allegedly inhibitive costs of an active foreign policy. The extent to which, and the ways in which, the interplay between elite restoration and social radicalism was a critical subsidiary determinant of expansion depended on the relative intensities of domestic cleavages and external conflict.

Domestic splits compelled transactions without insuring their compatibility with an effective foreign policy; external tensions and consequent insecurity promoted trust in the political elite so long as the outside threat was felt to be authentic and the safeguarding performance by the ruling class effective and materially disinterested. This being so, internal tensions and transactions conditioned foreign policy most directly during the preliminaries to the American entry into World War II and in the concluding stages of the cold war. A critical factor in the earlier instance was the gradually manifested relationship between restored full employment at home and full involvement in the conflict abroad; it supplemented materially the deficient consensus regarding the relevance of a still-remote outside threat for the United States. And, when the outside threat had seemingly waned in the later instance, compensatory domestic transactions gained renewed importance for carrying on with an expansive or dynamic foreign policy.

In the period opened up by the second Roosevelt, the transactions were the vertical ones between the ruling class and, since the classic mercantile middle class was fully participant in the ruling class, a seriously split new middle class and its lower-class extensions. Thus modified, the transactions were still more like the classic Roman and British transactions than like the earlier horizontal compromises among the sections before the Civil War or within the composite ruling class in the age of the first Roosevelt. As part of the latter phase of horizontal interrelations, the aristocratic element had been largely displaced to foreign policy before reversing its prior political dispossession and recovering fuller-scale domestic relevance by way of its role in reform. Within the vertical class setting of the later Roosevelt era, the aristocratic contingent traveled in the obverse direction. Starting from an initial mandate for internal system reform, the upper-class activists, rather than being displaced willy-nilly toward foreign policy, gravitated in that direction spontaneously as a matter of preference and presumed expertise. The trend was continued by the diversified cold-war ruling class, while a transformation took place in the social composition and the political attitudes of the middle class with even more immediately critical consequences.

x

The nativist Progressive middle class in the era of the first Roosevelt was not an effectually challenging counterelite. It was too widely separated from the alien, non-Anglo-Saxon, masses by ethnically motivated fears and suspicions; nor would it combine political tinkering with radical social reform on the economic plane, since it was either wedded to or dependent on the economic system dominated by the business elite. The Great Depression and World War II completed the work of World War I in attenuating the chasm between the nativists and the recent immigrants among the middle and the lower classes. But the subsidence of one split surfaced in due course other cleavages that radicalized the divergent elements in the new middle class in contrary directions. The more liberal segment of the new middle class dominated the liberal professions and included a significant Jewish component. It evolved ideologically toward doctrinal opposition to American "imperialism," in support for social justice at home. The innately, though in the period of its socioeconomic rise not patently, more conservative segment was less intellectual than vocational and included a strong Catholic component. It gravitated ideologically toward dogmatic opposition to foreign Communism and displayed increasingly a vested interest in acquired socioeconomic status at home.

The vocational middle-class stratum was lower relative to the professional stratum. Neither group replicated an ascendant mercantile middle class, to be compensated by expansion for continuing to tolerate the exercise of governmental skills by a (landed) ruling class. But the lower middle class was more self-consciously tied to the free-enterprise capitalistic system of production and distribution; it was consequently prepared to go on abiding by the wartime demonstration of the relationship between expansive foreign policy and domestic economic expansion, to which it had owed the first steps toward group prosperity. Coupled thus tentatively by material self-interest, opposition to Communism and support for countervailing foreign-policy activism were in the early postwar period consecrated by the lower middle class's Catholicism and consolidated by its predominantly East-Central European ethnic background. By contrast, the intelligentsia within the relatively higher stratum of the new middle class tended to be related to the capitalistic system either indirectly, through involvement in service industries of the liberal-professional kind, or critically, along radical lines. It was both inclined and able to minimize the threat from social change to individual and group status, while being sensitive to intimations of conflict between expansive foreign policy and expanding domestic reform.

The cold-war ruling class faced thus a middle class at once bifurcated in ideological orientations and stratified in terms of socioeconomic standing and self-confidence. If the lower layer of the new middle class was resisting merger with the racially heterogeneous popular mass, the higher middle class tended to be sympathetically concerned with the positionally safely remote lowest stratum. The opportunities for vertical interclass transactions that remained open to the ruling class were consequently fraught with conflict, liable to surface whenever either external threat or domestic elite performance were seen to decline. Pending such perceptions, however, it was possible to support or at least tolerate an expansive foreign-imperial reaction to the cold war in exchange for satisfactions derived or anticipated from a reform program keyed to expanding the welfare state and diffusing civil rights, and vice versa. There was no basic incompatibility between the foreign and domestic spheres so long as authoritative intervention abroad continued to be consciously or unconsciously equated, rightly or wrongly, with effective governmental allocation of the growing benefits of prosperity at home. It was immaterial in that connection that the key payoffs had shifted from full and secure access to markets and raw materials abroad, prized by the older middle class, to full employment and ever-widening social security. The presumption of beneficial congruence (between domestic and external interventionism) could continue, furthermore, so long as concessions to the civil rights movement in favor of the last major depressed ethnic group, the black Americans, went sufficiently far to establish symbolically a necessary minimum of coherence between racial policies at home and cold-war strategies for the global periphery, but not so far as to threaten only recently secured gains and all the more jealously guarded interests.

While the congruence (between cold-war requirements and welfare-state reforms) lasted, the viewpoints and prejudices of the self-consciously liberal and the latently conservative middle-class segments could be heeded without much friction by the progressively specialized foreign-policy elite within the overall composite ruling class. As a matter of fact, both main sectors of the new middle class came themselves to be increasingly incorporated into the expanding policy-influencing imperial bureaucracy (or "security community"), if perhaps in uneven numbers and at uneven rates, and were penetrating the opinion-shaping professions. In the process, the civilian and military imperial bureaucracy and associated professions (including the academic) came to constitute the key channels for upward social mobility, as a compensation for the new middle class provisionally continuing to concede the commanding role—or, at least, most conspicuous place—within the foreign-policy establishment to Americans of older stock. The ongoing disposition to concede the trusteeship role and status to the ruling elite hinged on its successfully coordinating the expansion of domestic economy and of politically participant society with politico-military expansion in the world at large; and coordination by the few had to occur without extraordinary material costs for the many, of a kind that would substantially abridge the economic and status gains won since the Great Depression. Gradually added to the critical interdependence between internal and external expansion was a second essential interplay, having to do with order and involving mutually reinforcing internal and external actions for containing the forces of disruption attendant on the twofold expansion.

The complexity of the performance was bound to increase with every decrease in the perceived threats to the physical security of the nation at large. In carrying on with the task of coordinating the two critical interplays, the ruling class had to underpin its trusteeship by largely implicit transactions with both the more liberal and the more conservative new middle class. This meant rewarding the liberal middle class for support and, as international tensions declined, compensating it for the mere toleration of an assertively implemented foreign policy by maximizing that policy's nontraditional liberal-reformist features. Economic aid, first for the decimated and then for the developing countries, along with institutional multilateralism, were the key external complements to domestic welfare-state and civil-rights programs and policies. The compensation was easy to effect, since the liberal bias in favor of diffusing economic well-being and social justice (or equity) as incident to, or an aspect of, expanding national power was congenial to the predominant temper and values of the specialized foreign-policy elite within the ruling class. The practical implications were, moreover, at the very least consistent with the economic interests of the business elite when foreign assistance created purchasing power through additional employment at home and facilitated economic access abroad. Conversely, any imperial system's intrinsic bias toward stressing order accorded less well with the liberal values of the foreign-policy elite. It provided instead the basis, if only a potential one, for an understanding, however inarticulate, with the inherently conservative lower middle class on two scores. One, the ostensibly costly liberal foreign-aid policies would be implemented in a way that would not diminish the material payoffs of the full-employment welfare-state system for the lower middle class. Two, an ideologically intensified and increasingly militarily implemented opposition to the Communist powers and, in due course, their left-leaning third-world associates, would do more than merely compensate for the liberal aspects of the imperial policies (such as development aid). It would, more importantly if implicitly, constitute a favorable external setting for containing threats to the existing domestic order as well. A threat to that order and to related distribution of group status could be easily associated with amplifying civil-rights and welfare-related policies, along the lines propounded by self-consciously revolutionary black Americans and their allies, to an extent imposing material and other costs on the next-higher, white, social stratum.

The cost of the more or less conscious and consummated transactions to the foreign-policy elite was unquestionably less tangible in kind, but no less real. Compensating or appeasing the two middle-class segments in ever more divergent and eventually opposite directions was liable to cumulate also foreign-policy commitments to both economic development and politico-military order maintenance, beyond the measure required by a strictly construed threat from the Communist great powers. The difficulty grew as the cold war subsided, the Sino-Soviet threat ceased to be unified, and the American domestic dynamic came to increasingly determine attitudes toward outside expansion as a result. As part of the dynamic, the ruling class regressed increasingly from gravitating to foreign-policy specialization as a matter of taste to being displaced in that direction by seemingly intractable domestic trends.

Notable among the domestic issues was the racial question. The degrees of homogenization effected by the two world wars, and of economic leveling produced by the depression and the subsequent recovery, shifted the most critical ethnic cleavage from one between Anglo-Saxon Americans and hyphenated Euro-Americans to one between lower-class whites and blacks, between the self-perceived carriers of a new Americanism and the self-styled Afro-Americans. The consequence was a tripolar pattern of one kind of American of older stock and two kinds of differently defined new Americanism. The racially colored domestic conflict released once again a powerful incentive for the incumbent elites to seek long-term resolution and immediate release within the largest possible imperial framework, as a preliminary to reestablishing eventually a pluralistic group equilibrium under the aegis of an only marginally renovated ruling class. But the same developments at home and abroad which enhanced the potential utility of the different compensatory transactions with the two middle-class segments tended also to make the transactions mutually incompatible, as some of the liberal middle-class elements grew progressively more radical and the conservative ones grew more resentful.

In principle, compatibility of transactions required a continuing congruence between the payoffs of the welfare-state and the requirements of the civil-rights agenda with challenges and responses in the several arenas of the cold war. That congruence faded when the spread of an apparently assured material affluence intensified conflicts in domestic group interests, attitudes, and demands, just when the external conflict with the major Communist powers appeared to subside; when the managers of imperial and foreign policy failed to replace the fading economic and physical insecurities and related anxieties with a convincing alternative rationale for social disciplines; and when progressively ascendant radical—or racially colored revolutionary—drives or demands interlinked the domestic with the international arena of conflict in ways that were either unmanageable or were not actually managed.

The accumulating developments were brought to a head by the American involvement in the protracted war in Indochina. The war itself grew out of a perverse confluence of the liberal and the conservative currents in American world policy, of simultaneous support for development in freedom and for stable order in the less privileged areas. While the military involvement climaxed the ideological commitments of both segments of the new middle class, however, it also managed to discredit the presumption of constructive beneficence flowing from both of the two critical interplays. One interplay, between expansion of the sociopolitical and economic systems at home and intense involvement abroad, had been of particular interest to the liberal middle-class element; the other, between the concern with order abroad and conditions of order at home, was the less clearly articulated premise of the conservative middle class. The newly emerging issue critical for the liberal middle class was the apparently direct competition for available resources between foreign war and domestic reform. Once affirmed, the competition raised dramatically the issue of the material cost of foreign involvement just when that cost was being aggravated by an apparently war-induced domestic inflation. The conservative lower middle class was likewise sensitive to the material cost; but equally critical was the status cost implicit in the satisfaction of increasingly radical demands by the militant black movement and its political allies. Such demands were, or could be plausibly seen as being, intensified by the real psychopolitical and the averred ideological connection between a "revolutionary" foreign war and domestic "revolution," the first effectively depressed to a militarily subconventional level on the remote battlefield, and the second intended to raise the level of effective social concern on the home front. The so far positive interplay degenerated into tension between enforced halt in external expansion and accelerating demands for internal system expansion. Intensified domestic disorders revolved around the issue of justice; they set the stage for a public disillusionment that crystallized around the issue of ruling-class competence and, eventually, integrity.

In the latter phase of the cold war culminating in the Indochina conflict, the essentially liberal foreign-policy elite failed to coordinate domestic and international expansion and order maintenance, empire and reform, without raising the material costs for both wings of the middle class and condoning status jeopardy for the lower middle class. The elite's failure undermined its standing with both segments; and the transition from liberal-Democratic management (in the Kennedy-Johnson era) to Republican auspices (in the Nixon administration) not only failed to substitute in full an increased lower-middle class for a declining upper-middle class support, but reopened also a division within the political elite over the issues of order vs. justice at home and the degrees of valid retrenchment abroad. Radical pressures from an allegedly new political left had by then joined reintensified reformism in surfacing incompatibilities, between the anti-imperial animus latent in liberalism and empire-induced effective conservatism, previously held in abeyance by a combination of repentant liberal anti-Communism, consensual conformism, and professional careerism within the imperial establishment. The incompatibility was bound to reappear when domestic and personal stresses originating in the Vietnam conflict mobilized the new liberal consensus of active opposition to the war, its imperial setting, and its foreign-policy rationales.

The war-induced frustrations suspended, if they did not terminate, the process of consolidating an American *grand empire* conjointly with a "great society." A relationship between full employment-cum-social improvements at home and integral involvement in the world had been suggested by two global wars and was largely validated through most of the cold war. Reversing the extreme formulation of the relationship in a certain kind of doctrinaire critique of the American socioeconomic system, it became henceforth fashionable to embrace the opposite extreme view and equate a full and effective deployment of American resources and energies in behalf of domestic society and economy with far-reaching international disinvolvement. As part of the attendant realignments, the younger elements of the upper class moved away from the imperial foreign-policy commitment of their fathers toward either outright domesticism or a species of humanitarian internationalism. The evolution may have expressed no more than a short-lived intergenerational dialectic, reversing the opposition prevailing in the 1890s between expansionist younger and anti-imperialist older members of the upper class. However, insofar as the more recent upper-class rebels merely followed a new, liberal-to-radical, middle-class leadership into the anti-war movement, the implicit reversal of the co-optation relationship to the detriment of the anterior ruling class may have been more significant in the long run than was any generation gap. Were it to prove enduring, the shift of leadership from one social class with a determinate ethnic background to less homogeneous groups was apt to engender unpredictable long-range consequences for foreign policy. In the short run, worse than uncertainty was created by the unwillingness of the older members of the political elite to restrict social transformations at home rather than disengage abroad when trying to deal with the temporarily deteriorated relationship between foreign-policy expansionism and internal reformism. The reluctance was rationalized by the instant need to limit both risks and costs overall; it had consequences that were immediately fatal to the trusteeship position of the elite and, concurrently, its official tenure predicated on ability to master crises in the last resort.

XI

Both segments of the new middle class were socially marginal to the original Anglo-Saxon American body politic. Being a major source of the impetus behind the drive for the internal and, interdependently, external expansion of the system after World War II, that social marginality was also the most potent instance of its kind in American history. So was the different, political marginality of Franklin D. Roosevelt, the renegade aristocrat mobilizing the lower-class hyphenates as part of securing a domestic power base by means and for ends reprobated by the bulk of the upper class. Similarly, the lapse of the cold-war ruling class and foreign-policy elite from trusteeship into near trauma in connection with the war in Asia was but the latest of similar consequences of failure in performance on the part of successive ruling-class generations in America. Nor was, finally, the ambiguous relationship between policies of world empire and of the welfare state the only case of a relationship between expansive foreign policy and domestic reform in the annals of the American Republic.

As a factor in expansion, the socially marginal "new masses" were more important in America than were socially marginal "new men," so significant in Rome and Britain. However confined it may have been by ethnic rigidities, social mobility was sufficient to enable forceful individuals to rise within both the socioeconomic and the political arenas without profoundly modifying or exuberantly glorifying either arena. And since the political system reflected social mobility in ancestral myths, such as that of the log cabin, and reinforced them by appropriate mechanisms, such as military-hero worship, both the presidential and the party-political planes could be, with relative impunity, biased against individuals self-consciously and aggressively at odds with the system's material base or political values. More according to the norm was the urge of differently marginal population groups to expand the critical universe so as to move nearer its center as a result. The marginality of the Western farmers having been geosectional at least as much as social, it was the attendant lack of a well-defined collective personality as well as the deficiency of a sustaining rapport with the older Eastern seaboard that were responsible for that group's particularly intense nationalism and aggressive expansionism. The rural West was succeeded by late-immigrating urban hyphenates as the major (and in their case unqualifiedly) socially marginal group imbued with compensatory Americanism. In the aftermath of a period of hyphenate isolationism, echoing the tone set by Anglo-Saxon "little Americans," a particularly intense Americanism found its full and mature expression in an integral anti-Communism and related expansionism, as part of the conquest of new frontiers within and without the continental United States.

The near-conquests of centrality by marginal new groups contrasted with the smooth and spontaneous co-optation of previously marginal new men. The "conquests" tended to occur as part of transitions to new patterns of policy and new distributions of power; and the habitually attendant crises were wont to inflect the political system toward a greater-than-usual tolerance for the self-assertion of aristo-demagogic leaders such as the self-made aristocrat Andrew Jackson, the two Roosevelts, and the two Kennedy brothers. These leaders were marginal to the dominant, ruling or upper, class either politically or socially. They consequently acted as both breakers of past sociopolitical molds and brokers in the transition to new ones, in rough conformity with the Roman and British imperial precedents.

Since there was no hereditary ruling class in the American political system, there was little occasion for a deliberate co-optation of socially marginal "new men" as a means to retarding larger shifts in the bases of political power and its tenure. By the same token, a fundamental challenge from assertive individual marginality was rare to the point of virtual absence. It was issued perhaps only by Alexander Hamilton as the self-conscious outsider in the relatively classic ruling-class conditions of early America, torn as such between the attractions of being fully co-opted into the system and converting it into a more congenial mold. The same circumstances intermittently enhanced the need for men only marginally marginal, willing and able to mediate shifts in social power because facing toward both conservatism and reform, old and new socio-ethnic forces, inward and outward. With this need went recurrent opportunity for authentically native and upper-class, Jeffersonian reformers. Inasmuch as major sections of the upper class perceived such individuals as renegades, they were (by our definition) politically marginal; they were aristo-demagogues insofar as they were allied with the "people" as a matter of both conviction, rooted in a sense of *noblesse oblige*, and political opportunism, relating ambition to democratic realities. The type reappeared authentically with the two Roosevelts and was incarnated, with modifications, in Woodrow Wilson as the self-conscious intellectual aristocrat. Social marginality due to only recent achievement of upper-class status clung residually to both Andrew Jackson as frontier-type aristocrat and to John F. Kennedy's new-frontier "imperial presidency," and was manifest in the imitative exaggerations disclosing the *parvenu* underneath the patrician.

Both of the Roosevelts aroused revulsion on the elite level, on the grounds of one form or another of class betrayal: Theodore among old-money reformist gentlefolk, Franklin on the part of the new-money, laissez-faire business elite. Conversely, all of the aristo-demagogues acted as powerful poles of attraction for activist members of both traditional and ascending, old-school and new-skill, elites of both Anglo-Saxon and more recent backgrounds.

The mobilization of non-Anglo-Saxons had begun with Jackson's electoral appeal to the Irish immigrants; it culminated with the recruitment of an authentically heterogeneous foreign-policy elite by Irish-American Kennedy, after a steady influx of new-skill elites to deal in succession with economic depression, cold war, and world empire. As they added acquired technical expertise to the inherited statesmanlike prudence of the relatively small numbers of politically surviving old-stock Americans, the newcomers tended to erode the monopoly and supplement the overall managerial experience of the older established group. The resulting provisional division of roles engendered, in turn, an independent impetus to expand official operations as a condition of harmony within the expanding elite and of reciprocal assimilation between its constituent parts. In regard to the masses, the aristo-demagogue was essential as the broker in the assimilation of socially marginal groups into an expanding system; he was thus inevitably also a breaker of traditional social molds in conditions of latent or manifest crisis. How essential he was had been demonstrated in America by the failure of the nonaristocratic Al Smith to achieve at one stroke a "revolution" to be carried out subsequently and in two steps by Franklin Roosevelt and John Kennedy, when wresting the presidency from old-stock political leadership with decisive hyphenate support and achieving the election of a Catholic hyphenate to the presidency. The obverse of its essentiality is the unavoidable opportunism of aristo-demagogic leadership. If the two Roosevelts had alternated emphases on foreign expansionism and the enlargement of domestic opportunities, John Kennedy's formula combined an expansive liberal foreign-imperial policy with a basically conservative approach to domestic reform, only to be inverted subsequently by a changed public mood into Robert Kennedy's mix of radical social reformism and populist anti-imperialism.

As the dual expansion process climaxed in the Kennedy administration, a liberally inclined multi-ethnic foreign-policy elite was closely associated with world empire by a buoyant doctrine and correspondingly activist declaratory policies. Moreover, the President's own ethnic ambiguity (Anglophile-Irish and Europhile-American) blended with a charismatic personality to largely eliminate from the foreign-policy arena the traditional ethnic idiosyncracies still lingering within both the upper and the lower social strata. The brief Kennedy tenure was, therefore, decisive for symbolically affirming the American world empire as ethnically neutral and socially progressive, independently of its less impressive substantial achievements.

Critically different from the suppleness of aristo-demagogues will be the fixed ideas of single-minded reformers, prominently including the notion of an inherent antagonism between domestic reform and foreign expansion. That particular belief was passed on in America from the Populists by way of the isolationist Progressives (such as Senators Borah and LaFolette) in the post–World War I era to the post–cold war radicals of the New Left; as a tenet, the belief is equally at variance with instances of constrictive conservatism within both the internal and the international arenas (typified by Cleveland Democrats as much as by Hoover Republicans) and with instances of a dynamic and positive interplay between reform and expansion. Expansion has not been historically simply a distraction from reform; instead, the frequent concurrence or alternation between the two expressed either "cynical" transactions, promoted by doctrinaire reformers only indirectly at best, or else "cyclical" transferences of impetus and energies from one arena to the other.

Reformers, from the Jackson Democrats down to the Roosevelt New Dealers, tended to fail in attempts to evolve effective economic policies within the domestic compass only. As a result, the search for equilibrium and equity would be extended in America (as before in Rome and Britain) to the external arena, not least in conditions of acute or recently incurred or apparently impending economic distress. Nor would external expansion leave domestic structures indefinitely intact or frozen.

Reform had coincided with expansion at one time, crudely, when the Jacksonian movement toward economic democracy and the continental push westward were married in popularly favored land-distribution policies. A more complex instance was the concurrence of world empire and the welfare state, evening out for a time the historically commonplace fluctuations between economic boom and bust, between tendencies to reaction and revolution, isolationism and interventionism, on the strength of the previously demonstrated bankruptcy of the rival conjunction, between economic laissez faire at home and diplomatic passivity abroad.

Alternating with concurrence of reform and expansion has been a form of dialectic between the two. The shift from reform to expansion, or vice versa, will betoken leadership strategies responding to prior exhaustion of either support or leeway for dynamic domestic or external policies and programs within a competitive pluralistic system prone to intergroup deadlock. The neo-Jacksonian Democrats turned to foreign-policy expansion in the 1840s after exhausting energies if not programs for reform. They did so in the hope, which was to be realized only in the much longer run, that the enlarged framework might somehow facilitate the resolution of the sectional crisis by recreating latitude for intersectional accommodation through gradual reform as part of economic growth. The dialectic unfolded in shorter time spans when individual aristo-demagogues balanced conservative reform-mongering with liberal empire-building. Theodore Roosevelt was responding to fluctuations in public moods and economic conditions when alternating expansive thrusts with reformist themes (the former in 1898 and via presidential "large policy" in the early 1900s and the agitation for war involvement in 1915; the latter after 1905 and immediately prior to 1912) so as to acquire the requisite popular basis for competitive-cooperative transactions with the dominant business elite or for head-on competition with radical tribunes (such as Bryan and LaFolette) or a fellow aristo-demagogue (Woodrow Wilson). The Square Deal and the New Nationalism were the domestic counterpoints to either militant or peace-making, but always ambitious, foreign policy. Similarly, when energies and possibilities behind Wilson's New Freedom had been exhausted by 1914 (witness his yielding on the regulation of railroads and regression on trust-busting), the subsidence of the reform drive was both a prelude and an incentive to the pursuit of a spectacular foreign policy that might renew the mandate for a further period of reform at a later date. After it had inspired Colonel House to urge foreign-policy initiatives on Woodrow Wilson in 1914, the prospect of a completed cycle intensified in 1919 the opposition of Lodge unilateralists to a League of Nations that would serve Liberal governments in the United States and Europe as a focus for coordinated social reform. The opposition aborted at one stroke both Wilson's peculiar brand of institutionally implemented globalism and the swing back to domestic reform. More successfully completed interplay was in evidence when, in and through post–World War II expansion, a prestigious cold-war elite corrected the earlier inability of the New Dealers to recreate the economic prerequisites to continuing socio-political reform by internal measures alone.

An exhausted or otherwise lacking leeway for peaceful reform will tend to stimulate the ruling class into foreign-policy activism (and make the public receptive to it). The obverse has been less commonly true. Suspended foreign-policy élan will commonly coincide with renewed emphasis on or call for domestic reform, but effective reform will follow less reliably a depletion in foreign-policy energies that may be just as easily attended also by domestic contraction. Whereas Progressive reform between 1904 and 1914 had come after the expansion consequent on the war with Spain, a striking new wave of reform did not fill the void created by the retreat from expansive foreign policy after either World War I or, immediately, the second Indochina war. When reform does actually follow upon an expansive phase in foreign policy, rather than coinciding with that phase in time, the sequence will appear to corroborate the thesis of the two being mutually exclusive. It may then be more accurate, however, to see in such sequence a proof for interdependence between expansion and reform, albeit one that is temporally staggered or, differently put, exhibits time lags in the transfer of energies from one to the other in a process of mutual, if sometimes seemingly perverse, stimulation.

XII

The obverse of an expansive interplay is one which encompasses political reaction and various restrictions as part of the defensive response to social mobility by adaptation-resistant members of a dispossessed or dispossession-prone upper or ruling class. Ruling-class trusteeship or interclass transactions have a direct and positive effect on expansion most of the time. By contrast, the effect of ruling-class trauma tends to be only indirect, and the underlying intentions will be negative on the part of ruling-class generations extruded from power before they had established a meaningful empire with which they could identify. The several generations of the discontinuous American ruling class forfeited political leadership as they failed to diversify and round off the functional basis of the trusteeship won previously by successfully resolving a specific national crisis. Since such a group had typically passed the zenith of dominant collective power in the fast-moving American political system before plumbing the depths of group trauma, the latter's impact on the body politic was automatically dampened. The impact on the dispossessed group itself was in turn diluted in one respect and aggravated in another by the opportunities which the selfsame sociopolitical mobility offered for individual re-entrants into ruling-class roles.

The major, but still only partial, exception was the integral group trauma of the Southern landed aristocracy following the Civil War. More in keeping with the rule were the splits that opened within the Federalist elite and the business elite in decline, and also the cold-war ruling class born of the twin crisis of depression and war. Fully and definitively traumatized and alienated were historically elite members unable or unwilling to adapt to social and ethnic dilution or (put differently) to assimilate with successive rising groups by accepting as legitimate the claim of such groups to the status of either old-stock Americans or authentic and representative Americans pure and simple—a self-perception that vitally eased the unfolding of social change. Alienation, attended or soon followed by withdrawal from politics, will quickly convert a traumatized political class into a social caste. The transformation was, in the American setting, more frequently manifest in retreat into gentleman-farming than into pseudo-aristocratic fascism; in individual expatriation more characteristically than in compulsive last-stage expansionism. Escape to the land or to more congenial lands typically followed a penultimate period of withdrawal from political struggles into diplomatic service, beginning with the high Federalists shortly before and after the Jeffersonian "revolution" of 1800. A more active or militant reaction than withdrawal into substitute arenas is, however, nostalgic regression into earlier political patterns and frameworks. In the domestic arena, nostalgic regression meant for a discontinuous ruling class the return to fundamentalist constitutionalism throughout and to integral Americanism most of the time. For the politically-minded Federalists, the basic Constitution meant the right of the best to govern in opposition to Jeffersonian mobocracy. It came to mean, in the views of the conservative anti-imperialists in the 1890s and of the anti-immigration isolationists of the 1920s, the right of the best to be properly self-governed by protecting the original ethnic stock against hybridization by unassimilable aliens. And for the orthodox-capitalist business elite in its period of trauma in the 1930s, the basic Constitution was reducible to the sanctity of the rights of property in the face of Roosevelt's big-government socialism.

The social elite's most innocent form of self-defense against alien intrusions was a return to English antecedents, consummating the positive reassessment of the British empire begun by the early Federalists. More forcefully defensive were the upper-class reactions to sociopolitical mobilization partaking of militarism and terrorism, however muted and ineffectual. Militarist in kind or inspiration was the scheme of the declining Federalists in the 1790s to enlarge the land army, in connection with current frictions with France, to a size usable also for repressing domestic opposition. In the late 1890s, the neo-Hamiltonian traditionalists desired war so as to evade group trauma via alliance with the momentarily bellicose masses against the timid "money power" of the post–Civil War business elite. And upper-class political parties with minority standing sought out repeatedly charismatic military heroes with presidential potential, as the remedy of last recourse. William H. Harrison had been picked by the Whigs in 1840 to beat back left-reformist Jacksonians; Generals Eisenhower and MacArthur were courted by different wings of the Republican party in the later effort to keep alive the two-party system and keep down the Fair Dealers. Terrorist in ultimate implications was, moreover, upper-class support or discreet sympathy for only superficially different expressions of pristine Americanism such as was the Red Scare of 1920, the Ku-Klux-Klan movement of the 1920s and 1930s, and the McCarthy hysteria of the 1950s. Individually varying, they all surfaced the reaction to forces perceived as alien by a status-insecure lower middle class at different stages of progression from anti-hyphenate Anglo-Saxonism to anti-Communist (and, in part, anti-Anglo-Saxon) Americanism.

The basic thrust of the collective psychoses legitimized sundry associated motives and objectives; it also created a potential mass base for otherwise ineffectual upper-class conservatives, including the orthodox businessmen of the Liberty-League variety in the 1930s and, in the 1950s, an orthodox politician (Senator Robert A. Taft) and an unorthodox military man (General Douglas MacArthur). Yet, if politically marginal aristo-demagogues would characteristically lead progressive reform, conservative reaction would be more commonly spearheaded by social marginals (or, in vast America, sociogeographic marginals). Thus the Irish-Catholic McCarthy from Wisconsin and the half-Jewish Barry Goldwater from Arizona would appeal to the fundamental moral and fundamentalist political values of the community in successive spurts of radical conservatism. In so doing, ultraconservative Goldwater partook somewhat of the dormant tradition of Alexander Hamilton, while sharing policy and value biases with one or two of Britain's one-time leading marginals. McCarthy was, by contrast, more the rabble-rousing popular tribune of Roman vintage, agitating in mutually exploitative tactical alliance with upper-class reaction against liberal aristo-demagogy and its liberal-professional middle-class allies.

As an expression of upper-class trauma in foreign policy, nostalgic regression was essentially limitationist without being confined to all-out isolationism. The attitude complemented in that way the stress on limiting governmental functions and containing socioethnic change internally. Since no declining American ruling class could fall back before the cold-war era upon an established empire as its historic achievement, it could not use empire as a platform from which to bid for an alliance with the people against less well-pedigreed claimants to power. As a result, nostalgic regression in foreign policy meant reversion to preexisting traditional patterns and scopes of expansion and involvement, by necessity more limited than the ones propounded by the alternative reformist-expansionist leadership at any one time. Dispossessed Federalists had withdrawn into the New England regional "empire" after failing to consolidate their dominant position against the expansionist Westerners within a "nationalist" politico-economic American system linked to the British empire; and antiexpansionist traditionalists looked back in the 1880s and 1890s to a preindustrial Anglo-Saxon United States, keeping unassimilable aliens outside a continental maximum. In the still later periods between the two world wars and immediately following the second global conflict, the isolationists had only the regional core-empire to revert to from war-related European and global entanglements. Thus, somewhat like the Federalists retreating into the politically impregnable New England fortress, Herbert Hoover would fall back in the global setting of the 1950s on a militarily impregnable Western-Hempispheric "Gibraltar."

Variously conjoined with regional imperialism, isolationism differed from unilateralism of potentially global scope. As exhibited by Senator Lodge in the first postwar period and by General MacArthur and Senator Taft in the second, the unilateralist posture was likewise backward-looking, however. It would either extend world-wide the single-handed approach adopted within America's hemisphere or perpetuate, through dissociation from multilateral institutions, the model of world-imperial expansion as it had been initiated in the Philippines in separation from, and apparent defiance of, the European great powers.

Self-isolation from the still essentially European, central balance of power immediately following World War I could go hand in hand with the economic diplomacy of the dollar. No less had the opposition of the conservative Mugwumps to annexations overseas been compatible in the 1890s with their support or even advocacy of what has since been called neo-colonialism. In all such cases, the desired limitation was on the scope or extent of responsible involvement by the United States, not of its influence. The undesired involvement in the 1890s had been in actual governing responsibilities via annexation; to be avoided in and after

1919, and residually also after 1945, was upholding the military-strategic balance and security by means of steady participation. Tactical deviations could accompany the pursuit of the highest political ambition, but gestures toward internationalism were as unrepresentative of Robert Taft's basic beliefs in 1952 as pledges of isolationist sentiments had been of Franklin Roosevelt's in 1932.

The successive forms of defensive-conservative limitationism were as diametrically opposed to Tory expansionism as they were to liberal internationalism. To favor limitation in foreign policy meant shielding the existing American framework, consecrated by tradition, from radical challenges and changes, arising out of either socioethnic mobilization or economic dislocation deemed likely to attend or follow expansive foreign policy or other forms of extensive involvement abroad. Alien impingements would result most directly from expansion introducing alien populations eligible for citizenship. Fears along these lines marked the Louisiana purchase and the annexations of 1898. A less direct impact from expansion could be tied up with warlike conflict or institutionalized peacetime cooperation. Both were capable of either mobilizing or legitimizing the claims of recent immigrants to full status as citizens and full access to the material attributes of citizenship. World War I had evidenced such a development, while Senator Lodge and ex-Senator Beveridge were among those who feared that its acceleration would flow from League membership. Even token involvements were held to upset domestic tranquillity most severely in the late 1920s and early 1930s, when they had apparently precipitated economic dislocations as a real ill and radical reformism as the pretended remedy.

Anti-foreignism, turned both outward and inward, stimulated isolationism in the 1920s before being aggravated by economic depression. Anti-foreignism merged with anti-reformism when the fear of internationalized reform and foreign interference with restrictions on continuing immigration via the League joined the concern for congressional war powers in prompting opposition to American membership. Anti-reformism moved into the lead and the ethnic aspect continued declining in significance in the late 1930s and early 1940s, when hostility to interventionist reform-mongering by the New Deal carried over into opposition to war-mongering by Roosevelt's interventions abroad. Intervening on the side of Great Britain in World War I had been a mechanism for self-maintenance by America's ruling class. But the actual war effort deranged the preservative mechanism by mobilizing the hyphenates sociopolitically as well as militarily. The triumph of Americanization over Anglicization was bound to disillusion major sections of the Anglo-Saxon upper class about the merits of an active and associationist foreign policy. The disenchantment was expressed either in pure isolationism or in mere unilateralism. Unilateralism was, in effect, a fusion of isolationism and imperialism, reacting to Britain's disutility as a social counterweight for the American upper class internally as much as to its decline as imperial surrogate for the United States internationally.

In the same class perspective, American isolationism has been either organic or opportunist. It was organic insofar as indiscriminate isolationism served as the appropriate, passive-defensive means for shielding the original ruling class from extraneous influences liable to accelerate social dilution and eventually dispossess that class in larger frameworks. The challenge and response applied principally to the authentic sociopolitical elite, but could be extended to the ethnically Anglo-Saxon populace as an elite of sorts. Ruling-class isolationism could be also partially opportunist, however. It was so when Henry Cabot Lodge appealed on that basis to war-disgruntled hyphenates or when conservative Republicans opposed Franklin Delano Roosevelt's internationalism along with the New Deal. Integrally opportunist was the specifically slanted isolationism of hyphenate Irish-Americans fighting friendship with Britain and German-Americans opposing warlike intervention against Germany; but generalized isolationism, too, was not free of opportunism insofar as it enabled recent Americans to scale the peaks of integral Americanism, and begin the ascent of the social pyramid at the same time, by sharing, if nothing else, the dominant elite's disillusionment with Europe after World War I.

The unstable identities of both the ruling and the middle classes had contributed previously to opening up the isolationist hiatus between America's regional and global expansion. An insufficient and insufficiently continuous thrust of the subsidiary domestic determinant after 1898 insured that the expansionism reaching overseas beyond the continental land mass would fade after it had climaxed prior shifts from predation to preclusion as the primary stimuli to expansion, and from geographic sections to social groups as the key subjects in mediating transactions, intermittently relieved by infusions of the elitist trust mystique in the early stages of successive ruling-class generations and associated spells of expansion. As a result, more or less authentically preclusive expansion was not kept alive beyond 1898 by U.S. reactions to active European and Japanese efforts to impede persisting American encroachments abroad; the international stimulus remained dormant until it was revived by the insecurities arising out of conflicts among non-American powers gradually intensified by the absence of a common anti-American concern among them. When the external threats to America's interests seemed to subside in the late 1960s and early 1970s, the previously activated rate, achieved scope, and revealed costs of global expansion were such as to strengthen the reemerging internal obstacles to the American domestic dynamics maintaining the expansionist momentum along the lines of the Roman and British models.

The American anomalies had at least two long-term consequences. One was to fragment the domestic impetus to expansion, displacing its effective salience from the middle or still later phase of global expansion to the extra-regional tail-end of regional expansion in 1898 and the onset of global expansion in the 1940s. In both periods a vertical alliance of the American varieties of aristocrats and populace was more for war (with Spain and the Axis, respectively) than for sustained expansion and was followed by horizontal transactions between old-family and new-money men in the first instance and between old-stock and new-skills men in the second instance. The divisions of functions on the elite level underpinned for a time a dynamic foreign policy in both cases, but were insufficient, in the absence of external stimuli (in the 1900s) or with their fading (in the 1960s), to reinvigorate and perpetuate expansion so long as stimulation from vertical sociopolitical interplays was inhibited internally by fluid group identities or rigid group ideologies and the actually occurring interplays proved to be inhibiting externally under the impact of ruling-class regression into trauma that accentuated any existing propensities to self-limitation. The other long-term consequence of the discontinuities was for the world-economic dislocations of the 1930s to impinge on a largely self-contained American economy that was neither protectively supported by, nor capable of restimulating through its needs, an established imperial posture.[3]

3. On domestic dynamics in America in different periods and from specific viewpoints (next to sources cited in chap. vi), see William A. Williams, *Contours of American History* (Cleveland: World, 1961); John C. Miller, *The Federalist Era 1789–1801* (New York: Harper and Row, 1960); Marshall Smelser, *The Democratic Republic 1801–1815* (New York: Harper and Row, 1968); David H. Fischer, *The Revolution of American Conservatism* (New York: Harper and Row, 1965); Glyndon G. Van Deusen, *The Jacksonian Era 1828–1848* (New York: Harper and Row, 1963); Robert L. Beisner, *Twelve Against Empire* (New York: McGraw-Hill, 1968); George E. Mowry, *The Era of Theodore Roosevelt 1900–1912* (New York: Harper and Row, 1958); Peter Kersten, *The Naval Aristocracy* (New York: The Free Press, 1972); Richard Hofstadter, *Social Darwinism in American Thought* (Boston: Beacon Press, 1955), and *The Age of Reform* (New York: Alfred A. Knopf, 1966); William E. Leuchtenberg, *The Perils of Prosperity 1914–1932* (Chicago: Chicago University Press, 1966); Selig Adler, *The Isolationist Impulse* (New York: Abelard–Schuman, 1957) and *The Uncertain Giant: 1921–1941* (New York: Macmillan, 1965); George Wolfskill, *The Revolt of the Conservatives* (Boston: Houghton Mifflin, 1962); and Gabriel Kolko, *The Roots of American Foreign Policy* (Boston: Beacon Press, 1969).

VIII

AMERICAN EXPANSION. *Economic Dilemmas*

A number of particular economic dilemmas have affected America's expansion into empire at different stages. But they are dwarfed by a basic analytic and practical quandary to which the economic factor itself, as a determinant of expansion, has given rise with special force in the American case.

Whereas the Roman empire had been distinctively military (and even militaristic), and the British empire started out as mercantilist and remained essentially mercantile, the American has been consistently neither one nor the other and was at different stages partially both. When the American pre-imperial community and, subsequently, continental empire had been released from the mercantilist cocoon, the Pacific-Atlantic regional empire was predominantly mercantile during the prolonged midterm lull in militarily or politically encompassed expansion including outright annexations. Highly opportunistic mixes of economic protectionism and quasi-liberalism drew then on the strength of a previously expanded free domestic market; and they did so from a doctrinally vulnerable position combining sweeping contention against different forms of economic control internationally with the selective practice thereof. When the American empire became global in due course, it acquired strong military overtones. The main emphasis on economic freedom in behalf of a meanwhile matured economy shifted from the domestic to the international arena; the materialistic ethos and the mercantile mentality became simultaneously less visible and salient as incentives to expansion; but the ethos found a compensating expression in method, in the guise of predilection for economic instruments, while the corresponding mentality remained latent in the dominant style of prudential calculation of costs and limitation of risks.

If the stress on economic instruments and a closely related managerial style denoted one kind of economism in an ascendant American empire, another kind had stood repeatedly for economic activism, avoiding politico-military exertions in isolationist lull periods; and yet another economism, and the most significant for any empire, including the British and Roman, entailed self-protective strategies at the stage of apparent economic decline.

I

Salient among the factors that influenced the impact of economic determinants on the American experience with expansion were atypical aspects of security and the ruling class. If the former is central to the international determinants of expansion, the latter is critical for domestic determinants. And if the peculiar character of the security most commonly at issue for the United States imposed a limiting constraint on the capacity of specific economic interests to press for or impede expansion, the peculiar character of the ruling-class issue weakened the capacity of the economic factor in the aggregate to influence expansion in a predictable fashion. Moreover, the two peculiarities in combination increased the importance of the interplay between the economic factor and security in the conventional, politico-military sense.

Since threats to physical security were insubstantial most of the time, the economic or "sustenance" factor ought to have been correspondingly promoted beyond its customary role in stimulating expansion. In actuality, and quite apart from the American propensity to simulate conventional insecurity for the national territory as a political good, security in the abstract came close to having its customary impact as a determinant of expansion. First, security had been initially equated with power, both symbolized and concretized in land as an economic good; second, it was progressively extended to encompass, and reformulated to focus on, the integrity of the indigenous economic system. Economic security evolved in the process from being an objective, first in a mercantilist and subsequently in a laissez-faire format, into becoming an achievement, to be defended in behalf of free-enterprise capitalism and its gradual welfare-oriented alleviations. In more directly threatened imperial communities, such as Rome and to a lesser extent Britain (or, even more so, imperial France and Germany), policy-makers were inclined to treat the integrity of metropolitan territory and the well-being of the politico-economic system as distinct and separate concerns, although always interdependent and most of the time inseparable for practical purposes. When the territorial base is secure, however, not only will the definition of what constitutes security be expanded, but (even more to the point) the central focus of insecurity fears will shift. In America's case, it shifted from physical or territorial integrity to the unconstrained functioning of the economic system and related sociopolitical institutions as the foremost value and the first line of defense. Even as the critical priorities undergo a subtle change, the controlling perception ceases to be one of practical interdependence between the territorial and the institutional aspects of security and insecurity and becomes one of their conceptual identity.

The location of principal insecurity influenced the economic factor's impact on American expansion throughout. On the one hand, if the economic system seemed intrinsically vulnerable or comparatively more endangered than other national values or attributes, its being the foremost arena of actual or potential crisis raised it to the status of the last resort or ultimate determinant of action. On the other hand, since a particular economic system was assigned a very high or even the highest social value as a matter of national ideology, it became automatically politicized. The functional autonomy of the economic system diminished overall as a result; and particular economic interests forfeited in some measure a specific or direct relation to and influence on public policy involving foreign expansion, especially when to give them priority might conflict with the requirements of the system through which their perception and evaluation would usually be processed.

The politicization of economics will have a similarly differentiated, fundamental as distinct from routinely operative, effect on expansion when it is due to the situation of the ruling class rather than to the character of the dominant national ideology. A so encompassed politicization will, however, affect less the degree of relative impact of economic motives and more the predictability of the impact's direction. When a landed ruling class is entrenched in power and authority over a mercantile middle class, it will politicize the economic factor by subjecting it to long-term considerations of class power and family status, individual career expectations, and group values, as these are tied to the structures of the internal and the imperial political arenas. Such close and enduring links will constrain the impact of specific short-range economic interests on public policy and will promote that policy's basic rationality and coherence. Politicization will change its character when a (landed) ruling class has encountered an ascendant (mercantile) middle class in a way that has converted the issue of relative political power between the two groups into one to be resolved before further and decisive shifts in the balance of economic power between the two classes can take place. Political transactions between the major sociopolitical groups, typically in the form of expansion-promoting compensation or appeasement of the lower class or classes by the receding ruling class, will then make the economic factor operational as the stimulus to expansion that is subsidiary and even indirect but relatively predictable and unequivocal in its directional thrust.

The American setting approximated the classic (both Roman and British) pattern only at key points of expansion, mainly in the late 1890s and in the period of the 1940s–50s. The always qualifying social background in the United States, and its dominating setting most of the time, was a highly diversified and only weakly hierarchical group pluralism. In such a group structure, interests and goals defined economically are the key stakes; and strictly economic leverage is critical for attempts by a group to wrest particular and fleeting advantages from the tendency of pluralism to settle into deadlock among group interests. Raw economic power will rise in importance, but will be also subject to the politicizing impact of intergroup bargaining and log-rolling within transient group coalitions, acting as the alternative to either anarchy or paralysis within the system. That kind of politicization will not, however, either constrain or channel expansion as continuously or predictably as does one attending either the primacy of a political class or a sustained, neat polarization between a ruling class and a middle class. Instead, divergences among plural economic interests and their political and administrative extensions or counterparts will influence expansion in largely haphazard ways and directions; and the divergences will have such an indeterminate impact even as they themselves are both amplified by a prior increase in the size of the domestic market and intensified by that market's crises of growth, changing the relative importance of the internal and the external economic environments.

Nothing could be permanent or unqualified in such a setting, including the early conflict in the United States between the outward orientation of the export-oriented agricultural interests and the inward orientation of the later-developing manufacturing interest. The eventual rise of organized labor was to add yet another, not always consistent or coherent, key group to American pluralism, while shifting balances of power and directions of thrust on the part of economically defined groups went on conditioning parallel interactions within the governmental structure (between executive and legislative organs and between different subgroups within each). Only a relatively marginal group, specializing in foreign trade or investment, was consistently committed to some form of economic expansion or initiative abroad. The other economic interests reinforced that concern only unreliably as real or imagined, material or mythical, needs and opportunities fluctuated in function, mainly, of harvests initially and later also business cycles and technological innovations. If the business cycles repeatedly raised the issue of production surplus and domestic underconsumption, as in the 1890s and following World War I, technological advances recreated a relatively self-sustaining domestic market after 1900 and eased the again growing dependence on external outlets following World War II.

Some of the features peculiar to the United States point to a more determining role for the economic factor than would be otherwise the norm for an empire that was not consistently mercantile and evolved into a military one. But other (or the obverse side of the same) features suggest a radical uncertainty. The actual impact that specific interests were apt to have (being constrained or politicized by the transcendence of the economic system as a whole) was no more certain than was the direction in which such interests or the perceived needs of the economic system itself would tend to influence policy (because of its bases in many-faceted pluralism); and both impact and direction will be as debatable as are the actually transpiring expansive thrusts that can be at all safely credited to the economic determinant in either its general-systemic or its more particularistic variety. Furthermore, the plural makeup or structure of the economic sector itself will be as responsible for such ambiguities as is the duality within the American politicization mechanism. That mechanism has assigned value primacy to the socioeconomic system in a manner that is ideologically both uniform and absolute; but it has been operationally fragmented as to process and diffuse as to product.

It would thus appear that American foreign policy, despite the high economic content of its domestic base and because of that content's highly variegated character, will most of the time depend on other than "purely" economic factors for clear focus and direction. A major disciplining factor will be issues that either fuse or closely interrelate the concern for the security of the internal economic system with the concern for external security within the politico-military balance of power, and impart operational priority to the latter even while offering no challenge to the implicitly postulated superior inherent worth of the former. Such interrelation was empirically plausible from time to time in the course of American expansion, whereas its factual grounds themselves either reinforced or were reinforced by the tendency to view as conceptually identical the physical and the institutional or systemic aspects of American security. The link between economics and strategy was relatively simple and straightforward when overland continental expansion aimed to enlarge both physical security and material sustenance. It grew more complex and problematic when widening cyclical fluctuations in economics combined with oscillations between imperialism and isolationism, as happened during the empire's fitful expansion from continental scope to first regional and then global circumference overseas.

The American empire grew from a materially strong home base, but at least in part independently of a variably intense, definite, and decisive economic determinant of expansion. As the empire grew in scope, its material basis was transformed from a primarily agricultural into a primarily industrial economy, while cyclical fluctuations were occurring in both of the principal sectors. In the process, imperial expansion went through the normal phases. Formative economic growth from an early position of inferiority, with the aid of predation (land) and protection (manufacture), produced in due course economic superiority; and superiority placed a premium on economic freedom also externally, before eventually displaying isolated signs of a relative decline different from sporadic depressions that inspired protective responses. But, when compared with the Roman and British patterns, specific mixes were deranged somewhat, regardless of whether they concerned warlike or less directly belligerent economic acquisitions in the formative stage or bore on protection, fairness, and freedom of trade as key stakes or concerns for the formed economy vis-à-vis the outside.

The distortions were due to the external environment in great measure. In the formative phase, the critical external environment was mainly politico-military, and it became mainly politico-economic in the maturer stages. Young America's politico-military environment on the North American continent displayed a sufficient paucity of antagonistically disposed resistant power to reduce the role of war in initial economic growth, without eliminating war altogether as a factor. The global politico-economic environment was contrastingly well-crystallized. It fostered, albeit unsteadily over time, a bias in favor of the extensible internal (or metropolitan) market as against the constraining or volatile external (or imperial) marketplace; but defensive self-insulation was repeatedly thwarted by definite extraneous incentives or inhibitions, inviting an offensive promotion of the American economic access abroad. Regardless of the thrust of the environmental influences and the relative quantities of internal and external economic exchanges, however, the conditioning factors originating in the external environment shared one aspect initially: they commonly predated internal developments in the American economy as regards doctrines and related policy dispositions as well as capacities. Insofar as the environment was primarily constituted by a dominant British imperial economy, it preceded the American development in both the mercantilist and the free-or-fair trade eras; outside developments ran largely parallel to specifically American developments only insofar as the outside consisted of German and Japanese economies and policies. The prematured mercantilist environment had been oppressive for the nascent American economy, not least when the environment functioned well; the post-mercantilist environment continued to inhibit the internal growth and external ramifications of the unfolding American economy, not least because it was liable to sporadic crises and eventually also to structural deterioration. While such defects were not unrelated to problems proper to the American economy itself, they did reinforce maladjustments in that economy's mature stage.

Starting out as chiefly British mercantilism, external obstruction evolved into the neo-mercantilistic practices of the continental European powers and Japan, notably in the Far East. The obstruction was initially matched by only localized opportunity for self-assertion, mainly in the Western Hemisphere. The combination of obstruction and opportunity was matched, furthermore, by the combination of gradual economic obsolescence (mainly British) and growing vitality (mainly German and Japanese). Facing the obstacles and directed to expanding the opportunities was the tendency of the maturing American economy and economic policy to press actively for free (or freer) trade in specific areas (Open Door) and with only some countries (early reciprocity treaties), before being ready to apply the free-trade principle more widely at large and at home. The consequence was to make the protective concern for "fair," i.e., non-discriminatory, trade coincide with growth of the American economy rather than with incipient decline (as had been the case for Britain), even while domestic protectionism behind a high tariff continued to flourish past actual capacity for more liberal trade practices. Promotive and protective features in public economic policies and related diplomatic initiatives were relatively constant in the course of America's fitful ascent to global empire. Once the latter became reality, it engendered noneconomic resources and leverages that would be only intermittently and provisionally necessary for dealing with particular failings of the matured internal economy, so long as that economy remained salient over a still more fickle or less controllable external economic environment.

All things considered, the sequence of formative war imperialism, informal free-trade imperialism, and protective formalized imperialism fits the American case only imperfectly. But positing the pattern may still make it easier to identify the evolution underlying discordant features at any one time and to highlight fitful progressions and regressions between the characteristic features of the several phases over time.

II

The United States shared the phase of formative war imperialism with the Roman and the British empires in general terms, implying basic similarity and specific differences. Generally, the notion encompasses and interrelates three components. One is the formation of the basic core-imperial economy as a distinctive process. Another is the coincidence of that formation with wars as a method intrinsic to the process of economic growth, even if actual growth will directly derive from specific wars in differing degrees. And yet another is the interdependence in and for expansion of economic (or politico-economic) factors and military-strategic factors (only including war). The interdependence is necessarily implied in the commonsense nonideological meaning of "imperialism" if it is to be distinguished from economic expansion or expansionism that is only remotely related or wholly unrelated to upholding a military-strategic framework. So defined, imperialism can accompany both a fully formed or developed economy, as informal (free-trade) imperialism, and a declining economy, as formalized (protective) imperialism. But a special and positive conjunction between the initial growth of an economy and military conflict is required for anything like formative war imperialism, inasmuch as economic growth can occur without wars and wars can be related to economic growth negatively as impediments or not at all.

American formative war imperialism was characterized by initial inferiority of the home economy relative to principal rivals, as its point of departure and incentive; by predation, as the method for correcting the disparity; and by political control over territory, as the immediate goal and longer-term means. Beyond that general similarity with the older empires, there were specific differences in regard to both events and ethos, specific developments and doctrines.

Early Roman wars had been fought mainly for strategic objectives, in keeping with the dominant military ethos. The ruling class had not sought primarily the incidental economic gains (booty and slaves), much as its members came increasingly to appreciate and covet the proceeds. The corresponding early British wars for empire were fought within the framework of the mercantilistic identification of trade and war. The fairly determinate strategic and economic prizes, commercial-naval primacy and colonies as the bases of a positive balance of trade, were broadly agreed-upon domestically under unifying dynastic auspices. An elusive but significant contrast was to attach to the early American wars, preceding the War for Independence and continuing through and beyond that war. Fought for an intersectionally controversial combination of economic and security reasons, the early military engagements had also individual and cumulative economic consequences that were either unintended or were not fully anticipated. But the aggregative consequence was massive economic growth by way of expanding land and population, trade, and manufacture. Seizing more land was crucial for developing the objects of trade in agricultural staples and minerals; and territorial expansion fostered manufactures by creating new capital, via agricultural exports and foreign investments in land and overland communication, as well as by expanding the market, via a growing population with rising consumer needs and purchasing power.

The central role of territory *qua* land to cultivate and exploit points to the fusion between security and sustenance, between strategic and economic factors. The fusion is as typical for expansion under formative war imperialism as is the complementarity of security with power, since the drive for power and the feeling of insecurity can readily supplement one another as incentives. Universally valid land-related equations were only fortified by specific local peculiarities when promoting American expansion. It was particularly urgent for an initially small economy to expand access to foreign trade within a constraining mercantilistic framework; a growing external demand for agricultural produce stimulated overland expansion, even while the advance was facilitated by a progressive decline of external resistance; promoters of an economy developing under the impetus of internal freedom exhibited a growing tendency to equate sustenance with an externally uninhibited continuous growth and, consequently, to identify physical security with the immunity of the evolving socioeconomic system; and, at the critical point of transition from agricultural to industrial economy and from continental-national to overseas-imperial economy, the major threat to that system changed from outside inhibitions to domestic tensions among the various sections and their increasingly pressing economic implications.

The basic characteristics of formative war imperialism, shared by the three empires, identify it as a universally occurring developmental phase. But they do not clearly delimit either the doctrine or the practice or the phase's duration. In doctrine and related practice, American formative war imperialism was not identical with either militarism along specifically Roman lines or with full-fledged mercantilism along Britsh lines; its evolving doctrinal base and practical manifestations can best be defined negatively, by differentiation from the earlier empires. Mercantilist features had been pervasive in the early American experience and remained long in force selectively. The decisive initial interaction was between superior and confining Britsh mercantilism and a developing resistant American counter-mercantilism. The overseas mother country had evolved disturbingly toward combining incipient economic freedom for the metropole with a continuing claim to ultimate regulatory control over dependencies; the colonists groped toward an "American system" that would combine advantages of privileged mercantilism internally and profitable trading license externally. Confinement and subordination of the American colonies, always implicit in British mercantilism, prompted secession only when they were further aggravated by a systematization of British policy. After secession, the mercantilist American system entailed in principle only a limited, progressive, and economically balanced outward expansion. In due course, however, a partial dismantling of mercantilistic constraints on the Anglo-American trading relationship (with respect to the West Indies, in particular) was roughly coincident with the shift, within the United States itself, to an unrestrainedly expansive laissez faire as public policy and to unchecked land-grabbing as populist predilection. The Jacksonian surfacing of this always immanent trend meant discarding the mundane compulsions of British-style mercantilism, as it had manifested itself in overseas colonies, for a God-given entitlement to continent-wide expansion American-style. The shift in doctrine and practice alike did not imply, however, a readiness to incur the costs of Roman-type militarism and of the related client system. American continentalism was different from both antecedents. It served the economic purposes peculiar to the British model, while preparing the basis for replicating the Roman model in the longer term and on an enlarged scale.

Being coterminous with neither mercantilism nor militarism, America's formative war imperialism on the continent partook nonetheless of the close connection between the two, manifested in the incidence of trade wars and implied in the systematic promotion of both agriculture and manufactures as the sinews of war. It also reflected the intimate link between war and land, insofar as military contest and conquest ineluctably derive from the finite supply of land, while land brings together most conspicuously the inherently unlimited expansive thrusts of national power and national honor. If power is tied to land as the critical primitive source of regular public revenues as well as of exceptional rewards for publicly useful service, honor is tied to territory as something that a self-respecting polity must not alienate by either sale or barter and that will, therefore, be properly the object of forcible seizure. But again, the intensity and the constancy of America's liability to militarism were muted by the relative mildness, brevity, and even rarity of the early wars. The wars were minor when compared with equivalent Roman and British wars as well as when measured against their effect on the American economy in the phase of formative war imperialism, before the increasing superiority of the economic potential over military effectiveness came to favor the United States in later wars.

Except perhaps for the French-Indian warfare of the 1740s, the early wars were fought either with powerful aid by others (the British before and the French during the War for Independence); they were fought among others (the Anglo-French Napoleonic wars); or they were conducted against only half-hearted or nearly powerless adversaries (the British in 1812 and the Mexicans in 1846, respectively). The engagements were no match for either Rome's great-power wars in the Western and the Eastern Mediterranean or Britain's contentions in the Atlantic and Indian Ocean areas in comparable periods. The major American war in the phase of formative war imperialism was actually displaced to the category of civil war, as a token of the increasing primacy of the intersectional crisis over interstate crises and consequent threats to security and sustenance. On the one hand, the Civil War compares with England's civil wars preceding domestic political stabilization under the Tudors, itself a preliminary to overseas expansion. But if overseas expansion by the British had coincided with formative war imperialism, the American outreach beyond the continent only followed upon that phase. On the other hand, American and late-Republican Roman civil wars were alike as harbingers of movements beyond formative war imperialism toward larger and freer trade, within East-West Mediterranean and

South-North American universes of unbalanced politico-economic integration.

Even though minor, American wars in the age of formative imperialism had about equally potent economic and strategic objectives from the viewpoints of both general and particular interests and public and private actors. The dual purpose of the pre-independence French wars was to thwart encirclement by the Franco-Indian alliance (with British military support) and to gain a monopoly of access to natural resources in North America (under the auspices of the British Board of Trade). Security and sustenance were even more strikingly fused as the objects of the Indian wars, continuing beyond independence, while both the Revolutionary War of Independence and the War of 1812 expressed American disaffection with the maritime as well as the mercantilist British systems. If the maritime system meant denial of free overseas trade, it also implied physical exposure to coastal assaults; nor was only one of the two discrete determinants responsible for the American reaction to overland British confinement before the two wars, with respect to the trans-Appalachian West and the Canadian Northeast. Finally, whereas the security objective was relatively far-fetched in the Mexican war, it was restored to parity with economic stakes in the Civil War. The free vs. slave labor dichotomy and the imperilled state of the cotton monopoly involved serious economic stakes; and security was endangered had a consolidated Southern sovereignty simultaneously fostered and placed under British auspices a multipolarized balance-of-power system in North America and the Western Hemisphere.

Economic objectives actually sought tended to differ from the immediate or ultimate and particular or cumulative consequences, however. In part, at least, the difference between anticipated outcomes and unanticipated consequences coincided with the difference between direct and indirect result. The pattern was set early by the War of Independence. It is immaterial in this respect whether the war was fought primarily against the new stringencies of British mercantilistic policies in America following from the (seven years' long) war that had been set off by the Diplomatic Revolution in Europe, or was waged against the broader and longer-term implications for the colonies of an incipient trend toward more free-wheeling economic policies anticipating the Industrial Revolution in Britain. Nor does it much matter whether the Americans sought to return to the reciprocally advantageous mercantilist system preceding 1763 or to move toward economic independence for a mercantilism of their own. The more significant fact is that the revolt's anticipated consequence, an improvement in the economic conditions in America, was not fulfilled for a decade or two after independence. Only conjointly with the successive later wars did assured political and increased economic independence begin to stimulate and amplify the productive interplay of land, trade, and manufactures underlying the growth of American economic power. The wars stimulated economic growth largely by raising governmental expenditures and prices for goods, while decreasing access to cheap foreign manufactures. A high tariff would be imposed during a war for revenue and serve to protect uneconomical war-born infant industries after the war's end (e.g., the long-lasting post-1812 and post–Civil War tariff); it would insulate America from foreign imports on a par with either generalized belligerency abroad (e.g., the Napoleonic wars between French land power and British sea power) or specific inhibitive measures inimical to the United States (e.g., the British embargo of 1808, terminating the prior latitude for American shipping and trade).

Ranking shifted overtime among ultimately interdependent land, trade, and manufacture as objects of concern provoking conflict and stimulating expansive drives and as rewards of war and expansion contributing to overall economic growth. The War of 1812 was fought less for land than over trade, and the obverse was true for the war with Mexico. The earlier war did eventuate in advantageous partial accommodation with the mercantilistic European empires; but its principal consequence was the initial growth of domestic manufactures, including textiles, with support from postwar expansion into cotton- and wool-growing areas. In the war in Mexico, the immediate concern for land acquisition westward was more intense than was concern for eastern trade, much as the two overlapped in agricultural staples as the predominating export item. But the major consequence of the war was to accelerate the industrialization that had been under way since the 1830s, with the aid of a transportation network inspired by the War of 1812. While foreign investments flowed into transcontinental railroads and land purchases, and the new land could secure domestic borrowing, the territorial frontier was replaced with an ever-receding functional frontier of technological innovation and economic productivity. The consequent shift was consummated when the Civil War completed the infrastructure for massive industrialization, provoked the tariff increase that was briefly alleviated only in 1913, and promoted economic integration between South and North by way of northern colonization under the name of reconstruction. The result was a free continent-wide internal market and transport network, both of which were to prove indispensable for the later and wider economic expansion overseas.

Fought over continental unity and cohesion, the Civil War engendered the economic impetus for the later sea war with Spain. It also removed the political inhibition to informal economic expansion overseas previously inherent in the intersectional conflict over the South's commitment to an annexationist slave empire in the Caribbean. Similarly, the Mexican war had prepared both the political and the economic terrain for the

Civil War. It removed the last vestiges of a unifying foreign threat on the continent, while incorporating the remaining territorial wherewithals of West-South complicities in managing a balanced expansion and containment of slavery; and it augmented the economic pressures for a final resolution of the North-South conflict on the basis of comparably costly labor when increasing the ascendancy and the attractiveness of the industrially more advanced North by way of a system of communications linking the North with the West. A similar dialectic interplay with unanticipated cumulative consequences had been in evidence also between the Napoleonic wars and the War of 1812, and between the latter and the Mexican war of 1846. Being thus interrelated, the early wars were also matched by internal contentions. Agricultural, mercantile, and (later also) manufacturing interests had only partially complementary objectives in regard to land and trade; they could be reconciled only by expansion. And the wars themselves first generated and then kept in being both the pressures for indigenous industrial production and its prerequisites. Although cyclically crisis-ridden, industrial production grew as a result overtime within an expanding internal market that was both insulated and financially invigorated from abroad. Since the wars were the most dramatic manifestations of the security factor, finally, they muted the predatory materialistic physiognomy of both economic growth and territorial expansion by providing a legitimizing complementary impetus and rationale.

The early wars played thus a critical role in the growth of America's continental economic power. The power arose in the last resort out of the functional interdependence between land, trade, and manufacture and out of the related sectional interactions between Northeast, West, and South; the midwifery of wars at its birth complemented the intersectional political transactions, which mediated the impact of the economic factors on continental expansion, not least when the West-South alignment with a bias against the Northeast (for war with Mexico) was replaced by the North-West alignment against the South (for the Civil War).

Had American formative war imperialism been coterminous with mercantilism as doctrine and practice, it would have extended only to the early nineteenth century in terms of domestic economy and all the way to the early or mid-twentieth century in terms of international-trade policy. If, on the other hand, militarism as either doctrine or practice were controlling, the phase might be deemed coincident in America with the so-called war economy or military-industrial complex extending from World War II to its cold-war aftermath. Instead, being either ambiguous or neutral in terms of both the mercantilist and the militarist doctrines, formative war imperialism climaxed with an event, the Civil War, and ended with the achievement of two conditions. One condition was a viable base for continuing economic growth within a secured habitat;

another, the sharp decline of interest in acquiring political control over additional territory. While insuring the first condition, the Civil War fostered the second. It shifted political predominance to the mercantile-industrial Northeast which, compared to the other sections, had been averse traditionally to territorial acquisitions as liable to displace indigenous labor to other parts; and it sparked a renewed post-bellum alignment between South and Midwest against cheap ("coolie") labor from overseas dominions that would inundate the ruins of the old West's expansionism for free land westward and the old South's for slave labor southeastward. In addition to impeding further annexations and introducing a decisive stage in economic growth, finally, the outcome of the Civil War also consolidated definitively the continental habitat in the so far crucial Anglo-American context by terminating British hopes for either reversing or modifying the verdict of the Revolutionary War for Independence (and the 1812 war) in North America and, by extension, the Western Hemisphere.

Just as the Civil War climaxed the period of formative war imperialism by securing a territorial and economic base for further expansion by different means, so the war with Spain was an intermediate phenomenon between two phases as regards economic determinants of expansion and two sets of wars. The Spanish war belonged to formative war imperialism in its Caribbean focus that consummated the security of the continental habitat, albeit without contributing to the preestablished economic home base or involving formal annexation. By contrast, the war's Asian-Pacific dimension relating to the Philippines overlapped into the next era of informal imperialism. The archipelago was to help secure anticipated overseas economic activities (the "China trade"), rather than the metropolitan base itself; and its actual annexation merely reflected the impossibility of confining acquisitions to a strategic base. The two world wars of the twentieth century differed from the wars of the initial phase even more completely than had the war with Spain. The interplay among America's wars continued insofar as the growth of productivity originating in the earlier military conflicts increased the importance of participating in later conflicts, so as to insure economic outlets overseas or bar the stifling effects of adverse war outcomes on domestic production. But the interwar dialectic was also subject to a fundamental discontinuity between the earlier and the later wars, in regard to their consequences even more than as to their causes.

All the major foreign wars, beginning with the Mexican war, were preceded by economic depressions or cyclical downturns (in 1843, 1896, 1913, and 1937). And both Woodrow Wilson and Cordell Hull identified structurally conditioned trade rivalries between expanding and receding economies and neo-mercantilist and quasi-liberal economic policies as the preeminent causes of contemporary major wars, in ways reminiscent of the war-trade equations dear to the mercantilists. Similarly, economically motivated American pretensions concerning the maritime rights of trading neutrals in wartime precipitated America's hostilities with Britain in 1812 and with Germany in 1917. Moreover, specific economic events preceded all the wars. Among them were the local land drives and speculations prior to 1812 and 1846; the geo-economic link-up between the West and the Northeast by way of the Erie Canal, and the concerted policy stand of the two sections in favor of protection, prior to the Civil War; and, prior to the three overseas wars, the German economic drive in Latin America and (secondarily) Asia and Japan's in Asia and (secondarily) Latin America for markets or raw materials or both. Likewise recurrently, economic stakes engendered in the course of a war between other parties became the stimuli for entering it actively. Just as the young United States benefited when France had acquired, in American debts to French traders and financiers, a special incentive to insure American independence, so the ability to collect on U.S. loans and other material aid to the Allies in World Wars I and II came to be contingent on American military support for Allied victory.

Economic antecedents were not, however, tantamount to either exclusive or self-sufficient economic causation for any of the wars—or for ensuing expansion. Built-in ambiguities prevent the economic factors from doing more than contribute to the total determinant in most cases and precipitate the onset of some of the conflicts. Important mercantile interests in New England had opposed the war with Britain in 1812 (and with Mexico in 1846), just as major U.S. financiers were to be opposed to the war with Spain. Such attitudes contravened the presumed economic objectives behind the two wars, in that they placed the immediate cost in socioeconomic stability of waging a war above the putative benefits of winning it for subsequent growth. Similarly, the protracted conflict between government policies in support of American and French agricultural interests led to only a species of trade wars at the most, whereas the less fundamental American-German competition over outlets for manufactures is supposed to have produced a fighting war unlike, furthermore, the comparable Anglo-American trade competition in Latin America and American-French (or American-Russian) trade rivalry in the Far East. If the necessity to lift the U.S. economy out of a depression by selling to some belligerents was largely responsible for America's movement into World War I, comparative capacities to pay entailed no compelling economic reason for not selling also or only to the Central Powers. Moreover, a victorious Imperial Germany could be expected not only to continue offsetting German competition with the growing size of a receptive German market but also to embrace economic policies at least as liberal as were to be those of economically declining Britain. And just as Germany, when compared with Britain before World War I, so Japan was both a more active competitor and a more receptive market than was China before World War II. In regard to expansion, finally, American participation in World War I culminated in genuine anxiety over economically rooted social-revolutionary upheavals in and beyond Europe without producing imperial expansion, in marked contrast to the consequences of concern with a military-security threat after World War II.

The never wholly economic causation behind American wars was subject to significant, if elusive, differences in successive phases of expansion. An increasingly speculative impact of external economic factors on a growing domestic market came eventually to hinge on such questions as the significance of marginal profits from foreign activities for internal prosperity in conditions of productive surplus, and the effective capacity or disposition of foreign suppliers to inhibit or deny access to actually or potentially scarce key raw materials. So updated stakes extend to the domain of economics the evolution from a predatory to a preclusive approach to war and expansion, especially in periods of economic pessimism; they can also relegate economic factors to the background, as either hypothetical or unavowed determinants, and maintain or even enhance their real importance at the same time. When an enlarged home economy has given rise to relatively liberalized economic policies, moreover, strategic and economic factors oriented respectively to security and sustenance tend to become more separate—or more readily separable—than they are when trade, war, and expansion merge in mercantilist and related navalist doctrines and, largely, practices, not least for a rising and assertive economy. Accordingly, the balances of power and trade had been fused for Americans facing antagonistic mercantilist constraints or even coercion in 1812. By contrast, a bigger economy in an expanded, even if actually or potentially quasi-mercantilist, environment made it possible for Woodrow Wilson or Cordell Hull to perceive and emphasize differently than did others the relative impacts on peace and war of trade rivalries and politico-strategic rivalries, of the balance of trade and the balance of power. Emphases could differ because determinants could be meaningfully differentiated for conceptual purposes, for related moral emphases, and for practical purposes of policy response. Once it has became separable, the economic factor will have only hypothetical implications for security; and it will be more likely than not susceptible of adaptations and accommodations by means short of coercion or conquest, despite its being ultimately interdependent and even circular with the factor of strategic security.

The increasing complexities and uncertainties which attend the transition to a mature economy relatively independent of the possession or control of territory will affect (next to the bearing of economic crises on war) the bearing of war on economic growth. While even a successful war can be judged to have had a disruptive rather than a stimulating economic effect, it is easy to exaggerate the negative consequence for the prenuclear period with respect to economies that have not been already declining. Since most American wars were followed by economic effervescence, together with a lull in expansionist élan, it is more revealing to differentiate the early and the late wars in terms of anticipated vs. actual, direct vs. indirect, and solely economic vs. broader politico-economic, consequences rather than causes. Anticipated consequences (i.e., the aims) of successfully concluded later wars may have accorded better with their actual consequences than had been the case for the earlier conflicts. One reason is that the earlier objective of acquiring or reinforcing highly disparate and specific economic elements was replaced at the later stage by the goal of protecting and projecting outward an already formed and integrated economy. Moreover, the direct consequence of success in early wars, in the form of conquest of particular assets, was apt to differ from their indirect result—the economic growth that was sparked by a productive integration of the newly acquired assets into preexisting structures. Direct and indirect consequences tend to fuse, by contrast, when a successful later war has removed prior constraints on the full internal and external deployment of an already developed economy. And leading up to yet another difference, if initial economic growth in the earlier war phase tends to be a function of a mix of strategic, economic, and political assets adding up to overall expansion, continuing economic growth in the later war period will be a function of such prior (economic) growth. However, if the early wars merely amplify a small or primitive economy, later wars translate previously developed economic power or capacity into external political manifestations as well. The issue in the earlier instances is cumulative economic growth, not fully anticipated as part of any one particular conflict; at issue in the later circumstances is more or less informal politico-economic expansion of a kind that was neither anticipated nor aimed at consciously during the initial formative period.

So much was true, within a growing scope and with increasingly durable postwar effects, of the overseas wars of the United States in its informally expansive phase, beginning with the war with Spain. Their intended general consequence, of translating economic growth into also political aggrandizement, entailed several complementary aspects. The specific objective was to create a politico-strategic setting for overseas deployment of continentally amassed economic power. Achieving the purpose depended increasingly on the capacity to exploit superior economic resource in an environment in which the threat to America's ultimate survival declined relative to both a paradoxically increasing threat to her military security (when compared with the continental phase) and, more importantly, relative to the concurrently growing threats to the survival of the other major powers or their internal regimes. As a result, when compared with the earlier formative period, America's politico-economic ascent was due to either the secular decline or the temporary decimation of others, directly or indirectly due to war, as much or more than to the economic growth of the United States itself. The two world wars tended to regenerate an already massive American economy rather than to qualitatively transform it. And economic advantage at the expense of other parties was gained both during and after each war. The United States took over Canada from Britain economically during World War I and Latin America during World War II, while American economic ascendancy after World War II inverted more lastingly than did the economic consequences of World War I the pursuit of economic independence through protectionist constraints into the pursuit of also political influence by way of economic freedoms.

The two world wars meant in these respects for the American empire what the chain of wars with Napoleon had meant for the British. They created the politico-strategic framework for an economically liberal, informal American empire. By contrast, it is the typical purpose of small peripheral wars, such as the later ones in Korea and Indochina, to maintain and only incrementally add to the framework of politically sheltered economic power. Actually weakening as they often are, such small wars can also be waged (or be retrospectively perceived as having been waged) to retard the relative decline of the imperial economy or of its political impact, just as the major wars had previously caused economic ascendancy to realize its full political effect. They mark then a transition from informal imperialism of the liberal variety to the third and last phase of protective imperialism.

Delimiting the qualitative difference between earlier and later wars helps date the transition from formative war imperialism to the immediately following phase. The key issue for the American case has not been whether the early wars were conducted primarily for strategic reasons of security or were waged more markedly for economic reasons than had been the comparable Roman and, even, British wars. That issue is largely a matter of different definitions of security in different settings, and its significance for the early phase is diminished by the tendency for the stakes of security and sustenance to fuse within the notion of either power or survival. That is to say, the main issue has not been to determine whether and to what extent the early wars, viewed in isolation or compared with conflicts in other periods, had economic causes and precipitants or only antecedents and concomitants. At issue instead has been primarily the question of the implications of these wars for economic growth, for the formation of the United States as a viable imperial base in material terms. The period from either the prerevolutionary wars or, at the latest, the Revolutionary War for Independence up to and including the Civil War integrally, and up to and including one theater of the war with Spain marginally, was one of formative war imperialism, since the wars in that period were intrinsic to economic growth. Early growth had been due to these wars in more critical respects than subsequent growth was due to later wars and was, by the same token, less of a self-sustaining, incrementally unfolding organic process independent of military conflicts. The result was a qualitative alteration of the United States, from being the secondary small-scale target of one or more European imperial economies to becoming a potential imperial economy and community in its own right.[1]

III

The war-studded American progression toward something like informal free-trade imperialism, that would foster and strategically sustain overseas economic expansion, was the result of factors that were not always unequivocal individually and were rarely if ever coherent in their sum. The factors comprised basic capacity, due to overall economic growth; incentives, reflecting both long-range shifts within the economic structures and shorter-range boom-and-mood fluctuations; and impediments, rooted in the American political system itself as well as in the economic environment.

For an actually or potentially imperial power to practice free trade it must first move from economic inferiority to economic superiority. America's flirtation with free trade soon after independence had, therefore, made policy precede capacity, just as indefinite protectionism evolved into a policy lag behind capacity in due course. And whereas the early pro-liberal policy had been a short-lived wartime strategy of defense against British mercantilism, increasing capacity was to be largely manifested at the expense of free-trading Britain. A still later conjunction of American capacity and policy was to approximate the free-trading British imperial model, finally, and challenge Britain's defensive retrogression into imperial neo-mercantilism. In terms of capacity alone, the American economy was quadrupled in the first half-century after independence and grew about tenfold in the half-century following the Civil War, until the U.S. manufactured output amounted to not much less than one-half of world output by the 1920s. American balance of trade had turned favorable in the mid-1870s; the United States began underselling Britain in steel in the mid-1890s; and America ceased being international debtor (chiefly to Britain) and became world creditor by 1914 (first to Western

1. The periodization just restated is superior to one positing several cycles—continental, regional, global—in the economic dimension of American expansion, each initiated by a formative-war imperialism phase centered on the Revolutionary War and the War of 1812, the war with Spain, and the two world wars, respectively; or, alternatively, to one extending the formative-war imperialism phase all the way to World War II, ignoring or downgrading differences between kinds and scopes of expansion as well as differences in categories of wars in economic terms.

Hemisphere countries and soon also to the European powers). Although informal economic expansion by way of free trade became fully possible when international financial primacy passed from London to New York after World War I, capacity for free trade was not matched by the level of foreign trade. After first declining from its high initial level and then rising again, the level remained relatively low even after World War II, and well below the foreign-trade dependence of the European powers in terms of per capita ratios. Nor did the secular trend from mainly manufactured imports and raw-material exports to the inverse composition of foreign trade ever nullify the critical importance of agricultural staples for American foreign trade and, eventually, policy. Similarly, while Europe's share in American exports and imports decreased in favor of Latin America and Asia, beginning with mid-nineteenth century, Europe never ceased being the principal economic partner. But even a quantitatively marginal shift had implications for policy, not least because the mainly agricultural exports to Asia were lucrative and the trade with Latin America was supplemental to major direct American investments and supportive of the Monroe Doctrine.

The growth in capacity entailed social (labor) and economic (production) crises, rooted in the prior shift from agricultural self-employment to a market economy and intensifying from the late 1870s on. More overseas economic outlets seemed required to siphon off social tensions along with agricultural and industrial goods, the surplus production of which successively replaced material deficiencies as the key stimulus of expansion. Moreover, since the rate of growth was declining from the late 1870s to nearly the end of the century, and depressions and recessions became more frequent and the overall socioeconomic crises more intense, business cycles supplemented economic capacity in intermittently pressing for economic expansion. Neither capacity nor crises did at first materially propel the United States toward anything like integral and world-wide free trade, however. Incentives were counteracted by equally powerful inhibitions, rooted in the very same structural shifts (from agriculture to industry) that had propelled growth and in the configuration of authority over the external tariff (lodged largely in a Congress keenly responsive to economic group pressures and sectionally induced internal deadlocks). Against the backdrop made up of a heterogeneous environment of differently mature if invariably competitive economies and a growing national capacity, the United States evolved as a result only fitfully toward informal free-trade imperialism. It did so through a progression of moods and myths, of general doctrines and more specific economic policies or strategies. The strategies contained only isolated elements of free trade and constituted at first only partial and differently one-sided antecedents to the full-scale model.

An ambivalent mood in matters economic befitted an ascendant early capitalist society that was not the first of its kind. Since the curve was ascendant (notably relative to the British exemplar), the fundamental mood was optimistic; since America's industrial capitalism was in its early stage without being original in substance (as had been Britain's), spells of pessimism reflected keen competition abroad and crises at home. Correspondingly dual was the tendency to aggressively anticipate future economic capacities and needs for fair and equal economic opportunities ("open door"), and to apprehensively and defensively delay free and equal economic confrontation (by means of domestic protectionism and regional preferentialism). Since the fundamental crisis, either immediate or long-term and either imaginary or substantiated by periodic depressions, was over production generating an agricultural and subsequently also industrial surplus, it was natural to look abroad for a cure and convenient to find the cure in the doctrine of the Open Door. Derived from its British version, the American doctrine was initially fed by the myth of an Asian (or Chinese) market that was in fact neither extant in its imagined size nor aggressively explored in its real size; and while the doctrine's purpose reflected the basic optimism, its propagation was exacerbated by the sporadically surfacing pessimism whenever the continental European powers (and Japan) were shown to be lagging behind Britain either in capacity or in disposition to expose the consequences of domestic glut to mutual adjustments or one-sided abandonments abroad. The resulting competitive tendency to engage in economic predation under the rationale of reciprocal preclusion was intensified on both sides, and chiefly with regard to extra-European markets, by two contrary extreme assumptions: the American, of imminent exclusion by European-imposed tariffs and other economic enclosures; the European, of eventual expulsion by a superior American production and trading potential.

For some time at least, the size of the internal American market diluted the dangers from economic surplus in the phase of overseas expansion, somewhat as geopolitical vastnesses had diminished external threat to security in the continental stage; and the more immediate or pressing economic surpluses of some other powers (Britain, France, and increasingly, Germany and Japan) operated to confront the United States with immediate problems of off-shore security, downgrading long-term economic dilemmas as stimuli to immediate action. In consequence, occasional economic depressions did not actually translate for long into a sustained economic drive abroad; partially unreal or unrealistic doctrines were expressed in a partially incoherent policy mix; and a comparably prolonged imbalance between economic and strategic factors affected the relationship of the two determinants within the imperial equation.

Since the foremost early surplus was agricultural, it was the agricultural interests that were the first to favor free trade. Their extraversion inverted the classic British sequence in the support for free trade, while reducing somewhat any discontinuity between the land-continental and the industrial-global phases of American expansion. This is not to say that the commitment of American agriculture to economic liberalism was either complete or consistent; just as the industrial interest combined protectionism with domestic laissez faire, so rural favor for free trade went with mercantilistic biases, beginning with early demands for publicly subsidized "internal improvements." Moreover, the contrast between agriculture and industry grew less when particular industrial interests began favoring free trade and major agricultural interests translated their fear of outside, notably Russian and Canadian, competition into greater sympathy for economic protection and, along with it, support for the political independence of areas replete with cheap wheat or cheap labor: Canada, in the 1880s and the Philippines, after World War I. On the whole, however, agricultural interests did help moderate the American tariff, notably in the decades before the Civil War, in contrast to the high-tariff industrial protectionism after the Civil War and again during the Great Depression. And, along with sundry other group pressures and coalitions, they played a role in the manipulation of reciprocal tariffs which, though deviating from the American stance of nondiscrimination, were among the early harbingers of the American progress toward trade liberalization.

Bilateral reciprocity treaties, briefly generalized in the McKinley Tariff of 1890, constituted one of the two main liberalizing elements in the mix of American foreign-trade policy. The second element, the multilaterally applicable principle of the Open Door, was most conspicuously formalized a decade later in the Hay Notes. Since each contributed to the American variety of free-trade philosophy, the two policy strands were potentially complementary. But historically, in the late nineteenth and early twentieth centuries, they stood in key respects for mutually contrasting manifestations of the underlying pessimistic-optimistic ambivalence in mood.

The reciprocity treaties were essentially defensive instruments, but effectively so; the Open Door as principle, declaratory policy, and paper reservation was offensive in thrust but ineffectual in impact. The treaties were essentially regional in scope and focused on the Western Hemisphere, with a bias in favor of American manufactures; the doctrine was inherently global in bearing, though immediately focused on Asia (China) and at least equally on agriculture-related American exports. And whereas nearly all of the nineteenth-century reciprocity treaties were concluded with lesser powers (beginning with Canada, the most significant were with Hawaii, Cuba, and Brazil), the target of the Open Door were the great powers. The reason for the differences lay in the objectives. The Open Door expressed opposition to spheres of exclusive political and economic influence by foreign great powers, anchored in military support points and either leading up to formal annexations or having practically equivalent effects. By contrast, the aim behind the reciprocity treaties was to create privileged trade relationships for the United States itself by lowering tariffs for American exports and raw-material imports. The Open Door was to permit the United States to stage economic inroads at large as they became needed and feasible; the reciprocity treaties would forthwith integrate dependent economies structurally into the American system in a manner approximating imperial preference and amounting to "neo-colonialism." Finally, whereas the reciprocity policy was discriminating (i.e., selective as to partners or targets and exclusive of major powers as potential beneficiaries), the U.S. version of the open-door principle was directed uniformly against all agents and forms of discrimination in both trade and investment, the formulators having withstood the temptation to favor the more liberal Britain and Germany over the more mercantilist Russia and France and to single out for emphasis either the more economically attractive Manchuria in northern China (with bias against Russia and later Japan) or the more strategically interesting Yangtze region in the Chinese south (in possible cooperation with Britain rather than, at German invitation, against her).

The real discrimination was one that juxtaposed the Open Door for Asia with the tendency to deny equal access to foreign powers in the Western Hemisphere. It was reflected in the way the United States applied the most-favored-nation clause so as to except at first all of the reciprocity treaties from the purview of a conditional clause, and to except still some (in treaties with Cuba and U.S. dependencies, although not with Brazil) when the United States adhered to the clause's unconditional variety in 1923. The most-favored-nation clause proved accordingly to be a low hurdle to clear when concluding reciprocity treaties and was for long a no more potent amplifier of free trade than was its conceptual twin and historical fellow-traveler. In the latter capacity, the Open Door failed to be vitalized by association with an aggressive private trade and investment drive and a supportive noneconomic official leverage; the most-favored-nation clause was by contrast impeded or even paralyzed by association with a tariff that was both high and (until 1934, with nonsignatories of a reciprocity treaty) nonnegotiable. Only disparate principles were thus broadly identifiable with free trade, and trade liberalization was but a halting process in the narrowest of scopes after the passing of formative war imperialism. The dynamically liberalizing, antidiscriminatory potential of the most-favored-nation clause was at variance with actual tariff rigidity; the reciprocity-treaty system instituted a mercantilist-liberal hybrid combining freer trade between unequal parties with the initial exclusion of strong outsiders; and the open-door principle of free (or fair) trade and equal competition was contradicted not only by a one-sidedly high domestic tariff (against finished products, though not some raw materials) but also by discriminatory preferences within the U.S. core-empire. For anything like American informal free-trade imperialism to come effectively into being required two developments. On the side of free trade, liberalization (through negotiated tariff reductions) had to converge with nondiscrimination more closely and on a wider basis; and on the side of imperialism, a similar conjunction had to occur between economic expansion and the strategic dimension of empire, however informal.

Meanwhile, the reciprocity treaties had built up a mixed record. One treaty managed to integrate Brazil economically into the American system to a large extent, both at a politically critical juncture in the early 1890s and in the longer run, while another failed to prepare the terrain for the political incorporation of Canada, and yet another, with Hawaii, was superseded by annexation only when the incentive from strategic security outgrew the economic impulse in determining effect. In the Philippines, finally, American policy used the first opportunity under the peace treaty to exchange Open Door for virtual reciprocity in order to reinforce U.S. political dominance by undercutting the trade dominance won by the British under the open-door system. Within the Western Hemisphere, the reciprocity treaties supplemented the off-shore annexations that had rounded off the core-empire with a more inclusive informal imperialism, avoiding annexations (of Cuba, Canada, and an array of Caribbean and Central American republics) and shunning permanent administrative responsibility for internal order.

Being informal for that very reason, the expansion was no less imperialism whenever it secured American access not only economically but also strategically (through naval deployments and intermittent military occupations under the Platt Amendment and the Roosevelt Corollary), while excluding rival powers from taking part in local crisis management on the strength of their creditor status. Informally imperialistic dollar diplomacy in the Caribbean was different from the diplomacy's open-door counterpart, which mainly the Taft administration promoted in Asia before World War I. It differed also from the diplomacy's extension to Europe by Charles Evans Hughes and Herbert Hoover among others, when the war had helped to replace American opposition to Europeans forcibly collecting on their loans in the Caribbean by American lending and attempted debt-collecting in Europe. Neither the weak American economic activities in Asia nor the more intense later economic activism in Europe constituted more than a kind of diffuse economic expansionism, differing from imperialism as activity (or process) and from expansion of the kind that attends imperialism as its consequence (or product). Contrasting with imperialism was the absence of strategic supports (other than the Philippine annexation), reflecting contemporaneous American isolation from the military-diplomatic balance of power; the difference in the kind of expansion resided in the consequent inability to consolidate economic gains and positions politically as part and parcel of the coincident structural lull in American expansion, situated between the Spanish war and World War II and fully consistent with economic exertions laying the bases for later expansion.

The American brand of informal free-trade imperialism emerged fully only during and following World War II, when nondiscrimination and trade liberalization had converged at last on a globally enlarged and strategically insured basis. Convergence was initially still one-sided, insofar as nondiscrimination preponderated over tariff reduction; and globalization of the new policy ran up against the rival Soviet-Communist socioeconomic system. But the outside threat helped keep alive the war-born structure for strategic security and supplemented it with a major noneconomic stimulus for converting into partially conforming postwar policy the wartime plans for multilaterally liberalized trade and monetary systems, embodied in the Bretton Woods principles and institutions. Both planning and policy reflected a basic fact and an immediate incentive, the fact being the definitive rise of the United States to economic supremacy and the incentive residing in the concern over postwar consequences of the war-bred increase in American productivity. If overall economic supremacy replaced the scarcity of capital that had still cramped the economic follow-up of the earlier, core-imperial expansion consequent upon the war with Spain, a new level of excess U.S. productivity in a war-ravaged global environment threatened to dwarf earlier sporadic crises once postwar domestic demand had been satiated. Moreover, although the competition with the Soviet Union was essentially politico-military, it did perpetuate the sense of a close connection between economic and strategic factors demonstrated in the prewar diplomatic interactions with Imperial Japan and implicit in the earlier apprehensions over the economic consequences of Nazi Germany.

By the time the two defeated, European-continental and Asian-insular, economic great powers were finally brought into the American system, they had been preceded there by the third and major, British, target of America's imperial economic liberalism. A newly authoritative American stress on nondiscriminatory opening of doors by others clashed with the defensive British emphasis on reducing the American tariff barrier. The divergent emphasis illustrated the continuing tension between the two techniques within America's peculiar free-trade doctrines and policies, while denoting a practical conflict over access. Whereas Britain would penetrate into the large American home market, the United States would undo in the British imperial-preference system a belated British effort to replicate the size of the same market and mount a last-ditch defense

against the American combination of economic dynamism and vulnerability to periodic depressions. The delayed consequence of Britain's
initial headstart over the United States in economic development and
doctrines was Britain's regression, in the 1930s, to equivalents of American policies for self-preservation and growth within the earlier, British-
dominated economic milieu. Pursuing core-imperial reciprocity (in the
Ottawa imperial-preference system) was accordingly combined with
efforts to revitalize and expand the home market with the aid of new
industries less dependent on foreign trade. But once the subsequent half-
hearted attempts to harmonize the British with the Imperial-Japanese
and Nazi-German varieties of neo-mercantilism had foundered on the by
then inveterate British preference for American alternatives intolerant of
contrary initiatives, British economic capabilities and policies had to be
adapted to America's invigorated economic liberalism. The adjustment
was promoted as much by wartime lend-lease transactions as by the end-
of-war negotiations over an American loan to war-depleted Britain.
American colonials had once sought political independence also as a way
to repudiate debts to British creditors, resulting from an unfavorable
balance of intraempire trade. Now, the necessity to submit to American
conditions for the loan (in the areas of imperial preference and currency
convertibility) signified the effective end of economic independence for
the British empire and nation alike.

The terms of the Anglo-American financial agreement (concerning the
loan) denoted America's accession to an informal empire of free trade. So
did the passage of the agreement by the U.S. Congress (in 1946) on
grounds of national security against the Soviet Union, in the wake of wartime congressional efforts to make lend-lease contingent on British concessions in matters regarding strategic bases and raw materials. The
widely recognized succession to Britain reflected the abrupt accumulation
of U.S. economic and military-strategic capabilities, but it also climaxed a
protracted development that had been replete with antecedents, crises,
and disappointments with alternative economic and strategic formulae.

Among the earlier short spells and partial symptoms of "free trade"
and free-trade "imperialism" had been Theodore Roosevelt's tentative
inclination to adjust the Monroe Doctrine to fit the principle of the
Open Door inside as well as outside of Latin America and to employ
generalized reciprocity with the great industrial powers as a counterpart
to concert diplomacy and conspicuous naval display. Similar in inspiration was Woodrow Wilson's design to couple the freeing of trade, with
the aid of a Federal Tariff Commission, and collective security, within a
U.S.-led League of Nations. Yet another, if weak, instance was the
Hughes-Hoover formula, combining adherence to the unconditional version of the most-favored-nation principle and negotiated reduction and
regulation of naval armaments. The underlying theory posited a direct

causal link between competition among mercantilistic trade blocs and war as part of recurrent economic crisis. Germany had been the principal object of concern in that context for the Roosevelt-Lodge team as much as for Wilson, while Japan was also of concern to the administration of the second Roosevelt and its secretary of state in particular. Before World War I, the German imperialists had feared becoming dependent on the United States for raw materials; this fear had strengthened their desire for overseas colonies and a trade bloc in East-Central Europe. Leading Americans responded before both world wars by apprehending a German industrial-export drive into America's own version of *Mitteleuropa* in the Western Hemisphere. The campaign against economic penetration by the Axis powers before World War II, and against continuing British entrenchment in Latin America also during the war, betokened the region's crucial role in America's defense and in her rise to world-wide economic ascendancy. Another such token was the initial concentration on Latin America of foreign trade strategies designed to lift the American economy out of depression first and recession subsequently.

Cordell Hull's updated reciprocity-treaty approach, which made the U.S. tariff negotiable, took initial shape in an American "free trade" bloc in the southern hemisphere (the Montevideo Conference of 1933); it was generalized by concluding reciprocity treaties also with major industrial countries headed by Britain; and was globalized when the United States as a belligerent reactivated its pressures to open the door also to the Middle East, next to Asia and Europe. But Latin America had to be first wrested economically from European and Japanese competitors, become itself secondary in importance and the former rivals economically subordinate, before U.S. economic policy would set out to synthesize trade liberalization and access equalization into one approach on a more-than-regional basis, and to extend beyond Latin America the institutional management of loans in ways capable of fostering U.S. exports and molding local economic development into patterns supplementing American needs and capabilities.

The decade-long transition from regional to economically near-global empire capped the more than century-long American evolution from mercantilism or near-mercantilism to freer trade that was to culminate provisionally in the Trade Expansion Act of 1962 and the subsequent round or rounds of tariff reductions. Both the secular trend and the telescoped transitions shifted the stress from agricultural outlets to manufactures; from underpricing abroad to tariff cutting; from a selective bias against discrimination to trade liberalization; and, essentially, from concern with competitively expanding American exports to concern with achieving that goal as part of a more widely shared expansion of international trade. Designed to avert or attenuate the succession of domestic economic crises, the free-trade bias expressed disillusion with an isolationism that would carry economic nationalism and regional imperialism beyond the life span legitimately allotted by either infant-industry or national-security needs and arguments. Over the decades preceding the 1930s, cyclical boom-bust variations and the more continuous diversification of big business had affected both the composition and the politico-strategic conceptions of the ruling class. As a result, while more strictly economic considerations conditioned attitudes to free trade, a latent receptivity to the larger set of policies comprised in informal free-trade imperialism expressed a more broadly based change in attitudes when disappointment with economic expansionism devoid of strategic complements joined the earlier disillusionment with annexationist colonialism to clear the ground for an intermediate approach.

Colonialism had proved disappointing in regard to the Philippines, as a matter of negative cost-benefit calculations from the viewpoint of both the American economy and the individual American consumer. A protectionism qualified by selective reciprocity-treaty regimes and open-door rhetoric could be viewed for a time as the superior alternative. Even marginally profitable outbidding or underselling of competing exporters abroad was thought preferable to overpaying for the administrative safeguards of privileged access in colonies and the naval safeguard around them; nor did producers for the home market look forward to losing that market to cheaper products from multiplying American colonies. But strategically unsupported economic policies and diplomacy, which had been frustrating in Europe after World War I, proved wholly abortive in Asia before the onset of World War II. They did little to help resolve satisfactorily the joint American-Japanese dilemma over the Open Door regarding the scope of its applicability in China and its relationship to the American reciprocity-treaty system in the Western Hemisphere. Nor did economic expansionism come anywhere near tackling either the unilateral American dilemma relative to Japan, as the most desirable economic partner and stabilizer in Asia and the greatest economic threat and potential expellant, or the problematic relationship between merely economic pressures and alternative responses to them. American pressure on Japan, begun in 1937 in substitution for prior appeasement attempts, only induced the Japanese to extend their expansion beyond China to European colonies. Once the United States had ceased to be deficient in both capital and business enterprise with respect to Asia, it was the American strategic deficiency in capital-ship deployment that became critical, along with its consequence, a surfeit of militarily unsupported diplomatic energy. More strikingly even than the similar case of Germany (as superior a customer of the United States relative to Britain as Japan was relative to China), the American-Japanese relationship highlighted the significance of the relationship between economic and strategic factors for free-trade imperialism once the United States had met the basic capability requirement in the form of overall economic superiority.

IV

When compared with Britain (and Rome), America's movement toward informal free-trade imperialism was subject to a more pronounced and longer-lasting discrepancy between mostly separately evolving domestic and external environments. A sustained interplay of economic and strategic factors and concerns took place as a result only following World War II, in a setting that combined an enlarged multiregional scope, a heightened level of strategic engagement, and an intensified rate and liberalized mode of international economic activity. Once it was realized, however, the new rapport consolidated also in the American case the previously only occasionally and transiently surfacing basic characteristic of free-trade imperialism, to wit, the operational priority of the strategic over the economic determinant of official policy (tending toward expansion), in conditions of a corresponding hierarchy between relatively separate public and private domains.

To be balanced were economic and strategic engagements and, more specifically, real or anticipated economic and strategic gains and costs. The U.S.-upheld strategic framework had become gradually underdeveloped as American economic capabilities and activities or ambitions grew, with the result of setting limits to stable economic achievements overseas. Only in the Caribbean may the naval deployments and bases along with military interventions have briefly anticipated the later movement toward equilibrium, as politico-military protectorates went hand in hand with economic paternalism, including financial supervision. And only on the Pacific side may the strategic posture have exceeded the economic potential for a while (due to the addition of the Philippine base to the Hawaiian), pending U.S. failure to extend strategic presence to mainland China after Theodore Roosevelt's fleeting urge to do so. The resulting strategic inferiority in China relative to the European powers and Japan was all the more galling since the powers were strategically and economically aggressive in direct proportion to their being apprehensive of American economic claims in the short run and potentialities in the long run. So long as the inferiority lasted, it reduced both the value of the Philippines as a strategic gateway to China and the level of possible trade and investment within China, inasmuch as reducing politico-strategic risks meant automatically curtailing material rewards in the area.

By and large, Theodore Roosevelt had recognized the implications of the imbalance in China as well as in North Africa (relative to Morocco) when reducing economic ambitions and attempting to fill partially the tangible strategic gaps with largely symbolic diplomatic initiatives and naval displays. By contrast, the succeeding Taft administration sought to simultaneously escalate economic activities in mainland Asia and lower the American strategic and diplomatic profile. The imbalance within official policy was saved from its anticipatable consequences only by the scarcity of the actually forthcoming private economic initiatives. The implicit dangers showed instead at a later date in Wilson's abortive attempt to harmonize a policy of strict neutrality in World War I with inadequate strategic-naval backing, and to combine both with a deepening one-sided economic engagement. After the war, only an ideally effective League of Nations with U.S.-supplied "teeth" could have adequately secured a likewise American-steered free trade in either Europe or Asia.

In reality, overseas economic activities devoid of adequate strategic backing alternated with intermittent spurts of imperial energy beyond the American seas. During the Hughes-Hoover era, a tentative economic-strategic equilibrium was briefly in existence in Asia when the United States acknowledged Japan's special economic interests in Manchuria after having contained Japan militarily (and thus also economically) in Siberia. The fragile equilibrium was not reinforced, however, by realizing the politico-strategic possibilities implicit in the so-called Washington Treaties and adjusting accordingly the American pretensions implicit in the open-door theses. The treaties by themselves neither insured sufficient long-term protection for China nor endowed the United States with leverage on a par with its economic desiderata; nor were they used as a basis for consenting to Japan's eventual accession to parity in either naval capabilities in the Pacific or economic access outside Asia. The disequilibrium deepened when the American policy on relative naval strengths provoked Japan and augmented Philippine vulnerability within the strategic sector, and when the theoretical inclination to accommodate Japan economically in China clashed with the actual policy of withholding loans for an effective (and thus peaceful?) Japanese entrenchment in Manchuria and refusing to abridge the American claim to equal access in all of China.

The refusal to surrender any hypothetical future U.S. exports to China matched the reluctance to see instant imports of goods from Europe repay the loans extended to the Allies during World War I, while postwar loans to defeated Germany were intended to promote America's own exports. A larger economic-strategic imbalance was simultaneously developing out of America's resumed isolation from the military aspects and diplomatic manifestations of the central balance of power in Europe and globally. More than creating it, the neutrality legislation of the 1930s merely institutionalized the disequilibrium insofar as it enabled the United States to enjoy "free" (in the sense of strategically gratuitous) trade in a once again war-torn Atlantic. But, even as the atrophy of trans-Atlantic economic transactions attendant on the world economic crisis and preceding the military cataclysm moderated the imbalance between economic goals and strategic supports, a nearly simultaneous U.S. naval build-up toward what was to become an effectively two-ocean navy also began to re-equilibrate the two dimensions. Although the build-up had been conceived as a safeguard for neutrality, it started extending into the Pacific and world-wide the near-equilibrium obtaining between U.S. strategic and economic engagements in the Caribbean regions, where the Hoover administration had anticipated both the Good Neighbor policy for Latin America and the free-trade imperial policy for the world by deemphasizing direct military interventions and favoring instead governmental support for permanent investments in infrastructures for development behind a naval-strategic American shield.

During World War II the strategic counterpart of America's role as the economic and military warehouse for the Allies evolved from the Anglo-American destroyers-for-bases deal in 1940, covering the Atlantic, all the way to the retention of formerly Japanese bases in the Pacific. The economic-strategic equilibrium escalated thereafter to initially ever higher levels. In Europe the Marshall Plan and its sequelae in the form of U.S.-European economic institutions and American investments were conjoined with the North Atlantic Alliance; in the Western Hemisphere, the Organization of American States and both covert and overt American military interventions under its aegis went hand in hand with both private investments and governmental economic assistance, culminating in the Alliance for Progress; in Asia and to a lesser extent Africa, military aid, extended in exchange or as a support for strategic facilities and as part of or a substitute for U.S. alliance with local parties and involvement in local wars, was matched by massive economic assistance for local development and American access to raw materials. The equilibrium was doomed to deteriorate when the conspicuous costs of the strategic engagement rose to the point of outgrowing their base in domestic support, notably in regard to Asia, and neither American strategic dominance nor U.S.-Soviet military bipolarity appeared to fit and contain any longer a changing distribution of economic capabilities or leverages world-wide. Even before any such degradation became visible, however, post-World War II American informal free-trade imperialism had been materially handicapped by the failure to insure political and economic access to China and to Eastern Europe by appropriate strategic measures. Whereas the failure imparted a tactical stimulus to the freeing of trade in the remaining "free world," it compelled an unpromising dependence on the economic weapon alone in regard to the Communist-dominated realm and induced not wholly successful attempts to evolve viable substitutions for the East European powers outside Europe and notably in the Middle East.

The very factors that reduced the geopolitical scope of the American free-trade empire intensified the military-political crisis and, with it, the operational priority of the strategic determinant in official American policy-making. Operational priority will be commonly assigned to the strategic framework whenever both economic and strategic involvements are extensive and acute insecurity prevails either at the center of the international system or at the frontiers of empire. Central insecurity attended the full-blown American free-trade period initially, whereas frontier insecurity had been critical for Britain's and Rome's free-trade period and was eventually to be also for America's. Even a mercantile elite such as the politicized business elite in the United States will bestow primacy on strategic considerations in suitable circumstances, and may then do so with the zeal of converts, while the primacy will come naturally to an aristocratic elite of the kind dominant in Rome, Britain, and, intermittently, the United States. At the same time, both kinds of imperial ruling class will adopt a similar attitude toward the economic costs or benefits of the strategic emphasis. Such incidental economic consequences will be commonly neither intended nor attended to in any one individual case; only in their sum and in a general way will they be the object of conscious awareness and concern. The situation differs from that prevailing in the phase of formative war-imperialism when it is individual economic prizes that are deliberately prosecuted and, along with parallel or consequent military conflicts, have in their sum either wholly unforeseen or not wholly intended general or cumulative consequences for the early growth of both empire and economy.

In the free-trade period, strategic and economic factors will be either separate or separable, in part because public and private domains stand in like relationship to one another. Although both the immediately preceding phase and the immediately following one tended to fusion on both counts, the difference could be only relative, since determination itself is elusive. Commingling of concerns with physical security and with economic sustenance had been in evidence ever since the drive of early Americans for animal furs had proceeded along with the search for a natural frontier, the preoccupation with sugar matched that with sea power, and before facilities for outward-bound communications were sought also as defensive posts against the outside. Prior to independence, Georgia had been added as both a buffer against Spain in the security interest of rich planters in the Carolinas and as an outlet for colonization by the economically less fortunate. At a later date, independent Texas was annexed to augment the supply of land as well as the feeling of security against suspected British designs on Texas and Texan designs on New Mexico and California. Strategic and economic motives were yet more intricately combined in the American approach to California, Hawaii, and the Philippines, intended to serve the interests of both New England merchants (among others) and the U.S. Navy; to Cuba, attractive for her sugar plantations and as the site for a military base at Guantanamo; and to the related isthmian-canal project.

Economic and strategic concerns became more easily separable as the American influence expanded from Georgia to Guantanamo and from the Mississippi basin to the Manila Bay. But there was no discernible concurrent evolution toward the established motivational primacy of either factor, in all circumstances and for different areas, not least in view of the problematic relationship between immediate and ultimate objectives and between deliberate objectives and incidental or unintended consequences. This indeterminancy was greatest in periods when the United States was exempt from acute strategic threat and its policy-makers were devoid of both responsible political reflexes and original economic thought. In such circumstances, the determinant that was intellectually dominant did not necessarily shape policy, not least because the submission of policy to the pressures of group politics grew in the absence of compelling economic and strategic needs.

Confusion and contention have been greatest in connection with the first period of overseas expansion. The strategic determinant was on balance primary in Hawaii and Cuba. Reciprocity treaties would have been sufficient to achieve the purely economic objectives in both islands; and, annexing Hawaii to make sure of the base at Pearl Harbor while being content with a protectorate in Cuba as a surety for Guantanamo, reflected accurately the different intensity of the apprehended threats to the domestic base threats from Japan and Germany, respectively. Conversely, the economic determinant predominated over the strategic in shaping approach to the Philippines, although in a way illustrating the circular relationship of the two determinants. The dominant economic interest was in China rather than in the Philippines themselves. If this meant that coveting a naval base in the archipelago was only ancillary to the ultimate economic objective, it also meant that any actually forthcoming economic gains would be incidental to the additional support and leverage deriving from the Philippine strategic asset. But, compared with Hawaii and Cuba, the salience of the strategic considerations in the Philippines was reduced by the insular asset being directly and indisputably related to home security only insofar as that security was ultimately tied to economic power and that power depended demonstrably on America's position in international trade. By best illustrating the strategic-economic circularity, the Philippines were for America what Singapore had been for Great Britain with respect to the China Sea in the early nineteenth century, when the then principal aspirant to free trade was facing the mercantilist Dutch in Indonesia.

Additional complications are possible. One takes place when expansion aims at a strategic position susceptible of improving access to an economically valuable terminal such as the East for Rome, India for Britain, and China for the United States, but safeguarding the strategic asset itself requires expanding into a hinterland that is possessed of only secondary economic significance. The expansive dynamic of the security factor was manifest when Hawaii was taken to secure Pearl Harbor and the Philippine archipelago to make sure of Manila Bay, just as the British had been previously "sucked" into Egypt to protect the Suez and drawn deeper into South Africa to safeguard the Cape Colony, while Rome had defended in the Macedonian hinterland both offshore Illyria and the petty insular and coastal states of the Eastern Mediterranean. There is yet another complication. Its source is the difference between mere preliminaries or immediate precipitants of a crisis eventually leading to expansion, and the actually or perceptually primary determinants of that expansion. The precipitants were economic in the case of Cuba and military-strategic in that of the Philippines, but the primary determinants were the other way round in both cases. Finally, strategic and economic factors may evolve in the period following expansion in ways that alter or even reverse the original hierarchy among determinants. Once the United States had failed to complete the annexation of the Philippines by acquiring a military port and a sphere of political influence in mainland China, the failure sapped the originally primary economic motivation, while commensurately strengthening the concern over the strategic vulnerability of the insular possession (placed under the U.S. War Department). As the declining economic concerns shifted from China to the Philippines, moreover, their internal balance was altered to favor disengagement from the archipelago.

While possible perspectives on individual instances of expansion can vary considerably, the discernible operational priorities on the part of individual protagonists oscillated within narrower margins. At a key juncture of the transactional phase of domestic dynamics attending early overseas expansion, the strategic priorities of Theodore Roosevelt were followed by the more pronounced economic preoccupations of the more big-business oriented immediate successor, William Howard Taft; the reemergence of strategic primacy under the stresses of the Wilson era gave way to the renewal of economic emphases in the Hughes-Hoover period; and the peculiar assortment of strategic purposes and economic instruments within the scheme of Woodrow Wilson for multilateral institutions was resuscitated by Cordell Hull following a period of nearly complete unilateralism and ostensible legalism.

Since Theodore Roosevelt was conscious of the need for naval counterparts to economic reciprocity overseas, he gave coming to terms with Japan's military-strategic needs in Korea operational priority over American interests moving into Manchuria economically. He also underlined diplomatic concert and parity with Britain in the Yangtze Valley as a precondition to reversing Britain's adjustment to an economic partition of China and to averting a British lead in extending such partition to Latin America. Similarly, the strategic dimension of a world order policed by the major powers took precedence for Franklin Roosevelt over long-term planning for the Bretton Woods economic and Dumbarton Oaks institutional frameworks during World War II. The ranking was vindicated when it became necessary to invoke the Soviet threat to economically weakened European allies and the German ex-enemy in order to refloat Hull's faltering scheme for the "developed" powers at the end of the war, and when economic assistance to the "undeveloped" countries came to be managed subsequently as an instrument of the cold war soon to follow. Moreover, if Japan's military expansionism had taken precedence over the economics of the Open Door to China in propelling America into World War II, postwar security for a stable Japan as a key element in the strategic balance and the strategy of containment vis-à-vis the emergent Soviet-Chinese amalgamation predominated even more clearly over any concern with Southeast Asian economic assets, including raw materials, in American foreign-policy-making councils. The priority of the strategic factor weathered, moreover, at that stage the reversion of governing responsibilities from aristocratic Rooseveltian to politicized big-business leadership, without there occurring any substantial change in the notion of security as comprising the well-being and stability of the socioeconomic system in its broadest meaning and in the last resort. The way the operational priority was actually implemented, however, became thereafter increasingly subject to the cost- and risk-calculating ethos and mentality of the business-cum-corporate lawyer elite.

The strategic will prevail conclusively over the economic determinant when there is a security crisis or when a political elite sees its special role and aptitude in maintaining a strategic framework to be made the best of by a parallel economic elite. As a response to insecurity, the strategic primacy will be both operational in the sense of effectively guiding action and structural in the sense of being inferrable from the given or affirmed state of the environment; as a reflection of elite specialization, the priority may be only operational. In the American case, unlike the Roman and the British cases, paucity of genuine crises originating abroad made the priority issue more than commonly questionable over long periods of time; and, when a major crisis did occur, its being located in either the economic or the strategic sphere influenced the ranking of policy determinants and the corresponding policy responses more decisively than did the complexion of the ruling class.

One reason why the make-up of the ruling class mattered relatively less was that even a routine interlocking of functionally diverse high-level personnel in the American free-trade empire did not wholly negate the tendency toward a separate functioning of private and public domains that is as peculiar to an economically liberal phase of empire as it is to a liberal state. The separateness was not sustained in America by a neat division of labor between a landed aristocracy and the mercantile classes; but neither was it strained by extreme fluctuations in pro- and anti-business governmental philosophies. It was instead fostered in the critical period by America's intense or intensely felt central-systemic security crisis. Whereas big-business elites moved freely into and out of an American government that came to comprise an expanding "security community," personal success at the highest echelons depended on an individual's performance as a crisis manager, measured by political criteria. A success so defined was sufficiently important not only for the governmental role but also for the eventually resumed business career to preclude subordinating strategic rationality to considerations of immediate economic consequences when recommending or formulating governmental decisions. For the American case to conform to the norm in essentials, moreover, intrinsic separateness did not have to mean systematic aloofness, and even less reciprocal aversion, between government and business in the aggregate. Instances of convergence between private and public interests and domains were sufficiently offset by cases of conflict; and convergence approximated but rarely the collusion between private interests and public authority that had been typical for the continental phase of expansion and had found supreme expression in advance financial speculation by public figures in the lands earmarked for annexation.

By and large, neither the actual extent of American strategic engagement nor the degree of pro-business philosophical bias in a particular administration made governments identify with private economic enterprise abroad beyond a certain point, not least but also not only if and when support might interfere with high priority political policies. Official policy in the pro-business and isolationist Hughes-Hoover era had been to withhold both guarantees and encouragement from private lenders abroad; governments at the height of the cold war and of free-trade imperialism abstained systematically from bringing business interests into the foreign-policy making process, even when requiring corporate assistance in implementing a set policy, and paid scant attention to the safety of private investments when pursuing important strategic interests. In return, corporate managers felt free to make decisions on profit-maximizing grounds and to pay scant attention to the U.S. balance of international payments when deciding what to do with a firm's assets abroad. Only accidental convergence occurred when, for instance, the private interest to see only noncompetitive, light or labor-intensive, industry implanted in the less developed countries either coincided with the development strategies espoused by government-financed lending institutions or supplemented the stress on infrastructures and agriculture in the development goals of public U.S. foreign-aid programs.

The official claim to autonomy was escalated to the assertion of primacy when private enterprise risked frustrating national political objectives. Republican pro-business administrations from Taft's to Hoover's matched the anti-business Wilson administration in that respect, e.g., when opposing the kind of loans to Caribbean republics that might stimulate, in addition to economic transactions, also palace revolutions exploitable by extra-hemispheric powers. Similarly, the U.S. government acted to dissuade banking interests from loaning to Japan in China after World War I (in order to prevent the integration of Manchuria into the Japanese economy) and from purchasing wholesale German economic assets after World War II (so as to prevent anything that might impede West Germany's eventual integration into the free world economy). And, if the post–World War I administrations had sought to bar loans to defaulting former allies in an effort to encourage repayments of wartime loans, the post–World War II administrations would yet more authoritatively prohibit trading in strategic materials with ideologically alien or politically hostile countries as part of cold-war rivalries generally and of competition over economic growth rates specifically.

Whereas the intensity of the governmental strategic engagement spelled only a minor difference for the basic character of the government-business relationship, degrees of intensity mattered when it came to positively promoting economic activities abroad either directly or indirectly. In a period of low strategic engagement and consequently weak capacity to back private enterprise effectively, neither the Taft administration nor its predecessors or successor were able to induce American banking interests to uphold the American national interest in the economics and politics of railroad concessions in China. Taft's incapacity was especially painful, however, because of the official commitment to economic diplomacy. After the United States had taken part in World War I, the government was comparatively more successful in opening the door for American oil interests in the Middle East. But, in general, the post–World War I proliferation of commercial and consular diplomatic services was no match, as a method for promoting and protecting American economic activities abroad, for the multiplication of American strategic positions abroad after World War II. Fostering a fair economic access for the dynamic American economic system was no substitute for insuring a modicum of world order as a precondition to free economic expansion. The most conspicuous feature in the expansion of both American and world trade was the explosive growth in the international activities of U.S.-based or controlled corporations—the so-called multinational corporations—in Europe and in the Third World. The growth was related to the expansion of the U.S.-upheld strategic framework of economic activities in a largely unwitting causal link that overshadowed the role of the international corporations as either a vehicle for American imperial expansion or its instrument.

Going beyond spontaneous complementarity between strategic and economic expansion, a more positive and deliberate governmental impact on economic activities abroad would occur mainly or only when the interest to be promoted or protected was that of the economic or cold-war strategic system in its entirety. In that vein, the U.S. government sympathized with the reluctance of American corporations operating abroad to be expropriated—i.e., nationalized without adequate compensation; but it also conditioned the extent of overt or covert support for nationalized corporations by considerations of diplomatic and military strategy, witness changes in the official attitude toward oil nationalization in Mexico with the approach of war in the 1930s and, subsequently, differences in the official responses to nationalizations in Peru in the 1960s and in Chile in the 1970s. It was consistent with their essential separateness within the framework of an informal free-trade empire, furthermore, to interlock private and public interests by tying economic assistance abroad to purchases from American sources of supply (a disguised subsidy to American farmers and industry faintly resembling the navy acts of the mercantilistic era) so long and insofar as the subsidy was a fair compensation to American enterprise for the special risks deriving along with advantages from empire-caused prominence in politically unstable and potentially hostile areas. And, finally, even where close links between private and public sectors gave rise to the so-called military-industrial complex as a manifestation of "warfare liberalism," the interpenetration was more an outgrowth of the cold-war setting than of free-trade imperialism itself, not least when involving direct or indirect subsidies for arms sales by private manufacturers to countries that might or might not host an American military mission.

How decisive the strategic engagement was for private-public interpenetration in the realm of economic and military assistance became apparent when it had taken the prospect of World War II to overcome a consistent previous distaste for government-to-government lending in the Western Hemisphere. The impression of sea change deepens when the modalities of cold-war foreign aid are compared with an earlier private-public entanglement, in the form of loans to the Allies in World War I and the subsequent attempts to collect on the loans that had been raised by private subscriptions to wartime bonds as a matter of public policy. Both transactions were in some degree and fashion related to the promotion of American exports; and even the ostensibly public foreign-aid grants and loans in the later era were also ultimately financed by private individuals in their capacity as taxpayers. But the foreign-aid outlays were purposefully and to a degree effectively administered so as to foster the U.S.-sponsored strategic framework, while the earlier policy of debt-collection had been an aspect of liquidating America's wartime strategic role. In large part as a result, the latter approach tended to undermine both the American and the world economic systems by the application of too-strictly economic or banking standards, whereas the former posture promoted both by applying essentially political criteria.

All things considered, neither economic nor any other interests abroad were demonstrably and lastingly served by assigning operational primacy to the economic factor as part of something like dollar diplomacy or economic diplomacy. By contrast, major economic gains derived incidentally from policies inspired primarily by the concern to develop and maintain the global strategic framework in and after World War II. Indirect promotion maintained substantially intact the intrinsic separateness, and infringed only marginally on the actual separation, of the economic and the strategic spheres and of the private and the public domains, even when informal free-trade imperialism was being managed by a politicized big-business elite.

v

American imperial expansion was primarily due in its global phase to the strategic stimulus, while the concurrent economic expansion was in large part incidental to it. Insofar as there was an economic agency directly or primarily related to expansion in the free-trade period, it must be sought less in the private economic drives of the American entrepreneur and the dynamics of the American socioeconomic system and more in the strategies of the American cold-war and empire managers, leaning toward the employment of economic instruments in support of political objectives. Economic instrumentalism is, however, not the same as economic imperialism. The latter entails using abroad existing economic assets in behalf of internal economic needs, whereas the former uses such assets for external purposes that are themselves only partially or marginally economic. A government may wish to keep aloof from some or most of the private manifestations of economic imperialism; it will be unavoidably the primary agent of economic instrumentalism. Both imperialism and instrumentalism are related to the military-strategic framework. But the first is so related mainly as an object of support by the framework and the second is itself a key support of such framework.

Different American administrations indulged in the overuse of economic instruments as a prime response to the challenge of Communist revolutions or threat of such revolution: mainly in Eastern Europe, including Russia, following World War I, and primarily in Western Europe and subsequently in the extra-European world following World War II. After the first global conflict, diverse forms of Allied military intervention were randomly juxtaposed with the employment of the economic weapon, prominently including food, in Central and Eastern Europe; the ambiguously mixed humanitarian and political purposes were soon blighted by locally converging forces of revolution and reaction. At the end of World War II, propensity to overdepend on the economic instruments became increasingly prominent in the wake of failures to adequately coordinate military operations with peace-related diplomatic transactions. Since the attempts to manipulate actual and prospective economic aid and credit for political ends likewise lacked supporting military-strategic measures, however, the desired results were secured neither from the Soviet Union nor Poland, nor, in due course, in China.

Overreliance on the economic weapon in the aftermath of World War I had helped intensify the domestic frustrations responsible for American isolation from the central balance of power. The longer-term consequence of the same propensity after World War II was to stimulate American expansion beyond the compass of the essential empire. American presence in Western Europe and Japan resulted from a strictly necessary response to the American-Soviet conflict, conditioned structurally by the war-created vacuums of military and economic power. Not only were those vacuums the very obverse of an overflow of competition over market shares; the paradoxical fact that economic instrumentalism intensified along with the progressive militarization of the empire confirmed further the empire's derivation from a central-strategic security crisis. Economic instrumentalism was gradually extended to the nonindustrial world as part of defense for a receding imperial frontier; and if the technique was by the same token only the executory arm of a subsidiary security determinant of imperial expansion, it was more demonstrably influential than was any more substantive economic stimulus, such as concern over access to raw materials. Not only had such access not been perceived as being in serious jeopardy at the time; America's political engagement in a revolution-prone third-world setting was liable to endanger that access at least as seriously as would have a politically self-effacing posture. At one and the same time, however, there was a supporting, in large part ideological, reason for using economic instruments on a massive scale. Just as the Axis threat before, so the Soviet threat had a conspicuous ideological exterior reducible to the economic factor as the real source of challenge, a fact that was aggravated by the postwar material plight of the European nations and later also of their former colonial dependencies. Being in that special sense ultimately economic, the challenge seemed to dictate a response in kind corresponding, moreover, to the likewise ideological American goal of a democratic or pluralistic politico-economic development for former victims of fascism and colonialism.

Applied ideology involved opposing Soviet state capitalism with American governmental capital, in the form of an increasingly politicized public economic assistance. The strategy extended from the United Nations Reconstruction and Rehabilitation Administration to the Marshall Plan and beyond; it came naturally once the avoidance of a militarily underwritten confrontation at the fulcrum of the world balance in Europe, that might have stemmed Soviet expansion from the start, had made inevitable a prolonged competition in depth over an ever-expanding arc of peripheral containment.

With growing competition, the use of the economic instrument in conjunction with military aid also intensified. The momentum was fostered by uncertainties about the nature of the primary threat: Communism or the Soviet Union; primary theater: Europe (and then the Soviet Union and decreasingly Communism) or Afro-Asia (and then Communism and only later China); and, correspondingly, primary technique of response: economic (if against Communism generally or China in Asia) or military (if primarily against the Soviet Union in Europe, following the European economic recovery, or Communist-inspired "wars of national liberation" in the Third World at large). The safest and least painful way of resolving both the uncertainties and the related controversies was to define the threat inclusively as to sources and theaters, and thus expansively in regard to response; and to combine the economic and military instruments in ways most suited to American material capabilities and to the ideal ethos of the governing elite. The massive American economic resource served to underpin the institutionalized business ethos of prudential risk-avoidance or at least risk-limitation, preferring management of programs over manipulation by diplomacy. Ample resource and allergy to risk were alike in favoring resort to the economic instrument, and a comparably conceived military-aid instrument, as the principal modes of day-to-day operations within the setting of an American strategic superiority. The method will be applied by most empires that are not strictly coercive; by virtue of its unusual scope, however, extending foreign-aid gratuities in exchange for overseas facilities became a distinctively American approach to foreign affairs, a continuation by other means of the earlier outright purchases of continental tracts from Louisiana to Alaska.

Whenever clear-cut security stimuli were present, the economic mode tended to do no more than attend and facilitate expansion. Economic mode would merge with economic motive in the resulting momentum only if and when foreign aid was used to insure access to particular raw materials, to foreclose forms of indigenous economic development contrary to American economic structures, or to deflect trade from former metropoles to the new imperial center. In most instances, however, economic instruments promoted expansion not so much purposively, by dint of serving specific economic interests and objectives, as pervasively, by virtue of their own lack of specificity compelling diffusion as a substitute for impact, while allowing the more concrete and determinate economic interests to appear to be actually determining official action in ambiguous circumstances.

In and of itself, the economic instrument stimulated expanding involvement because it was free of ultimate risks and uncontrollable costs for the American wielder; engendered for him marginal economic and political benefits abroad as a matter of fact or easy rationalization, so long as it was not put to a test revealing it to be a blunt and double-edged sword; and immediately appealed to ever more potential recipients of economic bounties as materially profitable, and to important sectors of the donor's domestic public as constructive, despite growing association with the hazy concept of neo-colonialism. Largely relying on the economic weapon in strategically less-than-vital arenas of the cold war shielded decision-makers moreover against politically motivated domestic charges of inaction, until such time as the conflict's decline emboldened a new category of critics to identify "creeping" involvements via economic aid as the source of undesired and seemingly unnecessary military engagements in the peripheries.

Although the economic instrument had an expansive bias also when used to underpin established military-strategic positions in depth, expansion resulted more indirectly and importantly when the instrument was compensating—and then more likely than not overcompensating—for insufficient or insufficiently vigorous use of force or threat of force. In contrast with the progressively militarized empire organization, American cold-war strategy was not one of military self-assertion. Force deployments preponderated over employments of military power most of the time, and a presumably cumulative force of economics was implicitly trusted over any precise calculations of the economy of force. Even the wars in Korea and Vietnam were in part at least caused by, as well as illustrating in their course, the American failure to master and manage the more difficult, force-related, branch of a broadly conceived political economy. During the post–World War I isolationist period, inadequacies of concept and irresolution in action had at the most perpetuated the easy to underestimate dormant perils; in the more strenuous internationalist or imperialist setting of the second postwar era, the same flaws helped disseminate challenges that were henceforth equally easy to overrate as clear and present dangers. The challenges stimulated reactive expansion by way of precautionary or deterrent commitments to economic assistance, and to military-strategic underwriting of that assistance in the last resort.

The stress on economic instruments was an ostensibly benign and benevolent form of economism. It conditioned American free-trade imperialism in its heyday and was different from the previous variety of economism in the form of strategically unsupported economic expansionism. The Marshall Plan and related institutions were designed to restore the European economies, parallel with the Japanese economy, as partners in trade and recipients of investments to be fitted into a military counterpoise to the Soviet Union within an American-dominated alliance system. The interplay of economic technique and strategic objective, partially and inconclusively applied also to pre-industrial conditions outside Europe at a later stage, was to terminate in events that raised acutely the issue of economic costs of the basic strategic framework (centered in Europe) and of peripheral military conflicts (clustered in Asia). An effective American free-trade empire had bridged meanwhile the time span between conception and crisis. The empire had originated intellectually, as a matter of wartime planning, in the sense of economic threat from surplus production at home; it took its actual impetus and shape from the military-political threat, as a matter of postwar realities; and, pending a later resurgence of the economic dimension, that dimension's role in the preponderantly military American empire was only subordinate as to causation and supportive as to operation so long as the U.S.-sponsored multilateral liberal economic order was thriving as both the dominant system in its own right and the primary instrument in the cold war.

Being an instrument in the confrontation with the Soviet Union, the liberal economic order evolved rapidly from a pure concept into a compromise on basics with the European and Japanese members of the essential empire. Since the economic system was initially successful, the compromise yielded in due course within the Atlantic industrial core to a conflict that became finally entangled with a structural crisis. The crisis opened up for the economic system the alternative of collapse or reconsolidation with the help of reexpansion, while increasing the salience of the economic factor overall, as did also the simultaneous subsidence of insecurity vis-à-vis the Communist great powers. It could be asked at that point whether one more (and for America novel) kind of economism, from relative decline or weakness rather than strength, was a symptom of late imperialism; and it was certain that both the crisis and the employed corrective responses displayed features characteristic of formalized protective imperialism. But, as the strategic framework remained by and large in place, while seemingly degenerating from a spearhead of economic expansion into leverage for economic concessions, there was still no conclusive evidence that the last stage had actually supervened and had superseded the largely, if not integrally, informal American free-trade empire along the lines of its Roman and British antecedents.

VI

The original free-trade concept had envisaged a politically neutral, multilateral economic and monetary system applying the basic rules of the liberal Bretton Woods scheme. The concept failed to be fully implemented institutionally; and it continued to bear the marks of tension between the ideals of a trade without discrimination and of a trade free of tariffs and other barriers, and between goals addressed to the volume of international trade and to the stability of domestic welfare. The system provided nonetheless a basis for substantial trade liberalization among non-Communist industrial countries. It did so, however, mainly because the political economy of the part-formal and part-informal American empire for, even if not immediately of, free trade was progressively making the apolitical vision of a liberal economic order fit for survival in the real world. Resulting compromises translated the nation's economic superiority into corresponding influence within multilateral organizations, while embodying America's politically motivated acquiescence in seeing the economically dislocated European and Japanese clients temporarily depart from fundamental liberal tenets bearing on currency convertibility, the most-favored-nation principle, and import quotas. American tolerance for the special needs of European (and Japanese) economic recovery during the decade following the cluster of emergencies in 1947 and 1948 counterpointed a largely unquestioning allied acceptance of U.S. politico-military leadership. The recovery itself was initially discriminatory with respect to the United States; and, when it had ceased being triggered by American economic assistance, continued to benefit from defense-related U.S. deficits in international payments and concurrent technological diffusion.

The underlying compromises were facilitated for a time by a lag in American readiness to match the tariff reductions taking place among the Europeans. They began to show strains during the period (1959–62) leading up to the climactic effort to expand intra-Atlantic trade liberalization (by means of the Kennedy administration's Trade Expansion Act). Just as a political challenge was then being issued by an apparently ascendant France-in-Europe to the American monopoly in NATO, so European economic exclusivism was being increasingly questioned in and in behalf of a United States that was experiencing the end of the postwar excess demand for American products. Responding to the new givens, the grand design of the Kennedy administration was to readjust economic and strategic factors by combining what would in effect be an Atlantic free-trade area in commercial exchanges with appearances of an Atlantic partnership in defense. The implementation of the first part required British accession to the European Economic Community; the authenticity of the second component was contingent on admitting France to co-leadership in the Atlantic Alliance. Neither condition was realized when (in the early 1960s) the Third World was emerging as, among other things, a source of future trans-Atlantic conflict as well as the principal recipient of American strategic support and economic assistance. American backing for cooperative third-world regionalism, viewed as a provisional shelter against and eventual bridge to the world-wide economic order for the less developed countries, was part of the United States defending the imperial frontier; it also saved the Europeans from either indefinitely upholding an embattled colonialism or seeing European control give way to indigenous or international Communism. Interallied difficulties began, however, when European savings were overshadowed by American initiatives suspect of substituting for the ex-metropoles in both politics and economics. If a compromise was ever achieved over the backward peripheries, it was even more unstable than had been the adjustments involving only the industrial members of the essential empire among themselves, also because tentative crystallizations in the empire's outskirts coincided with erosion in the more central relationship.

A policy of liberal economic assistance to less-developed third-world countries with a minimum of tangible strings was meant to insure eventual adhesion to economic as well as political liberalism; it did not prevent local nationalisms from rising and nationalizations from spreading, in the face of a growing volume of American investments. Likewise frustratingly, the Kennedy-round negotiations succeeded in reducing tariffs and increasing the volume of trade among the industrial countries in due course, but their very success helped erode further the free-trade coalition of agricultural, labor, and even business interests within the United States. The result was a revived tendency in favor of deliberately balancing U.S. imports and exports on the basis of reciprocity and of reemphasizing secure access to investments (American in Europe and in Japan in particular), to raw materials (in the Third World), and to exports (in both areas). The conflicts within the industrial world were escalating even before they were matched by the conflict between developed countries *en bloc* and the less developed countries. A basic issue was the proper relationship between economic independence and interdependence; and the basic option seemed to be between universal and regional or national systems, between the market economy's potential to foster economic expansion in the aggregate and the capacity and authority of individual governments and states to control and guide national economies so as to protect or augment existing country shares of world assets in conditions of uneven rates of inflation, internal taxation, and currency devaluations largely deriving from the prosperity of the 1960s.

While the most direct conflict between the United States and the European Economic Community was over protection of European agriculture, and was aggravated by America's need for agricultural exports being increased with every decrease in her competitive position in manufactures relative to Europe and Japan, the issue of discrimination was anything but dormant. It was reintensified by concurrent shifts in American and allied shares of economic transactions with the Third World and gave rise to often divergent ideological positions and actual policies (not least by the United States) on the issue of (mostly European) preferential trade agreements with the less developed countries. Exacerbating the competition over foreign trade were contentions over foreign investments. The preponderance of American over European and Japanese new investments in third-world countries or areas not clearly within the sphere of one major economic power was potentially at variance with short-term trends in trade favoring Western Europe and Japan; so was the concentration of American foreign investments in Western Europe, facilitating technological diffusion, at cross-purposes with the need to help maintain or further improve America's favorable trading balance with Western Europe as the critical positive item in the weakening U.S. balance of international payments overall.

European attitudes toward American investments were sufficiently different and ambivalent to be expressed in selective policies. The Japanese resistance was only one in a fuller range of protectionist features on both sides. And third-world economic nationalism was finding a parallel expression in investment codes discriminating against foreign capital. Simultaneously growing were controversies over standards of living within countries and the supply of raw materials between them. They highlighted the roles of both national governments and multinational corporations as attention shifted from production to equitable distribution. The issues of social welfare and justice rose to prominence not least within the industrially developed countries under the pressure of rising expectations, outstripping even the substantial increase in living standards; growing in acerbity for the preindustrial commodity producers (and, in due course, for industrial consumers) was the issue of fair terms of trade, under the impact of a both fluctuating and, over time, rising demand for raw materials. Short-term supply-demand fluctuations in third-world commodities reflected alternations between war and peace only more directly than did the variations in public moods concerning the enlargement and allocation of welfare goods within the industrial countries, prominently including the United States. Allocating resources ever more authoritatively among unequally privileged groups meant reconciling the conditions of an essentially free international market with a regulatory quasi-mercantilist approach internally. Any redistribution of economic power in the sense of access to real wealth in the domestic and the international spheres involved recasting existing relationships between productivity and consumption, among other things, while conflicts that had initially originated in the rapid rate of growth in the developed countries intensified with every intimation that the growth might slow down or actually come to a halt.

Even before generalized economic stagnation had become a possibility in the 1970s, domestic and foreign economic policies and priorities had been exposed in the United States in the 1960s to appearances of decline in growth rates and in the competitive trade posture, when compared with the peaks of postwar American superiority over the Europeans and the Japanese. Being a structural crisis or only a stage in transformation, the state of things derived from rising American labor-unit costs and declining efficiency in traditional areas of strength (such as steel production) to be compensated for in the area of high-technology capital goods and innovations. A concurrently rising dependence on returns from foreign investments signaled the United States having its turn as a mature creditor country liable to long-term degeneration into a *rentier* economy. America's disadvantage relative to her industrial competitors shrank whenever differential rates of inflation and social costs offset disparities in production costs; but the same equation also reduced the attractions of further trade liberalization in the Atlantic area from the European viewpoint, without appeasing the protectionism of American labor, drawn up in battle array against the unholy alliance of giant American international corporations with cheap foreign labor.

American-controlled multinational corporations flourished abroad on their superior capacity to productively borrow and implement economies of scale. In the process of continuing American economic dominance and expansion, however, the multinationals reflected also a lessened capacity of domestically produced goods to compete abroad; and even as they testified in consequence to a species of economic decline, they curtailed further the time span available for exploiting technological innovations within the United States itself. Moreover, they sapped the support for liberal economic policies by their very ability to adapt American free enterprise dynamically to the limitations on free trade implicit in European and third-world customs unions or regional markets. Whereas American labor taxed the corporations with exporting American jobs rather than American goods, and while U.S. business saw in the capacity of the multinationals to leap over trade barriers an alternative to free trade among nations, host governments in the Third World in particular were being propelled in the direction of economic nationalism by the very size of the multinationals and their alleged insensitivity to host-country needs.

An increasingly critical issue for the United States, overshadowing other derangements while mirroring them, was its unfavorable balance of international payments. The multinational corporations had profited from the imbalance (as a basis for credit abroad) before they could significantly help reduce it (by repatriating returns on investments); and the American balance-of-payments deficits had also helped liberalize the economic system at large insofar as they promoted economic recovery and technological diffusion in Europe and Japan. The overall system held so long as its cost in the coin of independence for the Europeans was neutralized by the likewise hard to quantify cost of interdependence for the United States. America's cost became both substantial and measurable when the margin of deficit in the balance of payments, due to outlays on overseas defense and foreign aid as part of imperial policies, was augmented beginning with the late 1960s by the erosion of the nearly century-long surplus in the balance of trade. Before the mid-1870s, the American trade deficit had been covered by European (mainly British) investments in the United States, and the subsequent American trade surplus was offset in stages by the liquidation of these investments, by private American lending after World War I, and by governmental outlays following World War II. The crisis due to the end of American lending in Europe in the 1930s reappeared in the 1960s when a trade deficit with Japan and West Germany (though not with Western Europe as a whole) aggravated the imbalance in international payments and dramatized as a readily focused phenomenon the worsening relationship of costs and benefits accruing to the United States from its imperial involvement generally and from the free-trade empire system in particular.

The open-door beginnings of the free-trade phase had witnessed a myth-creating exaggeration of the benefits to be derived from the China trade; the adult free-trade empire was exposed to another myth-creating exaggeration, regarding the economic sacrifices implicit in presumably unreciprocated postwar concessions within the essential empire and in presumably unrewarding material assistance for the third-world peripheries. From the American viewpoint, the international payments deficit was a burden of empire, imposed on the American economy generally and on the U.S. dollar as the key reserve currency in the liberal monetary system specifically. From the European perspective, the deficits were privileges that financed American direct investments and added fuel to European inflation. They were a form of imperial levy, conceded in return for military protection as part of an updated interallied compromise; and the effective costs of that protection to the United States were reduced whenever the Europeans shared the costs of supporting and equipping the American troops in Europe in ways that were, moreover, inimical to an integrated European production of military hardware among other things.

An inherently inconclusive trans-Atlantic dialogue over costs and benefits took place across increasingly fluid boundaries between the economic and the strategic spheres. It signaled the passing of the relatively simple and unequivocal post–World War II compromise under which the United States had compensated economically reascendant Europeans and Japanese for supporting America's hegemonial primacy. In a similar vein, the Roman senate had humored the trading Italian and eastern allies and Britain the white dominions, and (taking seriously the notion of an Atlantic "community" for the purposes of analogy) the Roman and British strategy-oriented ruling class had compensated the economically rising but politically self-denying middle classes. Compensation or, alternatively, appeasement gave way to competition when the increased economic strength of all European countries enhanced the political ambitions of some and restlessness in most. At that point, an officially unquestioning acknowledgment of American primacy was replaced by the quest for parity in the economic realm and equity in the relation of economics to the strategic realm. The groped-for formulas would have to reconcile the ancient value of independence with the new demands of interdependence, a revised posture of partnership with an unchanged level of protection; and they would have to do so within an environment that was, or seemed to be, increasingly multipolar economically, while continuing to be bipolar on the highest strategic level militarily.

Although real, the structural crisis in the U.S.-centered liberal economic and monetary system did not attain the severity of the world crisis preceding World War II. Nor did the decline of American economic superiority relative to its postwar peak equal in degree Great Britain's before World War I. If anywhere, the erosion of the Bretton Woods system in the 1960s had a closer parallel in the European free-trade system of the nineteenth century. The latter, too, weakened, barely two decades after it had gotten under way in the 1860s under British leadership, in large part over the protectionism of a continental European peasantry unable to cope with inroads by American and other new-world foodstuffs. When responding to an immediate crisis and to symptoms of long-term economic decline, the United States was able to mobilize more than the conventional economic remedies, be they tax and trust legislation to promote exports or measures to facilitate business and labor adjustments to diminished competitiveness in particular sectors. Any effort to inflect the free-trade system to fit an American conception of fair-trade and fair-labor practices could draw upon ample economic leverage. The United States was still the largest and most attractive market. As such, it was able to bargain with some effect to either reduce protectionist measures in both the industrially developed and developing segments of the world economy or facilitate adaptations to any transient or basic weakness of the American currency in the global monetary system. And the United States was, moreover, the world's leading food producer and was closer to self-sufficiency than either Western Europe or Japan in the critical commodity sector of energy derived from petroleum. It was, consequently, able to bargain with producers of raw material commodities in the food-deficient Third World over equitable access and terms of

trade, and over a whole range of issues clustering around the in-
dependence-interdependence dichotomy with all parties.

VII

Immediately even more important than any economic leverage was the
compelling strategic leverage implicit in America's role as the military
protector of both Western Europe and Japan. It could supplement or
wholly replace economic inducements and pressures whenever these were
temporarily in abeyance, due to either lopsided perceptions of interdependence or actually distorted balances of trade and payments. The
real relationship of forces was revealed in the summer of 1971 as part of a
New Economic Policy of the Nixon administration, when the Europeans
and the Japanese reluctantly concurred with trade and monetary measures designed to improve U.S. balances of trade and payments by effectively revising the Bretton Woods system without replacing the United
States as the economic and monetary centerpiece.

Linking a conspicuous remedy for economic difficulty with a leverage
deriving from America's imperial role in security went far toward refusing the economic and the strategic factors. The fusion signaled a deviation in the direction of protective imperialism, a fact more important
than any relation of the specific economic measures to protectionist economic nationalism. Both the readiness to depend on strategic leverage
and its efficacy in the economic arena were increased by the concurrent
decrease in the security threat as part of détente with the Soviet Union
(and normalization of relations with Communist China). Relaxation of
tensions made it less irresponsible for the United States to link strategic
and economic issues within the alliance system, and the allies' responsiveness to American needs was enhanced by the increase in American
options implicit in the new, flexible international diplomacy (to be
paralleled by the new flexibility in a monetary system based on floating
exchange rates?). Furthermore, and even more paradoxically, the resort
to strategic leverage was rendered more efficacious by the concurrent
deterioration in the U.S.-upheld strategic framework of the liberal economic system resulting from the Soviet surge to and possibly beyond
nuclear parity. The consequent erosion of the European (and Japanese)
confidence in automatic American protection by means of assured retaliation created an additional incentive for strengthening the American
strategic commitment by economic compensations. And, finally, since the
unfavorable outcome of the conventional military intervention in Indochina was liable to inspire critical third-world raw-material producers
with the sense of immunity to American reprisals against disruptive
pricing or supply policies, new and severe economic problems for both
Europe and Japan might be unmanageable without intensifying the

American commitment to the economic system by means of revisions to America's liking. Nor was it wholly insignificant that the near-overt resort to strategically backed interventionism in the industrial segment of the world economy coincided with lessened stress on economic instrumentalism in relations with the preindustrial segment.

At the climax of the free-trade empire, the United States had employed economic instruments to foster economic interdependence with recipients of assistance, with the result of consolidating America's politico-strategic hegemony while expanding its scope. In deteriorating conditions, the strategic leverage was employed to change the terms of previously evolved interdependence to America's advantage and reduce the net costs of continuing an irreducible degree of strategic performance. To the extent that the United States placed its strategic role on the scales of competing material interests, if only in order to be able to go on performing strategically, to that same extent conspicuously economic motivation from declining strength supplemented economic-strategic fusion in suggesting the tentative appearance, if nothing more, of economism attendant on late imperialism. Actual longer-term trends could be clarified only by the maturing of alternative responses to the dual economic crisis, within the essential empire and between it and the third-world peripheries. Short of outright collapse in economic warfare, the alternatives comprised a more deliberate management of the system and its further extension and were critically tied to the chances for consolidating the industrial core institutionally as a form of imperial expansion in depth. So long as institutional consolidation remained a practical possibility, however, American responses to the deterioration of the Bretton Woods system were unlikely to wholly efface the previously intruding features of formalized protective imperialism.

If the liberal economic approach to freer trade managed to absorb the dislocations of the early 1970s and resumed its course, it could expand further in kind as well as in scope. In kind, the removal of nontariff barriers to trade could be stressed as a complement to the prior reduction of tariffs to irreducible levels, along with more or less freely floating monetary exchange rates; and in scope, the liberal system could gradually incorporate the less developed countries equipped to produce labor-intensive industrial goods and revalue raw materials for export in sufficient magnitudes to pay for imports of both capital goods and consumer goods, including foodstuffs. The system might eventually associate selectively also the Soviet Union and its clients by virtue of a new fundamental compromise trading an enlarged access to the most-favored-nation principle and to Western credits and technology for the cooperation of the Eastern states in upholding an uninhibited commerical use of the oceans and a secure access to raw-material resources on economically sustainable terms. A wholly different kind of expansion might follow the failure of only economic bargains between industrialized countries and the industrializing commodity producers capable of helping set the free-trade system back on a pragmatically adjusted course, combining moderate redistribution of wealth with substantial expansion of trade. Were instead an escalated energy or comparable crisis to further aggravate economic strains in the unevenly vulnerable industrial world, the politically intolerable prospect might decisively reinforce narrowly economic incentives to relegitimize forcible means for reintegrating critical commodity suppliers into a U.S. -dominated politico-economic system.

Short of impending catastrophe, American policy-makers were reluctant to jeopardize either East-West détente or the South-North dialogue by forcefully safeguarding the economic interests of the industrial Atlantic-Pacific community. Nor were the empire's European and Japanese associates willing to pay with the only recently won degree of economic and political independence for the demonstration of an inescapable need for American protection, against economic aggression by the South along with the military threat from the East; they preferred to establish privileged economic and political relations with third-world countries generally and the Middle Eastern oil-producers specifically, also because they lacked the assurance that American protection against retaliation would be more assuredly effective in the economic than in the military field. Only if economic relationships such as illustrated by the U.S.-European (and Japanese) -Middle Eastern triangle threatened, at a future date, to intensify divisions within the essential empire far beyond the mainly procedural differences about the tripartite American-Soviet-Chinese interplay in the diplomatic and nuclear-strategic arenas, might it become necessary to formalize or institutionalize further the American empire as an alternative to system collapse and a supplement to wider liberalization or better management. Internal consolidation might then be either a requisite for dealing effectively with economic ills such as chronic inflation and unemployment that have been set off by identifiable unilateral actions from the outside, a consequence of an effective response to such actions, or the penultimate alternative to a forcible last-resort reaction against them.

A politico-military reexpansion in response to raw material-related pressures would mean more imperialism in the peripheries and, as reactions to such imperialism set in, less free trade outside the essential core and the provisionally reintegrated appendices of empire. Conversely, reconsolidating the essential empire institutionally without revitalizing intervention readiness at its peripheries might or might not entail more liberal economic policies outside, and more American imperial hegemony inside, the Atlantic-Pacific core. Much would depend in the latter contingency on whether the enhanced American responsibilities for both strategic and economic defense of the essential empire were compensated by mobilizing more active allied participation in the tasks of order maintenance and enforcement or merely solidified American control over the modalities of defense against a newly structured world crisis. As free trade was expanded further in both kind and scope, finally, the U.S. - upheld strategic framework might become eligible for revision downward in favor of increasing dependence on a partially arms-controlled mutual deterrence between superpowers on the nuclear-strategic level and of progressive American disengagement and devolution of responsibility to lesser powers in the conventional military and naval sectors. More free trade would then go with fewer imperial obligations in politico-military terms, although at the risk of a drift back to the frustrations of a strategically unsupported variety of economism in the guise of merely economic expansionism, aggravated by any possible intervening diminution of American economic strength.

Both the interventionist and the noninterventionist versions of institutional consolidation displayed the formalized feature of protective empire and imperialism most strikingly, without being alone in exhibiting that aspect. An essential characteristic was an increased tension and consequent interpenetration between public and private domains, amounting to a partial reversion to conditions usually preceding the free-trading phase. A basic tension in the United States and nearly everywhere else in the industrial world has been between the private character of the liberal international economy and the growing demand for intervention by public powers in the domestic sphere, directed at governments that were expanding functionally even as they were weakening morally and politically. A fair distribution of the benefits and liabilities deriving domestically and internationally from an essentially liberal world economic system was under such conditions increasingly contingent on a mixture of governmental promotion of the national interest and intergovernmental management of the international interest in restraining national governments from passing on to others either the domestic costs of international economic liberalism or the foreign-trade costs of domestic interventionism. Since a domestic-cum-international economy so managed could be shaped to be more neo-liberal or more neo-mercantilist, blurring the distinction between the two basic policies was apt to reduce the distinction between traditional European adherence to one (mercantilist) approach and the American ideological preference for the other (liberal) approach, while revising the historically experienced actual American assortments of either domestic mercantilism with international free-trading or laissez faire at home with protectionism externally. If a code of conduct were to be imposed by governments not only upon themselves but also on the multinational corporations, finally, the public and private spheres would be further interpenetrated without strengthening the case for identifying international corporations with neo-colonialism.

A growing tendency for strategic and economic factors, as well as public and private spheres, to interpenetrate was one consequence of dislocations in the American free-trade empire and in its strategic under-pinnings. So long as the dislocations stopped short of a survival crisis, the tendency was contained, but not without displaying traits peculiar to late empire or imperialism in all of the three crucial relationships. Progressive fusion or refusion of economic and strategic factors in interallied rela-tions had been exemplified by the nexus between the revisions in the U.S.-dominated economic order and the older issue of reductions in the U.S. military presence in Europe in the early 1970s; persisted in the require-ment to extend the American guarantee from the military-political to the economic survival of resource-poor Western Europe and Japan with re-spect to third-world commodity producers directly and to possible Soviet incitements to economic aggression by others, as part of superpower competition, indirectly; and was spectacularly in evidence whenever the requirements of the American and European national economies ex-tended competition over the procurement of arms within the Atlantic Alliance to sales of arms to less developed countries outside it.

In the second key relationship, with the Soviet Union, the rulers of the latter appeared to be increasingly more amenable (even as the allies were becoming less so) to tacitly linking problems in strategic deterrence with bargains over political and economic issues, specifically bearing on a balanced approach to détente, so long as Soviet economic performance could be enhanced at little immediate political or doctrinal cost inter-nally and at no visible cost to strategic position and geopolitical progres-sion globally. An essential barter in the U.S. view was between American credits and technology transfers and Soviet self-restraint or even coopera-tion on nuclear arms and in the world's peripheries. Any long-range gains were apt to be hypothetical, and few substantial economic advan-tages for the United States were readily apparent in the short run for either the balance of payments or domestic employment. Such limitations notwithstanding, the new diplomatic policy with the Soviets comple-mented the "new economic policy" vis-à-vis essential allies insofar as it liberated the United States from some of the constraints peculiar to the coincident climaxing of economically liberal military empire and American-Soviet hostility. In another respect, the détente policy was the obverse of the dollar-devaluation policy, however, since America's eco-nomic superiority over the Soviets was to compensate for decline in relative strategic posture, while strategic preeminence over the allies was employed to rectify a supposedly unfair balance of economic costs and benefits.

In the area of the third critical relation, with the so-called South, finally, strategic and economic factors interpenetrated in the issues of secure access and secure returns. The access to be secured was to essential raw materials and routes of communication over land and across the seas, in the face of actual or threatening restrictions on either. The returns to be guaranteed were on past U.S. private (and public) investments. Both were contingent on some form of American strategic presence in being or capable of being reactivated with a minimum of delay and provocation. As regards access, the speculative presumption that raw materials had been the original incentive to American imperial expansion was yielding to the practical possibility that a secure access to them would become dependent on continuing the imperial role in some form. As regards the returns, the myth that imperial expansion had originated in surplus capital's need for investment opportunities began to dissolve before the real, if remoter, possibility that a defensive *rentier* economy might come to require an imperial shield or safeguard against different forms of economic blackmail or outright spoliation.

VIII

With the growing interpenetration of economic and strategic factors, it became ever more difficult in principle and irrelevant for policy to differentiate, let alone evalute, the costs and the benefits of empire. These had been exceptionally hard to calculate even at the peak of the American free-trade empire. Given the doctrinally antithetical, illiberal nature of the adversary system, any effective strategic threat to American and Western security entailed the related danger of exclusion from economic access, while any threat to political freedoms comprised also one to the liberal-economic systen of free enterprise. In such a situation both immediate and long-term economic benefits of empire had to be subtracted from the costs of military defense. The issue was posed most sharply in Europe and Japan ever since economic and security considerations had been commingled in both the real motives and the official rationales for the Truman doctrine, directly with respect to Greece and Turkey and ultimately in regard to European economic recovery. Hard-to-calculate intra-alliance balance sheets comprised on one side the ostensible costs incurred by the United States as alliance leader and, on the other side, the militarily sheltered and economically profitable investments, arms sales, and sundry economic concessions and "offset payments." In the Third World, the cost-benefit ratios came to involve different degrees of immunity to unilaterally wrought economic disruption as a function of different strategic deployments. But, from the beginning, and even before a more advantageous cost-benefit mix was implicitly sought by way of the Nixon doctrine and the concomitant policies on foreign aid and preferential tariffs, the multifaceted imbrications of military and economic assistance policies confounded calculations and discredited any pat conclusions.

The costs of a maturing free-trade empire were dramatized by military involvements in Asia, most particularly including the war in Indochina. Conversely, a reduced imperial involvement after the war encouraged a politically motivated and economically disruptive employment of raw materials for political and economic leverage, notably by Middle Eastern suppliers. The residual imperial presence placed a ceiling on the resulting costs, however, by giving the moderate local regimes, politically insecure not least because raw-material rich, a stake in continued American support, while constituting a last-resort deterrent to conspicuous abuses of natural resource monopolies.

Nor were the direct outlays and inflationary domestic effects of the war in Indochina without some offsetting, though perverse, benefits. The troubled course and unfavorable outcome of the war helped improve the American economic position by making the allies amenable to the dollar-devaluation strategy and third-world parties psychopolitically ready for intensifying a commodity crisis less damaging for the United States than for its key allies. Moreover, the war was liable to set the stage for—or open the door to—an intensified American economic penetration in Southeast Asia in competition with Japan and also to promote in the longer run an economic as well as preliminary diplomatic normalization with China. It was equally futile, finally, to compare item-for-item the costs and benefits of the geographically limited free-trade empire during the cold war with the actual or hypothetical costs and benefits of political détente and trade liberalization with the Soviet Union, especially if such an effort was undertaken in isolation from concurrently induced alterations in the larger setting.

The costs and benefits of empire in all of the three critical relationships (with adversaries, allies, and comparative "neutrals") could be assessed only speculatively, in terms of hypothetical alternative pasts. One such possible "past" was the continuance of American economic and political isolationism, or of strategically unsupported economic expansionism, into post–World War II conditions. It was unlikely that the cost-benefit ratio of empire would greatly suffer from such a comparison, any more than it would appear particularly unfavorable in the optic of a hypothetical future. Such a future might consist, in a differently structured world crisis, of the hypertrophy of national protectionisms and regional neo-mercantilisms; and it could result from the United States extending its use of strategic leverages for economic advantage, mainly within the industrial world, and from radically constricting its strategic role, mainly in the nonindustrial world. An enforced economy in empire-like exertions, designed to bring external costs to a level compatible with unchecked domestic needs and demands, and a string of failures to meet outside provocations with an economy of force that differed from its atrophy, could be inspired by hopes to secure the benefits of world empire without its costs. Yet any experimentation with exchanging the labors of engagement for effortless equilibrium was more likely to throw the United States back eventually on formalizing an economically protectionist regional empire, including a Western Hemisphere that was in some of its parts straining toward the Communist East in revolutionary politics, and in other parts toward more or less alienated Western Europe and Japan in conventional economics.

The context was apt to combine a deepened economic crisis and a revived security crisis. The tentative, either isolated or latent, elements of formalized protective imperialism that had been previously in evidence would then be liable to evolve into a full-fledged instance of the genre, give it a protective cast, and expose the United States to the plight of both the Roman and the British empires in their final stages.

IX

In the period of informal free-trade empire the United States had more points in common with Britain than with Rome. Within the latter's equivalent of a free-trade empire, Rome was basically the military protector of trading allies and dependents, even as successive Roman political elites were gradually developing a stake in international finance and trade; nor was the overall economic setting closely comparable with the modern one. By contrast, the ascendant United States interacted with the British empire in a shared economic setting once the course of evolution narrowed and gradually turned to America's advantage the initial disparity, due to Britain creating the Industrial Revolution and the United States merely confronting its results. Having first lagged behind the British progression toward a free-trade empire, the United States eventually engaged Britain in effective trade competition over notably Latin America, when both parties were seeking to diversify their economic stakes in Europe; and it challenged Britain decisively over the principle of globally free (i.e., nondiscriminatory) trade vs. regionally preferential (i.e., intra-Commonwealth) trade as part of integrating a declining British into an ascendant American imperial system. It remained possible, finally, that the United States would more fully replicate the informal British free-trade empire at its apogee only at a future time, when intergovernmentally managed essential economic liberalization under American auspices had progressed further, while the strategic setting and the American involvement in upholding it had been relaxed into greater similarity with the plural great-power system of the mid-nineteenth century.

Barring that evolutionary path, the greatest similarity between the British and the American free-trade empires would lie in both having enjoyed but a brief climax before being eroded amidst balance-of-payments difficulties, experienced also by Rome. The sharing of fundamental traits was qualified, however, by differences that variously contributed to strains within the two Anglo-Saxon empires. Since the British had been the first industrial power, they tried (without success) to prevent the initial diffusion of the new techniques to Europe, while the United States fostered technological diffusion and with it future competition. Conversely, Britain readily accepted agricultural imports in exchange for manufacturing exports, whereas the United States neither did nor was very well able to do likewise, given its surplus in foodstuffs. Relatedly, the British accepted (mainly agricultural) imports in payment of prior loans during their rule as the principal creditor nation; the United States resisted imports from debtors when becoming the key creditor at a critical juncture of the liberal world economy after World War I. As the kingpin of the international monetary system, the British sustained the gold-standard mechanism from their (diminishing) balance-of-payments surplus, whereas the United States managed a dollar-based monetary system by means of a deficit. When financial conditions deteriorated, Britain tended to export deflation in the name of monetary discipline (e.g., when liquidating investments in the United States); the United States exported inflation in the name of international liquidity (while American investments were augmenting in Europe). The British seem to have managed fairly well the tripartite trade-and-investment pattern comprising India next to themselves and continental Europe on the strength of their major asset, the Indian surplus in the balance of trade. The United States was less successful, since relations with the nonindustrial third-world parties had become more complex and less controllable and American big business tended to concentrate both investments and export drives in the industrial European countries rather than (as had been the British practice) in the commodity-producing preindustrial areas of the empire.

When organizing the informal liberal economic system, finally, the United States stopped short of annexations even more than had Britain. But whereas the Americans inclined to institutionalize the system with the aid of international economic organizations and military alliances, the British were by and large content to rely on the unmatched resources and skills available to the City and on the Royal Navy. Full-scale transition to a formalized protective empire was, therefore, bound to be more (or differently) conspicuous for the British than it would be for the Americans. When in distress, both imperial centers of free trade sought to reconstruct to their advantage the economic and strategic-defensive relations with principal dependents. The British would reallocate costs and benefits of empire with less developed countries bent on industrialization —the white dominions. The United States dealt instead with the industrialized countries of Europe and Japan, at once more competitive than had been the dominions and less impelled toward the specific infant-industry kind of economic nationalism. In the area of uneven development, it was the principal Latin American countries that were for the United States what the dominions had been for Britain. Mexico, Brazil, or Argentina were consequently most apt to reproduce the efforts of Canada and Australia to escape from the imperial power center, if away from the United States rather than (as had been the case previously) toward it. America's industrial and Britain's preindustrial dependents were qualitatively different as potential parties to institutional consolidation. The critical difference became quantitative when internal pressures for socioeconomic revisions confronted, from broadly comparable liberal-radical sources, two home markets of markedly different sizes. As a result, if a formalized protective economic complex for Britain would have required the scope of something like the proposed Imperial Customs Union (and Federation), the United States could choose from a larger range of scopes at different costs. Consolidation could be confined to the Americanism of the labor unions; coincide with the Atlanticist framework dear to the internationalist elites; or extend to a kind of "Atlanticism plus" by selectively co-opting third-world political economies more or less liberal internally and externally.

American ruling elites inclined no less than had the British to escape from hard-to-manage domestic socioeconomic problems into the international sphere, and came to prefer informal cooperative adjustments of economic conditions without additional administrative and politico-military responsibilities in the international arena as well. But additional preemptive British expansion did take place in Africa and, differently, in China. The economic impetus was to insure British access to markets rather than to raw materials; the reinforcing threats to strategic communications came mainly from great naval powers rather than from maritime encroachments by lesser coastal powers (with the possible exception of the Boers).

The opposite either was or might well become the case for the United States in both respects at a comparable stage. Should, therefore, the American empire come under pressure to reexpand spatially as well as institutionally, it would move closer to the Roman than to the British antecedent. The Roman empire, too, underwent social crises and was reorganized administratively and institutionalized for greater efficiency in its protective phase, along lines dividing the Roman-Italian core and the East. Rome's growing need to protect the all-Mediterranean free-trade area from outside challenges and internal economic incoherences might be matched eventually by rising American responsibility to protect an embattled Atlantic-Pacific core for the European and Japanese equivalents of Rome's eastern provinces, likewise trade-dependent and economically vulnerable. Rome's original east-west axis in the Mediterranean was inflected in the later empire southward, toward Mesopotamia and beyond; the same would be true for any late imperial reexpansion by the United States, replicating the focus on the Persian Gulf of both earlier empires. A secure access to the black gold—oil—would then equal Imperial Rome's quest for the real thing in Dacia as a means to easing balance-of-payments difficulties. Similarly, Rome's concern with strategic communications overland via the Gulf to India and beyond to China had prefigured the urge of both Anglo-Saxon nations to secure mainly the maritime routes in the same direction. For the British, the Persian Gulf had been originally part of the security of the imperial frontier surrounding India as the key economic value. The subsequent discovery of oil in the area added strategic and economic incentives about equally. America's increasingly economic concern was related to the danger of a systematically hostile employment of the oil weapon; it has been reinforced by strategic preoccupation shifting toward the balance among American, indigenous (e.g., Iranian), and other extraneous (Soviet) naval deployments in the area and beyond.

It would take a survival crisis to fuse strategic and economic issues for the American empire as finally and dramatically as they had merged for Rome and Britain. Prior to such a crisis, all three empires had room for choice and maneuver between minimum and maximum responses to routine economic problems and dilemmas. A minimum response lay in the pursuit of fair terms for economic exchanges involving competitors and of equitable compensation by clients for imperial protection; the maximum possible reaction was institutional reorganization or territorial reexpansion. In either case, the economic factor rose in relative importance as part of a shift in both the governing perceptions of the manifold crisis and in the character of the (largely but not only economic) preliminaries to conflicts attendant on reexpansion. The economic crisis was sooner or later joined in the past with a strategic-security crisis; and the combined crisis caused the seat of empire to gravitate initially in the direction of the economically stronger segment or element, to the eastern branch of empire in the case of Rome and westward to the once-dependent "sister nation" in Britain's case. The economic reascent of Western Europe and Japan since World War II allowed for some deconcentration of economic power around the strongest of the dependent national currencies and economies. It did not produce, however, in the fragile new strength a reliable recipient for an empire that would be moving away from a declining United States toward a new principal seat of economic and financial exchanges (adopting Brooks Adams's term). Any major institutional or also spatial reexpansion of the American empire itself, employing new forms of control and cooperation, was conversely more than ever likely to originate in both internal and external

economic stresses and stimulants involving fairly specific stakes and interests; and the momentum would be sustained by diffuse moods and
expectations that had originated in an earlier economic environment and
were intensified by its deterioration into the economism of late imperialism within a formalized protective empire American-style.[2]

2. Concerning "economic dilemmas" (in addition to references in chaps. VI and VII)
see Herman E. Krooss, *American Economic Development* (Englewood Cliffs: Prentice–
Hall, 1966); A. G. Kenwood and A. L. Lougheed, *The Growth of the International
Economy 1820–1960* (London: G. Allen and Unwin, 1971); Brooks Adams, *American
Economic Supremacy* (New York: Harper and Row, 1947); Douglass C. North, *Growth
and Welfare in the American Past* (Englewood Cliffs: Prentice–Hall, 1974); William J.
Pomeroy, *American Neo-Colonialism* (New York: International Publishers, 1970); Julius
W. Pratt, *America and World Leadership 1900–1921* (New York: Macmillan, 1967);
Herbert Feis, *The Diplomacy of the Dollar 1919–1932* (Baltimore: The Johns Hopkins
Press, 1950); Lloyd C. Gardner, *Economic Aspects of New Deal Diplomacy* (Madison:
The University of Wisconsin Press, 1964); Richard N. Gardner, *Sterling-Dollar Dip-
lomacy* (Oxford: Clarendon Press, 1956); Gabriel Kolko, *The Politics of War* (New
York: Random House, 1968); William B. Kelly, ed., *Studies in United States Commercial
Policy* (Chapel Hill: The University of North Carolina Press, 1963); Karl Schriftgiesser,
Business and Public Policy (Englewood Cliffs: Prentice–Hall, 1967); Joe R. Wilkinson,
Politics and Trade Policy (Washington, D.C.: Public Affairs Press, 1960); Isaiah Frank
et al., *United States International Economic Policy in an Interdependent World* (Wash-
ington, D.C.: Report to the President submitted by the Commission on International
Trade and Investment Policy, July 1971); Harry G. Johnson, ed., *New Trade Strategy
for the World Economy* (London: Allen and Unwin, 1969); Charles P. Kindleberger,
American Business Abroad (New Haven: Yale University Press, 1969), and "U.S. Foreign
Economic Policy, 1776–1976," *Foreign Affairs* 55 (January 1977); Jack N. Behrman,
U.S. International Business and Governments (New York: McGraw–Hill, 1971); and
A. J. Youngson, *The British Economy 1920–1957* (London: G. Allen, 1960).

IX

AMERICAN EMPIRE.

Development and Defense

At the heart of empire management is a workable balance between central control or authority and peripheral or local autonomy. A deranged balance will mean in practice that there is overinvolvement or underinvolvement, as compared with optimum economy of control; and it will either signal internal mismanagement or create the appearance of external overextension. The American empire was never as centrally organized as had been either the Roman empire at its apogee or the first British empire before its dissolution and the second one before its decentralization. But the United States incurred the perennial problems sufficiently to warrant viewing the organization and defense of the U.S.-centered world order in terms of categories broadly identical with those discernible in the earlier empires, while allowing for significant contrasts.

I

At its climax the American empire resembled most the early Roman empire in that it combined internationalist features (bearing on America's Greeks, the Western Europeans) and imperialist traits. And it was like the second British empire when that empire came to differentiate colonial, imperial, and commonwealth features (the latter bearing on the white dominions, the equivalents of Western Europe and Japan in the American scheme of things). There was a basic difference, however. Despite elaborate multilateral structures, the American empire remained fundamentally informal. Consequently, the basic balance was between *de facto* control by the imperial center and effective autonomy in conduct by the dependents; and control was susceptible of being concentrated or deconcentrated and not, as is the case for institutionalized authority, centralized or decentralized. The difference was more than nominal. It imparted to the American empire additional elasticity in outward appearance, while depriving the pursuit of the internal equilibrium (between control and autonomy) of the temporarily stabilizing influence of institutionally ingrained routines, notably outside the essential empire made up of industrially developed powers.

Imperial authority was in evidence only initially, in the guise of the European colonial empires surviving World War II. But wartime events had by then begun to disjoin formalized authority from effective control, laying the foundation for synchronizing the transition to a new mode of control with the transfer of the means for exerting any kind of control. European authority was increasingly exercised as a matter of delegation from the West's true imperial center to subordinate allies, while the escalating indigenous drives for likewise formal independence were reinforcing morally even more than materially the parallel pressures for change emanating from the progressively intensified U.S.-Soviet conflict. The superpower confrontation made it urgent to enhance the economy and the efficacy of control for the West in the aggregate by eliminating the European intermediaries between an ascendant new foremost power and an emergent Third World.

The implied expansion of direct American involvement meant replacing tacit delegation of formal authority to the West Europeans by an "anti-imperialistic" United States with more or less enforced devolution of empire to America from the European metropoles. Involvement in depth complemented an expansion that had originated in a preclusive response to actual or suspected outside threats. It was to continue as the American imperial system groped inconclusively for an internal equilibrium, between the amounts and forms of overseas control sustainable domestically on the one side and, on the other side, the degrees and kinds of autonomy the dependencies would be willing and able to implement without contravening the irreducible requirements of a world order congenial to the United States. That order was no more universal than American latitude in shaping it was unlimited. Being a constraint as well as a stimulus, the parallel imperial system of the Soviets in Eastern Europe and, to a lesser extent, Northeast Asia was initially evolving into an ever more coercive one as internal weakness and external opposition confined Soviet power within the limits that had been set by the course and the immediate aftermath of World War II.

The change from delegation to devolution amounted to the transformation of a hegemonial American system with two layers or tiers into an American empire consisting of two segments or wings. The hegemonial system had superimposed overall American influence upon the Western

European metropoles and their colonial or security systems operative in the Eastern Mediterranean (via the British security responsibility for Greece and Turkey before 1947), the Asian East (via British, French, and Dutch colonial responsibilities parallel to the putative role to be played by Nationalist China in the new Far Eastern order-to-be), and, most thoroughly and longest, Africa. As a loosely unifying framework, the American hegemony was based on the nuclear capacity to deter any conventional Soviet counterchallenge and on the economic capacity to regenerate the European surrogates. Tacit delegation of primary responsibility in the peripheries to the surrogates went with an intermittently vocal opposition to its indefinite continuance, in ways only uncertainly consistent with the increasingly salient manifest function of the European metropoles in regional defense nearer home.

The two-tiered system was too precarious to endure. It broke down with the fading of the British in both the Eastern Mediterranean and Asia (India and beyond), of the French in Indochina, and of the Nationalists on mainland China; with the partially consequent direct American involvement in Korea on behalf of Japan, the previously only major direct "imperial" American responsibility; and with the coincident fading of American nuclear monopoly relative to the Soviet Union. The succeeding bisegmented empire arose out of the reduction of the European states from world-wide imperial surrogates to dependent allies in regional defense, and their replacement in the peripheries by a growing clientele of postcolonial independent states. Ideally, the new clients would convert their formal independence from the vanishing European empires into an effective role in defending the expanding frontier of the new informal American empire against the various forces and pressures originating in the ascendant Sino-Soviet heartland complex; an only ultimate American control, based on continuing nuclear and economic superiority, would delimit in the process a corresponding degree of effective client autonomy. And if autonomy grew with demonstrated readiness to deploy it within the framework of the "free world," it would be institutionalized in due course within multilateral regional alliances equalizing the status if not the function of the uneven members.

The two segments or wings of the emergent American system were Western Europe and Japan as the "essential" empire, and Afro-Asia and Latin America as the "peripheral" empire. The segmentation differed from the structures of the earlier American excursions into empire, centering on Latin America in the initial regional phase and on Asia in the first global phase. The shift in the core of the world empire to Europe (replacing Latin America) and Japan (replacing China) relegated the remainder to peripheral status. Similarly, the early Roman empire had been divided into Eastern (Greek) and Western ("barbarian") wings and the later British empire into the Continent-centered European balance-of-power system (eventually integrating the white dominions for strategic defense purposes) and the dependent or colonial empire. The distinction between the two, hegemonial and colonial, wings was only updated in the American case by the myth of community being introduced into the neo-hegemonial wing, as part of efforts to root control in consensus, and by newly devious mechanisms and instrumentalities of indirect control in the quasi-colonial segment.

As between the two wings, differences in the mode, the degree, and the object or purpose of dominance, sought or achieved, were near-polar along three axes of differentiation. One axis concerned the bases of relationship with the United States. The essential empire was based on comparable degrees of economic and political maturity and, as regards Western Europe, also on cultural affinity. Its members were basically familiar to one another, whereas the economically and politically undeveloped and culturally alien peripheral empire was unfamiliar (and, in the Graeco-Roman sense at least, "barbarian"). It was, therefore, mainly in regard to the first segment that the internationalist instinct could moderate and qualify the imperial imperatives. Another axis of differentiation consisted of perceived threats and consequent concerns. The essential empire was subject primarily to the danger of forcible subjection from the outside, contingent on the state of the central or strategic balance between East and West; the peripheral regions were chiefly vulnerable to internal subversion, supported or unsupported from the outside and entailing localized violence of the conventional or subconventional kind. The corresponding conceptual difference was between the balance of (military-strategic) power and a more complex balance of (sociopolitical) forces. The former was to be restored, along with national economies, so as to insure effective deterrence as an aspect of the strategy of containment; an effective management of the latter would insure a nonrevolutionary politico-economic development against direct coercion. And yet another, final differentiation was derivative, having to do with the principal means for implementing the imperial connection. In the essential empire, institutionalized association of broadly legitimate governments was expected to administer a partnership among the concerned nations and sustain a both steady and steadying American influence. In the peripheral empire, the typical effective link was not so much a multilateral alliance as an unevenly formalized unilateral U.S. guarantee or a bilateral alignment, addressed to currently dominant local elites and implicitly authorizing intermittent American intervention.

Contrasts such as these were neither complete nor static, any more than the two wings or segments were internally uniform. In the essential empire, core allies were ones situated in the military front line (West Germany), having a special relationship diplomatically (Great Britain and, later, West Germany), and possessing nuclear capability and extra-European responsibilities or concerns (Britain and France). They differed only in informal status and effective function from the secondary powers in Western Europe and Greece and Turkey in the Eastern Mediterranean. The circumstance that the major allies were not delegated any special authority or conceded any conspicuous advantage over the lesser allies insured the latter's loyalty to the transcendent American hegemony, while laying the foundation for a later challenge to that hegemony. Similarly, the clients in the peripheral empire were differentiated mostly, in fact only, by their strategic importance (proximity to the Communist-dominated heartland); their diplomatic importance (possession of alignment options and leadership roles in the anticolonial movement); their potential for politico-economic development (qualification to serve as a pilot country); as well as, most significantly, their involvement in an overt military conflict with Communist forces entailing massive backing or direct participation by the United States (Taiwan, South Korea, South Vietnam). The last-mentioned military allies were in fact or also in form most deeply penetrated politically, economically, and culturally; they came closest to resembling the essential allies in key formal features while approximating colonies in material respects.

In a parallel development, the geographically and otherwise marginal, mainly Mediterranean, members of the Atlantic core-system moved closer to the more favored among the members of the peripheral empire. As in the two earlier empires, particular overlaps evolved into a measure of reciprocal assimilation between the initially highly disparate wings or segments in both form and function. Even before the trend got fully under way, events had muted the early sense of the highly unequal strategic importance of the two wings, perpetuating the priority assigned to the European over the Asian theater in World War II. The two segments were factually linked when American belligerency in Korea and French military involvement in Indochina had a direct and positive impact upon the military rearmament and political rehabilitation of West Germany within alternative, European and Atlantic, organizational frameworks. The same events fostered the gradual extension from Europe to Asia of both the strategic concept and the institutional mode of military containment of the Sino-Soviet bloc.

II

The trend toward unified political organization and military strategies, reflecting both random interactions and deliberate efforts to deal with the problems of a two-wing structure, had first to overcome the initial bias toward differentiation. In broadest terms, "organization" covers forms and instruments of imperial control; "strategy" refers to forms and instruments of empire defense. The neo-hegemonial wing of the essential empire in Europe was organized, we have noted, by means of an integrated multilateral alliance, informed in its fitful development by the *telos* of an Atlantic community; the quasi-colonial wing's organization inclined toward informal ties consistent with either unilateral U.S. guarantee or unequal bilateral alliance. The military strategy corresponding to neo-hegemonial organization was to be the deployment of American military forces for forward perimeter defense, should the central-strategic nuclear deterrence fail. A primarily non-nuclear central or strategic reserve was conversely the main American contribution to the defense of the emerging peripheral empire, along with economic and military aid to local needs; a *de facto* delegation of front-line responsibility for defense to traditionally or recently independent client states at the peripheries, such as South Korea, Thailand, Pakistan, Iran, and (Hashemite) Iraq, replaced in that scheme the prior delegation of order-maintenance to outgoing European colonial empires. As constituents of reciprocity, American access to military bases and right to tender political advice in exchange for routine aid and last-resort guarantees matched in the peripheral areas the ideal of burden-sharing and division of labor in military matters among allies at the core of the empire. In addition to their function in global stability, peripheral bases would enhance U.S. capacity to intervene in support of protected clients, under exceptional circumstances, whereas burden-sharing was to ease America's more continuous involvement in the effective defense of her coalition partners.

Failures blunted from the beginning the thrust toward delegating responsibility for defense to peripheral clients and differentiating thereby the two wings of the rising American empire in regard to both organization and strategy. South Korea failed to implement effective defense against an outside threat to her security and survival in Asia; and the Hashemite regime in Iraq failed to lead effectively in evolving a new regional order in the Middle East. These failures compounded in the 1950s the earlier fiasco of China's Nationalist regime in Asia and the parallel setbacks of the colonial-imperial regimes of France and Britain in Asia and the Middle East; they recalled the abortive attempts, notably of Republican Rome, to adjust central control and local-peripheral autonomy within a patron-client relationship to be implemented by means of executory delegation. Nationalist China illustrated for imperial America the dilemmas of control vs. autonomy in client defense that lacked active and massive U.S. military participation. South Korea was to typify the dilemmas of a relationship comprising such participation, after epitomizing the insufficiency of backing local self-defense by no more than U.S. strategic reserve superimposed upon prior and continuing material aid. Once the South Korean performance compelled close alliance and direct massive American military involvement, the implied blow to theoretical and practical differentiation between the two empire segments could be minimized only by conceiving of the defense of South Korea as integral to the defense of the essential empire: directly of Japan and indirectly of Western Europe, viewed as being next in line for an unrestrained Communist aggression directed from the Soviet center of international Communism. Direct U.S. military involvement in South Korea thus pointed first to a subdifferentiation within the peripheral empire, between client-type and colonial-type organization, the former implemented by means of indirect American control and defense role and the latter by means of direct proconsular control growing out of a direct American defense role. Pending further developments that would clarify trends and complicate relationships, multilateral community-type alliance and *de facto* clientship remained in force as the two basic types of organization. They were matched by the two basic types of U.S. role in the military defense of empire, static-peripheral and in-depth elastic, the first based primarily and distinctively on perimeter deployment and the second on central-strategic reserve.

Central reserve had been represented by legions in the early Roman empire and by emperor-led armies in the late empire; it consisted of the Royal Navy in the British empire. The American variety was military and economic. The preeminent military component was nuclear capability, projectible by air first from land and eventually also from the sea as the back-up of last resort for similarly deployable conventional military capabilities. The conventional air arm was erroneously thought to be sufficient to bolster the defense of South Korea in the initial stage of the local war, and was briefly envisaged for use in support of the French defense of non-Communist Vietnam in its final stage; the naval arm alone was repeatedly activated in both the Middle East and in South and Southeast Asia, with seemingly greater efficacy. In relation to the major and ultimate Soviet adversary, and with consequences for both empire wings, the central reserve was inadequate when a temporary American advantage in one area (nuclear monopoly and long-range delivery) was being offset by inferiority in another (conventional-military) area; and when, subsequently, the reduction of the conventional-military gap by the United States and its allies was offset by the Soviet move toward stand-off in the nuclear-military sphere. The more insufficient the central military reserve proved to be in either its nuclear or its conventional dimension, the greater the weight that would be shifted to a central economic reserve made up of both potential and performance. Whereas that reserve was sufficient for dispensing massive economic aid, the aid was expected to substantiate local capacity for both military defense and stable economic-political development, initially in the essential empire and subsequently increasingly in the peripheral one.

In the final analysis, central reserve will be vital for an elastic defense in depth, however conceived and defined. For the British empire, this meant naval superiority in oceanic peripheries and economic subsidies to allies on the Continent. Central reserve was variably effective for the Roman empire as the both solid and submissive client states of the early era were replaced, in the ultimate stage, by barbarian and other static frontier defenses exposed to ever deeper hostile penetrations of the defense perimeter. And elastic defense in depth of America's essential empire meant relying in the last resort on nuclear retaliation to either discourage or break the back of conventionally irresistible hostile penetration. At the peripheries, the flexible strategy could mean reserving American military counteraction for two theoretically distinguishable contingencies. In one case an embattled client, having demonstrated basic capacity for self-defense, would be selectively accorded a marginal increment of American strategic power capable of tipping the balance in his favor. Under a different scenario, the United States, having previously tolerated a deep penetration by hostile forces against locally inadequate resources, would help intercept the inroad only after slowing down its momentum with the aid of merely punitive, demonstrative reprisal against the local source of the initially irresistible expansion.

The two possible military situations and strategies implied two different political and organizational strategies. An elastic in-depth defense stressing selectivity pointed toward a systematically discriminating allocation of American military and other material aid. Aid would go first and foremost to clients unequivocally committed to the United States, being the basic necessary even if not necessarily sufficient precondition to their capacity for self-defense. In return for preferential aid, the United States would acquire the corresponding right to deny last-resort support from the strategic reserve to clients that had nonetheless proved incapable of basic self-defense in a crisis, without the default causing fatal prejudice to its overall empire organization. On the other hand, if depth rather than selectivity was singled out as the key to elastic defense, a consistent strategy could avoid discrimination and distribute American material assistance impartially among both committed and uncommitted peripheral states and both conservative or authoritarian and reformist or nationalist governing and oppositional elites. Nondiscrimination would be in keeping with America's freedom (required for the interception strategy) to delay involvement while awaiting a local marshalling of resource and resolve that would maximize the impact of an eventual direct American input. In practice, the American conception of defense and organization for the empire did not face up to either the different variants of the elastic military strategy or to their diverse implications for policy and organization. Perhaps as a result, while leaning toward nondiscrimination in the distribution of aid, it evolved toward a nonselective static defense fought in tactical modes suiting the local enemy.

The meaning of elastic defense in depth was different in the economic realm. Adopting responsible fiscal-monetary and other internal economic policies would husband the central material resource as a basis for staying power in a prolonged contest and for a decisive use of power *in extremis*. The opposite was eroding and dispersing economic strength through inordinate governmental outlays in behalf of indiscriminately interventionist domestic and foreign policies, for welfare at home and local stability at large. For the purpose of elastic in-depth defense, protecting the economic base of American nuclear and conventional military power equaled efforts to minimize expense for the legions or the imperial field army at different stages of the Roman empire and for the home fleet in the British empire. If the key military safeguards symbolized the innermost essence of imperial power, concentrated geostrategically in the essential empire, a strong economy or an assured solvency would presumably help contain the unavoidable material and prestige costs of elastic defense in depth, and keep them below the costs of applying the static defense concept. In-depth defense entails fairly abrupt annihilation of material assets in the sectors of hostile penetration; it jeopardizes the confidence and undermines the loyalty of subjects or clients loath to be (even temporarily) abandoned or (only ultimately) rescued or liberated. Conversely, static-peripheral defense strategy that is based on the deployment of imperial forces at the perimeter of empire entails dispersion of resources at all times and their erosion or attrition in use over time. It will sap the capacity of the central power and the will of its people, loath to perpetuate actually or apparently unrewarding exertions; and it will cause friction with client regimes and populations.

The costs of dispersion are not least when imperial troops are deployed at the defense perimeter in peacetime on a standing basis, as U.S. troops were in postwar South Korea as well as in postwar Europe and Japan. They will be reduced when standing imperial presence is confined to military missions for training and equipment of indigenous forces. A so limited presence will tend to merge with the possession of imperial bases, and will be consistent with elastic defense anchored in central strategic reserve so long as the imperial power has proven able to either help defend clients or discourage hostile penetrations by reliably attaching punishing costs to immediately undeniable ones.

Interest in developing both capability and doctrine for waging full-scale "limited war" was first shown in American planning even before the North's inroad into South Korea. The interest constituted an early, tentative step away from in-depth to perimeter defense for areas outside the essential empire. When perimeter defense actually took place in Korea, it was tactically mobile and (in the advance north) counteroffensive, despite its strategically defensive purpose. The war's outcome produced a long-lasting U.S. involvement in the defense of South Korea.

Expansion of imperial involvement in depth exceeded the expansion of empire in scope, just as an enlargement in space consequent upon successful unification of Korea would have probably reduced the depth of necessary U.S. involvement and control in the area. At a later stage in Vietnam, the bombing raids in the North and the operational mobility in the field modified only marginally the static peripheral defense of the South that was in essence passive-defensive not only strategically but also tactically, and was such relative to both North Vietnam itself and, implicitly, its great-power sponsors and suppliers. Partly as a result, the defense of South Vietnam ended in a constriction of the empire's scope, and it did so in a pattern of cause and effect reminiscent of the increasingly passive perimeter defense of the Roman empire as it moved into decline.

Considering organization in the broadest sense of the term, static-peripheral strategy via local deployments will intensify central control over specifics while reducing control over basics. It will also subordinate freedom of strategic choices and options to influence over tactical implementation. The choices will include the critical decision whether and how to involve the imperial power directly in the defense of a client in the first place. That choice is present within the selective version of in-depth strategy, based on central reserve and delegation of local-defense functions to a preferentially subsidized client; and since that preliminary choice is basic to all other or subsequent issues of policy that can arise between the imperial power and its client or ally, likewise present will be essential control. By contrast, perimeter deployment for a direct defense role will concentrate control in a superficially impressive manner that will be dubiously effective when put to a test. A key question concerns the range of factors the imperial center can sensibly and realistically seek to control in conjunction with the different military strategies. As concentration is relaxed, the range of controllable acts will shrink even as efficacy is likely to increase on critical matters, and vice versa. Implementing the perimeter defense of the essential empire by means of NATO led the United States to penetrate both the domestic politics and the foreign policy-making of the allies as two interrelated processes critical for internal and international stability and, therefore, for the total U.S. engagement. Under an elastic strategy in depth that has replaced deployment with delegation, the range of relevant control will encompass only a smaller sum of factors and actions vital for an effective (and loyal) performance in defense or order-maintenance by *de facto* clients. And the range would shrink still further in a posture that replaced delegation by a farther-reaching devolution of responsibilities. It would then comprise only activities and factors apt to inhibit seriously the crystallization and continuous operation of near-autonomous regional balance-of-power systems that would have taken the place, in the devolutionary context, of a partially regionalized enactment of the global or central balance attendant on mere delegation.

A wide range of control will be implemented by fairly direct control over the actual policies of a "friendly" government; it will extend to mechanisms for selecting governments only when control over policies appears to be in jeopardy (e.g., postwar elections in Italy and Greece in the late 1940s and the 1950s). The more restricted range of control will habitually require only indirect control over policies, by way of insuring the identity of the dominant political elite in the client state (e.g., in Iran, as between the Shah and Premier Mossadeq in the late 1950s). And finally, the most restricted range of sought and attainable influence over fundamental dispositions toward patterns of local order will entail something like remote control. That technique will require the imperial power to behave in areas that are accessible to it (e.g., for the United States, South Asia in the 1950s and 1960s, the Middle East in the 1950s, and again the mid-1970s) in a manner that is sufficiently consistent to demonstrate for lesser powers in less easily accessible areas the outside bounds of tolerable action. For a dependent to challenge the most direct form of control will involve conspicuous acts, such as breaking up or out of the institutional framework (e.g., when France withdrew from NATO), without necessarily changing the underlying ratios of independence and influence if the dominant military strategy remains basically the same. Defiance of either indirect or remote control will be less conspicuous in form, but, since those control techniques focus on essentials, it will involve greater political risks and material exertions for both the major and the lesser powers when the former seeks to forestall, and the latter strives to consolidate, alterations in fundamental rapports and orientations.

A stable relationship between (military-defense) strategy and (political) control is in large part only a matter of logically implied tendencies and presumptions. The same is true for the characteristic relationships between military strategies and formalization of control in types of organization. An imperial power is likely to formalize relations with dependents when it is directly and visibly involved in their defense. Similarly, informal links between center and client will best suit the greater latitude that is requisite for a selectively effected elastic defense strategy. Informality reduces the prestige costs of default that is latent in in-depth strategy, while the potentially defaulting center's ultimate control is assured by the client's dependence and the center's freedom of choice. The nuclear factor will modify these logical relationships only marginally if at all when it constitutes the central reserve for an elastic in-depth strategy. When it is the key deterrent and ultimate fall-back in static-peripheral defense strategy, nuclearization will favor formalizing relations between center and dependents as an additional safeguard against either nuclear proliferation among dependents or other less drastic impediments to central command and control over timing and targeting the ultimate weapon. It did not require the nuclear factor, much as the development reflected and was rationalized by its existence, for the logical relationships between strategy and organization to be more than once deranged, in the actual American empire experience, in response to risks or as a consequence of responses to actual dangers. At first, multilateral alliances had spread beyond the essential into the peripheral empire as the presumed additional factors for deterrence, conjointly with strategic emphasis on central reserve for both segments. Subsequently, the self-same multilateral alliances were eroded in one and deemphasized in the other empire wing, concurrently with a climactic extension of static perimeter defense to the peripheral empire on the earlier model of the essential empire.

III

The eventual derangement was an outgrowth of earlier conditions and decisions. With the establishment of NATO in 1949, the defense of the essential empire had moved from the brief, both conceptually and chronologically preimperial, dependence on American nuclear monopoly toward static perimeter defense with nuclear-deterrent backing. *Pari passu*, the incipient decay of the European empires (the British in India and the French in Indochina) seemed to require an elastic American strategy of in-depth defense in the peripheries to maximize economy of force as well as control, and as a safeguard against overextension. Clearcut differentiation between the two segments was delayed at first by the war in Korea, which was to influence America's approach to the organization and defense of empire as crucially as it shaped her approach to the cold war and to containment. In the perspective of empire, the challenge in South Korea was premature as a test of in-depth defense, since the United States was no better prepared for the strategy than the client was for effective self-defense and, consequently, for a conclusive test of its eligibility for a selectively applied U.S. strategic-military backing. Moreover, judged by subsequent threats, the challenge was atypical. The military onslaught by North Korea was of a volume and intensity that foreclosed a wait-and-see strategy pending eventual interception of the North Korean armed forces in the peninsula, while the relevant Asian "system" was yet devoid of indigenous forces capable of resistance in depth to continuing Communist aggression.

In Korea the United States went beyond air strikes to perimeter defense on land in the periphery even before organizing perimeter defense in Western Europe. The resulting involvement illustrated the costs of prolonged static local defense, as military capabilities were dispersed abroad and as political support waned at home for the war and the

Truman administration alike. Since the defense of the French empire in Indochina carried the same lesson, it strengthened the reaction in favor of elastic defense in depth. However, that strategy had been likewise undermined by the self-same military events in Asia, even before it could be meaningfully formulated and the supporting structures organized. Both the Korean War and the first or French Indochina war raised dramatically, if somewhat hypothetically and speculatively, the issue of the cost of an immediately unresisted penetration by hostile forces. The cost came to be expressed in terms of the "falling domino" simile. Because of its physical connotation, the image did not supplement a valid insight concerning the tendency for an initial or first-stage hostile penetration to spread, with a matching insight into countervailing psycho-political dynamic of a progressively crystallizing will to resist. Such a frustrating dynamic was apt to blunt or even reverse the initial falling-domino effect, provided a central strategic reserve was available to support its local manifestations.

In its strengths as well as its shortcomings, the New-Look approach of the Eisenhower-Dulles era conformed to the historical context. The approach emphasized central strategic reserve to implement elastic defense in depth with the aid of two factors: one, self-imposed reliance on selective massive (nuclear) retaliation on the military plane; and two, on the political plane, a sweeping attribution of responsibility to the Communist great powers for even marginal or peripheral infractions of the imperial order. In the conventional military realm, the strategy favored the military build-up of formally independent and hopefully self-reliant postcolonial clients. A minimal capacity for selectivity was introduced into the otherwise incongruent institutional setting by the United States abstaining from membership in at least one of the multi-lateral alliances (the so-called Baghdad Pact, as distinct from SEATO). In case of need, a mobile U.S. strategic (if not necessarily nuclear?) reserve would be available in principle to supply the decisive margin of advantage for local defenses, whenever desirable from the global perspective and deserved by local performance in self-defense. Inspiring the New Look was the concern to avoid dispersing and dissipating the economic and military central reserve. In doctrine, the drive for economy showed in stressing the last-resort (nuclear and nonnuclear strategic) leverage as one with the greatest impact, and in aiming that leverage at the highest-level and best-crystallized agents of disorder (the Communist great powers) as the targets most likely to be sensitively responsive. In practice, economy meant deploying only limited seaborne and aerial resources (in Lebanon and over Quemoy-Matsu) and extending only indirect assistance through military material and political intervention (in Laos); it meant also avoiding an extensive management of control-resistant inferior actors and inchoate forces, growing out of a heavy investment in economic-development efforts in the peripheries. A logically implied trade-off was between economy in the outlay of resources peripherally and an increase in risk within the central strategic balance of power. The new resource-risk equation was viewed as the sole means for avoiding a real danger of incurring attrition and erosion of American power in a protracted struggle along a widening arc of imperial responsibilities. Going to the so-called brink in major-power confrontations was the postulated, and ostensibly preferred, alternative to courting certain bankruptcy from limited wars involving minor powers abroad and major budgetary and other imbalances at home.

In a not entirely avoidable contrast with the desire for economy, the New-Look strategy was liable to actually expand the scope of the empire. Stress on nuclear deterrence and retaliation implied the need to disperse striking power and multiply outlying base-and-aid facilities; the limiting effect on commitments of the stress on local self-reliance was weakened by including also indirect aggression against both internal and external security in the peripheries among the objects of deterrence. It mattered, therefore, that the implementation of the New-Look strategy was less than consummate and less than literally conformable with the doctrine's retaliatory-retributive component in the mixed international-domestic contingencies in Asia (Quemoy-Matsu and Laos) and the Middle East (Lebanon, Jordan, Iraq). More important were the flaws in conception, preceding implementation. Proliferating multilateral alliances was an incongruous institutional complement of the in-depth strategy, insofar as the alliances impeded the choice of American responses in crisis. And the concurrent failure to discriminate markedly in favor of committed against uncommitted or unaligned parties in distributing material aid weakened the right to distinguish effective from ineffective allies when allocating direct support in crisis. That which was lost in flexibility and latitude was not offset, moreover, by gains from implementing the multilateral third-world alliances. Neither organization nor planning nor integration were such as to constitute the third-world coalitions into theoretically effective instruments for first-line defense externally and for in-depth defense domestically. The omission was critical in the imperial peripheries, where alliances could not act convincingly as mere trip wires for activating a credible U.S. nuclear strategic reserve in response to clearly identifiable conventional transfrontier aggression, as they presumably could in Europe.

The chosen military strategy was applied incompletely in relatively minor crises; a maladapted organizational component was diluted antecedent to major crises; and no suitable link was forged between a purportedly elastic strategy and the shape of U.S. commitments. Moreover, just as the North Korean challenge to a latent bias in favor of in-depth peripheral defense had been premature in terms of conventional military capabilities of both client and patron, so the new strategy's official adoption under the aegis of nuclear retaliation came too late in terms of American capacity to either deter or punish the presumptive great-power sources of small-scale aggression or disturbance. The first attempt at rationalizing the American approach to empire defense was, consequently, but short-lived and, on balance, abortive. The New Look did not effectively unify the two empire wings by deemphasizing conventional defense in favor of nuclear deterrence all around and by imitating the Atlantic alliance system in the peripheries. Nor did the New Look's architects promote unity in strategy and organization by showing themselves receptive to coordination of policy for the peripheries among the principal NATO allies. They missed thus an opportunity to transmute the Atlantic system from a defense arrangement for one region into a key rear element or redoubt in the in-depth defense of the American world empire as a whole.

IV

The New Look was a scheme for rationalizing defense and organization for an incipient world empire arising out of decolonization. The New Frontier soon to follow was by contrast a complex of ideas and policies for adapting defense and organization to the accomplished fact of a *grand empire*, exposed to the challenge of the wars of national liberation. Whereas the Eisenhower-Dulles approach had sought to economize on resources in exchange for heightened, if calculated, risks, the Grand Design of the Kennedy administration sought to reduce the ultimate risk by expanding readily available resources with less concern for material costs. The New Look was keyed to an empire that was still growing in scope; but its guiding precepts were conservative and aimed at limitation. The key preoccupation was consequently to identify and manipulate reliably responsive surface leverages and readily accessible salient mechanisms, such as great-power interactions internationally and money-supply equations domestically, presumed to have automatic managerial and regulative effects on the more unwieldy underlying systems of small-power politics and welfare economics. The Grand Design was conceived for a fully grown empire; but its guiding precepts were essentially liberal in inspiration and expansionist in effect. Forswearing indirect manipulation, the New Frontiersmen aimed at a direct, interventionist management of both internal and external political economies in depth and at the grass roots. In the last analysis, theirs was an adaptation to the paralysis of the central nuclear-military reserve of the American empire that was destined, in its ultimate consequences, to precipitate the erosion of the empire's central political and economic reserve.

The American-Soviet nuclear stalemate cast a doubt on America's capacity and will to risk nuclear confrontation in behalf of allies. The decline in credibility resurfaced the always-latent tripartite structure of the two-wing empire, distinguishing the U.S. metropole from the essential or core-empire and the peripheral empire as the decreasingly certain beneficiaries of the American nuclear umbrella in a crisis. Moreover, the Cuban missile crisis split up the nonindustrial periphery for security purposes. Its course reaffirmed the Caribbean segment of the Western Hemisphere as forming part of the core-empire without conclusively demonstrating an equal readiness to defend the essential Atlantic-Pacific empire. With the waning of confidence in extended deterrence overall, the essential and the peripheral wings were evolving a new common denominator of sorts. The negative community of doubt (as to American protection) was operationally enhanced by the positive American response to the nuclear stalemate, reemphasizing conventional military forces as part of the strategic concept of flexible response. The new approach entailed augmenting American and, hopefully, allied conventional capabilities to permit waging simultaneously major wars in Europe and Asia and a limited or "brushfire" war on the periphery. A build-up of U.S. conventional and antiinsurgency capabilities took precedence over the military build-up of peripheral clients and allies requisite for elastic defense in depth. Rapidly expanding U.S. forces-in-being were expected to avert progressive paralysis of will (due to the conflagration or capitulation dilemma implicit in the massive-retaliation strategy) and of capacity (in the face of simultaneously activated specific crises, such as the current ones in Berlin, Laos, the Congo, and Cuba). The simultaneity of several crises replaced in immediate urgency the sequential unfolding of a single crisis, via deepening penetration and falling dominoes, peculiar to the antecedent strategy of elastic defense in depth. At the same time, if the expansion and diversification of American military capabilities increased tactical flexibility (as to the kind of response) in both wings, they did so at the expense of predisposition to strategic flexibility (as to decision to respond or not) on the peripheries. An implied commitment to perimeter defense in both empire wings was the chosen alternative to putting the strategic reserve to a conclusive test of credibility anywhere outside the American metropole and its immediate security orbit.

The tendency to standardize military defense for both wings was matched in the organization of empire by an uneven, but basically parallel, erosion of the multilateral alliance structures in both segments. While the American security treaty with Japan was under attack in the streets of Tokyo, the Atlantic Alliance was being eroded at its summits by de Gaulle's drive for more member autonomy and less direct American control by way of either integration or the interdependent partnership put forward by Kennedy as a substitute for a unified Atlantic community. Exceeding mere stagnation, decay was consummating the still-birth of the Central Treaty Organization (CENTO, a new name for the Baghdad Pact) and of its Southeast Asian counterpart. In the periphery, the alliance system degenerated into being only one of several formal pretexts and averred grounds for unilateral military intervention by the United States, most conspicuously in Indochina; in the essential empire, the alliance system was concurrently beginning to evolve from a force for military security into one of several frameworks for attempting inter-allied economic coordination and asserting American economic preroga-tives (along with affiliates such as the OECD, comprising Japan). As the multilateral alliances weakened conjointly with the ascendancy of the strategy of static perimeter defense, the result was one more derangement between strategy and organization that inverted and aggravated the earlier manifestation of the flaw in Dulles's New Look. The attrition of alliances accentuated the trend beyond alliance to a *de facto* colonial relationship in the peripheral areas of direct U.S. military deployment, and it undermined the potential of alliance for promoting community at the center of empire.

Overextension was a function of static deployment for defense in conditions of weakening imperial control. The decline in control grew out of the escalating drive for autonomy by allies and clients; but it resulted no less from an intensified American drift into commitment to on-the-spot defense, reflecting positive changes in U.S. military capabili-ties. Overinvolvement reflected, moreover, a heightened commitment of Kennedy's New Frontiersmen to anchor the imperial order in the peripheries less in the support of individual clients and more in generally supportive socioeconomic conditions. If the military defense concept became inherently static, the approach to political order through assisted economic development was intended to be dynamic. The static defense concept relied on diversification of both military capabilities and politico-military doctrines, the latter comprising counterinsurgency, graduated escalation, and tacit bargaining; it was put to a test in Asia. The drive for dynamic social change was predicated on U.S. economic strength and on the validity of theoretical doctrines covering the stages of, and the balances within, economic growth as well as its relation to political development; it was being tested most prominently through the Alliance for Progress in Latin America. A seemingly profound analysis of the sources of insecurity and instability in the peripheral empire was taken to dictate the means for dealing with the problem; and once in being, the means assumed control over policy ends and implementation. They did so even as control was declining not only over military dependents (as a result of a settled posture of intervention in conditions of a diminishing overall threat) but also over the political economy of the imperial metropole (as a result of the gradually unfolding costs of a specific military intervention abroad combined with socioeconomic interventionism domestically and globally).

v

The domestic and international crises attending the war in Vietnam broke the ascendant curve in the organization and defense of the American empire, as well as in the empire's expansion. They reversed the prior growth in the American equivalents of the three institutional pillars of the Roman empire at its zenith: an imperial presidency (in lieu of the deified emperor); a military and bureaucratic complex of professionals with careers keyed to the organization and defense of empire; and a parallel body of political and economic elites in the imperial dependencies tied to the metropole by education and technical expertise, institutional role, and economic and political interests. The approach to concentrating and consecrating authority was more subtle in the British empire during its ascendancy, but not basically different.

Likewise familiar to both of the older empires were events and experiences that either dampened or redirected the organizing élan and marked a turning point in expansion. Among these were, for Rome, disloyalty of the Greek allies-surrogates under the Republic and decimation in ambush of three legions led by P. Quinctilius Varus by ostensibly loyal client forces under the Principate; the American Revolution in the first British empire and the Indian Mutiny and the Boer challenge in the second. Nor was the United States spared similar tribulations. In Rome, empire realists and phil-Hellenic idealists had been equally disillusioned with the Greek surrogates, if for different reasons; so both the tough-minded Atlanticists and most of the Europhiles were to feel let down by some of the aspects of the political and material resurgence of America's culturally closest allies. Western Europe's reascent through semiautonomous unification was not translating into automatic concordance with American views and aims in the cases of either the Anglo-French "aggression" in Suez, the diplomatically and economically "subversive" Gaullism in Europe and overseas, or the American "aggression" in Vietnam. Similarly, in the peripheral empire, even before self-conscious empire realists came face to face with America's South African war in Southeast Asia, the experience of American sympathizers with India's nonalignment under Nehru or Egypt's revolution under Nasser had mirrored the disillusionment of British imperial romantics following the Indian Mutiny. It proved impossible to found a liberal imperial policy upon sympathetic alignment with either neutralist or any other variety of nationalism in the Third World without becoming an impotent captive to indigenous foreign-policy ambitions and before ceasing to be the indispensable lightning rod for domestic disaffections.

Matching the disappointment with the support given by actual or potential allies or clients in peace or war was the dissatisfaction of America's allies and clients with the performance of their imperial patron. The active American posture on Suez was as much a desertion when viewed from Europe as was, in the opinion of third-world loyalists, the failure to act to protect or avenge a client elite within Iraq two years later and to back the Pakistani ally repeatedly. Particular men or events will propel latent problems of organization and defense to the surface and set in motion either expansive or centralizing adaptation or retrenching devolution approaching abdication. Just as a Nehru or a Nasser exacerbated the drive for the multilateral alliances he opposed, so the American stance on Suez, Iraq, and Pakistan dealt one fatal blow after another to part-autonomous clientship as the key organizing principle of empire, while the course and outcome of the Indochina war eliminated the colonial technique of management as a practical alternative model for the American imperial system.

Of equal or greater import were the underlying latent dilemmas and prolonged drifts. The key policy question for the elastic in-depth strategy was whether to discriminate markedly in favor of loyalist clients. Next to minimizing occasions for American default (by making the client materially strong) and limiting prestige loss in the case of default (when a previously favored client proved unworthy of strategic backing), conspicuous discrimination would presumably maximize the client's attachment to the United States and the attraction of the client status for the uncommitted or even hostile parties; the attraction would grow if the United States implicitly penalized noncommitment and expressly blocked local or informal reprisals against pro-American engagement. The choice hinged on a subsidiary question: was it possible to reconcile discriminatory strengthening of the committed client before a crisis with occasionally necessary nondiscrimination between clients and unaligned parties during a military crisis? Just as discrimination was the psychopolitical prerequisite to a selective strategy for elastic defense within an international system that featured both clients and uncommitted parties to start with, so nondiscrimination might at some point become the technical military-political requirement for actually intercepting aggression in a geographically not unlimited, but systemically dynamic, depth. The final question was whether the practical difficulty also constituted an insuperable dilemma. The query was never put to a test by an imperial policy that would decide between an absolutely discriminatory, a but relatively or partially discriminatory, and an integrally nondiscriminatory approach, or that reconciled the different possible approaches in an outwardly comprehensible and internally coherent compromise approach. The American strategists were disposed neither to face up to the need for choice (between loyal clients and the others) nor to actually display nerve (before temporary or local penetrations by hostile forces). Whereas the refusal to choose was rationalized by international considerations, a major reason for shrinking from nerve-testing risk was domestic. It resided in the political penalty that attached at the peak of the cold war to an actively unresisted, and apparently irreversible, loss of a country to Communism.

The critical failure in the phase of perimeter defense strategy was of a different kind. It was rooted in the inability to reconcile growing autonomy and desire for autonomy on the part of allies with the requirements of interallied coordination in action under American leadership. The failure was of import tactically in the front line actually under enemy fire as well as in the imperial peripheries more generally. It was, however, most fundamentally critical in NATO, inasmuch as the failure in the area of action and consequently of function was foreshadowed in the area of status.

The status issue had been addressed when American policy-makers chose to declare an embryonic Atlantic community incompatible with the hierarchically stratified formulation of common policy being extended sufficiently to promote France on a par with Britain as a world power. Coordinating policy for the peripheries at the summit of the core-alliance would reflect changes in the immediately crucial role for the Atlantic Alliance from the front-line factor in Europe to the *de facto* military-strategic rear and potentially strategy-coordinating core of perimeter defense globally. The argument for such a role alteration was no more nullified than the American refusal was fully justified by the Europeans being only potential front-line participants in such defense; without consultation, the key European allies as spearheaded if not always represented by France were even less likely to contribute to controversial U.S. actions at the empire's margins. Since those actions might react back upon the center, the allies' desire for greater autonomy in the era of the world-wide American deployment was not wholly incongruent with the desire for greater influence on actually or potentially "forward" American actions at the deployment's extremities. The official U.S. reaction was to favor the small in size and modest in foreign-policy ambition of the allies, indifferent to meaningful consultation because both unable and unwilling to make a significant contribution. A possible world-wide strategy, and related organization of empire, were thwarted as a result for the sake of effective unilateralism in U.S. policy-making and of nominal multilateralism within a regional organization atrophying internally and receding in immediate importance externally.

For American policy to favor Atlantic loyalists at the center of the imperial system had as ill-fated a consequence for the strategy of perimeter defense as the refusal to discriminate at the peripheries had had for in-depth defense. Defense in depth had not been conclusively tried on the peripheries; nor was the New Look put to a test in the essential segment. Similarly, the architects of neither Kennedy's New Frontier nor Johnson's Great Society were able to unify the two empire wings conceptually and strategically through perimeter defense in the absence of intra-Atlantic coordination of policy for the critical theaters outside the essential empire. Inadequately faced choices and dilemmas were the prelude to an inadequately sustained drift, toward peripheral U.S. deployment from a dissolving core-imperial base and toward a direct U.S. defense function in relation to a demoralized client belt. America's capacity to continue protecting the European allies and Japan in the nuclear context was questioned as much as was her readiness to continue promoting or at least tolerating an expanding autonomy in matters political and economic. The consequent substitution of erosion for integration at the center of empire spelled America's isolation from her principal allies in regard to the peripheries; and the isolation aggravated an overextension that derived more from psychological, conceptual, and organizational shortcomings than from deficiencies in material resource. The American potential for effective control suffered correspondingly at both center and peripheries. At the center, the abstention of NATO allies from an active role in peripheral crises deprived the United States of even the precarious leverage implicit in effective engagement; and the wide range of control or only influence sought by the leading American ally within the community-type hegemonial association was increasingly out of line with the bond's narrowing functional and psychological foundations. On the peripheries, the American potential for effective control was minimized by an increased bias toward advance or near-automatic commitment to an active role in front-line defense, and the massive scale of involvement in defense once a commitment was actualized. The scale of American involvement tended to overwhelm both the small-scale local economies and the precariously poised, part-traditional and part-modernizing, indigenous societies; and the parallel enfeeblements, in American control and in indigenous structures, compounded one another most dramatically in local elite reactions to the many-sided social mobilization and alien penetration attendant on war-making by unequal allies. The conjunction stimulated the instinct of insecure client elites to seek in evasive license the antidote to absolute dependence, without correlating acts of self-assertion with the fluctuating efficacy of American protection.

While they were under way, the two major spells of groping toward uniformity-cum-rationality in defense strategy and organization expressed a natural desire. Any burdened imperial power will aspire to conceptual as well as material economy internally, as a prerequisite to efficacy externally. The slant toward reciprocal assimilation, or convergence, between the two wings was less marked in the American empire than had been the case for Rome in particular. Still, just as ties of alliance determined dependent status while shaping sentiments in favor of autonomy in both wings, so the initiation of a trend in one wing elicited either reaction or imitation within the other wing. And, as the Soviet control system interplayed increasingly with the American one in the setting of a containment that was becoming reciprocal, lesser parties were acquiring new latitudes for both reaction and imitation.

Earlier failures to break through dead ends in organization and strategy had intensified the sense of overextension. Anarchy became a possibility with the concurrent overassertion of autonomy by lesser states in the Third World, once the United States either lost or moved to surrender its privileged access to erstwhile *de facto* colonies, such as South Vietnam, Taiwan, and South Korea; once preeminent American clients, such as Turkey, Pakistan, Iran, the Philippines, or Thailand were seeking a new distance from the United States or new terms of rapport; and once a modicum of world order depended increasingly on self-restraint by the Soviet Union and Communist China. Even when present, the self-restraint was unreliable because it was tied up with a no more assured evolution from pseudo-ideological confrontation to neo-classic diplomatic transactions among the three great powers in the short run and because, in the longer run, it might prove to have been no more than a stage in a multiphase struggle between the two Communist great powers over imperial succession to the United States regionally and globally. The near-simultaneous movement by the lesser powers beyond ideological formulation of stakes was to material or economic preoccupations as the most prominent. The no longer so new states were becoming less concerned how to redefine moral and political legitimacy as part of their groping for Western-style nation-statehood and more concerned how to redistribute material wealth as part of a progression toward Western-style patterns of national economy and, mainly on the part of the materially better-endowed countries, national power.

The trend toward greater pragmatism in politics for all categories of great and small states meant that regional developments were being disjoined from the globally receding cold war and keyed to locally significant issues as controlling for both competition and cooperation. So released, however, the crystallization of regional systems under the nominal auspices of political equality could be even less than before disjoined from material inequalities among the local or lesser states themselves; it was in fact contingent upon such inequalities. Something closely or only remotely resembling regional balances of power appeared necessary to complement functional regionalisms, to concretize and routinize, if not immediately or safely resolve, the relationship of supremacy to equality, and hegemony to autonomy, among the regional middle and the yet smaller powers; only a basic political mechanism was

apt to contain, if only by scrambling lines of both conflict and cooperation, the disruptive effect of the discrepancies in actual or potential
material resource that prematurely close economic associations were more
likely to exacerbate than harmonize.

Meanwhile, whereas the two superpowers were preoccupied with
military-strategic parity between themselves directly, pressures grew for
accelerating material equalization of industrialization-capable members
of the ex-colonial "East" or "South" with the neo-capitalist industrial
"West" or "North." The issue was only imperfectly analogous with past
drives for redistribution. One such drive had been in favor of the lower
classes within the industrialized Western democracies, beginning with
late nineteenth century; another, in favor of self-styled dynamic totalitarian powers in the period between the two world wars. The objectives
which the rising less-developed countries sought by means of co-optation
into the Western industrial system were ostensibly economic; but they
were closely linked to the ambition to reallocate political power within
particular geopolitical arenas and were open to distortion by that ambition. On the one hand, the link between economic objectives and political aspirations was closer than had been true for the more single-
mindedly material, bread-and-butter concerns of the lower classes in the
West. On the other hand, the mobilizeable power of the less-developed
countries to disrupt existing arrangements and to impose redistribution
was clearly inferior to what had been the capacity of the militarily mobilized fascist have-not powers internationally; the third-world capacity
to disrupt might be second even to the capacity of a politically mobilized
lower class intranationally, were the theoretical possibility of a generalized denial of raw materials to the West revealed as being an inferior
replica of the myth of the general strike.

The oil cartel (OPEC) was a striking exception in the mid-1970s, even
though its disruptive impact was not necessarily repeatable without
provoking self-defensive Western reaction and was even more probably
nonreplicable by producers of other commodities. Even as circumscribed,
however, the claim to redistributive equalization increased the independently growing difficulty to manifest inequalities operationally; and
it was supported by the latest among periodic reversions to the sufficiency
of one outstanding constituent of power to engender leverage and enhance role and status for its possessors. For possession of oil deposits alone
to do all that has seemingly nullified the norm established in the just-
preceding, but not altogether representative, era in world affairs, associat-
ing power and effective independence or sovereignty with a materially
and psychologically broadly based capacity for mass mobilization in a
total and protracted conventional war. In the short run at least, control
over a source of productive energy has also temporarily overshadowed the
nuclear capability to destroy and has outdone nuclear stalemate between

two major powers in disproportionately enhancing the standing of otherwise minor powers. In spite of this, it remained uncertain how oil-based or otherwise generated economic and financial power would relate to politico-military power whenever the two were not harmoniously combined in individual countries, as was the case in the Middle East. Whereas aspirations for the redistribution of wealth were disrupting economies of key industrial countries, disparities and asymmetries in kinds of strength within the Third World raised no less critical issues for the national security and independence of lesser states when faced with bids for regional supremacy by regionally "great" if globally only "middle" powers.

It was possible that the question of whether economic objectives or geopolitically conditioned goals had priority would emerge as the critical issue for world order pregnant with international anarchy. In such a case it was an open question, finally, whether newly significant disparities and inequalities among the lesser states would deliver new instrumentalities of influence, if not control, to the major powers, including the United States; and, if so, what kind of instrumentalities. Although the superpower conflict over essential parity-or-primacy continued, antagonistic bipolarity was also inverted into something akin to cooperative solidarity on specific issues. To mute competition was a standing temptation on the highest strategic level; and it was sporadic and might become cumulative on the lower level, involving the preindustrial and coastal countries when they threatened the basic stake of the superpowers in defining the terms of both stability and change, and their specific interests as either advanced industrial or global maritime powers.

Pressures could prompt, and related opportunities permit, a shift in the American approach to world order, from imperial control to countervailing equilibrium. But the uncertain status and implications of both pressures and opportunities within the American sphere and the arena of U.S.-Soviet contention also favored caution, apt to defeat any new concept. One immediate consequence was reemphasis on Western Europe and Japan as areas of priority concern, less readily eligible for far-reaching devolution or disengagement than was the erstwhile peripheral empire in either theory or practice.

VI

The devolutionary strategy and its broadly organizational incidents could be identified with the so-called Nixon doctrine or associated more neutrally with something of a new diplomacy. However labeled, the strategy implied new structures of regional-global equilibria and new risk-resource equations.

Previously, only two sides had been facing one another directly as a rule in local military-political conflicts, such as those between South and

North in Korea and Vietnam, between Pakistan and India or Israel and the Arabs, as well as in civil conflicts, notably in Africa. The conflicts had, moreover, been treated as subordinate to the two-power global competition and had been liable to termination by cease-fire orders if and when ceasing to be relevant or becoming an embarrassment for the purposes of that competition. The new phase witnessed a tentative, initial emergence of multipower regional systems or balances of power. These were being accepted as something that might help sustain a henceforth three-power global interplay structurally, while being increasingly autonomous in operation and qualitatively equivalent. By the same token, regional defense arrangements under U.S. auspices tended to yield to local efforts at excluding interference by the major powers; and as political and technological developments conspired to reduce the American need for fixed and stable bases and other facilities, concern shifted on the peripheries increasingly from acquiring support points to avoiding being replaced by the Soviet Union. Any third power, be it a third-world middle power or a Communist China, was becoming acceptable as the more economical substitution for a costly exercise of the American imperial role along the geographic arc of one-time containment of the Sino-Soviet land complex, extending from the Eastern Mediterranean and the Middle East all the way to Northeast Asia. Regional imperialisms of lesser powers had been previously viewed as potentially auxiliary to the Soviet drive and nearly certainly obstructive of American access and had been unequivocally opposed as such. The changed perspective comprised more neutrally the varied, both positive and negative, potentialities of local middle-power hegemonies within the several fluidly bounded regions or subregions. Critical significance attached henceforth to the net margins of antagonistic or adversary power emerging out of, or surviving neutralization by, an increasingly complex checking and balancing process. The net margins replaced, as the object of a more relaxed preoccupation, gross accumulations of hostile power that might result from an unchecked local penetration.

Conforming to the changed basic outlook were new equations. They involved, in conformity with devolution, a substantially reduced range of sought control and, corresponding to the measure of discommitment, a hopefully increased efficacy of actually retained control. Moreover, reducing the invested material resource implied in logic, even if not always in practice, accepting greater, if deferred, risks in the longer run. The key risk resided henceforth in the difficulty to anticipate evolutionary developments and to control them from a sharply narrowed, if diversified, organizational base, including private and public multinational organisms subject to mounting pressures for inverting inequalities in favor of the host countries. Revising the ratios among the three interrelated features—range of control, risk, and resource—meant redefining the

American role as an essentially postimperial one, as well as post-postcolonial with respect to the anterior European empires. In keeping with the new posture was a new strategy, dominant by default and definable by a process of elimination rather than determinate in conception and capable of detailed execution in the absence of congressional support at home and suitable contingencies abroad. The strategy was centered less on military deployments outside Europe and more on political configurations within and among countries; and it was keyed less to the cheapest possible defense (by delegation or direct participation) against rival aspirants to empire, and more to disengaging from burdensome empire tasks at least possible cost in lost influence over the direction and rate of fundamental change.

The key problem was no longer to determine how much and how far to identify with clients as part of a global strategy of containment; the problem was increasingly to identify viable middle powers both suited and willing to act as surrogates in upholding regional security and order. Whereas the earlier critical issue had been to protect clients against forces of subversion linked directly or indirectly to the regional imperialisms of Nasser's Egypt, Sukarno's Indonesia, or Communist North Vietnam, among others, the new challenge was to decrease the liability to internal disintegration of variously heterogeneous micro-empires such as Ethiopia, Iran, Indonesia, and India without making their performance in regional stabilization more immoderate than effective. It was not certain in that connection how enduring and positively helpful a simultaneous change would prove to be, from two-sided local conflicts (such as the Arab-Israeli or the Indo-Pakistani), acting as both vehicles and pace-setters for one-power regional imperialism, to two-power axes (such as the Saudi-Iranian or Thai-Indonesian), potentially capable of restraining one-power hegemony as well as dynamizing local progress toward multipower equilibrium.

For a "newest look" to succeed where the New Look had failed, an illusory nuclear superiority of a growing empire had to be replaced by effectively sustaining conditions within and outside an apparently outgoing one. Military Vietnamization became the questionably conclusive test for the new strategy, replacing the inauspicious patterning of third-world on Atlantic institutions in the earlier phase. It seemed to make better sense for the longer run to match a relatively low-cost strategy *for* the periphery with readjustment downward of the value attributed *to* the periphery; and to supplement efforts to exhibit skill in manipulating and mediating local contests with demonstrations of official even if not national will in largely symbolic military deployments. The updated Nixon-Kissinger version of resource-economizing strategy differed less from the Eisenhower-Dulles antecedent than the two differed from the risk-minimizing managerial strategy in vogue during the Kennedy-

Johnson interlude. The main emphasis was restored to greater-power relations, even if to be exploited were henceforth not only the great-power handles on lesser forces but also balance-of-power mechanisms, including henceforth the greater among the small states, and the preferred, if fluctuating, emphasis was on great-power concert for conciliation (or "normalization"), as opposed to confrontation laced with threats of retaliation. A related stress was placed on treating one or both of the Communist great powers as responsive to the need for containing local crises instead of making them automatically responsible for such crises; on being flexible and tactful in counterpoising the two Communist great-power rivals against one another in the diplomatic arena rather than rigid in countering their supposedly combined or coordinated expansion at the nuclear brink.

The critical central reserve in the new strategy consisted increasingly of diplomatic options and decreasingly of America's headstart in material growth, the centrally important asset in the earlier context. Whenever it chose to exploit recession from the front line of conflict, U.S. diplomacy was blessed with a surplus of options relative to more intensely antagonistic powers, be it the Soviets and the Chinese globally or the Israelis and the Arabs and any other lesser-power contestants regionally. Increase in manipulative and diplomatic strength supplemented the still-vital military and economic background assets. It became more than ever possible to intercept rival penetrations in systemic depth by profiting from predictable politico-diplomatic rebounds of middle powers such as Egypt or Iraq or India from the henceforth more forward Soviet super-power, suspect of seeking too much or giving too little in either substance or support. A politicized in-depth defense strategy rested again on the continuing, if meanwhile abridged, U.S. capacity for naval deployments and demonstrations; the principal military cost was in equipping regional surrogates so as to make up for reduced American commitment and in reequipping a rebounding Soviet client, such as Egypt, so as to undo one-sided technological dependence.

The lowered cost and profile of the defense strategy was matched by relaxed organization; so was the rising domestic opposition to any determinate strategy, crystallizing diffuse popular disaffection into specific congressional inhibitions and revulsion from a particular war into restrictions on presidential war powers in general. A foreign-policy imperative was to delay or reverse a final erosion of outside confidence in the value of still-valued alliances. This required terminating or deactivating inessential associations (SEATO and CENTO), reaffirming the remaining ones, and discreetly backing discreetly friendly ones (such as ASEAN, the Association of Southeast Asian Nations). To safeguard an irreducible minimum of presence meant extending military (with residual economic) assistance, while engaging in profitable sales of arms and food. As control mechanisms grew more informal, they grew less influential; as official alliances for progress stalled, private activities for profit were reemphasized. Multinational disguises of American enterprise abroad were becoming increasingly meaningful; they began to shift whatever control there was over the home offices from the U.S. government to the host country, even as exploitation of the Third World by "late capitalist" imperialism was being subtly reversed into its opposite. A simultaneous compensatory drift was from overt military intervention to secret diplomacy and to clandestine intelligence and kindred activities; they were slated for paralysis, inflicted by hostile domestic reaction to their public exposure in a changed climate. Nor was deemphasizing the Third World, during most of the Nixon-Ford presidencies, assuredly adequate for dealing with the potential for disorder inherent in the simultaneous pursuit by peripheral players of economic equality with the industrial nations and politico-military superiority over neighboring states. The duality of stakes and ambitions threatened to nullify the degree of predictability implicit in the balance-of-power system so long as the equilibrium pattern of political action was only inchoate in the periphery. In consequence, a deliberate U.S. strategy for retrenchment in response to domestic pressures was likely to come up eventually against decreasingly only latent external pressures for one more reformulation of a basic American strategy.

Conditions in Europe and Japan were less precarious on the face of it. Both need and opportunity seemed intermittently present for reducing U.S. managerial influence. Instead, a tendency to discriminate against Western Europe (and Japan) when it came to devolution of role and responsibility denoted a reversion to emphasis on the essential empire and its cohesion. It was among the objectives of the United States to buttress its standing as one of the three great military powers, while retaining control over the rate and direction of any further increase of major power centers. It seemed advisable in that perspective to condone no more than a marginal updating in the early roles of the members of the essential empire, as peripheral surrogates in the post–World War II two-tier organization and as associates in central defense in the two-wing organization of the cold-war era. The United States would go on managing the essentials of military defense and deterrence vis-à-vis the Communist great powers, with maximum obtainable assistance from its principal auxiliaries; and it would continue to adjust the basics of world political order in an ambivalent relationship with the same Communist powers. On their part, Western Europe (and Japan) might supplement any waning in American assets by exerting economic attraction and seeking out political affinities in the Third World, without ceasing to be in all respects open toward the United States and cooperative in joint approaches to the outside. Although compatible with reverting to a species of partial and controlled delegation of function on the peripheries, the stress on cooperation militated against favoring Western European (or Japanese) independence that would result from a demonstrated capacity for either economic self-help (e.g., in the oil crisis) or nuclear self-sufficiency (supplementing the role in conventional defense).

Anything approaching a division of political and diplomatic labor with the West Europeans, be it for détente with the Soviet Union or for solving regional problems in Southeast Asia and the Middle East, was anathema to a succession of American policy-makers anxious to divide military labor only. If U.S. nuclear monopoly could be combined with an increased European conventional military performance, maximum interallied complementarity could be assorted with maximum U.S. control within an integrated organization. The American position on the nuclear issue was reminiscent of the British preference to have the dominions forgo separate navies and contribute instead financially toward the British naval monopoly. Only when naval proliferation had intensified in the world at large, did the British abandon the one-fleet principle within the empire, along with the two-power standard outside it; similarly, the United States held off abandoning the one-force nuclear ideal for the essential empire so long as it had an assured second-strike capability externally.

Among the dependents, empire-loyalist New Zealand had been unqualifiedly ready in the British setting to exchange naval abstention for participation in the making of imperial-defense policy, while the position of Australia and Canada had been more ambiguous. Loyalist West Germany abstained in the later context from any pretension to nuclear sharing without claiming codetermination globally; Britain claimed forms of consultation on policy without actually abstaining, but accepted far-reaching nuclear co-ordination tantamount to subordination; and fractious France demanded meaningful consultation without either offering abstention or admitting subordination. Creatively shaped by neither the will of the parties nor the weight of crises, both empires failed to evolve unifying institutions that would abridge the unilateral determination of policy by the imperial metropole and contain the continuing development of distinctive personalities by the major dependents. As a result, the British could not but be confirmed in their fear that naval proliferation without common political institutions would help dissolve the empire; and the Americans' fear of the catalytic triggering effect of nuclear proliferation for the U.S. homeland was doomed to go on rivaling inconclusively for priority the concern over nuclear diffusion's dissolvent impact on interallied cohesion.

There was in reality no necessary reason for dissemination to produce dissolution. Nuclear independence was apt to confer less of a secure immunity on the European allies than naval self-dependence would have given the overseas British dominions at the critical juncture; nor did America's major allies have a readily available alternative protector, of a kind the dominions were soon to find in the United States. Intra-alliance proliferation might, therefore, actually promote cohesion. Just as the lesser parties were liable to compensate for the potentially dislocative effects by intensifying consultations with the principal ally, so the ostensible discommitment of the alliance leader in response to nuclear diffusion was likely to enhance his effective control. Independently of any hypothetical future trends, however, the main basis for consolidating the essential empire was in the limited appeal that political and military independence had for most West Europeans and Japanese, so long as American policy did not deliberately expose them to the challenges of diminished protection or unwittingly convert them to rating the costs of self-reliance in the central balance lower than the risks from American provocations on the peripheries. The United States was consequently able to continue efforts to reorganize the two-wing empire by tentatively deconcentrating control and commitments on the peripheries and fostering elementary reconcentration after each crisis or setback at the center. Readiness to reduce organizational aims and strategic exertions in secondary areas was encouraged by every real or seeming increase in local resilience vis-à-vis rival great-power penetrations; every instance of instability enhanced the reluctance to go beyond controlled two-power détente and cautious three-power diplomacy at the vital center of the evolving international system.

At what was for the older empire and might be for the more recent one a late stage of development, the two shared the inability to combine devolution with reintegration in relations with key members inclined to blend assertions of independence with ultimate reliance on interdependence. If the similarity of the American with the British arrangements was essentially organizational, similarities with Rome were mainly in the realm of strategy, including delegation of supporting defense tasks to clients and the disposition of the imperial power itself to vary in locating the major defense effort at either the perimeter or in depth. But, in the last analysis, the American mode was intermediate between both earlier models in both organization and strategy; whenever U.S. patterns differed from the specific features of one of the empires, they automatically tended to resemble the other's. The American system evolved toward defense in depth, for instance, as had the Roman empire, but it did so more along the political lines of the balance of power reminiscent of the British strategies on the European continent than along the military lines of Roman imperial armies. Likewise, issues were in general more conspicuously or steadily military for the American than for the British empire in relation to the principal members; but they were less constantly military in character than were Rome's problems at the peripheries of empire.

VII

Just as with military strategies for unified defense and political strategies for uniform organization, so primary functional modes and physical or geographic foci of the American effort to maintain global order were undergoing changes that were partially cyclical. In the functional realm, an initial emphasis on economic instruments had expressed the desire to either avoid altogether an American-Soviet rivalry that would lead to sustained involvement or to limit the scope of an inescapable empire. Following unwillingness or inability to co-opt the increasingly rival Soviets by the economic means of end-of-war American credits, emphasis gravitated to restoring the major allies by means of the European Recovery Program. The next shift, to military instruments, reflected the insufficiency of the economic tool used in isolation from other tools. The military components of the aid to Greece and Turkey had started the trend, Korea surfaced it fully, and the militarization of the American approach to global stability and order climaxed in the Indochina war. To be sure, the economic dimension was never wholly ignored or really neglected in external dealings. And the Vietnam war deranged economic equations sufficiently within the United States itself to compel a re-emphasis, as part of liquidating the war and responding to the increased economic challenge from the earlier recipients of material American aid, be they allies or clients or neutrals. The recipients had been materially reinforced by America's use of the economic instrument within a U.S.-centered world economic order, but they were not coincidentally conditioned by politico-military instruments to fit the ramifications of their economic rise into a continuing U.S.-centered strategy and organization for imperial order.

Likewise revolving was the physical or geographic focus of the Americans imperial exertions. The focus had first moved eastward, from Western Europe to Afro-Asia, as outside political and military pressures were in part deflected and in part fragmented and dispersed. The deflection followed a broadly concurrent consolidation of the American and Soviet systems in Europe; the fragmentation mirrored the disintegration of both the European colonial empires and the Sino-Soviet conglomerate. Disintegration of colonial holdings augmented the range of indigenous actors and stakes; dissolution of Communist bonds reduced the unifying effect that concentrated hostile onslaught might have had on the Asian periphery. An independent China became instead a fresh revolutionary challenge adding a new dimension to the largely conventional intergovernmental modes of competition in the Third World. The Chinese bid was seemingly for a geographically contiguous regional orbit to match the Soviet one in Eastern Europe and the American one in the Western Hemisphere. The bid's climax (in the 1960s) intensified the American determination to bar any significant, and not least an uncompensated, Communist access to what, from different strategic perspectives, was either a periphery of the U.S. world empire or the soft underbelly of the American metropole in the Western Hemisphere. Alternately mobilizing and ignoring the Organization of American States, America's half-concealed and half-conspicuous interventions in Guatemala and Cuba were to culminate provisionally in the direct and doctrinally buttressed intervention in the Dominican Republic. Only when the politico-military and ideological stakes and instruments receded again in favor of economic ones, did the principal defensive American concern return to the Euro-Japanese industrial powers. It did so within a postulated pentagonal structure of world-economic power, to be repolarized on a South-North axis when the politically emancipated and ideologically postrevolutionary periphery moved to assert its economic leverage. That leverage had always been latent in the existing distribution of raw materials and processing facilities; it came into full play when it had ceased to be checked by the industrial West's politico-military pre-eminence, successively lodged in Europe and in America.

Fluctuations in functional and geographic focuses did not reflect basically changing conceptions of America's role, interests, and commitments; these were definable fairly early as keyed to promoting a congenial global environment or upholding a stable world order. Nor were the shifts primarily a function of either an expanding environment or a gradually restored "minimum" order, after World War II and before the sense of being overextended and overwhelmed arose out of the Vietnam war and its sequelae. More than any of these factors, the shifts reflected perceptions of prime external challenges or threats successively rising and leveling off on the part of the Communist great powers, neutralist new states in the Third World, and major industrial allies, until oil monopoly replaced armed mobilization, and economic revisionism took over from territorial revisionism, in the change from interwar to post–cold war have-not challengers to the status quo. American responses to these challenges were just sufficiently efficacious externally to displace their most damaging implications inward. The imperial posture spawned a multifaceted crisis for the American polity, changing the perceptions of both vital interests and viable scope and organization of empire; deficiencies in the empire's internal economy exceeded any shortcomings in its external efficacy. A change in the most basic principles and perspectives became due when the visible material and moral or psychological costs of static defense strategy outran hypothetical savings in the risks supposedly inherent in strategies of elastic defense. A reversal in the relative incidence of internal and external pressures in favor of the former caused an empire that had grown out of a contest over predominance to evolve into the quest for a peaceful way out of empire, to be found in a stable new internal equilibrium and a newly dynamic international equilibrium.[1]

1. Comprehensive treatments of issues discussed in this chapter are to be found in Seyom Brown, *The Faces of Power* (New York: Columbia University Press, 1968); Walter LaFeber, *America, Russia, and the Cold War 1945–1975* (New York: Wiley, 1976); Raymond Aron, *The Imperial Republic* (Englewood Cliffs, N.J.: Prentice–Hall, 1974); Amaury de Riencourt, *The American Empire* (New York: Dial Press, 1968); and Claude Julien, *America's Empire* (New York: Pantheon Books, 1971). The defense strategy options are most clearly identified in Edward N. Luttwak, *The Grand Strategy of the Roman Empire* (Baltimore: The Johns Hopkins University Press, 1976). For decline and decay in American society, see Andrew Hacker, *The End of the American Era* (New York: Atheneum, 1970).

X

AMERICAN EMPIRE.

Decline and Dissolution?

Broad similarities between the fundamental defense strategies and organizations of the American and the Roman and British empires could be subsumed under identical categories. There were, however, also sufficient differences in both the inner resources of the metropoles and their larger environments to qualify the similarities in organization and strategy and to render speculative any findings about the American empire itself when the perspective shifts from development and defense to decline and dissolution.

I

The most critical equation for a changing American empire continued to center on authority and autonomy. Just as authority entailed the range of *de facto* control which the United States sought and that which it actually secured, so meaningful autonomy for clients meant not only political self-assertion but also a corresponding effort at self-reliance for external security and internal stability. A right balance would define the right scope of imperial effort, ruling out both overextension relative to the capacity of imperial power and underinvolvement relative to the needs for empire-type order maintenance. It was not achieved in the neohegemonial setting of the essential empire by either an "Atlantic community" in the integrated mode or a "European Europe" in the Gaullist mode; nor was the balance attained in the peripheral empire by either the initial Americanization of the war in Indochina in the period of strategic advance or its attempted Vietnamization in the phase of strategic retreat. The range of ineffectually sought control was excessive in the instances of American initiative and leadership, while the readiness and capacity of the dependents for effective self-reliance was insufficient when that leadership was questioned or relaxed.

The basic quandary had been also that of Britain and Rome. There was a critical contrast between the American and the two older empires, however. When casting about for a stabilizable scope and internal balance of empire, Rome and Britain acted on the strength of institutionalized authority, but from a base relatively weak in material and human resource; the American groping unfolded from an inverse position of largely informal influence anchored in massive material, including manpower, resources. In principle at least, the surfeit of substantive resource could be useful, and might have been necessary, to compensate for the comparative institutional deficiency; it was both useful and used to induce ostensibly spontaneous responses to American directives and desiderata. By the same token, combining symbolic potency and coercive potential within institutionally formalized authority might make up for deficit in material resource.

Both methods of compensation worked about equally well in periods of expansion and ascendancy, when the physical disparities among the three empires were least significant. The British empire was managed at that point within an international system which was only fitfully in need of British material and manpower resources at its center. Only as time passed did British financial subsidies or expeditionary forces in Europe grow in scale and the proportions between them change. Moreover, the colonial or dependent segments of the British empire were largely self-supporting financially; and the central strategic reserve in the form of the Royal Navy, although costly, tended to pay for itself by shielding profitable trade and invisible exports without too often provoking Britain's (incidentally benefitting) trading partners and competitors into rival naval build-ups. The Roman legions and empire organization were likewise largely self-financing, within a more overtly coercive and exploitative framework, without initially causing fatal injury to the supporting material assets in the empire at large. By contrast, the American rise to empire was virtually coterminous with the need for massive expenditures of material and manpower resources in behalf of a disrupted international system and of non-self-sustaining dependencies, and the resulting empire rested on a central strategic reserve that was not directly productive. For a time at least, however, the outlays tended to be offset somewhat by indirect or covert returns, including "tied" foreign aid and the technological "fall-out" of both nuclear and conventional armaments. More fundamentally still, the empire framework stimulated materially and safeguarded politically an ever-expanding productive economy, while fostering an eventually revenue-producing economic involvement and investments abroad.

The assortments of institutional authority and material resource worked less well when expansion and ascendancy had faltered. One set of reasons had to do with the relation of material resource to its functional complement, organizational or managerial resourcefulness. The very narrowness of the Roman and British material and manpower bases had stimulated initially a creative search for compensations in the form of both sanctions and inducements, ranging from calculated terror to sophisticated attraction; the large resource base of the American empire warranted efforts to substitute constructive for compensatory techniques of management, conspicuously infusing resources into economic recovery or development of dependents with a view to preventing their politico-military subversion. The older authority and control systems' insufficiency of resource had unhinged them progressively in favor of extreme centralization in the Roman case and premature decentralization in the British; an inordinate deployment of resource and its invariable limitation in military use in the American control system encouraged dispensing with both "calculated terror" and "sophisticated attraction," and proved differently self-defeating. Prior U.S. deployments turned into a source of debility when no adequate techniques made up for the waning effectiveness, and eventually also diminished availability, of material and manpower resources within an increasingly deconcentrated field.

Critically supplementary to both material resource and managerial resourcefulness was, traditionally, the capacity to co-opt client elites into the imperial systems. Effective co-optation will facilitate both indirect and direct control by metropoles; it will be altogether decisive for forms of indirect control devoid of supports in either legitimized authority or compelling sanction. Similarly, it will take cultural and ideological assimilation, by means of education or indoctrination, to foster the co-optation of *clientelae* into an imperial system; but only continuing positive perceptions of self-interest and an irreducible minimum of self-respect can permanently attach the client elites. Self-interest concerns the material perquisites of co-optation into empire; self-respect will sooner or later require participation in the management of empire. Moreover, effective protection must complement both perquisites and participation. Next to being rewarded both materially and ideally, the co-opted elites must be also shielded against internal and external adversaries. And they will shun alternative options only if they are shielded in a way that is, at the point of threat, sufficiently effective to satisfy the ultimate self-interest in survival and, at other times, sufficiently discreet to preserve a self-respect that is ultimately contingent on enjoying the elementary respect of their people.

The Romans had managed all three of the requirements well. Beginning with the Italian allies, the participation by a both geographically and culturally ever-expanding circle of client elites was instrumental in fostering the long survival of the empire from a precariously narrow indigenous base. The British empire scored at first fairly high as regards client perquisites and protection. Its narrow manpower base encouraged extending participation locally by way of indirect rule and colonial self-government. But, at a critical juncture, British tribal mentality and parochial outlook proved to be still narrower than the manpower base. It ruled out participation by even the self-governing dominions in central governance at a time when the metropole was losing its ability to protect dependents without outside help. The sucessor American empire's strong resource base generated in its turn ample direct and indirect perquisites for clients willing and able to be co-opted. But empire management failed in the areas of participation at the center and protection at the peripheries. An explicit denial of the French bid to participate in directing global strategy, in the late 1950s, implied rejection of the view that such co-determination was a fit corollary to sharing the burdens of empire defense regionally and the risks accruing from U.S. defense of the worldwide imperial frontier. In the peripheral empire, the question whether and how conspicuously to favor committed client states in distributing material perquisites was compounded by the question whether and how to protect the committed parties against external and internal foes other than America's major adversary.

The specific questions involved more basic ones. As viewed by the friendly or allied client elites, was commitment to crystallizing an indigenous nation-state-to-be compatible with commitment to the U.S.-centered world imperial system? And were the two frameworks reinforcing one another in promoting the survival of the elites in power and privilege? The corresponding questions for the U.S. empire managers bore less on compatibility and more on priority as between commitments. Was the priority to secure any particular committed elite or to avoid alienating a dependent country or collective as such? Adopting the second alternative meant, in practice, espousing any alternative or successor elite willing and able to abstain from injuring the local or global interests of the United States. On balance, American policy tended to apply the narrower definition of the national interest over one comprising the imperial ethos and to choose, correspondingly, the dependent-country option over the committed-elite option. Faced with the decision whether to protect or, at least, demonstratively avenge an embattled friendly elite beset or brought down by internal enemies, American policy-makers failed to do either—from Iraq in 1958 to Ethiopia in 1975.

No less common was the tendency for the American definition of vital strategic or security interests to prevail over the client elites' identification of their critical external adversaries: most conspicuously so in the case of Pakistan in relation to India and, at a later stage, also in the case of Thailand in relation to Indochina. American policy undermined to that same extent any inclination of the client elites to identify both their group interest and their country's national interest with the U.S.-centered imperial system. It failed by the same token to compensate the elites for the additional internal and external liabilities that the American connection was engendering for them in an ideologically anti-imperialistic environment. The political liabilities were great enough to exceed, and in specific cases did exceed, the material benefits or perquisites accruing to the committed elites from their status as American clients.

A surfeit of material resource stifled resourcefulness in the managing of empire; a matching excess of a self-consciously pragmatic realism in approaching the issue of loyalty to committed client elites on the plane of high policy (as contrasted with middle-level bureaucracy) militated against introducing into imperial management a saving dose of empire romanticism. An ingredient of romanticism in central direction will express a matured ethos and will help weather reversible short-term crises, as it did in the older empires. A great power, acting in a crystallized international system of balanced powers with settled interests and traditions, may profitably disregard sentimental loyalties. The same is not wholly true for an imperial power dealing with only emerging political actors and sectors, likely to abide by a hierarchical conception of politics within and among states in fact even if not in official tenets. In such a setting, direction of policy will be highly contingent on the identity and orientation of the dominant local elites, and the latter's intense psychopolitical and even physical insecurity will convert unconditional support by the outside patron into a key yardstick of his utility. A record of both demonstrated and demonstrative support will be the indispensable reverse side of legitimately imposed and freely accepted imperial counsel or control. It may consequently reduce the occasions for supportive interventions by improving elite performance over time; and even if a resolute protective effort by the imperial power has finally proven unavailing, it may still confirm others in loyalty and convert even the opposed counterelites to cooperation in due course.

Avoiding the risks and costs attached to calculated forays into feudal-type relationships with peripheral clients, such as Iraq, Pakistan, or Thailand, was eventually to put a premium upon replacing the American client system with regional balance-of-power systems. At the start of their empire, the Romans had managed regional balances in the Eastern Mediterranean and in North Africa in both the positive and the negative senses. They delegated management to lesser-power surrogates, impeded lesser-power imperialism, and policed the right of the minor actors to both self-defense and self-aggrandizement. In the British context, the divide-and-rule approach to the institutionalized empire proper supplemented the balancer role and the balancing strategy in relation to the hegemonial European sector. American policy was evolving in the direction of balancing only when deconcentrating the empire and was, consequently, less imperative in both design and impact.

At the root of the particular differences were different relationships to the larger setting. A multiunit system receded as the Roman empire rose in the Mediterranean; such a system's emergence in Europe had preceded the British empire, but its fuller crystallization (and initial decomposition) was parallel with the empire's expansion and stabilization; and whereas a superficially global system was retrieved from Europe's existential ruins and normative traditions concurrently with the foreshortened life span of the American empire, it began to be subdivided regionally only along with the empire's seeming contraction and decline. Prior to that, the larger system's origins, expansion, and organization were most closely related to the course of a sustained, systemically dominant conflict. By contrast, the Roman influence had arisen out of a range of successively acute external conflicts that eliminated comparable rivals one by one; and the overseas British imperium was generated by less determinate and sustained external incentives than was either of the two other, more markedly military and security-related, empires. It was in keeping with such differences that the requirements of a largely mercantile empire equaled the imperatives of insular security during British ascendancy, when it came to influencing policy attitudes toward both the unevenly self-governing dependencies and the unevenly self-generated conflicts on the European continent; and that, conversely, the American imperial organization and strategies only mirrored the immediate requirements and the predominantly reactive dynamic of a single global conflict. It was, moreover, only jointly with waging the cold war that the management of empire contributed importantly to the multiplication of viable actors and autonomous conflicts as the not always fully intended consequences of either impetus. The multiplication was in due course to help defuse the dominant bipolar conflict and act as both cause and effect of the empire's movement toward "dissolution."

In the critical formative period, however, the U.S. empire's close connection with the crudest possible, because only two-power, contest meant that the national bias in favor of short-term pragmatic problem-solving would mold its organization and strategy. Likewise typically, the emphasis was on organization in its most elementary guise of agencies and programs, as distinct from basic approach or doctrine, to a more marked extent than had been true for either the Roman or the British empires. Concurrently, there was little if any self-conscious imitation of either of the older empires, and certainly less than had been the case for the British in relation to the Roman. The habitual belief in the historical uniqueness of the American experiment continued until the last, and actually postclimactic, phase of empire; self-persuasion fostered self-deception about the nature of the patterns of associations with dependents that were arising out of the dominant antagonism. As a result, the American empire developed, both spontaneously and reactively, within a psychological and conceptual setting imbued first with its nonrecognition and subsequently with its rejection.

Empires tend to be exalted only after they have passed their zenith; but the American empire was up to that point barely recognized for what it was, let alone acknowledged as useful or necessary. Its nonestablishment was partially responsible for the failure to resolve, or even to discern, the persistent, if variably structured, inconsistencies between the institutional side of empire organization and the improvised defense strategies. Just as elastic defense had been contravened by formalized alliance commitments on the periphery of empire, and American nuclear near-monopoly in the West had been ill-assorted with denial of institutionalized consultation or co-determination at the center of empire, so later attempts at flexibility in strategic and diplomatic responses at large were exposed to conflicting executive-legislative rigidities domestically. Nor could any of the many balances—between authority and autonomy, internal constraints and external pressures, realism and romanticism—be properly adjusted so long as fascination with a fluctuating contest blocked out ephemeral opportunities for stabilizing configurations within the resulting empire. Ignored or aborted regarding the whole empire were differentiation by segments and unification by a single strategy; regarding the metropole, ranges of feasible control relative to resource investment, risk acceptance, and resourcefulness; and regarding the clients, effective control, meaningful consultation, and mutually sustainable co-optation, reconciling client autonomy with checks upon its arbitrary exercise.

II

A big and protracted conflict over the central balance was the most important single determinant of America's imperial expansion and organization. It fell to a small-scale peripheral war in Asia to become, in keeping with the Roman and British experiences, the singularly potent precipitant of crisis. It accentuated the forces and surfaced the trends that pointed in the direction of something akin to decay in the imperial polity and decline and dissolution of the empire itself.

Small wars of the three empires were similar in their causes, conduct, and both specific and general consequences. Relatively minor conflicts will erode empires most seriously when no other major power is directly and conspicuously engaged on the adversary side. Accordingly, the small wars in Spain and Africa damaged the Roman empire in the Republican period more than did conflicts engaging Rome with the Parthian empire;

the war in South Africa against the Boers enervated the British more than had the Crimean War against Russia; and the war in Indochina disrupted the American national polity and imperial psyche more deeply than had the war in Korea, which presumptively encompassed the Soviet Union, actively engaged Communist China, and was widely perceived as affecting the security of the major European and Japanese allies. Even if no direct threat was inferred to the security of the continental United States, the Korean War was sufficiently linked to the initial incentive to American expansion to foreshorten its internally disturbing repercussions. The Indochina war originated less compellingly in concern with basic security and grew instead out of the raw structural fact of radical disparity in sizes, stakes, and standards between the United States and a minor polity pursuing a locally self-assertive, expansionist or imperialist, policy.

Once activated, such fundamental disparity will make an unequal military conflict sooner or later inevitable. It will also make the sources and rationales of the quintessentially imperial or even colonial war open to challenge, denial, and many-faceted distortions, within the imperial body politic no less than outside it. Opposition will grow and become more effective when objectives that are legitimate within the imperial power's frame of reference have been vitiated, and their prosecution undermined, by more or less self-inflicted flaws in the conduct of a "small" war. Any one particular small war will be automatically justified up to a point by the predictably adverse consequences for both imperial authority and the wider order of systematic inaction in a setting of structurally conditioned disparity in stakes and standards. More specific justificatory rationales will bear on the small-scale adversary of the imperial power (if only as a matter of previously withstood or lastingly intolerable provocation); on the interested third parties (if only as a matter of the need to avoid larger conflict by upholding prestige); and on general or abstract concerns (if only as a matter of continuing protection of access to endangered clients and assets of various kinds). One of the flaws confounding the fundamental justness of the ultimately unavoidable war will be incremental drift into an uneven limited conflict, devoid of a convincingly formulated rationale; another, the war's hesitant conduct reflecting, on the one hand, too narrowly conceived requirements for achieving the immediate objective and, on the other hand, too widely cast apprehensions regarding the intervention's possible ramifications.

As it grew in length and scope, American participation in the war in Indochina became vulnerable on the count of origination. It shared, moreover, the main characteristic flaws in the conduct of small wars with the British and Roman empires. An inadequate material mobilization, due to insufficient political motivation, will be a handicap in the field; so will be, on the home front, insufficient political understanding or skill.

Ineffectual conduct of the war, along with its inconclusive course and prolonged duration, will cause the imperial belligerent to transgress both humanitarian norms and technical-military principles of warfare, and push the transgression beyond the measure inherent in any contest between adversaries unequal in total power and asymmetric in specific strengths. As methods are debased and the costs of protraction rise, furthermore, the public will be alienated by governmental policies that failed to either inspire support for the war by the way it was managed at home or to insulate the domestic rear from its impact by the way it was managed in the field. Insufficiencies in motivation and of mobilization will reflect the ostensibly minor scale of the immediate stake and antagonist; conjointly with the insufficiency of either inspiration or insulation they will, furthermore, reflect leadership preoccupation with larger, if hypothetical, internal or external threats. One key concern will be to avoid either provoking or being distracted from the supposedly real, major external enemy, another, to uphold economic and political normalcy internally. The priorities will not, however, be matched by the corresponding requisite capacity and will to effectively intimidate potential great-power backers of the small-scale adversary and to effectively insulate the domestic arena from the external conflict.

When indulged in the early stages of the small Asian war, normalcy without insulation was damaging to both the national and the imperial American purpose. It updated the damage that a precipitate return to normalcy for isolation had done after the first, and in a muted form also after the second, world war. Ultimately self-defeating normalcy during the Indochina war meant retaining peacetime standards and expectations regarding, among other things, civilian vs. military primacy in directing the battlefield operations and the priority of short-range political expediency over long-range economic stability in defraying the war's material cost. Unabridged civilian control over military minutiae was being combined with unlimited consumption by the public in an overall strategy that commingled the strict construction of a constitutional principle with loosely unprincipled obeisance to the habitual practice of mass-democratic politics American-style. Broadly comparable, in the intimate aristocratic politics of predemocratic Britain, had been the persistence, into Crimean and South African warfare, of the conventions of intraelite tolerance for individual incompetencies and idiosyncracies, as well as the persistence, into the Roman wars with Jugurtha, of the ambiguous ties of clientships with foreign potentates in the Republic's oligarchical senatorial politics.

The self-inflicted vices in all such cases reinforced the flaws unavoidably adhering to a small-scale imperial war that impinges upon largely peaceful international and domestic political systems. If the lowered intensity of its engagement deprives the imperial power of rapid and decisive victory, the absence of victory will assume for political purposes some of the appearances and entail most of the consequences of a military defeat. This fact will benefit the small-scale adversary, while also of benefit to third powers will be the presumptive absence of a massive threat to the national security of the imperial belligerent, inferrable from the low intensity of his engagement and liable to shield third-party exploitative or provocative acts from the deterrent risk of probable reprisals.

A low-intensity peripheral involvement will be, moreover, peculiarly apt to change qualitatively the nature or identity of the imperial state itself. Militant involvement in Egypt had transformed insular Britain, in effect, into a vulnerable continental state, by supplying the European great powers with an area accessible to pressures and a cause propitious for blackmail. Comparably, America's involvement in Indochina both consummated and surfaced her gradual prior transformation into an "imperial" state and an "Asian" power. That which elevated America to a higher class of statehood from one perspective, however, degraded her from another viewpoint to being a state like any other. If, as previously in Great Britain, the ethic of the American critics of the Vietnam war evolved into a repudiation of war in general (with very limited and particular past and potential future exceptions) as a matter of moral sensitivity, the small-scale imperial war itself was also condemned on specific grounds. It mattered little whether the rejection was impressed with a sufficient measure of political sophistication when examined in a long historical and a wide systemic perspective. The increasingly prevailing view excluded automatically alternative perceptions of the war itself, as a virtually unavoidable symptom of structural and attitudinal disparities in the system at large, and of the merits of a resolute conduct, as a symbol of maturing civic disposition to uphold the U.S.-centered world order against even peripheral and hypothetical threats in deference to a self-imposed necessity.

The repercussions of small-scale wars on domestic polity and on external conduct or commitments, often exceeding those of many a major conflict, have not radically varied across time and empires. In the American case alone, the Mexican War in the mid-1840's owed its origins to the corruption of public life, associated with land speculations. And insofar as its outcome had promoted the disruption of the political party system, associated with sectionalism and slavery, America's moral "conquest" by Mexico culminated in the American Civil War. More loudly proclaimed was to be the indirect subversion of American values by those of decadent Spain in the war of 1898 and its guerrilla sequence in the Philippines; subsequent recoil from an expanding world role by the United States, if by no means directly causing World War I, helped create the conditions that made Europe's own "civil war" eventually appear unavoidable to many. Compared with a later one, the two earlier small wars of the

United States had a politically redeeming, if ethically aggravating, advantage. They were self-consciously conceived and decisively conducted against a materially weak opponent for an anticipated major gain located, moreover, outside the principal theater of combat. Such was not the case with the Indochina war at the provisional end of the American empire-building career. The Asian war thus produced no material compensation for something akin to a moral conquest of the United States by the Vietcong specifically and by assertive third-world elements generally. The Vietcong "conquered" America only temporarily, at the radical extreme of antiwar counterelites bent on overthrowing the established internal *political* order with the aid of outside leverage. The "conquest" by the Third World had the appearance of being more enduring and fundamental at the prudent middle of the partially renovated liberal political elite. It translated into the elite's postwar and apparently postimperial responses to external pressures for a new world *economic* order.

Vulnerability to moral conquest by the physical enemy was only the most dramatic domestic consequence of America's small wars. In the broader compass, internal consequences of the specifically imperial wars bore on general or objective economic, military, and political conditions; elite credibility; and specific consensus.

The objective conditions comprised the visible economic consequences of the small wars and their supposed economic causation. Economic consequences in the form of massive inflation attended both the Korean and the Vietnamese wars; the economic interpretation of causation was prominent only in the second of the two wars and coincided with the decline of the straightforward ideologico-strategic interpretation that had been accepted as sufficient for the first. The economic consequences were of greater concern to the traditional political Right, while the economic causation was both a fetish and an obsession for the "new" radical Left. The massive inflation consequent upon the failure to meet the unfolding costs of war with fiscal and other compensatory measures alienated principally the lower- to middle-income groups, even as reducing the causes of war to the economic factor was winning over the middle- to high-brow intellectuals. Both the manifest consequence and the pretended cause involved the operation of the capitalistic economic system, the former raising questions about that system's performance and the second impugning its propensities. The victims of the consequences were impressed by the apparent incapacity of the capitalist system to combine internal economic expansion with external politico-military defense without raising the cost of living by runaway inflation. The critics of causation stressed the dependence of the system for performance on a steadily satisfied propensity to expand both economically and politico-militarily as an alternative to economic depression and system-disintegration. In conformity with different analyses, the would-be preservers of the system inclined to prescribe changed political and military strategies for a "cheaper" international equilibrium, compatible with internal economic stability. The would-be displacers of the politico-economic American system sought remedy in changing it for a more "just" equilibrium intra- and internationally, expressive of greater social equity everywhere.

The political and economic spheres displayed ample parallels, notably with Britain. In the military sphere, reminiscent of Roman as well as British antecedents, the issue was less causation and consequences and more control and commitment. Cause and consequence were at stake in the question as to whether the mere possession of conventional and subconventional military capabilities induced direct combatant involvement. Such capabilities had been absent before and largely again after the Korean War; they were supposedly overdeveloped before a fighting role became largely overt in the Vietnamese War. An inquiry into the problematic relationship between deterrence and defense in relation to limited wars was secondary, however, to the practical consequences of the small war becoming protracted. The resulting tendencies were to increasing civilian control over military operations and to declining civic commitment to military service in the field. Civilian control meant questioning the competence of the military professionals by the political superior (backed up by self-professed strategists) as a matter of abiding constitutional principle reinforced by recent experience (e.g., the Bay of Pigs); civic dereliction compelled substituting a professional force for the citizen army as a matter of political expediency or even necessity, but not soon enough to affect the course of the war. In Republican Rome the control issue had been obscured by the fusion of political office and military command, but not so the issue of civic commitment. Obversely, the British tradition of first mercenary and later professional soldiery isolated for critical significance the issue of civilian and military control and direction within a comparatively elastic practice in peripheral conflicts. The more rigid American way of waging imperial wars was subject to both problems critically, if with changing salience. Insofar as the Truman-MacArthur controversy had been symbolic of widespread disaffection among the top-echelon military, the control issue enjoyed prominence in the Korean War; a more pliant military high command in the American sequel to the French war in Indochina allowed the issue of the drafted "contingent" to predominate.

Near-universal disaffection of free citizenry with obligatory military service in low-level warfare and the consequent spread of defections will express and further deepen the crisis of a consensual political order. They will do so, moreover, at that order's vital, if normally hidden, center. America's actual crisis coincided with a transitional state that differentiated the Vietnamese from the Korean setting. The weight of frustration over dealing with a minor Communist power grew as the counterweight of fear emanating from a major Communist threat became less potent. The lessened fear weakened the disciplines acceptable to the polity at large; the intensified frustration depressed the self-confidence of the political elites and stimulated the counterelites. The bipartisan cold-war/imperial coalition was fractured if not split over both Asian wars, but, in the Korean case, the elite fission was insufficient to produce a leadership vacuum. The Truman-Democratic section of the political elite had endured long enough to permit the substitute, Eisenhower-Republican, elite to negotiate the war's termination. The general fabric of the cold-war/early-imperial system was upheld as a result with sufficient firmness to prevent a counterelite from widening any incipient breach between the bipartisan elite's basic strategy and the public's tactical support. By the late phase of the Vietnam War, much larger defections and much deeper cleavages had occurred within both the Democratic and the Republican wings of the liberal cold-war/imperial elite. The resulting vacuum of effective leadership created an opening for two kinds of substitute elites, differently anti-Establishment in orientation. A wholly extraneous radical counterelite would terminate the war instantly as a prelude to expanding the domestic and constricting the foreign-policy system. Their very excesses reduced the radicals gradually to the status of a disavowed assault column and publicized foil for a conservative alternative to the liberal Establishment, typically bent on doing no more than retool the domestic and foreign-policy systems for less costly and more effective management.

The difference between Korea and Vietnam was not unlike the difference between the Crimean and the South African wars in the British empire. It corresponded, in the American case alone, to two more basic differences. On the side of ideology and demagogy, the difference was one between (Alger) Hiss and (Cordell) Hull as the successively impugned arch-villains in first a Communist and subsequently an imperialist conspiracy, and as prime targets for marginal elites or outright counterelites from the extreme Right and Left. In the first case, the charge was one of subverting, in the second, of consummating, inherited American values and doctrines. On the side of practical politics, the difference was one between the liberal Republicanism of the Eisenhower brand and the conservative Republicanism of the Nixon variety, each brought into office in order to "honorably" (i.e., gradually) terminate the war and marginally revise the system. The ideological issue denoted the peculiarly American dialectic between extremes, as the Vietnam-related (leftist) "antithesis" to the Korea-related (rightist) "thesis" was safely delayed beyond the point of the latter's exhaustion and avoided producing any stable or coherent new synthesis out of a collision of extremes as a result; and the only superficial and transient impact of the ideological extremes on sociopolitical evolution and practical politics was illustrated when the Nixon group, having been helped into the saddle by the reaction to one (leftist) counterelite, briefly tempered underlying institutional continuity by the display of social and psychological characteristics suggestive of the other (rightist) counterelite.

The state of the American political system and process had been defined in the Korean context by the fact that the ideological and military loss of China could, and in a sense had to, be converted into winning an American empire as the loss's strategic and psychological corrective, beginning with saving at least some of Korea. Conversely, the gradually unfolding impossibility of saving some of Vietnam with the means actually available could, and in a different way had to, be parlayed into the diplomatic recovery of China for a new system of foreign policy. The later event dramatized the evolution in the informational system toward greater flexibility and diversity; it betokened also a domestic American system that had done little better than veer from both single- and simpleminded anti-Communism to a no more nuanced or sophisticated antiimperialism; and it followed the cold-war/imperial elite's move from undisputed trusteeship into a trauma surfacing parallel with the evolution of the system. The Eisenhower-Dulles Republican elite segment had sought to be provident in both military-strategic and internal-political arenas, with the aid of an economizing strategy of nuclear deterrence or retaliation. The approach turned out to be more correct conceptually than feasible practically, and to be as obsolete militarily (with the passing of the American nuclear monopoly) as it was premature politically (before the onset of major-power pluralism). The succeeding Kennedy-Democratic elite set military-strategic prudence above more broadly gauged providence when proceeding to diversify U.S. capabilities. While the revision made pragmatic sense, it also invited political disaster by forging the means for a nonviable protraction of low-level international conflict.

It fell to the Johnson climax of the Kennedy approach to a small imperial war to set in motion the war's domestic consequences, suggestive of internal decay, as a prelude to its foreign-policy implications, suggestive of the decline or dissolution of empire. The overall credibility, or integrity, of the incumbent elite bore on military-political as well as economic issues and had a social aspect. At issue was the competence of men and system alike to manage an imperial war for global order without jeopardizing domestic peace in the short run and domestic prosperity in the long. Public confidence in the imperial elite had begun to decline in Britain during and in the aftermath of the Crimean War; following a brief spell of popularity for empire in the Victorian twilight, the declension was accelerated by the South African war. A similar early mistrust had sprouted in the United States during the Korean War, was suspended by the cold war, and erupted all the more dramatically in the second half of the Vietnam War. The crisis of credibility related superficially to the questionable veracity of official pronouncements on the war's progress; but governmental integrity was more fundamentally tainted by deferring the war's costs to future generations, as if this could be done without incurring an immediate economic penalty. And the issues of both credibility and integrity were controversially at stake on the yet deeper level of social order and justice, in the regime's implied pretension that domestic social sensitivity was a function of successful global stabilization; that the Great Society could and would be an offshoot of a grand empire. The official doctrine of simultaneity of world power and national well-being was defensible in regard to long-term fundamentals. But, in the midst of a faltering war effort and forfeited credibility in both the military and the economic spheres, the expansive social doctrine was certain to be overwhelmed by the contrary assertion of incompatibility between empire and reform. The proposition holding that the disaster of war must be brought to an end to give birth to a peace dividend carried the day, only to be soon lost from sight amidst rising postwar pressures for either supplementing or supplanting interethnic domestic with internation redistribution of wealth and power.

Public disenchantment with the performance of the governmental function had meanwhile created a mass base for elite recoil from the concentration of presidential power. And if elite criticism grew in volume as it spread from ideologically radical counterelites to electorally pragmatic congressional elites, it also denoted a certain inconstancy. It was the liberal elites that had begun to promote the "imperial presidency" during World War II as a prerequisite to an internationalist involvement conforming to their ideological beliefs and political principles; the same kind of elites were to recant in the course of the later war in the name of a different, constitutional, principle as a matter of both opportunity and opportunism. The turnabout came when grass-roots isolationism, ideologically obsolete in the face of big-power totalitarian challenge Soviet-style, assumed the more acceptable form of divorce from an imperialism entailing resistance to small-scale challenges Vietnam-style as well.

The culminating consequence of the war in Asia was the breakdown of the national foreign-policy consensus. It reflected the deterioration of both objective conditions and of subjective confidence, the public's in the elite and of the elite in itself. The vanished consensus had had the characteristic virtue of uniting the elites on ends, while linking them to the mass public by competitive soliciting of support for alternative means; the breakdown of the consensus was accelerated by the rhetoric of opinion-makers without responsibility for results. Since instructing the Romans, the verbalizers of discontent merely moved from the forum to the floor of the U.S. senate and from the circus to the campus, while traversing only the small distance separating yellow journalism from the multicolored television screen since the similar British experience. In the resulting climate, the dominant elites defected from the prior consensus in order that its revision might forestall the drive of counterelites for a revolution in policy installing a new consensus; they sought to contain (where the others aimed to exploit) end-of-war disillusionments; and they would replace the waning faith of anti-Communism with the old-new religions of either pragmatic utilitarianism or humanitarian idealism as antidotes to ideological materialism. The proffered alternatives to the shattered consensus ranged correspondingly from expediency to exaltation; from restoring a world balance-of-power system, within which reduced foreign-policy goals would enhance America's diplomatic independence, to installing the millenium of domestic and global welfarism, anchored in growing economic interdependence. The extreme goals and conspicuous costs of an empire would be either reduced or more basically transformed, but in either case without admitted detriment to its largely ignored covert benefits.

III

The responses to disarray were neither original nor conclusive. They could be discounted as tokens of war-end deflation or be taken more seriously as surfacing longer-developing demoralization and decay. A more than commonplace disillusionment ensued after most or all of both major and minor American wars. The reaction could be temporarily contained only by an immediately following challenge, such as the cold war after World War II. Profound disillusionments were the reverse of unlimited self-confidence; they reflected the exceptional American capacity to inflate beyond the mundane norm both the ideal expectations and the material expenditures attendant on wars. In connection with the direct American involvement in Vietnam, psychological deflation was aggravated by economic depression-cum-inflation. The two together caused the empire-related civic commitments to shrink ahead of the empire itself and the shrinkage to be attended by the lowering of at least some of the private expectations as to the material good life, possibly pending one more rebound from depression into reexpansion internally or subjectively and externally.

Pending more evidence either way, the American body politic was not altogether lacking in superficial symptoms of institutional and material decay, unhinging the prior social equilibrium. Whereas the adult sociopolitical elite was losing self-confidence at least temporarily, its adolescent offshoots were toying with defection to either counterculture or counterelite. And whereas the dominant elite's shaken political tenure coincided with an explosion of demands on the mass level, declaratory commitments to increased political participation contrasted with signs of retreat into privatism by the bulk of society. Diffusing too widely and abruptly the effective right to mainly the material perquisites of citizenship risked repeating the ultimately debilitating effect of an indiscriminate conferral of formal citizenship in the Roman empire. And for the younger members of sociopolitical elites to identify with the pseudorevolutionary "proletariat" or authentically revolting "slaves" was, among other things, also a symptom of decay that, reappearing in different versions since Roman days, was wont to infiltrate moral relaxation through the conduit of pretended value conversion. Included in the latter in America was an unfocused humanitarianism that could be broadly compared, while it lasted, with the role of primitive Christianity in the Roman empire and of missionary vocations and activities in the British empire.

Conjointly with these evolutions, the previously felt primacy of external security crises with domestic repercussions was yielding to the primacy of a domestic crisis with external consequences. The domestic repercussions of international crises had assumed the shape of bipartisan consensus of the governing and a modicum of social discipline of the governed; they had tended to be damage-limiting. By contrast, the internal American crisis escalated the economic and other exactions addressed from the outside to a morally if not materially weakened America. Yet another earlier and causative shift had been from the heroic-expansive style and strategy of the political leadership to a husbanding-diffident mode and mood spreading from the leadership downward. The change from a Pitt or his son to a Baldwin or (Neville) Chamberlain at the head of government in the British empire was matched in the telescoped American trajectory by the change from a Forrestal to a McNamara or Clifford at the head of the civilian defense establishment. On a collective scale, the post-depression and post–World War II "new" middle class shifted similarly from unqualified commitment to its socioeconomic expansion internally, parallel with an expansive implementation of containment in foreign policy, to a gains-conserving attitude stressing domestic security coincidentally with demands for retrenchment abroad. Such mutations could be only partially explained by the difference between inception and consolidation, in regard to either America's world role or the ascent of a social class, in conditions of a growing challenge from below for both.

Implicit in the sociopolitical crisis was both a thrust toward new postempire values and subsidence back into old preimperial states of mind. Coincident with either trend was some decay of the national institutions themselves. The diminution of the moral authority of the presidency, attendant on "Watergate," was but an aggravating circumstance which facilitated the assault on its powers, consequent on "Vietnam"; and the abuse of public powers at the summit was no graver for the long-term integrity of the political system than was the widespread assertion of a private right to interpret civic obligations, including military, to which the official abuse was either a pendant or a reaction.

The diminished authority of the imperial establishment as a whole was more deeply caused by that establishment's failure to adapt sufficiently to its internal growth in size and to the growing scope of its activities abroad. Adaptation was not forthcoming in the conceptual realm, starting with the sheer recognition of the fact of empire; nor was adaptability displayed in the realm of organization, concerning either the political problem of relations between elites (executive and legislative, civil and military, and interallied) or the economic problem of transitions between peace and war. Instead, a spurious adaptation occurred from weakness, in the guise of disowning previously affirmed methods and objectives and redefining domestic and foreign challenges in response to changes either confined to public moods or exaggerated by those moods. While the elites were avoiding hard choices, the public became receptive to the morally charged but, in part at least, ideologically inspired aspersions on the conduct of both low-level warfare (My Lai) and highest-level political office (Watergate). The crises of conscience and of legitimacy may not have significantly altered the structures of national military security and political decision-making in the longer run; but they did seriously diminish both the inherited faith in key institutions and the contemporary confidence in their transient incumbents.

The main assault on policies and institutions came from societal elites farthest removed from the productive process, such as college students and professional intellectuals and media men. The Great Depression had been redeemed by economic growth during and after World War II. A new socioeconomic middle class arose without being, however, sufficiently secure socially and economically to realize the potential of an authentic middle class for being politically stabilizing. The 1960s saw instead the destabilizing convergence of climaxing domestic affluence and prolonged peripheral warfare, while the early 1970s witnessed a continued groping for a substitute political elite in conditions of economic stagnation (or "stagflation"). An affluent society was increasingly vulnerable to chronic inflation and periodic recessions; an imbalance in international payments was susceptible to only precarious remedies; and, as governmental expenditures rose without basic reform ending the evasion of fiscal obligations by the most affluent, a concurrent evasion of military service by both upper- and middle-class off-shoots transformed one more privilege of citizenship into a career for the underprivileged—too late to be of immediate use to imperial foreign policy, possibly too soon for a post-imperial polity that was being integrated at too uneven rates in its different segments.

An apparently declining propensity to risk-taking and innovation in traditional productive industries coincided with the growth of consumer-materialism and of service industries. Yet weaknesses in the traditional economic sector suggestive of long-term decay were at variance with continuing innovation in the most advanced sectors; so was the conspicuous loss of political élan out of keeping with undercurrents of social resilience. Discrepancies of this kind made it difficult to assess the several facets of decay, beyond noting their similarity with manifestations in earlier empires in decline both individually and in their sum across a wide spectrum, from declining birth-rate to assertive feminism. Instead of reflecting the authentic decay of a but inchoately stratified mass polity confronted too soon with climactic challenge, they could merely denote a growing sophistication of sorts within a maturing society which, more surely than deviating from ancestral fortitude or longer-surviving optimism, was merely dispensing with the more naive features of the American dream and discarding the self-satisfied attitudes behind that dream. Moreover, the more difficult it was to assess "decay," the more complicated was the always ambiguous cause-effect relationships between internal decay and an empire's decline relative to outside forces ending in its final dissolution. Decay can be the profoundest ramifying cause of empire dissolution and, being long subterranean as it gathers momentum gradually, may be fully surfaced only by a far-advanced external decline and appear then to be the decline's consequence. Or decay can be only the last-stage prelude to, or precipitant of, decline when it has caused an externally beset empire to be widely and suddenly perceived as one that is unmanageable, undefendable, and unnecessary. It is then such a perception that translates decay as a social condition into public policies aimed at liquidating a political order.

IV

Just as dynamic management of empire tends to engender further expansion, so the belief in the empire's becoming unmanageable will promote readiness to accept constriction deferring to the altogether relativistic sense of overextension. One reason lies in the fluidity of the distinction between management and defense, between the empire being manageable and its being defendable. An empire is manageable when public support or tolerance and elite cohesion are sufficient to permit mobilizing adequate effort and resource for the defense of the empire at a materially and psychologically bearable cost. To be bearable, the cost must be neither back-breaking at any one point nor must it exceed over time the perceived material and other than material benefits of empire even as they come to be taken for granted and include the forward defense of physical security and a widespread network of influence underpinning economic (and, relatedly, political) stability. Being increasingly elusive, the costs and benefits of empire will be also relative to alternatives in organization and strategy that are neglected, forgone, or avoided by adhering to the imperial formula. When needs have ceased to be in accord with either disposable means or the perceived net costs, strains will set in; and as the strains set off a movement toward restabilizing the needs-costs equation, the eventual consequence will be to either supersede the empire by a more viable imperial successor or to phase it out in favor of an alternative form of international order.

In terms of will and perception of the elites, the American empire at its vastest and most centrally controlled ceased to be manageable when its external and internal hinges collapsed, its domestic support weakened, and its original international setting was no more. On the hinges had been suspended the core-values sustaining the empire; and the values in turn engendered both the internal rationales and the domestically produced resources for the empire's rise and continuance in the world at large.

One key hinge was the negative ideology of anti-Communism, with strategic implications; another was a positive sentiment with material implications, which supplemented anti-Communism with the vision of community with Western Europe (and, secondarily, Japan). Anti-Communism had been sentimentally intensified by the loss of China to hostile force; it fittingly faded as preconditions grew for recovering China diplomatically. The role of the idea of a wider community was emotionally and materially equivalent to the role played by the East in the Roman, and by India in and for the British, empires. Atlanticism had been intensified as the amputation of Eastern from Western Europe brought risks along with relief from the responsibility for managing a regional powder-keg. It weakened as the Western Europeans moved to either affect independence or practice what Americans perceived to be unequitable interdependence, substituting criticism of American actions for contributions to imperial defense in Southeast Asia or the Middle East and converting politically motivated U.S. economic infusions into assets in economic competition, devoid of counterparts in the upholding of a common stake in world order. The mystique of the essential empire expressed community-generating anti-Communism in the present; it faded conjointly with the erosion of a related myth, defining the ideal future in a still wider spatial compass and updating the British ideal of progress to colonial self-government within an ever-wider and forever-loyal commonwealth. The updated myth was embodied in theories of world-wide economic development via free enterprise and political development for free institutions that would supplement, when they did not reproduce, conditions of the economic and political stability in the United States itself. The developmental theories constituted one more intellectual hinge, with long-term political implications, on which hung the American commitment to action. They may have been the ultimate distillations of the will-to-power in the most liberal of garbs, but they were also a profession of the capacity of the "first new nation" for transcending power in a purpose for pan-human ends. Since the principal theater for the testing of the myth was on the peripheries of the empire, India was again the focus, despite her self-consciously cultivated estrangement from the American system. The myth waned fittingly, therefore, as India's updated "mutiny" against American succession to Britain was simultaneously manifest in economic regression, domestic autocracy, and regional domineering with Soviet support.

The weakening of core values and key expectations went with the decline in domestic support for empire, viewed as the source of material burdens and moral blemishes. Already suspect as the source of war-induced costs, external expansion came to be widely perceived as the occasion for profit-motivated exports of capital and for politically motivated easements for imports of manufactured goods from the Third World, both draining off employment into areas of lower labor costs. A growing propensity to be close-fisted materially traveled, moreover, in an incongruous tandem with the desire for an institutionally more open foreign policy, as if reductions in available resource did not have to be compensated for by all kinds of greater resourcefulness requiring different measures of secrecy. An abruptly reawakened public sensitivity at large repudiated with little advance warning the technical standards of bureaucratic professionals that had been cumulatively evolved to wage the cold war and perpetuated to preserve its gains. The perceptual disparity recalled a somewhat different one in the late British empire, between a public increasingly indifferent to empire and a colonial administration increasingly zealous in improving its management. If the war in Vietnam engendered revulsion against methods of mass killing, its aftermath produced a severe condemnation of the once-acclaimed selective and secretive methods of political warfare. Public disapproval shifted from special forces to special intelligence; but the public's image of foreign activities was not any the less misshaped by renewed exposure to moralizing abstractions than it had been by the failure to properly internalize the ethical relativity of action.

Internal strains were magnified by an international setting of increasingly diversified, diffuse, and, in consequent appearance, diminished pressures. Intersuperpower bipolarity and the once monolithic Communist bloc were giving way haltingly to pluralism in power and policy; America's and, to a lesser and more forcefully resisted degree, Soviet alliances evolved away from one-power hegemony. As equality graduated simultaneously from being an empirical fact of limited application to the status of a major value issue for policy, the once near-equal exposure of the two superpowers to influence- and aid-maximizing playoffs by third-world neutralists gave way to different, and no more constructive, leveling.

For one thing, governments of both aligned and nonaligned smaller third-world countries came to be about equally disoriented as they searched for bearings in the new political and diplomatic game, occurring henceforth among three principal powers and largely outside the nuclear-military sphere. For another thing, depolarizing and demoting the cold war meant that conflicts were diffused more evenly, but it meant also that the modes of waging conflict, already lowered by the nuclear stalemate, would be depressed to basest forms of violence both within and between national and tribal societies. Moreover, equality emerged as a more than usually potent aim and questionable prospect in a third-world setting rendered hierarchical by the rise of a fourth, collective and economic, power in the guise of an oil cartel turning one face toward the great expectations of the "fourth" world (of the resource-poor unequals) and another face to the high politics of the three major powers. Taken together, changes in the international setting seemed inhospitable to any practicable effort at adjusting local autonomy and central control within anything like a traditional empire formula, much as they may have augmented the need for structures of order. They seemed also to displace the even but theoretically plausible framework for co-opting foreign elites away from a U.S. -centered politico-military empire for defense and power, to a transnational economic equilibrium for development and production which, even if modeled on it, would not necessarily be lastingly centered on the West.

As the diminished sense of need for imperial-style American protection and promotion spread abroad, it dampened the feeling within the United States that an increasingly costly empire continued to be necessary. The once felt complementarity of reciprocal needs with friends and dependents was replaced by a conjunction of downgraded threat and a deteriorated defense posture. Capacity for defense had been diminishing and threats diversified even before the onset of changes and revaluations set in motion by the Vietnam War, as the Soviet Union learned how to imitate American techniques and approximate American capabilities and the lesser third-world powers came to insist on changing both the rules and the stakes of the superpower contention to which most of them had owed their birth. The Soviet Union grew stronger and more ambitious as elementary outside containment made it change internally into a more conventional power. Successive attack waves from the Third World came as the periphery evolved from ideologico-political to pragmatic-economic radicalism, from the quest for national liberation to that for transnational equity, from self-containment by internal divisions within a pressure group aiming at unity to interstimulation consistent with outward solidarity in conditions of uneven national capacity for individual growth. The lesser-power challenge was the U.S.-centered empire's functional equivalent of the small-power (or "barbarian") invasions and subversions that had beset the older empires; when it became America's turn to see her initial key military and economic assets and strengths devalued, these turned once more into so many pressure-points and hostages for the expanding range of rivals and would-be global or local successors.

Narrowly military defense became more difficult in regard to a Soviet great power moving toward quantitative parity in capabilities; in regard to the lesser powers, problems arose mainly from qualitative changes in weapons technology favoring defense. And if quantitative change discouraged U.S. military intervention, qualitative change threatened to facilitate local ability to thwart an intervention that would be undertaken nonetheless. In the nuclear realm, different constructions and assessments of parity between the superpowers transformed the strategic reserve for the American empire into a seemingly self-sufficient rationale for a U.S.-Soviet détente that left unclarified any corresponding change in the rules of superpower conduct on geopolitically significant regional issues. In the realm of conventional and subconventional land warfare, the Vietnam experience had reawakened the "never-again" reaction to the Korean War. Only the residual, typically imperial, naval and amphibious capabilities remained theoretically available for employment. They, too, were subject to critical inhibitions, however, responsible for the widely held belief in the impossibility to ever repeat the effortless seaborne intervention of 1958 in Lebanon. Increased Soviet naval capabilities and the demands of lesser states for wider margins of control over coast-adjoining seas reduced U.S. capacity to largely symbolic and dubiously persuasive naval deployments. The same changes exposed the United States and its major allies to the possibilities of offensive or retaliatory harassments of trade routes and naval communications by either the land- and sea-based instrumentalities of coastal states or the surface and subsurface naval capabilities of the Soviet Union.

Closely related to the military was the political and economic deterioration from interacting erosions. Erosion affected United States alliances, the distinction between allied and nonaligned powers, the prior Soviet inability to acquire quasi-allies in the Third World outside the reach of the Red Army, and the straightforward simplicities of the American-Soviet conflict and the West's economic ascendancy. The relatively easy U.S. access to military bases and political links on the periphery in return for protection and economic promotion was simultaneously replaced by interallied competition over arms (and food) sales; the reluctance of precariously prosperous European and Japanese economic "haves" to purchase security by U.S. defense cost-reducing concessions was overshadowed by questionably satisfiable demands of unevenly endowed third-world "have nots" for revision of the world economic order. A politically valued conservative and regionally stabilizing posture, such as Iran's, went with radically aggressive leadership in formulating economic demands, while the obverse combination of economic opportunism with political radicalism was illustrated by Iran's local rival, Iraq. So confusingly assorted in its constituents, the economic threat from the Third World was yet more strikingly uneven in its impact on the United States, its major allies, and key interests within each. Holding the American system together under the circumstances required reducing differences in both hardships and responses to opportunities; but defining a transcendent common objective was no easier as a way thereto than was sustaining tactical flexibility in individualized approaches over time.

With the growing plurality and diversity in the environment, the empire appeared to be increasingly unmanageable and undefendable, while the positive sides of the new conditions made it also appear increasingly unnecessary. A minimal management of the empire within its outermost geographic scope had become so costly as to make its defense along the increasingly multifaceted functional frontiers appear impossible. One resulting redefinition would reduce the perceived strategic requirements in upholding the (irreducible) balance of power, with especially the Soviet Union, in such key areas as the Persian Gulf, the Indian Ocean, and the South Atlantic, not least by relying more on local or other countervailing powers; another would expand the opportunities for moving toward new terms of trade or exchange (broadly conceived) with the relatively minor powers, notably by means of co-opting local elites into the Western system politically by the economic route. The co-optation's conspicuous costs would be presumably offset by incidental benefits as the sections of the South capable of industrialization learned to appreciate their stake in the economic well-being of the industrial West; and both costs and benefits would be individually contained by the continuing politico-economic competition within both the southern and the northern parties to the newly salient relationship, as it ceased being a confrontation and became a dialogue.

Without being assuredly sufficient, reductions and revisions in perceptions and premises were genuinely needed as to both needs and interests if a dimished will and capacity for defense were to be accorded with an evolving situation. A widening diffusion of modern military technology went with a shrinkage of support facilities readily and reliably accessible to the United States in the world at large; a fictitious shortening of the physical frontier of empire by new declaratory foreign-policy and defense doctrines went with the frontier's functional extension, as economic threats supplemented military-political ones. In the empire's beginnings, its physical defense frontier had been extended by the Atlantic Alliance deflecting the key conflict with the Soviet Union to the Third World, in compliance with Western material strength and putative Soviet ideological strengths; in its twilight, the frontiers were acquiring new dimensions with every increase in the West's material vulnerability and psychological disarray, not least when compared with an ideologically discredited but militarily reconstructed and materially relatively self-sufficient Soviet Union. The new weakness of the West was expressed in doctrines and ideas liable to undercut the will to defense, without necessarily producing its fruits; in circumstances only problematically amenable to adjustments by solely economic measures and means, reduced will and capacity for self-defense could be at any moment faced with the stark option between submitting to economic aggression and implementing economic self-defense through acts having all the outward appearances of military aggression, between revitalizing the American empire on a new basis and allowing the Western industrial system to succumb to the ancient tendency for members of a disintegrating system to cultivate the means for deflecting threats from one to another. To be so diverted were, in the contemporary context, either economic aggression or the economic costs of nondefense against such aggression; were it to grow unchecked, the tendency could transpose into modern conditions the experiences of the decaying western and the surviving eastern parts of the military Roman empire in their respective hours of truth and need.

While the United States empire was undergoing a transformation akin to dissolution, basic reorientations were from efforts to control forces in most spheres to counterpoising powers mainly in the politico-military sphere; and from efforts at a single-handed management of the world economic and financial systems to taking part in its reform and revision on more diversified and flexible foundations as only one, if the strongest, among narrowly self-interested players. The effort in the politico-military sphere, to reduce critically significant threats to the net margins of potentially damaging hostile power that survived reciprocally neutralizing competitive interactions, would be facilitated by an increase in America's diplomatic options; the contrasting effort to enhance the reequilibrating potential of the still considerable margin of American economic superiority, ranging from technological innovation to massive food production, would require continuing readiness to apply politico-economic sanctions and inducements in relations with parties or partners in the industrial sector and also military sanctions in the last resort against acts of economic radicalism in a politically increasingly pragmatic and even conservative Third World.

v

The American empire appeared to have become unnecessary when the international, economic, and domestic stimuli behind the earlier expansion were replaced by a choice. The choice appeared to be between leadership in and for a beneficial new equilibrium internationally and isolation from the most disturbing features of the emergent global environment in the interest of a stabler new balance domestically; the first course spelled "interdependence" and its success promised keeping the essential benefits of world power, while shedding the costs of control and empire; the light at the end of the second course was "independence" offering an opportunity to fully exploit potent national resources without the costs of sharing and involvement. The pressures behind expansion were at least provisionally lessened in all three of the critical spheres.

The principal international determinants of expansion into world empire had been concerned with security, and operated through preclusion of major-power threat and frontier defense. In the new setting, pressures to preclude offensive encroachments by the major powers were reduced by the reciprocally offsetting Sino-Soviet competition over a widening range, and by the apparent stabilization of the nuclear stalemate. This new tripartite balance of power, along with half-powers of Western Europe and Japan, constrained the Soviet Union in Europe and the Middle East and both the Soviet Union and China in Asia. Neither of the greater powers seemed capable of effectively seeking succession to the American empire globally in short or medium terms. The same factors militated against overt military challenges to the imperial frontier in ways reminiscent of either the Korean or the Vietnam wars. Neither of the two Communist great powers could presumptively have an incentive to encourage a small power to reactivate the global balance of power militarily in any one place or region, including Korea itself, if only because it might thus improve America's political relations with the other Communist great power. And insofar as the developing triangular relationship among the major powers was both circumscribed and underpinned by the advances, however halting, toward relatively autonomous balance-of-power systems in the several regions, it was unlikely that local conditions of a kind that had found expression in the Vietnam conflict would either arise or give rise to comparable American assessments. With luck, global stability would be secured by a combination of nuclear stalemate and diplomatic flexibility among the great powers, while even an intensified competition in the several regions would be inherently stabilizable and be largely managed locally. Regional theaters would then become impervious to irreversible imperial-style takeovers by either Communist great power, without ruling out a gradual and moderate reapportionment of access and influence among all three of the great powers and the "half-powers."

An unresisted spontaneous process of deconcentration in the global balance of power could be expected to reduce the necessity for the United States to play a role in local defense. A concurrent measure of deliberate devolution in favor of friendly third-world middle powers—and, to a lesser degree, allied Western Europe and Japan—would restrict also American responsibility for such defense. It would do so, moreover, without a significant risk of any sudden and major influx of hostile power into the henceforth many-compartmented structure and many-sided interreactive dynamic of the world system.

Just as enlarging the range of available American options in defense and diplomacy, so merely recasting the elements in the capacity for economic sanctions and inducements permitted envisaging a movement from empire to equilibrium. The latter-day economic stimulus to expansion was associated with formalized protective imperialism; the apparently readily available alternatives to pursuing that route beyond its sketchy manifestations in the Nixon years included reversion to modified free trade internationally or (regressing still farther backward) to outright protectionism within national or continental confines. A new liberal economic system would remove nontariff barriers to trade among industrial countries and phase out governmental subsidies to agriculture within the United States; a revised complementarity of industrial and industrializing countries would evolve beyond relations between producers and processors of raw materials to exchanges of variously labor-, technology-, and innovation-intensive manufactures. And whereas the new system might include the extension of most-favored-nation treatment to the Communist countries in exchange for functionally comparable relaxations, it would even more certainly decentralize institutionally the responsibility for managing the economic and monetary systems worldwide. Foreign aid for traditionally backward countries tied to U.S. exports would become subordinate to ties of economic interdependence with the new rich; co-opting ex-revisionist third-world elites into the management and enjoyment of the new world economic order would decolonize these elites also psychologically and fully assimilate them culturally into Western-style industrialism.

Finally, the elite vacuum engendered in the United States by the trauma of the Vietnam-related elite replaced the one-time domestic stimuli to expansion with domestic influences adverse to keeping the empire in being. The transitional post-Vietnam foreign-policy elite was fluid and heterogeneous. Its make-up created the room, and enlarged the need, for a more enduring successor elite translating a recrystallized collective identity into a new dominant consensus on objects, techniques, and values of foreign policy. Elite fluidity favored deferring commitment to any well-defined foreign-policy strategy; being necessarily onerous in one way or another, a determinate strategy was as impossible to contrive among rival elite groups as it was potentially compromising for its proponents. Opportunistic manipulation of existing forces and proliferation of insubstantial formulae had a clear advantage in such circumstances over sustained generation and management of power for either imperial or national ends.

It will be easier to let go of empire in favor of a radically different structure of order than it is to surrender control to a qualitatively identical rival and successor. The Roman empire was succeeded in the West by the institutionalized Church and assimilated barbarians; the former was to become the spiritualized substitute for the role of Rome in centrally focused order, the latter looked as if they might become the Romanized replacements of empire within an incipient pluralistic system. The British empire was replaced by the U.S.-centered liberal economic system and military-political equilibrium, both comprising the former British dominions along with the metropole. The new order enabled Britain to depoliticize and, especially, demilitarize the prosecution of her perennial economic needs and stakes. At the later stage of America's retreat from empire, it became the American purpose to reallocate the costs of defense among major allies, while retaining most of the performance undergirding the essential hegemony and hierarchy within the principal alliance; to divide the labor of containing the rival (Communist) great powers between these powers, while being foremost in shaping the resulting equilibrium; and to subcontract peripheral order maintenance to local surrogates, while defining the basic norms of the new and increasingly multipolar order. Differences in the settings of their eclipse made the outgoing imperial states differently capable of shaping the future. Western Rome's bequest of the world to the Church had been less self-conscious and less immediately effective than was Britain's to America; and America had a clear advantage over Britain in any attempt to deflect the line of succession to an alternative format rather than to a more vital force. Superior U.S. assets included a material base that made potential independence or self-sufficiency into a key bargaining counter; the wider range of diplomatic options, determined by ranges and intensities of conflicts with and between other powers; and the centrality of geographic position in relation to the major land masses and oceans.

So favored, Americans could hope to fare better than their predecessors while fending off an imperial succession. They could hope to shed the military-political burdens, analogous to those of the later Roman empire, rather than further institutionalize the organizational structures and commitments of empire; and they could look forward to shedding the "colonial millstones" around their necks in an informal plural system, comparable to one that had briefly sustained a similar ambition of Britain's mid-Victorians in regard to the balances of both power and trade. In the radically different conditions of disorder, neither the ecclesiastical nor the secular elites of emergent Europe regarded either the Roman empire or a re-edition thereof as unnecessary. Both assumed instead that a substitute was required that would relate the universal principle, perpetuated by the Church, to the finite territorial principle, reaffirmed by the secular realms, while containing the ascendant principle of divisive nationality by the cosmopolitan principle of ethnic neutrality perfected by the late Roman empire. Much of the subsequent evolution of the European state system merely recorded the travail involved in transforming the presumed normative necessity into adaptations to a practical impossibility. Conversely, the British empire came to be perceived as unnecessary fairly quickly in retrospect, once the United States was manifestly insuring basic stability and access while Britain's declension was being softened by an Anglo-American special relationship that seemingly realized the earlier anticipation of global co-management. Completing the spectrum of attitudes based on either experience or expectations, America's "responsible" political elites, intellectual dissenters, rationalizing interpreters, and impressionable public joined together in treating the empire as unnecessary prospectively, even before it was actually dissolved or forced into dissolution. To perceive the British empire as unnecessary had been a factor in easing mental adaptation to its actual disappearance; in the American case, the perception was itself a factor contributory to a possibly final dismantling of empire. Whereas the British mechanism partook of self-consolation, the dominant American hypothesis was of the kind that amounts to self-fulfilling prophecy.

VI

Just as with the declining sense of need for empire, so the declining capacity to uphold empire encompasses all of the areas within which, under other signs, were previously lodged the well-springs of expansion. Decline and dissolution occur habitually under the converging impact of uneven pressures from great powers outside the empire, lesser forces within or without the empire, and strains within the metropole.

Big wars with great powers will weaken empires in depth even if the metropole has withstood the major pressure and ostensibly won the war. America's cold war with the Soviet Union (and Communist China) compares in that respect with the wars of the Roman empire with Sassanid Persia (in the third century A.D.) and Britain's two wars with Germany and one with Japan. Large conflicts with powers of comparable magnitude and technological civilization compel the mobilization of both material and psychic resources; they will consequently cause deep-seated moral fatigue and psychic or physical erosion that permit later subversion by lesser agents. Unlike the big wars, minor conflicts with qualitatively different lesser powers occasion a less full mobilization and expenditure of resources, but agitate greater overt resentments and inflict deeper latent decay when they are only half-won militarily and practically lost politically.

Coming on top of debilitating victory in major conflicts, terminal external blows will be commonly dealt directly or indirectly by actually or only metaphorically peripheral or barbarian lesser powers. The blows will be backed by force and pressure that may be inferior even to forces and pressures involved in small organized wars; and whereas such wars commonly enervate by combining half-victory with half-defeat, the inferior force or pressure will be applied in behalf of goals and tendencies of peripheral elements that are half-assimilated and half-alien in relation to the dominant traits and values of the imperial state. The duality of the challengers will rule out single-minded resistance by the imperial center, whose enfeeblement will matter more than can any enhancement of assault capacities resulting from the attackers' improved coordination or the attack's expanded perimeter, out into the sea against Rome or way into the metropoles themselves against both the British and the Roman empires. No less affecting will be the tendency for the small-scale peripheral forces to be somehow allied with both the greater-power rivals and the internal enemies of the receding empire. The "Germans" had been aligned in effect with the Huns of Atilla and many British colonial elites with the Axis powers; more recently, the radical postcolonial elites were similarly aligned with one or both of the Communist great powers in the political realm, while even conservative third-world regimes implicitly joined forces in the economic realm with America's major adversaries. The chain of more or less overt and conscious complicities is fully forged when the metropolitan counterelites have derived political strength from the outer barbarians or their replicas and the dominant political elites have subsided into intellectual bondage to the principal theses of their would-be successors. The latter bondage will condition policy not least after the counterelites have failed to parlay *de facto* alliance with the stronger external revolutionary force into formal power within the metropole; it will have helped by then to transmute the chain of alliances and complicities into a silken cord for strangulating the empire, as it were, without a sound.

Terminal blows will strike at the shell of an empire that has been hollowed out about equally by a prior exertion in conflicts and attendant erosion of consensus. Even a weak impact will then create an opening sufficient for allowing anti- and postempire doctrines to be drawn into the vacuum left behind by the receding imperial elite. And finally, the internally ramifying pressures by even weak peripheral forces will be fortified beyond their inherent strength insofar as the forces ostensibly uphold a purpose that is intrinsic to the larger empire, even while they assault the empire's structures. In the Roman case, the purpose was cultural assimilation and in the British emancipation for political self-government. It has been economic and related political development in the American system. The added potency makes resistance to the peripheral onslaught appear illegitimate on the plane of values, even as both empire and its defense have been rendered apparently unnecessary in the realm of facts.

In the external arena, decline and dissolution are a function of largely indirect interplays involving great or "civilized" and lesser or "barbarian" powers. In the narrower domestic sphere, decline and dissolution pertain instead to a direct interplay of dominant with insurgent or dissident political classes. An empire is ready for dissolution when three trends converge and add up to a drift. One such tendency is for the intellectual and other opinion-shaping elites to be hostile (when they are not subservient) to the exercise of power within their own polity and even more markedly by it (not least when such exercise is faltering). Another tendency is for dissident political counterelites to clothe in sweeping doctrine their natural instinct to exploit specific weaknesses in the established structures of power for the purpose of replacing those structures. And yet another, third tendency is for a crisis-shocked dominant elite to temporarily or lastingly lose faith in inherited or internalized guidelines for the exercise of power tested in previous spells of successful exercise. When they are effectively operative, the pragmatic guidelines of the political elite will be largely free of ethical and doctrinal rationales; the counterelites' pursuit of practical goals will overstate doctrinal rationalizations; and the intelligentsia's propensity to criticize on explicit ethical grounds will reflect a less translucent psychological motivation whenever an unavowed need and ineffectual desire for authority is diverted into a contrapuntal interplay between the cult of foreign idols and the condemnation of domestic incumbents.

The various elite trends will converge most disastrously for an empire when an escalating internal struggle for the material and immaterial fruits of power coincides with an outside conflict of limited dimensions. Among the examples is the conjunction of civil wars in the late Republic and succession conflicts in the late Empire with Roman wars of conquest or defense; in the British case, colonial imbroglios interacted with the intensifying conflict over Irish home rule and social change on the home front; and in the United States the racial and welfare issues discharged passions that ricocheted into the Asian war issue and vice versa. In such a setting, the intellectual elite and the ideological counterelite will find it easier to dissolve the inherited myths of the tribal polity as preliminary or concomitant to eroding its acquired imperial might; easier to lift themselves upward in the pyramid of social status by promoting the ascent of still-lower strata, and to rise in the scales of social power by depressing the authority of the state; and, even if the counterelite itself is conjointly dissolved as a coherent and effective force, easier to carry off the essentials of victory by diluting the identity, undermining the will to power, and reshaping the purpose of the dominant political or foreign-policy elite.

The facts and forces which encompass the dissolution of an empire constitute a seamless web wherein the climactic event, if any, will do duty for the nonexistent single cause. Erosion of institutions and functions sets in with the fading of the stimuli to expansion; and material exhaustion or emotional disgruntlement at the base are no more damaging than is the loss of nerve at the commanding heights. The immediate precipitant will be the perception of either an unbearable burden or an easier to bear alternative; the perception will translate diffuse decay and specific deficiencies into effective dissolution.

Deficiencies developed also in the United States not only among the original determinants of expansion but also in the supports maintaining the finished empire. One such prop is commonly the pivot or pinnacle of political authority, be it the deified emperor or the exalted Crown-in-Parliament or the "imperial" presidency, supported by the oligarchy of senatorial or aristocratic or just vaguely ruling-class (or "Brahmin") power. Another support is the critical military-strategic reserve, be it the unconquerable legion or commanding sea power or nuclear superiority. Yet another is the infrastructure of a self-confident imperial bureaucracy which, open to talents, is shielded from attacks inspired by criteria extraneous to its specific missions and traditions. And likewise supportive is the magnetic attraction which the center exerts on the peripheries, over and beyond any shared empire ideology, by such boons and benefits as freely accessible imperial citizenship, freely traded goods, or freely granted material aid and physical security for empire loyalists.

Even if it were possible to make the requisite fine distinctions, it would not be decisive whether first to weaken was the material or the moral basis of empire, its institutional and organizational structure, or its external setting; whether external wars or internal contentions were more responsible for moral decay and material decline and for steering both in the direction of moral-political dissolution. And if the perceptions of whether empire is practically necessary and the pronouncements on its being morally legitimate are commonly interwoven in the process of the empire's becoming destructible, so are the views on whether the empire is still effectively manageable internally and defendable externally instrumental in formulating the seemingly abstract criteria of need and right themselves.

Impenetrable as the empirical cause may be, however, the possibility remains of a historically informed judgment. The judgment bears on the arena outside the murky sphere of the right to, and the need for, empire as contrasted with alternative structures of order; and it concerns the side to which the balance between outside pressures and domestic solvents has tipped in the final phase of dissolution. Empire can fail dramatically before outside pressure, as did the last redoubt of Eastern Rome. It can combine fall with dissolution under a near-even conjunction of forces within and without the empire and the metropole, after a gigantic last encounter, as did the British. Or the quite sudden fading of empire can be due principally to internal factors, as has been the American case. The fall, in the first case, can be judged heroic, because the pressure was both resisted and irresistible; the combination of fall and dissolution in the second was honorable, because it was long avoided and in the long run inevitable. Contrasting with both, the apparently concluding events of empire in the third instance have been mainly uninspiring and would be humiliating for the imperial polity if they did not allow for doubt about their finality and ultimate significance.

Whereas the American empire had not been expressly acknowledged even as a series of official doctrines attended its expansion, it seemed to be stealthily abandoned while other doctrines were being enunciated to screen its constriction. Truman's doctrine for the Eastern Mediterranean culminated in Johnson's war for keeping the door effectively open to Southeast Asia; Nixon's finally unimplemented Guam doctrine was further deflated in Ford's unremembered Pacific doctrine; and the latter was only one among the declaratory statements on continuing American world role, about equal in their weight and impact to such erstwhile exercises in ersatz diplomacy as Hay's notes in favor of the Open Door and Stimpson's doctrine of opposition to closing that door by aggression. The empire's nonrecognition was effected by using value-laden terms like "free world" and neutral ones like "involvement"; its abandonment was camouflaged as retrenchment and disengagement. The manifold benefits of empire had been enjoyed without recognizing the connection. A belated, and then adverse, acknowledgment of the existence of an empire was integral to the very process of its abandonment. Recognition of the fact entailed legitimately the obligation to inspect more closely its moral price and material cost. But the suddenly awkward truths about the past could seemingly be borne only by giving the lie to the view that the flaws were organically of a piece with the accomplishments. The previously passive or condoning public would once again absolve itself by immolating the more active performers of deeds to be left behind; Vietnam and all that was associated with it was to be the Vichy of the simon-pure conquerors of evil in a bigger and unquestionably just war.

When the American empire was dismantled, it was in response less to compelling pressures and more to an irresistible temptation. Dissolution was, in the last resort, an abdication. And the seemingly compelling causes of decline, contemporaneously identified as deep-seated and structural, were in large part also but the symptoms of a somewhat shallow and subjective public desire for either release or just change. To affirm abandonment as a matter of official decisions reflecting public desires neither invalidates the analysis nor nullifies the acts and events understood or understandable in terms of decline and dissolution; it qualifies both, however, and makes it possible to raise questions about the finality of the dissolution. To the extent that the dissolution of the American empire was more a matter of free, uncoerced decision than had been the disappearance of either the Roman or the British, to that same extent it was reversible by the exposure of the determining conditions to change.

CONCLUSION. *The American Experience with Empire: Universality and Uniqueness*

For the American empire to resume its interrupted career, to reexpand in scope or institutional depth, one or several conditions would have to be present, converting reasons for the slackening of energies into so many stimuli and replacing reactions to depression with responses to dangers.

In the central balance impinging on national security, both Soviet Russia and Communist China, acting separately or in restored coalition, might stimulate a counterexpansive or consolidating American response. Whether a genuinely hegemonic drive expressing a predatory mood or reacting preclusively to a denial of parity may yet inspire major-power policies has become the key background question of international politics. It controls the possibility or probability of a qualitative change in directions that would make the strategy of classic balance of power only residually viable and the structures of empire obsolete. But even if the quest for hegemony proved to be anachronistic for major industrial powers, it might still remain a commonplace objective for lesser powers acting from an earlier stage of politico-economic development to authoritatively integrate regional arenas or preventively contain their own liability to disintegration along the multiple fissures or cleavages (ethnic or tribal as well as economic and political) besetting most of the Third World. As an international determinant of reinvolvement, finally, a regional vacuum of power inviting major-power penetration dangerous to global equilibrium might match or outdo an excess in regionally coercive middle-range power, to be contained for the sake of protecting the smallest powers against extinction in the interest of either an intraregional or the interregional balance of power.

Both hegemony bids and fragmentation on the part of middle-sized powers could readily translate into events in the Third World causing economic hardships for the industrial world, including the United States. A dynamic American response would then have to ensue to protect domestic (or allied) prosperity already lowered in critical areas (e.g., food and fuel) as a result of the prior disengagement. Efforts to deal with internal distress would point to pulling together the scattered pieces of protective (formalized) imperialism; the aim of orderly economic expansion would suggest pushing on with free-trading (informal) imperialism. Finally, either conjointly with setbacks for international security and economic stability, or independently of either, new impulses might be forthcoming from the American domestic dynamics. A renovated political class might reinvigorate the American posture as it reacted to the leadership weaknesses of either traumatized traditional or time-serving transitional foreign-policy elites. The new elite's complexion and mood would then combine with the state of the external environment to determine whether an empire-type American reexpansion would be largely unilateralist or, broadly speaking, Atlanticist; and whether consolidation would be chiefly geographic, constricting the larger prior scope, or institutional, revising the prior equations of authority and autonomy.

For an institutionally reconsolidated empire to be distinctly multilateral, more change would have to take place in the function of the Atlantic Alliance. The roles of alliances as regulators of the balance of power by interallied checking on and of individual gains, as restraints on forward allies by the major ally's conservatism, and as shields for insecure allies, came to comprise their functioning as sanctuaries for system-transforming policies by dissatisfied allies. In conceivable future circumstances, transformation might be redirected from enhancing multipolarity in the international system (as manifest in the Gaullist phase of the Atlantic Alliance) to promoting a more genuinely pluralist make-up of a participant empire. Evolution along that line in the function of America's major alliance or alliances would then have to coincide with the maturing of American nationalism from a parochial into a more open, imperial variety. Such a metamorphosis would end the narrowly nationalist era of the United States, begun when the original ex-colonies rejected self-confinement within the Atlantic coastal realm or system in favor of an expanding empire; and it might offer a more attractive alternative to the possibility of having to regress in the future from the American world empire into a narrowed and narrowing regional orbit.

There has been a continuing tension between a regional and a world-wide scope for American expansion and empire, just as different roles were open to the United States in various global configurations, more realistically before than after World War I, and possibly again in the aftermath of the cold war. Determining how real the role alternatives were entails assessing the actually achieved against the necessary extent of American expansion, in historical perspective as much as in hypothetical speculation about the future. If the fundamental American choice in foreign affairs was between empire and equilibrium, it was   *eo ipso* a choice between intermittent responses to pressures and incentives, eventuating in fitful expansion and contraction, and the employment of resources and espousal of risks in behalf of a more constantly alert and active diplomacy. As is usual, contention over the fundamental strategy options was appeased by alternating between them within more or less prolonged time spans, even as conflicts over the specific directions of expansion were reconciled by eventually combining all; less usual was the frequency with which the exhaustive character of the two basic options (of empire or equilibrium) was being denied in an effort to extend further the already vast American leeway for choice, and as both cause and consequence of the failure to identify the options clearly enough and pose them insistently enough.[1]

Steadily active involvement would have facilitated self-limitation; liability to intermittently ongoing expansion was ultimately caused instead by the always reappearing urge to self-isolation. It was possible in principle to consolidate initially, within and with the aid of a dynamic North American balance of power, the well-defined coastal realm won in the War of Independence. The realm depended for economic viability and strategic security on only marginal enlargements in the St. Lawrence-Newfoundland area in the north and in the lower Mississippi and, possibly, Cuba in the south. (Similarly, Rome confined to Latium would have had to be safeguarded in the Adriatic and England, juxtaposed with independent Wales and Scotland, safeguarded from the seaside in Ireland and across the Channel). The both safeguarding and stimulating balance of power would have comprised other autochthonous entities, progressively emancipated from European control by way of asserted independence (from Spain) or consented imperial devolution (by Britain). The possibility was abrogated for all practical purposes when the fledgling United States acquired Louisiana as an outright, non-

1. On basic American foreign-policy options, see the Introduction to George Liska, *Quest for Equilibrium* (Baltimore: The Johns Hopkins University Press, 1977), pp. xi–xiii; the same volume discusses the several functions of alliances (chaps. 1 and 10).

autonomous dependency. Once annexation foreclosed an autonomous course for that huge area, even while loose confederation had been discarded for the American political system, further expansion became inevitable. American pretensions and encroachments bred enough of impotent opposition to engender as many stimuli and gave rise to sufficiently irritating resentment to create a reliable supply of pretexts for further expansion.

Effective countervailing power to America's could be found henceforth only outside the North American continent; and for the growing United States to cope safely with the potentially counterpoising great powers in the long run on the basis of parity as the minimum, the necessary resource and (consequently) next possible resting place was a two-regional empire extending through insular positions into the Atlantic and Caribbean toward Europe and in the Pacific toward Asia. A purely continental United States, whether including or excluding Canada, was by the same token neither a sufficient compass nor a logical terminus for expansion. Underlying the case for the continental solution were cultural cohesion, constitutional propriety, and economic coherence (in the sense of agricultural-commercial balance); they all ran afoul, however, of the vital criterion of strategic security within a viable balance of power comprising the world policy-minded Europeans and Japanese and conditioned by the existing military technology and economic expectations.

American expansion could have stopped thereafter indefinitely within the bounds of regional empire and interregional equilibrium. But just as Louisiana had materially linked the Atlantic coastal realm with the two-regional core-empire by making obsolete the former and impractical a scope narrower than the latter, so the Philippine annexation linked the regional empire to the global one. It did so at first only symbolically, however, by advertising periodically surfacing material incentives and anticipating future strategic vulnerabilities. If the reasons for the annexation gave a preview of the deteriorating strategic balances (reducible to the central one in Europe), the circumstances attending the Asian conquest testified to reviving sentimental ruling-class biases (reducible to attitudes toward England) in the United States. Both made the regional empire unstable, or hard to stabilize, within its limited scope and released pressures for global expansion.

By-passing transient opportunities for self-limitation, the American polity progressed from an inchoate regional state system (of the original colonies) within an empire to a world empire within an inchoate global system of states. At the latter point the United States could have synthesized the several traditional or innate opposites in an empire that was both land- and sea-power oriented, military and mercantile, central-systemic and peripheral, centrally coordinating and respectful of effective autonomies. Such an empire would be universal in character to a previously unequaled extent and might become so in potential scope as it was progressively further decentralized; it might point to a way to end the indefinite sequence of approximations and second-rate alternatives to both *imperium* and *libertas*. In actual fact, however, the American performance inclined in different time periods and situational contexts toward stressing alternatively one or the other sides of the paired characteristics and failed as a result to achieve either coherence for an accomplished individual uniqueness or cosmic relevance for aspirations to universality.

The initial, preindependence period had been one of fused maritime and mercantile conception in an (American) empire within (the British) empire; the subsequent shift was to land as the salient feature in the continental expansion. But there was no concurrent shift to an essentially military empire, not least because the early expansion's direction was away from the then central system. The emphasis on land was reminiscent of Rome, to the point of involving the issue of plantation slaves; the mercantile emphasis was more like that of Britain. Reliance on sea power for both trade and triumph in war and peacetime diplomacy resurfaced when the United States had extended itself, like Britain as well as Rome before, into the central and in the circumstances Eurocentric balance of power. It so extended itself at first only marginally, in the Pacific-Asian area, and only in due course also as a key actor in the Atlantic-European arena. The involvements carried with them a shift from mercantile to military emphasis in a fitful motion, culminating in World War II and its outgrowth—America's second overseas empire.

At that point, the military trend was consolidated by a reversion to land-power emphases in the guise of a massive overseas presence of American "legions" and the pervasive overseas influence of America's nearest facsimile of civilian and military proconsuls. Like Great Britain's before, the basic capacity of the United States to involve itself with effect in the central system had taken shape during a period of self-insulation from the European balance of power. Thereafter, America asserted herself from a continental basis closely analogous to that of Rome in Italy and in the Western Mediterranean (including North Africa). The directors of American statecraft were neither able nor willing, however, to consummate (by transforming Europe as a whole) the resulting drives and pulls, similar to the incentives and imperatives that had led Rome from preeminence to imperium in the Eastern Mediterranean Hellenistic system. If Germany was twice America's Macedon in Europe, an also Asiatic Soviet Russia proved to be more effective than had been one-time "Asia" (or Syria) and less passive than Parthia. Consequently, the American experience of empire could not but gravitate toward the British model as American expansion by-passed the but half-dominated and consequently

polarized center of the system into its peripheries. Direct involvement
and presence on land did not, however, immediately begin giving way to
mainly offshore maritime deployments; neither did economic stakes
automatically change from having been incidental to a primarily military
empire (with chiefly strategic emphases) into becoming causative incentives behind a primarily mercantile empire with conspicuous, but none
the less only incidental, military consequences. Economic consequences of
strategic considerations were more important than were purely economic
incentives in the origins, the course, and the sequelae of World War II,
while economic considerations had been salient, albeit within strict limits, in the Spanish-American War and the American entry into World
War I, before inspiring efforts to move past the cold war out of the world
empire.

   Throughout, oscillation in emphases on land-based and sea-based and
on military and economic power was a function of America's relation to
the changing character of the European, or Eurasian, balance of power.
Land-power emphasis had initially reflected America's immunity to a
stalemated central balance and marked subsequently her direct involvement in an either deadlocked or fatally lopsided balance; stress on sea
power (if on any kind of power) reflected, by contrast, repeatedly a more
marginal relationship to a central balance that was relatively dynamic
and autonomous, largely impervious to impact by an either only rising or
provisionally receding American empire, because needing neither the
additional outlet nor the extra weight with sufficient urgency. Roughly
corresponding shifts from military to mercantile, or from strategic to
economic, emphases reflected also the various degrees in which Americans
deemed sufficient their capacity for either economic autarky or politico-
militarily unsupported access to commerce abroad. Insofar as optimistic
assessments were grounded mainly in domestic considerations, feelings of
economic self-sufficiency or invulnerability encouraged recurrences of
politico-military irresponsibility. But complacency failed repeatedly to
survive the acid test of an actuality comprising either real or only hypothetical threats to America's access outside her continental domain and
regional hegemonic orbit.

   While it underwent such alternating emphases, the American experience evolved, even more markedly than had the British, from the empire
of settlement (on the American continent for both countries) to an empire of only indirect or informal control. Beyond that very broad similarity in fundamental technique, the geostrategic pattern of American
expansion resembled the Roman model more closely than the British.
Rome's early competitors in Italy equaled the European colonial powers
and Indian tribes on the North American continent. Rome's subsequent
progression to mastery over the Western Mediterranean was equaled by
America's in the Western Hemisphere. If the price had been paid by

Carthaginian sea power in one case, it was charged against Great Britain and, secondarily, Chile in the other. Roman power had been extended toward the adjoining Dalmatian coast into Illyria as the strategic link and counter to Macedon; mainly Cuba in the Atlantic and Hawaii and the Philippines in the Pacific were to play the same roles in relation to Germany and Japan. If Rome was to be drawn, as a result of earlier expansion, into the Hellenistic balance-of-power system, so was the United States to be drawn into the European system and, via Japan the second time around, the Eurasian system. And, finally, Roman dominion had advanced by dint of both external and internal political dynamics ever further east into Asia and into the barbarian West. America's involvement advanced correspondingly into the Afro-Asian Third World and veered back to Latin America.

Parallels in the paths and patterns of American with Roman expansion were not necessarily matched in the area of either style or spirit. They were anchored instead in a comparable configuration, though not necessarily in precisely matching weights, of outside power and pressures. The pragmatic mentality behind the varying motives and modes of expansion was more intimately shared with Britain's and was rooted in comparably constituted, though (again) not identically assorted or compounded, elements of national power and societal values. The similarity with Britain tended to reduce the practical bearing of the similarity with Rome and may have nullified it in ultimate effect. Both similarities were, moreover, qualified by significant differences between America on one side and Rome and Britain on the other.

Different was the global environment as well as the domestic scene, the policy-determining external system as well as the ruling-class situation within. The common denominator of the differences was the comparative weakness, in the American case, of survival threats to either security or sustenance as clearly defined environmental pressures responsible for likewise well-defined domestic polarities relative to a ruling class. When they are determinate, such pressures and polarities will habitually act as the clearest determinants of external action and the resulting evolution.

America's geopolitical distance from a constraining international system comprised both her physical remoteness and the ineffectiveness of the European powers other than Britain initially present on the (North) American continent. America's initial advantage was also a major drawback in the longer view, however, insofar as it ruled out a full equivalent of what Carthage had been for Rome in the critical phase forming American values and attitudes. That the deficiency was vaguely felt showed whenever the young American statecraft exaggerated beyond reason the postindependence British threat (from the Caribbean south to the overland Canadian rear), the Spanish threat, and the more or less associated

Indian or Mexican threats. How weak the environmental constraints actually were was shown in the Civil War, the one and only critical threat to the imperial American Republic. British favor for the South and the French intrigue in Mexico were alike incompetent and equally insufficient: the former, to set the Southern Confederacy on an independent imperial career, competitive with the North's and more authentic in its feudal-aristocratic-agricultural original foundation; the latter, to confront the reunited states with an effective indigeneous rival in the Western Hemisphere. The failures made it impossible to draw gradually either the North alone or the United States as a whole into a confining, but also expanded and dynamized, central system. America was sucked instead, much later, into domineering expansion of her own by a precariously stalemated, embattled, and reserve-poor system. Failing the Civil War, it took Pearl Harbor and the cold war to present the American Rome with Carthage-like threats in the variously ill-fitting shapes of Asia's Japan and Soviet "Asia"; a fear-inspiring counterweight to complacency delayed for once America's tendency to evade prolonged systemic involvement on a rebound from brief warlike exertions, without fully compensating for the earlier and protracted deficiency.

During the earlier period, a policy dilemma of Britain as the principal and, considering the original's initial make-up, intrinsically genuine Carthage-substitute had aggravated the effect of the deficiency by concealing its extent. Being simultaneously hostile to the new United States and to the old Continental powers, British statecraft's objective was to exclude the Europeans from the Western Hemisphere without thereby enabling the Americans to freely expand to the point when they both could and would expel Britain herself. The irreconcilable duality in Britain's purpose kept alive the ambivalence in America's perception of Britain herself, as both target and protector, all the easier to identify as a threat the less urgently or avowedly the former mother country was welcome as a shield or buffer; it helped neutralize real if diffuse psychic insecurities with a largely imaginary but focused sense of physical insecurity, as a supplement to purely doctrinal means of fostering collective self-reassurance. The mechanism served the United States well, and may have served it too well.

The major consequence of insufficient environmental constraints, itself fraught with a range of secondary consequences, was the insufficient consolidation of an original ruling class. Only a prolonged, and in the end successful, testing by an external danger could have helped overcome a geographically and economically conditioned cleavage within the heterogeneous political class that had masterminded the ascension of the several American colonies to independence. Only a protracted ordeal would have been capable of entrenching in a likewise prolonged trusteeship the more martially qualified and politically stable landed Southern aristocracy, giving that feudal element the strength and the time to assimilate members of the mercantile wing in terms of both interests and values, at least in part. Instead, transactions between ruling-class segments and among geographic sections projected domestic power plays into an expansionary process that was precipitate and, when compared with the Anglo-Roman model, may have been premature. An uncommonly early ambiguity beclouded as a result the respective primacy of international and domestic determinants of expansion, compounding corresponding uncertainties with regard to security and sustenance. An assured trusteeship of a materially saturated and politically unassailable ruling class will be initially best suited to contain domestic dynamics and channel the outside projection of that dynamic. The same early condition will help politicize even essentially economic stakes, whereas sustained polarization between the ruling class and a gradually rising mercantile middle class (on top of a slowly awakening populace) will subsequently compel such politicization. Either ruling-class primacy or inter-class polarity will politicize economics more reliably than could the fluid elite and interest-group pluralism prevalent in the United States.

In the actual course of events, the initially near-classic pattern of the domestic American scene was quickly changed in favor of near-kaleidoscopic mutations on the part of plural, co-dominant or alternately dominant, elite groups. But, even after the Founding Fathers had become a mythical ruling-class substitute, America was not wholly devoid of residual, periodically recurrent, and (in crises) popularly respected, ruling-class elitism, with political pretensions based on social pedigree, economic performance, or ethnic parentage. However imperfect, the approximations related the American domestic scene loosely to the classic ruling-class pattern as it bears on expansion into empire and its maintenance. Similarities to Roman and British domestic dynamics were not sufficient, however, to engender in America a dominant ruling-class ethos capable of imparting internal unity or coherence to either expansion or the resulting empire, any more than similarities with British economic dilemmas could nullify differences in the way domestic and external economic environments were aligned for the two Anglo-Saxon polities. Anything comparable to an imperial ruling-class ethos in American history was as a result both transient and insubstantial because either imitative or derivative: imitative of nonrepresentative early native (Hamiltonian) or contemporaneous foreign (British) values in the first empire wave; and derivative from the actual process of acquiring an empire after World War II, albeit in the image of a predominantly corporate or bureaucratic elite.

Yet more serious than derivation of ethos from the fact of empire was the discontinuity or discrepancy between empire and ethos in kind, which impeded the derived ethos from maturing into a separate and sustaining force. The shortcoming was due to limitations in both cultural adaptability (reflected in the empire's delayed recognition) and time in which to adapt (on account of the empire's foreshortened growth). The British empire had been sustained by correcting the mercantile taste for the opportune with an aristocratic stress on obligation, while the accumulated political sagacity of a self-perpetuating oligarchy struck a rough balance between the two perspectives. The Roman empire had embodied in its apogee yet more intimately the interplay of the military ethos and the materialistic ethic of the senatorial ruling class. In America by contrast, neither the acquisitive predisposition of the society at large nor the dominant elites' cost-calculating and risk-limiting propensities were adapted to the requirements of a preeminently military empire; the cause of empire was bound to suffer when the imperial polity's materialistic ethic, far from being offset by either an aristocratic or a military ethos, was compounded by the intellectually mercantile mentality of the corporate-cum-bureaucratic imperial elite.

Stressing material incentives was plausible in such a setting; the emphasis remained problematic, not least because the ambiguous economic factor itself is commonly both an incentive and an incident to otherwise constituted aims and achievements. If the economic determinant is neither artificially overburdened nor artfully overrefined, it will be seen as decisively affecting imperial expansion only in the earliest "predatory" and last "protective" phases. The early fusion of sustenance and security needs typically consummates expansion under the impulse of buoyant vital energies; the later fusion will coincide with decline of empire, be an attempted response to it, and will consequently give rise typically to but inconclusive inclination or unconsummated tendency toward expansive remedies in space or depth. In other periods and circumstances, the economic factor will impact positively on expansion and maintenance of empire only if the political class is able to compensate via empire-created opportunities the domestic self-restraint of the middle class (e.g., Britain in the late nineteenth century and intermittently in a modified fashion also the United States); if the populace can be appeased by establishing a credible link between expansion abroad and controlled material prosperity or progress at home (Republican Rome extensively and briefly also the post–World War II United States); or if empire managers erect a sufficient strategic framework to serve as the direct safeguard of, and an indirect impetus to, private economic initiatives (Britain in and past the mid-nineteenth century and the United States past the mid-twentieth century) or if supporting the framework itself elicits public commitment to the use of economic instruments (e.g., the United States in the cold war) in a widening compass. Without such political mediation or strategic matrix, economic expansionism will not lead to empire when occurring from strength (e.g., interwar United States), any more than late-empire economism from weakness can alone sustain past accomplishments in empire-building for long (interwar and post–World War II Britain, post–Vietnam United States).

Economic causation will plausibly appear to predominate throughout only if an essentially materialistic view narrows power to its material component as the ultimately controlling incentive to, and reduces power to wealth as the ultimate object of, self-assertion; if an idealistic view equates empire with corruption in the last analysis and reduces corruption to economic temptations and manifestations; or if a practical necessity reduces a polity to seeking constantly on the outside an always precarious access to the wherewithals of material existence.

The American course of expansion and empire could be properly understood even less than the British and the Roman by resorting to either form of reduction. Britain's imperial expansion, its climax and decline, were readily subdivisible on material grounds into differently mercantilistic and liberally free-trading phases; the dialectic between and within the two basic economic doctrines and practices has been more nuanced and has been even less controlling of political acts at critical junctures in the case of an America more self-sufficient than Britain as a market and less continuously instrumental in shaping the larger economic environment. Similarly, it is not wholly false to subdivide the Roman empire, within a broad view of the economic factor, into early-Republican virtues and late- and post-Republican corruption; likewise more complex has been the recurrent alternation in America between collective self-attribution of exemplary virtue and compulsive self-purification from materially or morally contaminated or otherwise tainted actions, implemented collectively even when not so concerted. While the two themes in self-perception have interacted constantly, one or the other theme tended to predominate in successive phases of each expansionist wave. An initiating illusion of innocence, not uncommonly sustaining predation, culminated habitually in the illusion of omnipotence; and when either the use of seemingly unlimited power or the need to adjust to the revealed limitations of policy had dwarfed the affirmation of unqualified right, self-doubt would replace self-satisfaction and the sense of omnipotence would veer into the feeling or attitude of impotence. If impotence has not meant so far inability to strike at a mortal enemy in the last resort, it has meant the incapacity to strike and perpetuate a viable balance between predation and preclusion; between indulgence in an expansionary drive and endurance of the expansive dynamic of effective defense; between sustaining a necessary role abroad and soliciting an ideal equilibrium at home.

Self-consciously aristocratic leaders of the American democracy in the 1890s tried to imitate contemporary British imperialism. Their effort was even less effective and lasting than had been either the sensitivity to philhellenic ideas of the early Roman imperialists or the pragmatically disciplined urge of the British imperial elite to assimilate the indigenously derived ethos to the intellectually idealized Roman exemplar. But the later American failure to match (mercantile) ethos and (military) empire showed that differentiating oneself self-consciously from past imperial models may be a still less constructive state of mind than studied imitation had been. The first and brief period of overseas expansion had mirrored an oversupportive or permissive international system, combining only token resistance to American dynamism with a hypertrophy of readily imitable expansionist symbols and slogans. More critical for the more organically evolved second overseas empire was intellectual insecurity or skepticism regarding its real (as well as legitimate) motives or determinants. Both forms of doubt were rooted in the American background of a highly ambiguous relationship between predatory drive and preclusive expansion, finding its fullest expression in the predatory taint that will attach to even preclusive responses to threats to economic well-being as distinct from physical security. Moreover, a permissive international system had one trait in common with plural ruling-class structures. Both stimulated the early American inclination to grandiloquence about imagined threats, as a substitute for the solid grandeur achieved in withstanding real ones. The result was a record of frequent abuses of a legitimate rationale. The record was always susceptible of exposing to moral doubt or moralistic indictment officially affirmed grounds for either preclusive-defensive expansion or forceful maintenance of empire; in a relaxed environment, the temptation became overwhelming to downgrade even genuine security issues into mere replays of the artificial scares or contrived occasions for sordid gain remembered from the past.

A prolonged absence of even but localized major security threats after the early pioneering days had been responsible for advancing the onset of many-faceted intergroup and intersectional transactions; and the same absence was responsible for the more prolonged persistence of the myth of national uniqueness. Just as essential security failed to produce a pre-eminent ruling class, it also failed to compel manifestly commonplace remedial responses to challenges from the outside. Ruling-class deficiency fostered group pluralism; comparative safety proliferated ever-changing but uniformly ideological rationales for American expansion;[2] and the deficiency was like the hypertrophy in that both harbored motives and designs less exalted and disinterested than were the averred ones. The key element in the myth of American uniqueness has been a both egalitarian and competitive individualism sustaining group pluralism. Individualism constituted the common denominator for the plurality of

2. See Albert K. Weinberg, *Manifest Destiny* (Baltimore: The Johns Hopkins University Press, 1935).

doctrines rationalizing expansion. It served also to lend verisimilitude to the companion myth of a single-factor, economic, causation and underpinning of American imperialism. Stressing the economic factor made it easier to explain expansion as the natural expression of the problem-solving pragmatic mood whenever the more distinctively political determinants were indeterminate, and easier to condemn expansion whenever the moral ambiguity of political action was overshadowed by the conviction of the empire's immorality.

All rationalizations of expansion had worked well for an early continental expansion that was as arduous for its pioneering spearheads as it was facile for the supporting official statecraft. All turned sour sooner or later in the politically ambiguous world outside the continental bounds. Hypocrisy as to one's motives and goals allowed them to appear qualitatively different from any other imperial expansionist's; the same hypocrisy proved eventually to be only the other side of hesitancy regarding the proper response to the motives and the goals of others; and jointly the two persistently beclouded the issue of the legitimate arena and proper manifest structures for America's "manifest destiny." An unceasing and often complacent self-examination was not surprisingly the offspring of America's peculiar opulence in material goods and feasible goals; it was just as fittingly the surfeit's torment.

Uncertainty about and vacillation between basic assessments and related strategies produced at all stages variations in the empire's actually extant or apparently unavoidable spatial compas and internal control mechanism. In the long run and most basically, however, the hesitancies about strategies and structures were reducible to, while aggravating, ambiguities in the spirit that inhabited the American polity and molded the intermittent empire-type expansion. Accordingly, the latter-day decline of the empire grown to world scale derived in large part from the failure to recognize the dominion and acknowledge its implications for what they were. The climactic nonrecognition of empire externally was inseparable from the long-standing refusal to recognize the existence of a social hierarchy internally; while ascendant, the empire had not been self-consciously linked to a status-sustaining political role for a domestically retreating ruling class any more than its sustenance-enhancing economic utility for the lower classes was laid bare when the empire came under attack in a war setting. At that point, conjointly with a belated and then negative recognition of the empire, the prior failure to acknowledge its identity in time had contributed to an omission and a self-limitation. The omission was in the refusal to offer the public (contemporaneously described as the "silent majority") the fullness of choice between upholding empire at one cost and jettisoning it at another; the self-limitation was to confine appeals for endurance to the modalities of the empire's dismantlement.

A self-consciously conservative administration failed in the process to seize upon an opportunity to reach over the heads of a dispirited liberal political elite and professional middle class to the masses (including the conservative lower middle class) on the basis of the defense of empire in exchange for disciplining the mode of social change. The failure was as much the consequence of the administration not perceiving itself self-confidently as being the inception of a legitimate substitute ruling elite as it was the cause of its not becoming such; it unleashed the full effects of prior deficiencies in the stimuli to sustained effort in all the critical arenas: in the international arena, insofar as the foreshortened rise and ebb of the cold war could neither substitute for prolonged insecurity nor instill a prolonged response to a provisionally overcome mortal danger; in the domestic arena, insofar as the interclass dynamic in the late cold-war/imperial phase was circumscribed by the ruling elite being blinded to the link between internal and external order-maintenance by its liberal ideology and to that between politico-military exertion and economic access by the ever-reappearing strengths and elasticities of the mature American economic system, inspiring the dominant political ethos of prudential adaptability; and in the strictly economic domain, insofar as the normally expansion-fostering features of economism in protective imperialism were born of a crisis at a time when the degree of revulsion from the implications of empire exceeded the degree of intensity of the economic crisis itself.

Nonacknowledgment of the American empire at a critical juncture may have constituted an avoidable superficial error, spawned by an ingrained group determination to reject America's commonality. Alternatively, an unwavering group instinct may have rightly affirmed the sense of America's individuality against a contrary superficial impression. Each of the two basic assessments will have implications for the validity of any analysis that postulates the comparability of America and her empire with other powers and their dominions.

Such notable differences between the Roman and the British empires as, respectively, military and mercantile, based primarily on land power and on sea power, superseding and merely impinging on the central system of the day, and progressively centralized and decentralized, were bound to enhance the value of any unifying generalities about evolutionary patterns and operative mechanisms that could be abstracted nonetheless; and any such generalities were plausible points of departure for examining the so-far traversed path of the United States in the perspective of expansion tending to empire. America's failure so far to forge a coherent new order capable of universalization out of the several characteristics and tendencies peculiar to empires was equally apt to diminish the practical value of the American experience insofar as it tended toward realizing one of the great utopias haunting mankind. And America's peculiar differences from the historical prototypes of empire were, on balance, even more certainly responsible for reducing her capacity to move a real-world empire beyond a partial and provisional realization. Taken together, America's long-term propensities to change and her unsteady latter-day performance may have reduced also the interpretive utility, or theoretical value, of projecting the American experience against an analytic framework, or ideal model, patterned on those of acknowledged and authentic empires. But, again, a refusal to idealize the American historical record as unprecedented and unique, in conformity with the orthodox view, has not depended for vindication upon a compelling counteridealization of that experience as one conforming in every particular with variously ancient patterns.

Elements of uniformity with the two older empires individually and conjointly appear clearly enough to a viewpoint adjusted to disengage broad outlines in sweeping retrospect; they suffice to identify America's career as partaking in important respects of the empire phenomenon in its traditional meaning. Moreover, the disengaging of divergences from past patterns itself will perform a useful service whenever findings intimate, to the satisfaction of some, why the United States has failed so far to measure up to the challenge of empire in attitude or action; and when they reassuringly suggest to others why the United States has managed to avoid and may continue to evade the fullness of the imperial predicament with the aid of peerless internal resilience, unprecedented environmental latitude, or both.

An effort to uncover both a common and a coherent basic anatomy of superficially diverse empires neither had to explain nor could it explain America's checkered career in world affairs in all of its particulars. Notably the cleavage and embattled balancing act between states leaning primarily on land-based power and those with a chiefly maritime orientation have been sufficiently critical both for the multiple state system and for the role of the United States in that system to loom large in America's total experience.[3]

A balance-of-power analysis complements logically the analysis of and from expansion to empire, just as the realities of balancing relate to the fact of empire. They do so not only by way of countervailing resistance to immoderate expansion but also by the advantage which an initially marginal position relative to the central balance of power (and, incidentally, dominant civilization) of the day has had for a long line of future

3. See George Liska, *Quest for Equilibrium* (Baltimore: The Johns Hopkins University Press, 1977), for the other line of analysis. The balance-of-power alternatives for American foreign policy in the global and the regional settings are also discussed in the author's *Beyond Kissinger* (Baltimore: The Johns Hopkins University Press, 1975) and *States in Evolution* (Baltimore: The Johns Hopkins University Press, 1973).

metropoles of empires-to-be—including Rome, Britain, and the United States. Moreover, combining the two complementary foci for viewing the present in the light of analogies with the past constrains the range of plausible anticipation about the future. That constraint is particularly useful at a time of mutually reinforcing tensions. One such tension has emerged between tendencies toward stabilizing imperial control and toward flexible balancing on the part of the principal beneficiaries of the most recent gravitation to power to the margins of the superseded older system (also Russia and China next to America). Another has pitted the need for an accelerated diffusion of technological, and in part also political and economic, features of Western civilization against the lingering threat of one more onslaught from the peripheries turning back upon that most recently dominant civilization its former strengths. And, last but not least, traditional tenets and tendencies of interstate relations have lost some of their force, and world-community relations have remained stubbornly resistant to cumulative growth, in conditions where neither mode guarantees an order-promoting conjunction of either national power and interests or transnationally operative functions and manifested needs, while each is impervious to meaningful synthesis with the other in either speculation or statecraft.

INDEX

Empire (in general): decline and dissolution of, 92–94, 98, 106, 320–21, 330–35; defense of, 81–82; enemies of, 47–48, 92–93, 106, 331–32; and expansion, 3, 269 (kinds of, 7, 148); and hegemony, 14, 156, 270–71, 337; organization of, 73–74, 269, 303–6; and state system, 5, 100–2, 156, 306, 307, 336; and subimperialism, 29; utility of concept of, 349–50; and world-community models, 351. *See also* American empire; British empire; Roman empire

England. *See* Great Britain

Equilibrium. *See* Balance of power

Expansion (in general): and empire, 3, 269; and conflicts of expansionist strategies, 37–38; kinds of, 4, 53, 54–55; lulls in, 22–24; sources of, 3, 7–8, 24–25, 31–32, 46–47, 107; stages of, 5, 52, 105–6; types of determinants of, 3–6, 31, 53, 106. *See also* American expansion; Great Britain; Rome

Federal Republic of Germany, and American empire, 273, 297. *See also* Alliances; Germany; North Atlantic Treaty Organization; Western Europe

Ford, Gerald R., 296, 334

Forrestal, James V., 318

France: and American empire, 251, 271, 234, 235, 239, 281, 288, 297, 302, 305; and American expansion, 109–10, 113, 114, 116, 118, 123, 136, 167–68, 182, 218, 222, 228, 343; and British empire, 62, 63, 68, 84, 92, 99, 101; and British expansion, 15, 17–21, 22, 38, 44, 107; imperial expansion of, 9, 24, 28. *See also* Alliances; North Atlantic Treaty Organization; Western Europe

Franklin, Benjamin, 163

Free trade (U.S.): and Bretton Woods, 232, 242, 251, 257; and British economy, 226, 228, 232–33, 251, 258, 264; domestic attitudes toward, 229, 235, 252–53; and external tariff, 219, 229, 231, 232, 234, 251, 252; and "fair" (or nondiscriminatory) trade, 214, 230–32, 244, 251–53, 256; movement toward, 226–32, 233–36; perspectives for, 258–60, 328. *See also* Economic determinants of expansion

Germanic tribes, and Roman empire, 76 81, 82–83, 95, 96, 98–101

Germany: and American expansion, 118, 123, 125, 126, 133, 135–38, 144, 182, 213–14, 222, 228, 232, 234; analogy with Macedon, 15, 151–52; appeasement of, 135; and British empire, 15, 21, 28, 38, 63, 65, 67, 83, 84, 89, 96, 100, 107; and the United States, x, 135. *See also* Federal Republic of Germany

Gladstone, William Ewart, 38, 39, 44, 45, 50

Goldwater, Barry, 203

Gracchus, Gaius Sempronius (the Younger), 39, 40, 43, 49

Gracchus, Tiberius Sempronius (the Elder), 39, 40, 43, 49, 89

Great Britain: and American empire, 271–72, 288, 297; domestic determinants of expansion of, 19, 24, 34–51, 65; and early American expansion, 118–20, 123, 125, 342–43; (economic) decline of, 63, 65, 93, 96, 232–33; economic determinants of expansion of, 15–18, 20, 23, 29; foreign-policy options of, 9; and formalized protective imperialism, 54, 63–70; and formative war imperialism, 54, 55–58, 71; and formal free-trade imperialism, 54, 58–63; interclass dynamics in, 38–47, 49–51, 71–72; international determinants of expansion of, 9–10, 15–22, 26–28; lulls in expansion of, 22–24; marginal men in, 43–45, 49–51; middle class in, 40–41, 43–47, 96–97; ruling class of, 32–37, 40–42, 46, 93, 96–97, 182; and sea power, 10, 15, 16–17. *See also* Alliances; British empire; North Atlantic Treaty Organization

Greek city-states and leagues: and Roman empire management, 75–76, 80–81; and Roman expansion, 10–14. *See also* Roman empire

Grey, Sir Edward, 39

Hadrian, emperor, 82

Hamilton, Alexander (*and* Hamiltonian), 165, 168, 169, 170, 174, 175, 181, 182, 198, 203

Hanna, Mark, 179

Hannibal, of Carthage, 11n, 14

Harriman, Edward H., 188

Harriman, W. Averell, 178, 188

Harrison, William H., 203

Hastings, Warren, 23, 29

Hay, John, 134, 181, 229, 334

Hiss, Alger, 314

Hitler, Adolf, 4, 48n

Hoover, Herbert C., 144, 187, 199, 204, 231, 233, 237, 241, 243, 244

House, Edward M., 201

Hughes, Charles Evans, 144, 231, 233, 237, 241, 243

Hull, Cordell, 221, 223, 234, 241, 242, 314

Imperialism: differentiated from economic expansionism, 53, 58, 231, 235, 237, 241–